WITHDRAWN

ALFRED G. MEYER was born in Bielefeld, Germany, in 1920, and received his early education there. He came to the United States in 1939, and served during World War II with the American Army in Europe. After the war he studied at Harvard University, where he earned the master's and doctor's degrees and was Assistant Director of the Russian Research Center. He also taught at the University of Washington and directed Columbia University's research program on the history of the Soviet Communist Party before going to Michigan State University, where he is presently Professor of Political Science. Professor Meyer is the author of *The Incompatible Allies* (with Gustav Hilger, 1953); *Marxism: The Unity of Theory and Practice* (1954); *Leninism* (1957); and *Communism* (2nd ed., 1962).

The Soviet Political System

AN INTERPRETATION

ALFRED G. MEYER

MICHIGAN STATE UNIVERSITY

RANDOM HOUSE   NEW YORK

THE
SOVIET
POLITICAL
SYSTEM

An Interpretation

First Printing

© *Copyright, 1965, by Random House, Inc.*

*All rights reserved under International
and Pan-American Copyright Conventions.
Published in New York by Random House, Inc.,
and simultaneously in Toronto, Canada,
by Random House of Canada, Limited.*

Library of Congress Catalog Card Number: 65-23338

*Manufactured in the United States of America by
The Haddon Craftsmen, Inc.,
Scranton, Pennsylvania*

ACKNOWLEDGMENTS

This book is the fruit of over fifteen years' study in the field of Soviet government and politics, and of ten years' experience in teaching the subject. I acknowledge my indebtedness to the numerous colleagues and friends whose books I have read and whose ideas I have absorbed. The subject matter is so complex, the source materials of such vast dimensions, that all scholarship in this field (as probably in most others) is of necessity a collective enterprise. It remains the individual author's task to order and interpret this material for and by himself. This is a lonely and individualistic task; and perhaps this is a very individualistic book, not only because of its author's stated prejudices. I have written it in a somewhat personal style. I have written it primarily for myself, in order to come to grips with the material it contains. And I have written it by myself, in the spare moments between teaching duties and bureaucratic–academic busywork. I owe gratitude to my employer, Michigan State University, for releasing me from my teaching duties, once for a ten-week period and more recently for an entire sabbatical year. A fellowship from the John Simon Guggenheim Foundation, which I gratefully acknowledge, has enabled me to complete the work. Some of my undergraduate students, especially Mrs. K. P. Grzelkowska, Mr. Martin Kalb, and Mr. John Love, have been of great help in gathering information and checking references. Miss Anne Dyer Murphy of Random House not only did an admirable job of transforming my draft into a publishable manuscript, but also had to muster a great deal of patience in the attempt to maintain her friendliness in the face of an obstreperous author.

31390

CONTENTS

Part

A NOTE ON TRANSLITERATION
OF RUSSIAN WORDS

All transliteration systems for rendering the Russian language in Latin letters have their peculiar inadequacies. In this book I have used a modification of the system used by the Library of Congress. It doubtless is unsatisfactory for linguists, but it may be useful to English-language readers by rendering approximately the Russian sounds. The apostrophe in the middle of a word indicates palatalization of the preceding consonant. Where end consonants are palatalized, the apostrophe has been omitted. Russian words fully adopted by the English language, such as "intelligentsia" or "Soviet," have been spelled in English dictionary fashion.

The Soviet Political System
AN INTERPRETATION

Introduction

This book is dedicated to a type of person who is becoming more and more dominant in modern societies of the American and Soviet varieties, and therefore increasingly deserving of our careful attention and study—I mean the bureaucrat. As our societies become ever more mechanized and automated, as familiar institutions within the economy, the educational world, entertainment, politics, and the entire broad range of human endeavor turn into giant machines, the bureaucrats who manage them and lead managed lives within them face us in a bewildering variety of roles—and with a thousand different faces. We are often inclined to malign the bureaucrat, to blame him for interfering with our lives in seemingly arbitrary fashion. Yet the professional student of the bureaucratic way of life may come to the conclusion that administrative chiefs and bureaucratic hierarchs should be forgiven rather than maligned; for not only is their work essential, they also rarely know what they are doing.

I hope that the bureaucrats to whom I so respectfully dedicate my work will also read it. If such a reader happens to function as an administrator in the Soviet system, the book may make him aware of features in his own environment of which he has hitherto been unconscious. Should he be a member of an administrative hierarchy in the West, he may gain insight into the workings of his own system by looking into the mirror of Soviet bureaucratic politics. Naturally, I am hopeful that the book will also be of value to college students and to the general reading public, as a general *introduction to Soviet government and politics, and even to the scholar in the field, who may find stimulating the manner in which I have arranged, explained, and evaluated material with which he can be expected to be thoroughly familiar.*

In this book I attempt to present a general picture of the entire Soviet system and to acquaint the student with its most important components, including institutions, practices, processes, and the very vocabulary of Soviet government and politics. Most if not all the material in this volume is already available in English, although the reader might have to search extensively for all the details presented here.[1] Still, I wish to stress that I have not come up with important new information. My contribution, if any, can lie only in the compilation and in the manner of presentation. Whatever originality this work may have consists, not in the facts offered to the reader, but in the way that known facts are interpreted.

One element in this manner of presentation is the author's bias. The nature of this bias must be made clear from the very beginning. In some of my earlier books I confessed the intention to practice as much objectivity as possible, to present the subject of my studies more dispassionately, fairly and coldly than most other writers dealing with such hotly controversial topics as communist theory, institutions, and policies. I suspect today that in fact I never lived up to my intentions, but that, instead, the biases I now confess pervade everything I have written in the past.

These biases may be summarized as follows: I am suspicious of people in positions of power and authority and of the institutions which place or maintain them in these positions; in my work I seek to penetrate their pretenses and shatter their legitimacy. My sympathy lies with the citizens, whom I tend to regard as the victims of political systems and of the rhetoric with which those systems justify themselves. I am preoccupied with the discrepancy between a system's (or a person's) aims and promises, on the one hand, and its (or his) performance and achievements, on the other.

[1] Also, because institutions and practices in administrative structures are changed with comparative ease, details of Soviet government have a habit of suddenly being outdated.

I tend to take political ideology seriously and to use the professed values and aspirations of a system as a mirror in which it can view its own reality.

Preoccupied with the search for a social and political system that provides maximum freedom and dignity to all its members and enables them to function as autonomous, confident, aware individuals, I am suspicious of the vast bureaucratic structures that have been created as the by-product of technological advances. I tend to regard them as inhuman or antihuman institutions, even though I cannot deny that they are essential servants to mankind in the job of rationalizing the management of ever more complex social machineries. At times they are dysfunctional to the very purposes they are supposed to serve; and, like all human institutions devised for rational goals, they usually become ends in themselves, enslaving and degrading men as much as they aid them. In short, much as I recognize the need for rational management of human affairs, I am appalled by the threat modern bureaucracy poses to freedom. Freedom seems to be withering away in entire societies or in subsocietal structures run by vast impersonal administrative machines, managed and operated by people without individuality or identity. Although freedom and diversity can lead to inefficiency, frustration, immobilism, or chaos, I confess a strong prejudice in favor of heterogeneity and diversity, because I believe that men can enjoy freedom only where there are choices to be made, and that truth emerges only out of conflict. My bias is individualistic and libertarian.

This romantic individualism may seem to the reader hopelessly outmoded, quixotic, and as thoroughly utopian as machine-wrecking in the days of the Luddites. Obviously, large-scale organization and its rational management, bigness and bureaucracy, are in our world to stay. They cannot be wished away, nor would any ideology which exhausts itself in attacking them be satisfactory. Ideology is the search for self-orientation in the world of man; it will inevitably contain a value system against which to measure existing social institutions; but it is not complete if the resulting critique does not lead to a more acceptable alternative—a utopia—and a program of action designed to make the utopia into reality. To be sure, individuals in modern societies can still escape the demands the bureaucratic masters of the social machines make on those who wish to get ahead. They may escape into the obscurity of the great mass of the indifferent, or they may be fortunate enough to have financial or occupational security so they need not conform to the norms of the machine men. But the former solution tends to stifle creativity, or at least to remove the escapee from the mainstream of social life. And the latter solution is a luxury available only to a happy few; it cannot become a general prescription. In short, I have no generally applicable practical proposal for combining the advantages of bureaucratic rationalization with the blessings of freedom and individual autonomy. I suspect that such a synthesis will be found only after a fundamental re-examination of the concept of freedom, and a consideration of the ways by which it might be modified in the world of automation, computers, and giant bureaucracies.

Until such a synthesis is found, quixotic adherence to an obviously old-fashioned romantic individualism seems to have a rationality of its own. It maintains the memory of individualistic values which often are lost in the course of human progress. It reasserts human needs which civilization stifles. To be sure, it may reassert them in disorderly and irresponsible fashion: the rationality of freedom turns quixotic when it confronts the "crackpot realism" of the social machines, those who run them, and those who adjust to them. But, by keeping alive the faint memory of lost human values, this quixotic commitment may make possible later syntheses combining the old values with the technical and administrative achievements of modern civilization. For the time being, however, my approach remains negative and thoroughly subversive. And this fundamentally subversive attitude underlies the entire presentation I have given of the Soviet political system. It affects not only the book's content, but also its style. For the interaction of moral values, aesthetic styles, and scholarly con-

clusions is something that cannot be avoided in the study of man and his institutions.

But the style of a book in the social sciences depends not only on the author's biases; it is related also to his method of analysis. Very generally, my method might be called inductive–deductive. We know a great wealth of facts about the Soviet political system. In our attempt to give meaning and order to these facts, we construct models of the total system into which they can be fitted. These models, in turn, are not speculative constructions based on mere imagination, but are empirically derived from our knowledge of how other societies function.

I accept Easton's and Lasswell's definition of politics as the process which determines who gets what, when, and how, provided we restrict our view to include only the "authoritative" distribution of "socially accepted" values. This definition combines the consumer-oriented interpretation of politics with necessary emphasis on the decision-making machinery: politics is a process of values distribution, but also a machinery for producing decisions with regard to this distribution, decisions which take the forms of policies, laws, and administration. Because this definition of politics is, essentially, an application of economic categories, one can describe the political process in terms of input and output; the output consisting of decisions and policies, the input, of interests (values, expectation) and the people who have these interests. Political institutions and processes constitute the machinery which changes input into output by transforming interests into decisions. It is clear that the political system comprises all of society. The political scientist studies the same subject matter as his colleagues in sociology, economics, history, and other disciplines, but he sees the entire society as a machinery for carrying out specifically political functions. The political system is the entire society organized for the purpose of allocating socially accepted values in authoritative fashion. In practice, the process comprises a fantastically broad range of decisions, from the action of a town clerk in marrying a couple or of a policeman in giving a traffic summons to the action of a constituent body in shaping the system itself; the values which are allocated include virtually every form of reward and punishment, advantage and disadvantage, that can be bestowed upon individuals or groups.

In analyzing any political system, the student must ask such questions as the following: Who makes decisions at various levels of the system? What kind of people are they, and how are they re-cruited? Precisely what kind of power do they have, and on what is it based? How do they secure and perpetuate their rule? How do they justify it to themselves and to others? What relations prevail among them? What counter-elites, if any, are waiting to replace them, and how does the system provide for such a movement of elites?

What is the culture within which the decision-makers operate? What classes, groups, nationalities, and other elements make up the population, and what values, aspirations, traditions, and habits prevail among these various groups?

What are the principal objectives of the ruling group, and how are these aims related to the political norms of the constituents? How responsive or responsible is the government to the con-stituency?

What is the political structure, that is, the institutions comprising the machinery of decision-making and decision-executing? What is the political process by which this machinery actually operates?

Chto komu'—who gets what, when, and how? What are the rewards and sanctions with which the system seeks to control the citizens' behavior? Or, from the citizen's point of view: what's in it for the individual?

Every one of these broad questions gives rise to a host of sub-sidiary questions, leading to an exceedingly complex analysis. More-over, once the political scientist has carried out his task of describ-ing the system in its structure and process, he will want to evaluate it against a variety of standards; he must ask not only how effective it is in fulfilling the tasks it sets itself, but also how it stands up to political norms that others, including himself, may have developed.

Finally, in a very different kind of evaluation, he may attempt to fit the system into the typology of political systems that political scientists, from Plato to our contemporaries, have sought to establish.

The difficulty in dealing with such complexity on all these levels of analysis lies in the fact that any one bit of information must be placed under many different headings, so as to fit it into the various approaches that lead us to a full understanding of the political system. Every datum must be examined many times—as part of the political culture, as part of the structure of institutions, as a weapon in the struggle for power, as an element of various functioning mechanisms, and so forth. If carried through consistently, this kind of description would be unbearably tedious and repetitive. Any actual description will therefore have to compromise by sacrificing pedantry to readability.

In other words, to present a coherent and reasonably clear image of the system he wishes to describe, the social scientist must be selective; and in social science there is no agreement on what must be selected—one man's essential elements are another man's trivia. Hence, from the point of view of social science as a whole, every actual analysis is a distortion of reality.

The organization of the present volume is based on the following considerations. First, in line with the sociological orientation of contemporary political science, the book stresses processes rather than institutions, informal patterns rather than formal arrangements or tables of organization—all this in an attempt to be realistic, to look for actual human relationships behind the façade of laws and institutions. Moreover, I attempt to treat all the citizens as participants in the political process, rather than to fix attention excessively on the top leadership. I do not mean to imply that other scholars have neglected to discuss the relationship between Soviet government and the common man in the USSR, only that my emphasis on this relationship may be stronger. Such an approach necessitates increased attention to the differences between various groups of citizens, hence to a view of Soviet society as heterogeneous and differentiated. The book thus turns its back on those interpretations which regard Soviet politics merely as an eternal struggle between the top leadership and the masses, or as a conflict within the top elite, and thus give the impression that the masses are an undifferentiated, monolithic body of helpless victims. Again, this is a matter of different emphasis rather than absolute disagreement.

In its attempt to explain the political system of the USSR on the basis of its historical, cultural, and other determinants, the present work is pluralistic and eclectic rather than monistic. This is another feature that puts it into contrast with other interpretations, the most commonly prevailing being attempts to interpret the Soviet system primarily as an institutionalization of Marxist–Leninist doctrines or as a manifestation of the power struggle among the highest echelons of the political elite.

Finally, I have made continual attempts to compare the Soviet political system with other systems, particularly that of the United States—a comparison in which striking similarities as well as sharp contrasts can be expected to become apparent. Comparisons are useful in several ways. For one thing, political science may make significant advances by comparing and classifying phenomena in different systems and fitting these into broad typologies. Second, comparison is a useful didactic device, because we understand the unfamiliar much more easily when it is presented in terms of the familiar. Conversely, we may gain better understanding even of the familiar by seeing it reflected in the warped mirror of unfamiliar but related phenomena.

The difficulties of presenting a coherent and meaningful analysis of the Soviet political system are multiplied by the relative scarcity of authoritative and verifiable factual material. An immense wealth of information is available, of course. We may obtain it from Soviet publications as well as from direct observation; and there is so much of it that no individual scholar can survey even a small fraction. But the available data in all their abundance may not be the most significant ones. In the Soviet Union, in contrast to some other political systems, a far greater proportion of really important political processes goes on behind the scenes; far more is hidden from public scrutiny, especially that of foreigners, than in the "open societies," as Karl Popper has called them.[2] Moreover, the investigative survey work which political sociologists conduct in the West cannot be done in the USSR. Nor, finally, does Soviet society indulge as much, or as openly, as the West in critical self-appraisal of its own institutions and processes. To be sure, criticism is voiced. But a substantial proportion of whatever is published in the Soviet world must nevertheless be characterized as self-advertisement, or public relations literature. Its usefulness for scholarly purposes is limited. Consequently, Western descriptions of the Soviet political system must remain impressionistic, and the line between political science and journalism in this field is tenuous. What presents itself as an analysis of political processes and human relationships is often no more than mere speculation. The reader should be aware of these limitations. At the same time, they should not prevent the scholar from attempting to describe and understand. Historians describe the civilization of Sumer, of imperial Rome, indeed, of Elizabethan England, on the basis of infinitely scantier factual material.

[2] *For a brief discussion of the concept of the "open society" see Part VI, Chapter I.*

Part One

Determinant Factors

Chapter I
The Land and the People

The land, climate, soils, and natural resources of a nation are given facts with which any politcal system has to reckon, regardless of its structure and ideology. The influence of these basic factors can be exaggerated and misunderstood, and in the case of Russia a good deal of fanciful speculation is rife. Again and again, Russian as well as Western writers have explained certain character traits attributed to the Russians as a consequence of the landscape and the climate of their country. The broad sweep of imagination and the all-embracing warmth attributed to them have been linked to the endless expanse of the Russian plains; a penchant for mysticism to the overpowering Hansel-and-Gretel atmosphere of the northern forests; the apathy and laziness of many Russians to the helpless stupor which the harsh winter imposes on the peasant; and so forth.[1] All these hypotheses become dubious as soon as we realize that the forests were as mighty in upstate New York, Pennsylvania, and Michigan when these areas were first occupied by the white man, that the plains are as flat and wide around Kansas City as they are near Volgograd, and that winter in Minnesota or Saskatchewan is, if anything, harsher than in the central Russian provinces—yet despite these similarities land and climate obviously did not make the inhabitants of North America like Russian

[1] For examples of such writings, see the pertinent chapters in Wright Miller, *Russians as People* (New York: E.P. Dutton, 1961); Klaus Mehnert, *Soviet Man and His World* (New York: Praeger, 1958); and Wladimir Weidlé, *Russia: Absent and Present* (New York: Random House, 1961).

peasants. We must therefore be very cautious in assessing the influence of geographic factors. Nonetheless, the basic facts about the land and peoples of the Soviet Union must be stated here.

The Union of Socialist Soviet Republics, more often referred to as the USSR or the Soviet Union, is one of the world's leading powers. One of the simplest reasons for this eminence is the sheer size of the country. Comprising close to 8.6 million square miles, almost three times the area of the 48 states that made up the United States until recently, the USSR stretches over the entire northern side of the Eurasian continent, from Japan to Poland, and from the Arctic Ocean almost to the northern borders of India and Pakistan. The distance between the western and eastern edges of the country is roughly 6000 miles. A substantial part of this huge area, however, is barely fit for human habitation, at least under contemporary conditions of technological development. A severe continental climate and the tremendous distance from the ocean of large areas have given much of the country extremes of temperature combined with a grave lack of precipitation. Consequently, outside the Central Asian oases and the Pacific littoral, the inhabitable parts of Asiatic USSR seem like a thin wedge precariously inserted between southern deserts and arctic wasteland. Many agricultural areas are marginal because of poor soil or periodic years of drought, although intensification of agriculture through heavy investment in fertilization, irrigation, and other modern methods could doubtless raise agricultural productivity significantly. As for other natural resources, however, the USSR is amply endowed. Although in considerable part her mineral deposits and sources of energy still await exploitation, some of them being in remote areas where the climate imposes severe hardships, the country is close to autarky in all but a few essential resources.[2]

In the earlier decades of this century, most important industries were concentrated in a few areas of European Russia, Transcau-

[2] See Dimitri B. Shimkin, *Minerals: A Key to Soviet Power* (Cambridge: Harvard University Press, 1953).

casia, and the Ural Mountains. The Soviet regime, especially since World War II, has made efforts to establish important industrial centers or entire industrial regions in proximity to newly exploited energy or raw material resources in Siberia and Central Asia. This effort has undoubtedly been impeded to some extent by the poor state of development of the communications system in some of these areas, which in turn is partly due to the difficulties imposed by climate and soil conditions, to say nothing of the tremendous distances to be bridged. Thus the process of transforming the vast country into one closely integrated industrial empire is still going on today.

The Soviet Union is inhabited by 225 million people, about 35 million more than in 1953. Official estimates for 1956 gave the country a population of roughly 200 million.[3] The 1959 census counted close to 209 million.

Until recent decades, the age composition of this population formed a fairly even pyramid conforming to the typical demographic pattern in nations with comparatively high death rates and even higher birth rates. In this generation, however, the height of the pyramid has risen and the base narrowed, because of a fairly sharp decline in both death and birth rates, so that in time the population of the USSR can be expected to conform to the pattern which, until the postwar baby boom in the United States, was considered normal for industrial nations. The Soviet pyramid, however, shows marked gaps in several layers of the middle-aged population especially among males. These gaps are the result of severe population losses as a result of World War I, the subsequent revolution and civil war, the severe famines and epidemics of the early 1920s and 1930s, and other major political upheavals. Moreover, as a result of World War II the USSR lost at least 20 million people, half of them military personnel.[4]

[3] *Narodnoe Khoziaistvo SSSR* (Moscow–Leningrad, 1956), p. 17.
[4] Thirty million according to Hermann Schubnell, "Bevölkerungsprobleme in der Sowjetunion," *Osteuropa* VII, 3 (March, 1957), 157; 40 million according to estimates of Erik Boettcher, "Nachwuchsbedarf in Staat und Wirtschaft der Sowjetunion," *Osteuropa* IX, 2–3 (February–March, 1959), 114.

Soviet society is a melting pot of nationalities, religions, races, languages, and cultures—although it is different in several respects from the American melting pot. First of all, even though linguistic differences linger in American society, we can say, on the whole, that all Americans speak the same language. This is not the case in the USSR, as we shall see. Also, cultural and religious differences in the Soviet Union are greater than in the United States, although, on the other hand, no class distinctions in Soviet society are so deep as that between Negroes and whites in America. Finally, the nationalities of the Soviet Union, unlike those which compose the American people, are distributed unevenly through the country. Various national groups are concentrated in frontier areas, forming distinct national regions in which Russians may still constitute the minority population. The situation is somewhat analogous to that existing in French Canada.

Counting every minor tribe, Soviet statistics in 1917 listed as living on Soviet territory almost 200 separate nationalities speaking close to 150 different languages. The major nationalities, however, are far fewer. As of 1959, slightly over three fourths of the country's population, about 160 million people, were of Slavic origin; among these, 115 million were Great Russians, 37 million Ukrainians, and 8 million Belorussians. Slightly less than one eighth of the population, about 25 million, were Muslims, living in Central Asia, along the lower Volga, in the North Caucasus region, and scattered in other places. Most, but not all, of these Islamic nationalities speak Turkic languages. The country north and south of the Caucasuses is a jumble of nationalities, languages, and religions. The most numerous among them are the Armenians and Georgians, nations with ancient cultural and political traditions of their own. In the northwest, the three Baltic nations of Estonia, Latvia, and Lithuania were added to the USSR two decades ago. Other important, though less numerous, minorities include Finns, Moldavians, Mongols, Koreans, Persian-speaking Tadzhiks and Azerbaidzhanis, Jews, and Germans.

A precise profile of Soviet society by professions is not available to us. But the growth of the industrial working class, white-collar workers, and professional groups has been steady. In 1926, no more than thirty Russian cities had a population above 100,000 and 82 percent of the nation lived in rural areas. According to Soviet estimates for 1956, the number of cities with a population over 100,000 had risen to 134; many of these cities, especially in the Asiatic part of the country, had not even existed thirty years before. And the rural population had been reduced to little over half— 56.6 percent, to be exact. By 1962, the urban population had outstripped the number of rural dwellers. Almost 112 million people (a little short of 51 percent of the total population) were reported to live in towns and cities, as compared to 26 million (18 percent) in 1926. Of this urban population, more than half lived in cities of more than 100,000 inhabitants.[5]

Soviet society on the whole shows surprising similarities to the occupational breakdown of the population of the United States. The main differences are two: the proportion of rural and agricultural people is still much greater in the USSR, and the range of occupations does not include the independent businessman. Furthermore, if exact data were available, we should notice a very different distribution of many individual professions—more teachers and physicians per capita than in the United States, for example, and far fewer attorneys and people engaged in the distributive side of the economy. Lacking precise figures, we may nevertheless be able to bring out some of these differences in our description of the political system.

One final geographical factor is of great importance for understanding the history and political system of the Soviet Union. Having as her immediate neighbors such countries as Japan, China, Iran, Poland, and Finland, not to mention the United States just a few miles across the Bering Strait, the Soviet Union stretches over the entire breadth of Eurasia, forming the roof of the entire Old World. This geographic location may be seen as a symbol of

---

[5] In the United States, the urban population comprises about 70 percent of the nation. Soviet urban dwellers live primarily in cities between 100,000 and 1,000,000 inhabitants; the American urban population is found more predominantly in cities over 1,000,000 and in towns under 100,000 inhabitants.

the fact that historically too Russia has been part of Asia as well as of Europe, and the impact of Asia on her political developments has been considerable.[6]

[6] By making this statement I have no intention to subscribe, in whole or in part, to the highly controversial views expressed by Karl A. Wittfogel in his *Oriental Despotism: A Comparative Study of Total Power* (New Haven: Yale University Press, 1963) and summarized in his "Russia and the East: A Comparison and Contrast," in *Slavic Review*, XXII, 4 (December 1963), 627–643.

Chapter II
History

Even the most revolutionary political systems have their roots in history. A country's institutions and behavior patterns can be seen as the products of social and economic development in which every phase and every conflict, every issue and every resolution of an issue have left, like geological deposits, some laws, some institutions, traditions, or methods of administration. Every historic event leaves sediments, and the political system is composed of such sediments and crystallizations. In the case of a revolutionary regime such as that of Soviet Russia, the institutions, behavior traits, and aspirations at any particular time only very inadequately portray what might be called the "geological history" of the system, for two reasons. First, the revolutionary regime bluntly repudiates all of the past and deliberately seeks to destroy all historically accreted features—usually however, without complete success. Moreover, it may take decades or generations for a revolutionary system to settle into relatively stable forms; until this occurs, those who rule often feel free to experiment with institutions and behavior patterns, to create and destroy, to set up elaborate structures only to abolish them when they prove undesirable. All this has been true of the Soviet political system. But the past nonetheless has a persistent tendency to reassert itself; and this applies to both the tsarist past and the more recent postrevolutionary experiences. We shall therefore be unable to understand Soviet government if we are not acquainted, however sketchily, with the society out of which it developed.

TSARISM AND ITS HERITAGE

Medieval Russia, its center in Kiev, was a member of that group of nations and cultures we call the Western world, a civilization which shared the heritage of Greece and Rome, of Christianity and feudalism. Because of the vicissitudes of history, however, the path of Russia separated from that of the West, with results that have remained important. One essential feature of Old Russia which is still a political factor is the Orthodox brand of Christianity Russia received from Byzantium. As we shall see, the church hierarchy as well as the believers, traditionally used to accommodating themselves to any political rule, have had great difficulty in achieving an accommodation with the Soviet regime.

The increasing contact which Kievan Russia had with the Western world, and which integrated her in many ways with Western civilization, was disrupted in the thirteenth century when Russia was conquered by the Mongol empire and remained under its rule for about three centuries. For the people of Europe, most of Russia during that time was an unknown part of Asia; maps made in the West until well into the sixteenth century usually show vast blank spaces to the east of Poland, marked only by the name "Tatary" (from the Tatar tribes which claimed suzerainty over Russia). In turn, the West was utterly unknown to almost all of Russia. The consequences of this separation were profound, for the centuries of Russia's isolation were precisely those in which the groundwork was laid for the scientific, technological, and economic development of the West. Once the Tatar domination had been overthrown, the Russian state which again came into increasingly intimate contact with its Western neighbors was in a state of technological and economic development comparable, roughly, to the Europe of Charlemagne, facing a world that had gone far beyond this stage with its flourishing town civilization, its crafts and trades, its scientific pioneers and political experimentation.

A Carolingian Russia face to face with an Elizabethan Europe— that situation spelled backwardness for Russia, a state of economic underdevelopment as measured against her new Western neighbors.

Economically advanced nations usually are regarded by their less fortunate neighbors as presenting a threat to themselves, and much of Russia's history can be explained in terms of her reaction to the technological—and hence military—superiority of the West. Political leaders in underdeveloped areas face a great dilemma: What they regard as the threat of economically advanced nations can be mitigated only by adopting the technology that is the basis of the presumed threat. The underdeveloped country must westernize if it wants to survive. The rulers of Old Russia ever since the sixteenth century were well aware of this need; indeed, some of the tsars were nothing less than revolutionaries who tried to transform radically the society over which they ruled. But they faced two major difficulties. For one thing, for any nation that wishes to maintain its established culture and traditional way of life, the need to Westernize is painful, and all those of its people who do not wish to see their culture disrupted or their high status dwindle will resist westernization. Second, the introduction of Western technology, science, and administrative skill may also endanger the political system and the very rule of the crowned revolutionaries. Aware of this danger, the reformer-tsars aimed to westernize selectively. But here they did not succeed. On the contrary, with Western technology and administration came Western progressive ideas and movements of reform, while at the same time westernization was resisted by the more traditional elements of society.

Old Russia was ruled by emperors who claimed absolute power, as their European colleagues did in the seventeenth and eighteenth centuries. Their arm of government was a civil and military bureaucracy, the officers of which were recruited mainly from the landowning aristocracy, a privileged leisure class whose wealth was measured in land as well as in serfs. They had obtained their privileges as compensation for services rendered to the tsars, in line with feudal and absolutist practices. But in the eighteenth century, again in conformity to practices and developments in the West, they were freed of their service obligations while retaining their privileges. Indeed, service itself became a privilege of the nobility. After the nobles were freed of their duties, the serfs remained in bondage for about another hundred years. They were released only in the second half of the nineteenth century, almost simultaneously with the emancipation of the slaves in the American South. But the conditions imposed on them in this settlement were so unsatisfactory that the Russian peasantry, constituting about nine tenths of the population, remained a dissatisfied class.

Toward the end of the nineteenth century, industry began to develop in Russia, and with it grew a working class which found itself laboring and living under conditions as poor as those of the working class in the early periods of capitalism in the West. The Russian workers, therefore, made up another seedbed of discontent. Furthermore, with the growth of industrialism, a middle class of merchants, financiers, and professional people arose. This class at once claimed the right to participate in the political process, if only by virtue of their being educated, and also began to advance the aim of free enterprise. But in tsarist Russia, demands for free enterprise and democracy were revolutionary demands.

If to these dissatisfied classes—the peasants, workers, and the middle class—we add Russia's numerous national minorities, whose representatives demanded equality, autonomy, self-determination, or other such rights denied them by the tsarist regime, we obtain the picture of an entire society seething with discontent. This image, however, is only partly correct. The grievances of millions of Russians were deep, and the political system under which they lived was unable, or at least too dilatory, to satisfy them. At the same time, awareness of this frustrating state was alive only in a minority. The vast majority of Russians doubtless felt that their needs and hopes could and would be satisfied by the tsar and his government. Only dramatic crises of confidence would jolt sufficient numbers out of this belief and would cause revolutionary upheavals.

At the same time, the tsarist political system can be partly explained by the rulers' ever-present fear of the people. Tsarist government, in this sense, was continual warfare between the ruling group and the nation as a whole. In this respect, of course, Russia resembled Europe in the age of absolutism (the difference, however, was that in Russia the age of absolutism lasted much longer). The principles of government and administrative traditions of tsarist Russia generally corresponded to those of absolutist Europe, with some crucial exceptions. First, the Russian system had completely eliminated the medieval tradition of autonomy, self-government, or some sort of popular participation. Second, the urban middle class, which in Western Europe came to constitute a formidable counter-elite, entered the Russian scene much later and in much smaller numbers. Finally, the philosophies of limited government, which in the West arose well before the absolutist princes were overthrown, were late imports into Russian society. Hence despite traces of countervailing forces, the bleaker side of royal absolutism was accented in tsarist Russia and became its peculiar political heritage. The ruler claimed absolute sovereignty. All his subjects, from the highest government officials to the lowliest serf or prisoner, were as slaves before him. He claimed the exclusive right even to discuss public matters; hence all expressed social thought on the part of his subjects was in itself subversive. He ruled his vast country through a bureaucracy as strictly centralized as the means of communication permitted; everything that went on in the remotest corners of the empire was, at least in theory, subject to control from the capital. One prominent feature of tsarism was the predominance of the military in the government. In many parts of the empire, especially those that were newly acquired or had non-Russian inhabitants, military government was more or less the normal form of rule; this, again, was typical of royal absolutism, where military needs usually overrode all other political considerations.

Having conquered vast areas inhabited by alien populations, the tsarist government also took on some of the features of colonial rule. Early attempts to integrate the subject populations, whose cultural levels ranged from high to very low, later gave way to a policy of discrimination and oppression and attempts at wholesale russification.

The general political climate of tsarist Russia might perhaps be characterized by the word "statism." Even though the idle rich were free of obligations, the political culture stressed the ideas of

service and duty—that is, of obligation not to society, but to the
sovereign ruler. For the poor, the burden was increased by their
substantial obligations and their utter subjugation to the landlords.
For all subjects of the tsar, it meant exposure to the high-handedness
and bureaucratic stubbornness of brutal, narrow-minded, crude,
arbitrary, and self-seeking officials, recruited primarily from the
landlord class. Life in tsarist Russia was life in a state in which
the scope of governmental activities was wide, in which, overtly or
covertly, officialdom poked its nose into the private life of the
individual and dictatorship was mellowed only by inefficiency and
corruption. It was a society, therefore, in which hatred of the regime
smoldered, if only subconsciously, in the hearts of the population.
This hatred would, occasionally, erupt with the bloodiest violence;
most of the time it would be smothered by religion or drowned
in vodka. Or else the people would console themselves with the
benign image of a benevolent Father Tsar, kept poorly informed
by his evil advisers of the crimes perpetrated in his name, but who
would sooner or later punish his officials and redeem his oppressed
people. In other words, unchecked autocracy in Russia was made
acceptable to some by paternalistic rhetoric.

This dreary picture of tsarist society was not without its contrasting features.[1] Repeatedly, emperors or their advisers sought
to reform their society in the image of Western constitutionalism,
or at least in that of the state-according-to-law, and made feeble
attempts in this direction, most notable among them the reform
of the judicial system in the 1870s. But all such efforts were
counteracted by the more pervasive features of the absolutist police
state. Civil rights flourished briefly after the revolution of 1905,
were suppressed again, and burst out anarchically only after the
fall of tsarism in 1917. In the last decades of tsarist rule popular

[1] Nor is it generally accepted. For instance, Nicholas Timasheff argues
in *The Great Retreat* that tsarist Russia before 1917 was well on her way
toward joining the industrialized urban civilizations of the West, that her
social and political institutions were becoming similar to those of the most
advanced countries—that Russia, in short, was overcoming her backwardness. He regards the revolution of 1917 as a temporary mad aberration
which deflected Russia from this inevitable and gradual development, but
argues that the cultural counterrevolution of the 1930s indicated that the
prewar trends of development had reasserted themselves.

participation in political affairs was only in its feeblest beginnings. A national representative assembly, the State Duma, created in 1905, was ineffective as a law-making body, although it was effective as a public forum and political training ground. Local organs of self-government, the *zemstvos,* created late in the nineteenth century, were more important beginnings of civic autonomy, although during much of their existence they were harassed and hampered by the tsarist regime.

The entire picture is complicated by the fact that on top of this society of illiterate peasants and barbarous officials floated an educated minority, tiny in numbers but outstanding in its contributions to science, art, and letters, a cultural elite which could well measure itself against its counterparts in the West. This intelligentsia, as it is called in Russian, also became the moving force behind the revolutionary movements that developed in the nineteenth century.

Because of the relative apathy of the masses of the population, political movements in the nineteenth century took the form of small conspiratorial circles formed almost exclusively of members of the intelligentsia. From Europe these self-conscious critics and apostles took the most radical notions of the day and tried with utter earnestness to apply them to their own society. Living in an autocratic society which would never allow their ideas to be tested in practice, they tended to think irresponsibly, in sweeping, grandiose, absolute terms, fancifully developing the idea systems they took from the West. They moved in a world which consisted of ideas that had become more real than reality itself; they were therefore addicted to dogmatism and sectarian quarrels. Their whole lives at times had an air of unreality, increased by the circumstance that all their discussions were by definition subversive, so that they had to carry on even the most intellectual and theoretical pursuits in conspiratorial fashion. This tradition of underground organization and activity left a lasting imprint on Russian political history. Incidentally, it also led to chronic infiltration of all political movements by the tsar's secret police.

Russian revolutionary movements in the nineteenth and early

twentieth centuries echoed the broad aims of Western European liberalism and socialism. Almost all the political reformers desired the participation of all, or at least all the educated, in politics. They usually demanded constitutional government, some kind of national self-determination, and broad civil rights. But from the very beginning of the twentieth century, socialist thought came to predominate, as a vague commitment to social and economic equality as well as to cooperative forms of social organization merged with an increasing antagonism to capitalism. In many Russian thinkers, liberal and socialist views were joined in interesting fashion. For instance, the broad current usually described as populism (*narodnichestvo*) might with equal justification be labled "peasant socialism" or "Jeffersonian–Jacksonian liberalism." Even the Marxist movement, which clearly demanded the establishment of socialism through a dictatorship of the proletariat, sought the fulfilment of liberal aspirations as its intermediary goal.

Whatever the specific aims of the various discussion groups and conspiratorial circles, they were in general agreement on certain broad questions. Most of them tended to be collectivist, asserting that man fulfills himself only by serving society, whereas government is justified only so long as it serves men and provides for the welfare of all. Almost all of them manifested a touching and at the same time disturbing earnestness and single-mindedness, a puritan disdain for all endeavors that did not directly serve the cause of social reform they were promoting. They tended to be stern utilitarians who wished to measure all things and actions by the benefit they provided for the relief of misery and the liberation of the oppressed; hence many of them manifested the zealot's intolerance for the pleasurable and beautiful refinements that graced the lives of the rich and cultured. Such a renunciation, not to say condemnation, of worldly pleasures was typical both of those who came to the revolutionary movements from among the wealthy or high-ranking nobility and of those who had risen to the intelligentsia from below. Both types were characterized by a burning idealism, by readiness to renounce all comforts, security, and career prospects, by eagerness to sacrifice their very selves for the sake of saving the people, for in their eyes there could be no personal happiness until society had been thoroughly reshaped. Liberals, socialists, or anarchists, they consciously modeled their lives after the characters in Chernyshevski's novel *What's To Be Done?*, a book that inspired whole generations of professional revolutionaries.

Throughout the history of Russian revolutionary movements, a number of controversies persistently came to the surface, providing, as it were, the main themes on which each new political movement improvised its own variations. One of these was the issue of elitism. Granted Russia had to be saved from her present state of oppression and misery, who was to do the saving—a small elite from among the intelligentsia who through education had acquired consciousness of the need to reshape society, or the masses of the people rising up in elemental ("spontaneous") revolt? Did wisdom lie in a formal education, or in the allegedly unspoiled minds of the illiterate peasant? Could salvation be brought by a tiny band of dedicated professional revolutionaries, or would a mass movement be necessary? The problem of the ideal relationship between leaders and masses, between the educated and the illiterate, was intimately linked with questions about the organization of the revolutionary movement and the nature of the society to be created. Obviously, faith in the wisdom of the common man led to a belief in democratic organization, whereas exclusive reliance on an elite spelled dictatorship or, at least, temporary tutelage. But in most of the revolutionary movements the alternatives were not so clearly outlined. Ideas about the relationship between leaders and masses were often complicated, and so therefore were the revolutionaries' notions concerning decision-making processes. Similarly, there was often a good deal of open or hidden ambivalence on the related questions of revolutionary tactics; under conditions prevailing in tsarist Russia, even the most temperate reformer at times had difficulty renouncing the use of terror or other forms of violence to promote his aims.

Another very different complex of problems with which all political movements in Russia had to deal was the attitude to be taken to the West and to the machine age. This question was very controversial in the age of nationalism, and in a country whose intelligentsia was afflicted with a sharp national inferiority complex. On this question some thinkers, again, took extreme positions, but in most cases the attitudes were quite ambivalent: Russian nationalism mixed with adulation of the West; Western doctrines used to defend Russian exclusivism; hopes of adopting Western technology or Western democratic institutions without having to take capitalism in the bargain; and similar positions.

The number of people actively engaged in subversive discussion and agitation during the nineteenth century was very small, but their influence was tremendous. Actual political movements did not form until the last decade of the century, and they became established as functioning political parties only in the early years of our own century, receiving their baptism of fire in the revolution of 1905. This revolution for the first time mobilized all those dissatisfied with tsarist rule—and it seemed as if this category comprised the vast majority of the population. The revolution was prepared by the galloping social dislocation gripping the Russian empire; it was precipitated by recklessness and stupidity on the part of the tsar and his government, and, most immediately, by an unsuccessful war with Japan which Russia had unleashed for the very purpose of diverting popular discontent into "harmless" channels. The last ruler of the Romanov dynasty was an innocuous gentleman who would have made a first-class forest ranger or a very friendly corner grocer, but who was not prepared to hold together a tottering political system. The grotesque character of the advisors with whom he surrounded himself became an open scandal. Many Russians regarded the court as corrupt and discredited; hence the most important element in the regime's paternalistic rhetoric was undermined. To be sure, the revolution of 1905 did not lead to the overthrow of tsarism. By making belated and half-hearted concessions to liberal demands, the emperor succeeded in pacifying at least some of the revolutionary groups, so that afterwards the continuing revolt of the irreconcilable radicals could be drowned in blood. A brief period of emergency government by firing squads helped restore order, so that most of the concessions made to appease liberal opinion could be taken away or rendered inoperative. For a few years, tsarist Russia seemed to sink wearily back into a state of government-as-usual, even though rapid social and intellectual transformations continued to take place. Given a few more decades, the impact of these changes might have compelled the tsarist political system to adjust much more drastically to Russia's modern age. But this time was not afforded to tsarism. The whirlwind of World War I once again shook the system to its very foundation, and this time the regime was unable to save itself.

THE REVOLUTION OF 1917

The revolution of 1917 was the product of several factors: an oppressive, corrupt, and discredited regime; a disastrous war that had ruined the country's economy; and the agitation and propaganda of revolutionary parties. The political system of tsarism was so unpopular that it fell at the first feeble blows. About the positive aims of the revolution there was, however, no agreement. Instead, a number of burning issues were debated throughout the first year of the revolution. The most important of these issues were:

1. *Peace or war:* The vast majority of the people, especially the peasantry, wanted peace, but many others were in favor of continuing the war against Germany.

2. *Redistribution of land:* The peasants wanted to seize the landlords' estates at once and distribute the land among themselves. Many political leaders either did not favor such dramatic action or wished to see it performed in orderly, constitutional fashion, on the basis of laws still to be passed.

3. *A constituent assembly:* Most Russians agreed that a democratic government should be organized and a constitution written by a constituent assembly freely and openly elected by all the people. The speed with which this assembly should be convened became an embarrassing political issue.

4. *Nature of the new regime:* Liberal leaders thought of the

coming democratic regime as a parliamentary Republic; radical
leaders hoped that it might be a government of councils (soviets)
representing spontaneously organized workers, peasants, and
soldiers.

5. *The economic system:* Principles of free enterprise were pitted
against those of socialism.

6. *The national minorities:* The striving of national minorities
for autonomy or self-determination clashed with the aspirations of
those who hoped that the territories of the Russian empire might
remain united.

After the hurried abdication of the tsar in March of 1917, no
organized government was able to establish itself for several
months. Instead two governments which, singly or jointly, did not
have full control over the entire country existed, so to speak, side
by side. One of these governments was by origin a committee of
the State Duma which had reluctantly assumed command when
power slipped from the tsar's hands. Its members were representatives of the middle-of-the-road Constitutional Democrats (Kadets)
and the conservative Octobrist Party—in other words, people from
the upper classes, the wealthy, the educated, those endowed with
rank and status. At first only one representative from a moderate
socialist party, Alexander Kerensky, agreed to join this so-called
Provisional Government. But in subsequent months its political
center of gravity shifted to the left; other socialists joined and took
over some of the portfolios; a number of conservative members
dropped out, and Kerensky became head of the government.

The Provisional Government, with its tenuous ties to formerly
existing institutions, asserted the most legitimate claim to authority
until a constitution might be written and a fully authoritative
government installed; but in fact it existed and operated only by
toleration of another authority, which in effect exercised a veto on
all its policies. This was the Petrograd Soviet of Workers' and
Soldiers' Deputies. Soviets (councils) were action committees
spontaneously created within factories and troop units and, later,
also in villages and towns. During the revolution of 1905 they
had sprung up in many parts of Russia and, in some areas, had

become the local decision-making centers of the revolution. Disbanded and suppressed when the revolution was defeated, they had acquired a certain revolutionary halo as a form of self-government which better than any other permitted the lower-class citizens to participate in making vital decisions. Soviets, in the eyes of many radical-minded Russians, were institutions of direct democracy. Through them the voice of the people could express loudly and clearly the general will of the community. They were the people's answer to the hypocrisies of complicated electoral systems and the bewildering intricacies of constitutional arrangements.

Soviets were created throughout the empire when tsarism fell. That of Petrograd, the capital, was akin to a shadow government, while regional and national congresses of soviet delegates became something like self-appointed popular parliaments. The Petrograd soviet issued orders directly to the entire Russian population and exercised far-reaching control over the actions of the Provisional Government. Yet for the time being it refused to assume direct responsibility, preferring to work in the background. "All Power to the Soviets!" was, however, a slogan that increasingly appealed to those among the poorer classes who rebelled against the caution and procrastinations of the Provisional Government or who resented the fact that government was still in the hands of upper-class people.

Although the soviets were, by origin, genuine mass organizations and, because of their flexible organization, extremely sensitive to the changing mood of the masses, their direction, especially in the executive organs of the Petrograd soviet, was concentrated in the hands of the political leaders. These were prominent members of the various socialist parties, which therefore were also known as the soviet parties. They included the Socialist Revolutionaries, a party based primarily on peasant support, with an ideology derived in the main from *narodnik* ideas, and the Social-Democrats, the Russian section of the international Marxist movement. Both of these parties were divided. The Socialist Revolutionary Party split into a left and a right wing in disputes over

various issues raised by the revolution itself; by the end of 1917
these two wings constituted separate parties. The Russian Social-
Democratic Labor Party (RS-DRP) had formed two factions almost
at the very moment of its creation, around the turn of the century,
and as early as 1912 these two factions existed as separate parties.
Of these the Mensheviks (literally: minority faction) were the
more moderate party, akin to the democratic socialists of Western
and Central Europe, while the Bolsheviks (literally: majority faction), led by V. I. Lenin, who a year or two later renamed themselves Communists, advanced more radical revolutionary ideas and
pressed for an intensification of the revolution.

Throughout the spring and summer of 1917 the more moderate
socialists were in a comfortable majority. It was they who resisted the clamor for an exclusively soviet government and who
pressed, instead, for the convocation of a constituent assembly
which might give Russia a democratic parliamentary constitution.
Only the Bolsheviks endorsed the mounting popular pressure for a
purely lower-class government by soviets, aware that this would
amount to the complete political elimination of the old ruling
elements. Moreover, in taking a stand on the various issues the
revolution had placed on the agenda, the Bolsheviks backed the
most sweeping demands made by the poorest of Russia's peasants,
workers, soldiers, and national minorities. This unyielding radicalism of the Bolsheviks was one of the factors producing their
eventual victory. Other factors were the strict discipline of their
organization, and Lenin's determination to seize power when the
moment was propitious—not to mention the vacillation of all other
parties and the growing impatience of the masses with slow and
piecemeal reforms. By September, the Bolsheviks had attained a
majority in the Petrograd soviet, and similar shifts in the balance
of political power took place in other parts of the country. At this
point, the Bolsheviks decided, at Lenin's insistent prodding, to
overthrow the Provisional Government and seize power in the name
of the soviets they now dominated. A relatively bloodless coup
took place on 25 October 1917 (according to the old Russian or
Julian calendar; 7 November according to the modern or Gregorian

calendar). It is therefore known as the October Revolution, even though its anniversary is celebrated in the USSR on 7 November.

THE ANATOMY OF REVOLUTION

In his provocative comparison of the English, American, French, and Russian revolutions, Crane Brinton tried to show that all great revolutions have gone through similar phases of development.[2] At first, a discredited and hollowed-out autocracy is assailed by demands for reform. Concessions are made, but the demands become more sweeping. After a brief struggle for survival, the old autocracy, despite its concessions, is swept away; power slips into the hands of the revolutionary mob or its representatives from among the most radical intelligentsia. Civil war breaks out; terror is unleashed; the counterrevolution is defeated. But, with the victory of the revolution, the radical forces have overstrained their resources. They are now swept away, and forces of moderation and compromise take over, ushering in a new upper class with a vested interest in law, order, and stability. But due to instabilities inherent in such a "thermidorian" regime, it in turn will be replaced by the dictatorship of a military hero, a Bonaparte, who will give the revolution a pseudo-radical direction. Using the slogans of the revolution, he will in fact bring back many conservative and traditionalist features, yet some of the essential changes brought about by the revolution will be preserved. The cycle is closed when the Bonaparte is overthrown by a restoration; but even this cannot turn back the wheel of history altogether, and the most essential gains of the revolution will be preserved. A new ruling class will establish itself, and the cycle can begin anew as society is transformed.

A pattern roughly like this emerged from Brinton's comparison of the four major revolutions. It will be controversial to fit the history of Soviet Russia into it, chiefly because in the Russian case there is a seeming continuity of rule that was absent in the

[2] *The Anatomy of Revolution,* rev. ed. (Englewood Cliffs, N.J.: Prentice-Hall, 1952).

other revolutions. For example, in the early radical phase the Bolsheviks came to power but, unlike the Jacobins in France, their party was never ousted from its monopoly of power; on the contrary, it is still in charge today. One explanation of this seeming continuity is that the party leaders had been careful students of past revolutions, especially the French, and were intimately familiar with the phases through which they had gone. Moreover, they tended to draw analogies between themselves and the French Jacobins as well as the English Puritans, and, being thus forewarned, tried hard to forestall the fate that radicals had suffered in previous revolutions. They were also aware of the possible ebb and flow of radical sentiment among the masses, and, instead of fighting against overwhelming popular sentiments or political trends, tried to swim with the current in order to be able to harness it.

To what extent the Communist Party has managed to control history, and to what extent events have controlled the Party, may become apparent in the discussion to follow. And in the long run, any analogy between the Russian revolution and its precursors in the West may break down completely because of the explosive implications of modern technology and its application in promoting economic growth and new methods of government.

PHASES OF SOVIET RULE

The development of the Soviet political system can be regarded as a sequence of major readjustments of the entire society to new and troubling problems facing it—readjustments in organization, functioning, and policies. The principal goals pursued by the ruling party in successive periods might be summarized as follows: preparation for revolution; the waging of civil war; reconstruction; industrialization; and, finally, coping with the problems of an industrialized society. Each of these major preoccupations has put its stamp on shorter or longer eras in the history of Soviet society.

The Period of Civil War. The October Revolution was relatively bloodless, but in their revolutionary fervor Lenin and his fellow

Bolsheviks excluded or antagonized all other soviet parties and established a dictatorship of bolshevism. Moreover, driven in part by their own boundless enthusiasm and partly by the impatience of the Russian masses, they sought in all seriousness to transform Russia into a socialist society at once and without delay. However popular their early measures may have been with Russia's peasants, workers, and national minorities, their attempt to reach utopia stirred great numbers of people to desperate resistance. Vast areas of the country had not yet been subjected to firm control by the new government, and in these areas the counterrevolutionary forces organized themselves. A bloody civil war, complicated by the intervention of foreign troop units seeking to aid the counterrevolution, raged for about three years, ravaging a country that had already been bled dry by participation in a costly international war. The Communist regime had its back to the wall and was close to extinction several times. Fighting desperately for its very existence and at the same time attempting to reach a utopian goal, the party governed by sheer violence, imposing the emergency rule of a besieged fortress on the entire country. Food supplies and raw materials needed for the war effort were taken from whoever had them in his possession, usually the peasants, direct producers of these commodities. Everyone possessing any skill or knowledge or simple muscle power was pressed into service, willing or not. The workers, in whose name the regime claimed to govern, were forced to work under unbelievably hard conditions. Control over many economic enterprises, which they had seized in the early months of the revolution, was wrested from their hands, and their unions were subjected to the command of the party. Police terror deliberately sought physically to destroy all remnants of political opposition. Military force was applied to recapture the areas that had belonged to the Russian empire but had set up their own non-Bolshevik governments.

A number of reasons can be given to explain why the Bolsheviks won the civil war against what often seemed overwhelming odds. Holding only a small portion of what had once been the vast Russian empire, they had, perhaps, the advantage of being able to shift small armies quickly from one front to the other as the situation required. This advantage was multiplied by the fact that the counterrevolutionary forces did not succeed in coordinating their efforts; indeed, they were at odds with each other. More important, the civil war forced the population to choose between two extremes—Bolshevik rule or the return of landlords and tsarist officials. Extreme situations tend to eliminate all compromise solutions and all counsel of moderation. Unpalatable as both of the extreme alternatives may have been to the majority of Russians, many—perhaps most—of them seem to have dreaded a restoration of the old order more than the uncertain fate awaiting them under Lenin and his followers. At the same time, a sizable number of people, especially among the workers and the young, took a much more positive attitude toward the Bolshevik regime. In their eyes, it was the defender of the revolution, and the revolution meant the destruction of an ugly, reprehensible world and the dawn of a truly humane society. The revolution had the effect of lifting millions of people in Russia to the enthusiasm of crusaders, and of releasing tremendous untapped human energies. In men and women thus affected it awakened the belief that liberty and equality had indeed been won, that the rule of the Bolsheviks had at last made it possible for all men to be brothers. They felt themselves ennobled by the experience of these years, and showed by their actions that the revolution was a cause for which they would gladly give their lives.

Of course, they were also ready to take lives for the cause. Boundless confidence and enthusiasm were mixed with boundless hatred of those who seemed to stand in the way of the millennium. This coexistence of lofty ideals with ruthless practices was perhaps most aptly exemplified by the personality of F. E. Dzerzhinski, the head of the revolution's security force. He was a man of refined taste and ascetic disposition, a burning idealist whom many of his colleagues considered almost a saint. Yet his political principles during the years of the revolution and civil war seem to have been that communism could be achieved by killing off all members of the former ruling class; and in this he was no more than the Red counterpart of the many White (counterrevolutionary) officers who seemed to assume that the revolution could be defeated simply by killing off all workers or all Jews.

This mixture of ruthlessness and idealism pervaded all features of the early Soviet regime, including the formal structure and self-image. In its own pronouncements, as typified by the 1918 *Program of the Russian Communist Party (of Bolsheviks)*, it proclaimed itself a dictatorship, that is, a violent and arbitrary government. It was to be a dictatorship of the proletariat; and in fact the working class was exalted as the ruling class. Workers were given a great variety of material and psychological benefits, whereas people from the old ruling and propertied classes were reduced to the status of barely tolerated pariahs. According to the Party's pronouncements, a dictatorship of the proletariat is an acceptable dictatorship because the proletariat constitutes the majority of the people; indeed, when the poor peasantry is added to it, these workers and peasants are The People, and the dictatorship of the proletariat, or of the toilers,[3] is therefore the dictatorship of the many over the few, of the people over their enemies. Moreover, claimed the spokesmen of the regime, this dictatorship of the people over their former exploiters is democratic because it operates through the institution of the soviets, which, they claimed, was the most simple and direct form of democratic rule yet devised.

These soviets, formally the authoritative governing organizations of the country, were elected by the enfranchised citizens in army units, villages, towns, or city wards. (The constitution disenfranchised members of the old ruling classes and their progeny and weighted the votes of workers and peasants so as to counteract the overwhelming numerical superiority of the peasantry.)[4] Delegates from these grass-roots organizations came together to form soviets for higher territorial units, which in their turn sent delegates to provincial soviets. The apex of this pyramid of dele-

[3] The word "toiler" during the revolutionary years signified everyone and anyone working with his hands, hence the proletarians *and* peasants.

[4] Cf. Article 25 of the 1918 Constitution: "The All-Russian Congress of Soviets is composed of representatives of town soviets, on the basis of one deputy for every 25,000 electors, and representatives of provincial Congresses of Soviets, on the basis of one deputy for every 125,000 inhabitants."

gated delegates was formed by the All-Russian Congress of Soviets of Workers', Peasants', Cossacks', and Red Army Deputies, which, according to the Constitution of 1918, was to meet at least twice a year.

But the soviets as formally constituted had their limitations as governing bodies. Even the Petrograd Soviet of Workers' and Soldiers' Deputies, which had coexisted with the Provisional Government, had been an unwieldy institution and had therefore operated more and more through its committees and executive organs. The semi-annual Congress of Soviets, with its thousands of members meeting for but a few days, could not be expected to function as a national parliament, although formally it was the sovereign decision-making organ of the republic. More meaningful debate and decision-making could be carried on only by a smaller body meeting more frequently. To some extent these functions were carried out by the All-Russian Central Executive Committee (Vtsik), a permanent committee of around 200 members set up by the Congress of Soviets and formally responsible to it. According to Article 31 of the Constitution, the Central Executive Committee was to be the "supreme legislative, administrative, and controlling body of the Russian Socialist Federal Soviet Republic." In turn it appointed a cabinet to carry out the functions of a national executive. This was the Council of People's Commissars, headed by a Chairman, whose role was thus closely analogous to that of a Premier or Prime Minister in Western cabinets. In addition, the Central Executive Committee formed some agencies not under the direct authority of the Council of People's Commissars. On each territorial level, from the village to the federal republic, each soviet or congress of soviets was, according to the Constitution, the supreme authority. Each was organized in a fashion analogous to, although simpler than, the all-Russian institution: a representative assembly which elected its own executive committee. At the same time, all lower organizations were subject to the decisions and decrees of the higher soviets.

This early soviet government machinery was remarkably unstable, partly because of its own structural features, and partly for extraneous reasons. Structurally, the pyramid of soviets was an unstable mixture of pronounced centralism and equally strong centrifugal tendencies, and these two trends were forever clashing. The urge to practice grass-roots independence on a local level was, of course, fortified by the chaos of civil war, which often forced autonomy on large or small areas and prevented the central government from exercising effective control or even guidance. Such tendencies toward autonomy were reinforced by the spirit of the revolutionary period, which had manifested itself in a general burst of spontaneous autonomy practiced by the peasantry, the soldiers in the field, the workers in factories, and others, and which many of its practitioners took to be the goal of the revolution.

Many even in the Communist Party believed that syndicalism, egalitarian military organization, national autonomy, village self-government, and the like, were part of the Communist goal. This misconception (as it turned out to be) was linked to the exuberant optimism of the revolutionary weeks, which had expressed itself in the belief that the people henceforth could govern themselves, that professional civil servants were no longer required, that, instead, even kitchen help could have a turn at running the government. In its most extreme form, this faith was soon abandoned by most communists; but for a time the belief persisted that a member of the Communist Party could automatically be assumed to perform well in any governmental assignment he might be given, and that consequently the government machinery could safely be staffed with Party members almost at random. This belief, too, turned out to be unrealistic. The Party leaders came to recognize that the qualifications of a good professional revolutionary were not necessarily those of a capable administrator. Hence, as it organized itself seriously, the Soviet regime faced a chronic and almost overwhelming recruitment problem. It had to find administrative and executive personnel among a population in which the rate of literacy and political sophistication was very low; and it was forced to recruit such personnel among the less-educated layers of the population because the qualified people were products and often adherents of the old order. Whatever their actual political convictions, the latter were clearly bourgeois and hence could not be entrusted with the tasks of governing the proletarian dictatorship—if they could be trusted at all.

The chaotic situation during the civil war, the economic ruin and social dislocation prevailing everywhere, forced the government to improvise and experiment quickly, boldly, even desperately, while struggling to maintain and widen control. Under these circumstances, obviously, any plans the communist rulers may have had for conducting the business of state were condemned to failure (and in fact they had no such plans). Instead, government in the early years of the revolution inevitably came to be a tangle of improvised policies and hastily established agencies, an administrative mess that at times seemed unbearable. At such moments, Lenin's typical responses were either to fire those who had shown themselves incompetent or to create new centralizing and supervising agencies. Such measures could not, however, improve the situation, and the creation of a stable government service turned out to be a very long-range task of organization and recruitment.

A problem more quickly and effectively solved was that of overcoming the centrifugal tendencies inherent in the soviet organization, curbing the autonomy of grass-roots government, and taming the soviets into an obedient tool of the ruling party. The very instability of soviet institutions aided the Communist Party here, because it weakened their structure. Deputies to soviets were subject to immediate recall by their constituents, and in the early years the voters made frequent use of this device, which was praised as thoroughly democratic. Indeed, if shifting public moods represent the will of the people, the soviets were obviously quite sensitive to public opinion. But at the same time they were defenseless against those who might sway the mood of the voters; and for doing this the Communist Party had a variety of effective devices, ranging from coercion and threats to persuasion and incentives. As we have seen, moreover, the strong centrifugal—not to say anarchic

—tendencies of the soviet structure were matched by an equally strong centralist bias spelled out clearly in the constitution of 1918; and it did not take the Party long to impose central control on the regional, provincial, and local soviets. The central government gradually established its field agencies; in cases of special need, extraordinary emissaries would be dispatched for the purpose of establishing control; and at all times the political police, the Cheka, was ready to mete out summary revolutionary justice to anyone alleged to stand in the way of the regime's policies. Meanwhile, the Red Army served as the main instrument for re-establishing control over some of the scattered parts of the Russian empire.

A more subtle method of taming the soviets, however, was Party control. The soviets were grass-roots organizations of the lower classes, and the delegates felt themselves to be representatives of their entire constituencies. But they were also members of the various socialist parties. Those soviets in which the Bolsheviks formed the majority by this very token became instruments of the Communist Party, because, although the structure of the soviets was loose and flexible and the individual delegate was not restricted by intricate rules, the Bolshevik members were expected to act strictly within the bounds of Party discipline, so that the caucus of Bolsheviks within any soviet organization became in fact the decision-making center. To be sure, Bolsheviks did not constitute absolute majorities in many soviets, not even on the national level. But in the course of the civil war the regime first harassed and then outlawed all other parties, drove them underground and, after a long and stubborn struggle, managed to destroy them completely. In this fashion, all political opposition was shattered while the Bolsheviks remained well organized. Even a minority of Bolshevik deputies, acting as a disciplined caucus, could dominate the entire system of soviets. In a surprisingly short time, the central agencies of the Communist Party and the soviet system found themselves able to control the personnel of local soviets and even to assign to them staff people from the center. "The strengthening of local state organs with experienced personnel transferred from work at the center was regarded by Lenin as one of the measures which could ensure [the unity of local and state interests]," says a recent Soviet source.[5]

By the beginning of 1921, the Bolsheviks had at last won the civil war. To be sure, all of the former tsarist lands had not yet been reconquered; nor had all foreign troops been ejected from the country, nor all areas of unrest and rebellion pacified. But the major struggle was over; the regime was in the saddle. The methods by which this victory had been achieved, however, had been so harsh that the ruling party had lost the sympathy of most of those people who had helped it win. Even as the last serious counter-revolutionary attempt was put down, the Party seemed to disintegrate in violent disputes; peasants in various parts of the country were in open rebellion, the working class seemed about to disintegrate, and in one of the bastions of proletarian bolshevism, the naval fortress of Kronstadt, the workers revolted against Bolshevik rule in the name of the soviets.

Having thus lost almost all of its political capital, the Bolshevik regime staged a careful strategic retreat of retrenchment, known as the New Economic Policy (NEP). It began as a fiscal device instituted to stimulate agricultural production and gain the confidence of the peasantry, but it soon had many economic, political, and social ramifications, and led to the re-introduction of private enterprise in agriculture, crafts, retailing, and lesser industry. The NEP therefore resulted in what we might call a socioeconomic interregnum.[6] For a number of years capitalism and socialism coexisted more or less peacefully within Soviet society, even while in the political realm the Party attempted to retain sovereignty or proletarian hegemony by continuing to dominate and guide the system of soviets. Ideologically, too, the 1920s were an interregnum. Outside the Party, various intellectual currents not in tune with communism were grudgingly tolerated, and within the Party

[5] A. Denisov and M. Kirichenko, *Soviet State Law* (Moscow, 1960), p. 199.
[6] In Soviet writings, it is always called the Transition Period. For a recent Soviet definition and discussion see, for instance, P. I. Nikitin, *Osnovy politicheskoi ekonomii; populiarnyi uchebnik,* 2d ed. (Moscow, 1962), pp. 193–217.

debate and controversy flared up once again. The immediate cause
for this renewed disunity was the prolonged illness and, ultimately,
the death of Lenin, which deprived the Party of the authoritative
command he had wielded. The bitter debates in the Party were
therefore part of a struggle for power which shook it from about
1922 to 1927, with repercussions that were felt long afterward.
For this reason, the various contestants were vitally interested in
problems of Party organization, management, and membership.
Those who lost did so very largely because they could not, or
would not, rebel against the principles of centralism, discipline,
and managerial supremacy which Lenin had given his political
machine. But problems of organization were not the only matters
of conflict in this crisis. The larger issues were real enough; they
concerned the meaningfulness, in communist perspective, of the
socioeconomic and ideological interregnum—how long it should
last, whether or not it should be replaced, and, if so, by what kind
of order.

The Advent of Stalin.   The decision was made after J. V. Stalin,
the Party's Secretary General, had emerged from the power struggles as the undisputed leader of the Communist Party. It was
decided to industrialize Soviet Russia as rapidly as possible so as
to lay economic foundations on the basis of which socialism, or at
least the survival of the Soviet state in the midst of a hostile world,
would be possible. This new policy unleashed a new revolution in
Russia, for the Party now undertook no less a task than that of
thoroughly changing the entire social system, destroying entire
classes and creating new ones, altering the entire national way of
life. In the process the independent peasantry that had risen out of
the revolution was destroyed and replaced by the collective farm
system; the autonomy of the labor unions was severely curbed;
minority strivings for self-determination were outlawed; and the
system of soviets was emasculated more thoroughly than ever before. An entirely new class, the Soviet intelligentsia, was created,
and the regime began to wrestle with the problem of how to assure
that the educated elite be both competent and submissive. Mean-

while, impressive achievements were made in creating a broad industrial base.

In trying to transform society in this fashion, the regime resorted to the most thorough methods of ruthlessness and violence, and at the same time evoked, at least for a period, a measure of dedication, enthusiasm, and heroism that remind one of the crusading spirit awakened at the time of the civil war. In effect, Stalin tried to achieve in the course of a few years a transformation which in other countries had taken generations of organic development. In this effort he seems to have felt that all humanitarian considerations were misplaced, that the attempt would fail if any attention were paid to the needs of consumers or the happiness of citizens. His program of industrialization turned out to be a crash program, hastily conceived and executed in a burst of revolutionary euphoria that had little to do with rational planning. It therefore had all the unfortunate consequences of crash programs—tremendous waste of lives, human energy, and material resources; bottlenecks; duplication of efforts; outright failures; and the hysterical search for scapegoats every time something went wrong. A whole generation was deeply affected by the spirit of this crash program, and even today many features of the Soviet political system can be explained by it.

Setbacks, inefficiency, and widespread suffering notwithstanding, Russia under Stalin was transformed from a predominantly rural society into a leading industrial nation. In the process, a dictatorship of a new type was imposed on the people—new in the sense that it subjected Soviet society to as stringent and far-reaching controls as had ever been imposed on a nation. In addition, the internal structure of the government was thoroughly changed. In the 1920s Stalin had gained leadership over the Communist Party; he now proceeded to fortify this leadership into an impregnable personal dictatorship not only over the Party, but also over the country.

Lenin had ruled the Party by virtue of his prestige. Stalin ruled the nation by virtue of his tight control over the political machine. His most important steppingstone to power had been the Party

Secretariat; his most important organ of government was probably his personal secretariat which, formally if not politically, transcended the framework of the Communist Party. Below this personal secretariat were three parallel structures of power, a trinity of institutional networks that worked with and against each other, all serving the one man who controlled their policies, organization, and personnel. This trinity consisted of the Communist Party, the Soviet government apparatus, and the political police, none of which could in truth claim to be superior to or sovereign over the others. For the sovereign was Stalin. Before his ascendancy the Party had been the supreme decision-making organization in the USSR; therefore, this was a significant change in the structure of the political system. Indeed, it must be pointed out that, as he rose to dictatorial power, Stalin not only shoved the Party aside but in a sense destroyed it. He did so not only by altering its role within the political system, but also by physically eliminating most of the members who had belonged to it before the revolution, thus killing off a major portion of those who had remained from Lenin's party. Finally, the destruction of Lenin's party was sealed by an ideological transformation, which some students of Soviet history have called a "cultural counterrevolution." This was a turn away from all those elements in Marxist and Leninist thought which stressed liberal values such as freedom and equality and which guided men to radical criticism of all institutions of exploitation and domination. Furthermore, as we shall see, this "cultural counterrevolution" was a perversion of all Marxist aspirations toward scientific verisimilitude; instead of being a means of scientific self-orientation (which at least Marxist–Leninist ideology had striven to be) it became an ideology of self-justification and self-glorification.

The Postwar Years. By the time the October Revolution was twenty years old, Soviet Russia was just beginning to settle into this new mold, and the outlines of what might be called the Stalinist political system were becoming established. Soon after, the nation was involved in a very costly war which at first brought the regime close to military and political collapse. The nation rallied, however, and the Soviet Union emerged from the war as one of the world's most formidable powers. Still, a tremendous task of repair and reconstruction lay ahead; and in trying to cope with it, while simultaneously engaging in a global cold war and armaments race, the regime forced its people once again to undergo scarcely tolerable hardships of many kinds. In the postwar period, therefore, the regime became more oppressive.

Yet simultaneously new social forces were growing which were opposed to the Stalinist system of government. For various reasons, the postwar years saw a discernible growth of popular dissatisfaction with the policy of economic austerity, an increasing desire among the population to see some material results from its years of backbreaking toil and miserly self-denial. In addition, industrial development brought with it the rise of a new educated elite characterized by a variety of anti-Stalinist trends. For one thing, as in all industrial societies, the need for more and more professional and specialized personnel led to a rapidly growing differentiation among the Soviet Union's citizenry, and hence the development of something resembling broad interest groups, each with different aspirations, methods of work, and ways of looking at the social system. Both the pressure for improved living standards and the changes in outlook brought about by education and professional life were intensified by differences in outlook between the old and the new generations. Furthermore, the Stalinist dictatorship promoted recurrent (albeit muted) claims for some degree of autonomy among various sections of the population, among them not only the creative intellectuals and professional experts in various fields, but also, perhaps, the leadership of the Communist Party. All these trends were bound to intensify as the USSR became a mature industrial society. They came to the surface when Stalin's death, in March 1953, forced the political system to reorganize itself, and they are still operating today. In short, the Soviet Union has crossed the threshold of industrialization and has become a society which most Western scholars would identify as "modern." This transformation cannot but affect the structure and functioning of its political system; and without doubt the changes that have been going on, now reluctantly, now rapidly, in the last ten years or more, can be regarded as the reorganization of that system for the new tasks: having solved the problem of industrialization, it must now seek to manage the complex economy and society it has thereby created. This task of restructuring is complicated by the ever-present struggle for power within the top ranks of the leadership.

The struggle that ensued after Stalin's death among the leading figures and the grouping they represented resulted in the emergence of N. S. Khrushchev as the political leader who maintained himself in the top-ranking position for almost a decade. Most Western observers seem to have taken for granted that he represented the upper echelon of the Communist Party, especially its provincial and regional satraps, and his victory was considered as part of the restoration of the Party to the sovereign position it had held in the first ten or fifteen years of Soviet government. When I first drafted this book, Khrushchev was still in power, and it seemed difficult to imagine how he might be dislodged. Yet even then it was obvious that the Soviet political system in the 1960s is in far greater flux than it was a decade ago, and observers should have been aware that any reorganization, or any resolutions of power struggles, might be quite transitory. As this is written, Khrushchev has been ousted by two experienced leaders very closely associated with him, one of them a lifetime Party official, the other a successful career civil servant who on his outstanding merit was co-opted into the highest ranks of the Party. The arrangement by which they share authority within the political system is obviously more unstable than was the leadership position of Mr. Khrushchev; hence the need for caution in assessing the permanence of present arrangements is all the greater.

Chapter III
Political Culture

The term "political culture" denotes the subjective ideas of the members of a political system regarding that system and their own roles within it. These ideas constitute different images or perceptions of the actual existing social order, and they also include various sets of values, expectations, and aspirations. The manner in which a polity is perceived and the hopes, fears, and strivings it generates can be assumed to vary from one group of the population to another and from individual to individual. True, some views and attitudes may be common to all people in a given system. Still, differences may be significant, and therefore a survey of the political culture must be based on a preliminary survey of the major social groups—hence, of the social structure. In addition to perceptions, expectations, and values concerning politics and government, political culture also includes the ingrained habits of people, their actual political behavior which, when it becomes traditional, takes on the character of an institution. The boundary between views and expectations, on the one hand, and actual behavior, on the other, is uncertain; in fact, ideas and actions can be explained in terms of each other, for instance, by reducing behavior patterns to role expectations. At the same time, one might attempt to fix the boundary by distinguishing between implicit or latent political culture, on the one hand, and manifest or overt political culture, on the other. The former is expressed in actual behavior and expressed attitudes; the latter, in codified laws, constitutions, and official ideologies.

The manifest, or overt, political culture of the USSR is easy to summarize. The implicit culture, however, is very difficult to present because our ability to study the actual behavior of the people of the Soviet Union and to survey their views and aspirations is very limited. An understanding of this latent political culture is obviously important for an analysis of the Soviet system, but the statements made in the following pages are offered with great diffidence because they are based on very impressionistic evidence. To verify them satisfactorily is impossible under present conditions.

GROUP INTERESTS

Social Stratification. As an industrial society, the Soviet Union is stratified in a manner not too different from the United States. Such a statement can be made more precise by specifying the differences in stratification that distinguish the two societies. The most well-known difference is the lower level of the general standard of living. Profession by profession, layer by layer, the Soviet citizen consumes fewer goods and services than his American counterpart. Furthermore, entire components of the American stratification pattern are absent, among them that stratum we would call the "very rich." Although a small handful of men in the highest political posts probably enjoy all the material advantages they might desire, the USSR does not have the hundreds of millionaire families which form the apex of the United States' pyramid of wealth. We have already noted that a number of professional groups important in the United States are either less important or totally absent in Soviet society. Furthermore, those professions that predominate in both societies are at times evaluated somewhat differently. The relative status of any occupation can be measured either by the esteem its members enjoy among the population—and the esteem given to any one group may vary from one section of the population to another—or by the material rewards the particular profession earns. The two societies' ranking systems may or may not yield the same results: physicians are held in high esteem in America and are also highly rewarded, but farmers, although held in high esteem by public opinion, are near the bottom of the standard-of-living scale. The physician in the USSR is very highly regarded by the people but is low on the pay scale; farmers are close to the bottom not only in material rewards but also in the popular regard. Until a few years ago, it would have been necessary to mention the inmates of labor camps as the lowest class in the social structure of the USSR. Today, their number appears to have decreased so much that, perhaps, they should no longer be taken into account, just as an analysis of the American social structure would not consider the inmates of prisons and penitentiaries as a class by itself. Teachers and professors have a far higher prestige in the Soviet Union than in the United States, and professorial salaries are much nearer the top than in the United States. Lawyers, in contrast, are far nearer the bottom both in esteem and in remuneration.

In the Soviet Union, as compared with the United States, differences in social prestige and material reward are, it seems, somewhat more closely related to differences in educational level. In other words, in the USSR more education is somewhat more likely to lead to higher pay, greater responsibility, and greater esteem. There is also a closer correspondence of all the above factors (education, rewards, and esteem) to the degree of urbanization: all three factors tend to rise with the size of the community in which the individual lives. This phenomenon is so striking in the Soviet Union that one might say that both the regime and the population have a strong urban bias—the regime, because of its interest in industrialization, its preference for workers over peasants, and its suspicion of the rural way of life; the population, because of the material, cultural, political, and status advantages enjoyed by city dwellers.

One important similarity between the societies of the USSR and the United States is the tendency of status differences to be related to differences in national origin. The Soviet Union's society, like that of the United States, is a melting pot of nationalities, and in both countries the population tends to assign different prestige to various groups. Owing to lack of precise information it would be extremely difficult to construct a scale of relative status for Soviet nationalities, but we probably are safe in asserting that both the official regime and popular opinion attribute to the Great Russians a status roughly similar to that enjoyed by white Anglo-Saxon Protestants in the United States. For an analysis of the political system this fact is relevant because it gives the favored nationality unearned privileges in the process of elite recruitment. In other words, Great Russians, like white Anglo-Saxon Protestants, seem to have better chances, all other things being equal, to rise higher in many career lines than do people of different origin.

Citizens of the USSR appear to be both rank conscious and egalitarian. The two attitudes might possibly be explained as long-ingrained traits of the Russian national character; at the same time, both have been strengthened by the Soviet regime. The egalitarian belief in equal opportunities for all is an integral part of communist doctrine and is carefully fostered by the Communist Party. Belief in equality of opportunity is, of course, easily compatible with the notion that rank has its privileges and that differences in performance should lead to differences in status or material reward; this doctrine, too, has been carefully promoted by the regime. At the same time, there is a latent groundswell among the Soviet people of hatred of all higher-ups, a leveling egalitarianism which rejects the very idea of rank and salary differentiation.[1] This feeling, too, has been part of Russian national traditions; it also was encouraged by the ideology of the revolution. To be sure, Stalin and his successors subsequently rejected it, but there are occasions when the Party seems to be making use of such popular feelings of resentment.

Social mobility in Soviet society, like the class structure, corresponds in general to the pattern prevalent in the United States. Revolutions, of course, thoroughly shake up the previously prevailing social structure, and the Russian revolution was no exception. Entire classes and professions were eliminated; the top

[1] The Polish sociologist Stanisław Ossowski in his brilliant discussion of class structures and class images has convincingly shown that the underprivileged majority (those who are less wealthy, less powerful, and perform less desirable labor) are more likely to have a dichotomous view of society, dividing it into "us and them," poor and rich, working class and leisure class; whereas those endowed with greater power, wealth, leisure, and agreeable work tend to see society structured in several or many layers with fluid boundaries—a classless though unequal society. See *Struktura Klasowa W Społecznej Świadomości* (Łódź, 1957); German edition: *Klassenstruktur im sozialen Bewusstsein* (Neuwied, 1962).

and the bottom of the social pyramid were to some extent reversed. Out of the chaos and class warfare of the revolutionary years a newly stratified society has emerged. From the point of view of social mobility, this new society is far more open than was Russia under tsarism. This openness itself is undoubtedly a result of the revolution. Even more, however, it is the consequence of Soviet economic development, of the transformation of a comparatively primitive society based mainly on agriculture into a mature industrial society. This transformation has been so rapid that the need for technical and managerial experts has—at least in the past —been almost insatiable. Hence it seemed that there was virtually unlimited room at the top—not at the very summit, to be sure, but among the professional elite. Anyone with the desired talents and the necessary drive could rise in the new Soviet society. Surely this must have been an important factor in the political socialization of the younger generation. And yet, two features of this mobility have surprised Western observers. One is the piecemeal rate of social mobility, from one generation to another: mobility does not, as a rule, take the form of a dramatic leap from very low to very high social status even though the Soviet elite, like the American, contains its share of people who have started near the very bottom. More frequently, the individual moves from one status group into the next higher or lower one, and he is likely also to articulate his life's ambition in terms of moderate advances. Such a piecemeal pattern of mobility is similar to that prevailing in the United States. Even more surprising to the Western observer has been the realization that prerevolutionary status advantages have persisted far more stubbornly than the violence of the revolution would have led us to assume. To be sure, the old upper classes were destroyed, their members eliminated or reduced to the status of pariahs. But the new Soviet elite, in terms of education, status, and material reward, contains a surprisingly high proportion of people who are descended from the old upper strata.

The Peasantry. Perhaps the most significant difference between the societies of the USSR and the United States is the glaring contrast between urban and rural life. Small towns and villages in the United States are, as a rule, simpler, smaller, and perhaps poorer copies of cities. The inhabitants of the former and the latter enjoy similar goods, services, and facilities, and, broadly speaking, share the same views and way of life. In Soviet Russia, in contrast, what might be called the peasant way of life still distinguishes large parts of the rural from the urban population. The reason for this is that the city and all it carries with it has not yet managed to penetrate as deeply into the Russian countryside. The Soviet regime has not yet succeeded as much as it wished in making the peasant a child of the twentieth century. The peasant way of life can, in most general fashion, be explained by the fact that the farmer lives according to the rhythm of nature rather than that of the machine and the clock. The sun, the winds, and the seasons determine most of his activities, which to the urban dweller therefore acquire a disturbingly and stubbornly irrational, planless, and erratic character. Since the special wisdom which allows such careful attunement to the rhythm of nature is age-old and is transmitted in highly traditional forms, the peasant tends to be strongly bound by traditions, customs, and superstitions. Living in relative isolation within the narrow bounds of a village, rarely venturing further than the nearest market town, the typical peasant also develops strong attachments to the primary groups within which he is born, lives, and dies—his family, his village, his church, and his national or language group. These groups form his universe. They therefore become mainstays of his personal and emotional security.

The peasant is naturally hostile to the city and feels it as a distinct threat to his entire way of life. The city spawns new-fangled ideas which corrode peasant tradition, religion, customs, and prejudices. Its way of life promises liberation from the peasant way of life to all who wish to rebel against it; cities therefore represent a deeply subversive attraction which lures away the more enterprising peasant youths and thus threatens to destroy the bonds of family and village. The city with its financial power is seen as the exploiter of the peasantry. As the administrative center, it becomes the seat of hated bureaucrats and officials, of military recruiters and police jails. Among the Russian peasants, such feelings were common and still may be widespread. They were best symbolized, perhaps, by the contempt and envy of the peasants for all other professions, by the feeling that tilling the soil was the only labor worthy of a man. Therefore, the peasantry was the salt of the earth, all others being parasites—the most objectionable parasites, according to this attitude, being those who do not work at all with their hands, the educated, the professionals, the intelligentsia.

The Russian peasantry has, traditionally, shown a lack of interest in politics, an attitude that irritates believers in democracy or socialism as systems requiring popular participation, who must inevitably find it stupid. Politics, of course, can mean several things. It may mean active involvement in current, day-to-day public issues; or it may mean conscious planning for the future through the elaboration of long-range political programs, platforms, and utopias. It might be reasonable to assert that, on the whole, the Russian peasantry has been apolitical in both senses. As a severely underprivileged class, it has tended to think in terms of very short time spans and, therefore, has not been very receptive to utopias—or, indeed, to any kind of political program involving planning, saving, the postponement of gratification, or a life led primarily for the purpose of improving the lot of one's children. This, at least, is the general impression one gets from reading the history of the Russian peasantry.

As for day-to-day politics, the Russian peasants' general lack of interest may, to some extent, be due to the fact that a rural population anywhere is difficult to organize. Second, the statist political culture that prevailed under tsarism and still (or again) prevails today[2] prevents a deep sense of involvement from develop-

[2] To be sure, Soviet statism is very different from tsarist statism. Tsarism was on the whole paternalistic. It left decision-making to the ruling bureaucracy and was satisfied if the subjects obeyed and acquiesced. Soviet statism, as we shall see, desires the active participation in public life of all citizens. At the same time, the transition from the old pattern to the new has been slow and difficult, nowhere more so than in the countryside and in the national minority regions. In those areas, the Party chief and government official, in their relations with the peasantry, still bear striking resemblances in many respects to the paternalistic tsarist bureaucrat.

ing in those who are told that citizenship is primarily a set of duties, that citizenship is obedience. Although the Communist regime sedulously seeks to inculcate in all the people a sense of responsibility—often by means the outsider might regard as contrived—large numbers of people, especially among the peasantry, seem to lack a sense of civic responsibility and to disdain participation in public life as meaningless, except insofar as it serves their individual purposes. What is in it for me? How can I get by? How can I beat the system? Those are the questions many Soviet citizens seem to ask themselves, showing a highly pragmatic view of public institutions that has little to do with active citizenship. Thus, power corrupts . . . those who are subject to it.[3]

In the case of the peasantry, political apathy may also spring from an awareness that politics is part of city life and therefore one of the many ways in which the urban population deceives and despoils the peasant. Politics is thus suspect, and so is government, with its bureaucracy and administration and all the institutions the city has imposed on the countryside. The attitude of Russian peasants to central government has been described in seemingly contradictory terms. On the one hand, they have been lauded for their meek submissiveness, their Christian resolve to bear all evil without resistance. On the other hand, they have been described as anarchists who repeatedly unleash bloody revolt against all authority. In fact, the two images are not at all contradictory. True, the Russian peasant, under tsars as under Bolshevik commissars, has rarely had the power to resist, and has therefore developed extraordinary meekness and humility. At the same time, the very extreme of this kind of behavior imperceptibly shades into an attitude that can only be called antisocial. Overtly meek behavior may be the mask that hides sly evasiveness or even a habit of deliberately sabotaging the directives of authorities. The church has served to console the peasant for his bleak life. Another consoler to which he has turned with equal fervor is vodka; and vodka may release pent-up resentment and destructiveness. (In

[3] For a pertinent discussion of apathy as an inevitable reaction to the bureaucratic way of life, see Robert Presthus, *The Organizational Society* (New York: Knopf, 1962), Chapter 7.

the last few years the television set has been added as a third vehicle by which the Russian peasant may transport himself into a dream world beyond the harshness of everyday existence.) Finally, the antisocial attitude of the Russian peasant is expressed by his chronic hostility to all attempts on the part of the Soviet regime to press him into collective enterprises. Almost all peasants in the USSR have for many years been organized in collective farms, but the regime has always had difficulty getting the members to put in a sufficient amount of effort to operate these enterprises. Russian peasants have always preferred to spend as much labor as possible on their own little garden plots, the produce of which they were allowed to sell on the free market. In this sense, if not more generally, the Russian peasant reveals a seemingly ineradicable devotion to his own homestead and his own property, as well as to the right to dispose of it freely in the open market; and he shows an equally unceasing hatred for the system that has been imposed on him.

The Working Class. It may be argued that the entire course of Soviet history has shown a persistent tendency to eliminate the peasantry, or at least to change its entire way of life.[4] Telling testimony of such a trend is the reduction of the peasantry from about four fifths of Russia's total population in 1917 to about one quarter in 1962.[5] The revolution was made in the name of the proletariat, and the regime has made repeated efforts to convince the workers that they were its chief beneficiaries. In the society that claims to have eliminated class antagonisms, the working class

[4] In making this statement, I disagree with those scholars who would explain the Soviet regime or the present-day Russian national character as a manifestation of the peasant culture of Old Russia, or who would explain the behavior of Communist chiefs as the typical behavior of the toughest and most vicious types of Russian peasants. Two such attempts, very different from each other, have been those of Nicholas Vakar, *The Taproot of Soviet Society* (New York: Harper & Row, 1962), and Geoffrey Gorer and John Rickman, *The People of Great Russia* (New York: Chanticleer Press, 1950).

[5] For the 1917 figures, see Nicholas S. Timasheff, *The Great Retreat* (New York: E. P. Dutton, 1946), p. 286. For the 1962 figures, see *SSSR v tsifrakh v 1962 g.* (Moscow, 1962), p. 22; also *Narodnoe Khoziaistvo SSSR v 1961 g.* (Moscow, 1962), p. 27.

is praised as the first among equals and "the most consistent champion of communist ideals. Among the working class there are incomparably fewer survivals of the psychology of property-owners such as is characteristic of part of the peasantry, or of individualism, which persists among some representatives of the intelligentsia. The traditions of socialist mutual assistance and comradely solidarity have their deepest roots in the working class."[6] In almost all periods of its history, the Communist Party has favored workers and their children in recruiting new members, thus providing easier access to positions of leadership to the working class. Until 1936, moreover, the influence of workers in the governmental apparatus (soviets) was deliberately increased by weighting their vote as against that of the peasantry. In other ways, as well, workers have been given favored treatment, for instance, by the establishment of discriminatory quotas for admission to higher educational institutions and by the provision of special educational facilities only for workers, so that they more easily than other groups could improve their status. Such opportunities still exist today, in the form, for instance, of evening schools and correspondence courses, and workers are still urged to take advantage of them. But one can read complaints in the Soviet press that at times even graduation from night or correspondence school leads the worker nowhere; he simply stays at his present job.[7] In any event, the climb is hard for a person whose energies are spent in the workshop, and the rate of both failures and dropouts is high in such institutions.[8] In the first decades of the regime, the drain from the working class into the professions was considerable. Standards were low because personnel for leadership was at a premium. Today there is less room at the top; or, rather, there is a very great demand for people with professional skills and education, but the public school system provides an adequate number of graduates. Standards are rising, and, for many reasons, the

[6] *Fundamentals of Marxism–Leninism; Manual,* 2nd ed. (Moscow, 1963), p. 596.
[7] See *Trud i zarabotnaia plata,* No. 9 (1962), p. 37.
[8] For a discussion of the high rate of dropouts from evening schools, see *Uchitel'skaia Gazetz* (June 24, 1961).

educational screening process tends to favor the children of the professional classes. Of course, the educational ladder is not the only method of elite recruitment. Especially for recruiting its political elite, including such institutions as the police, the political system of the USSR has often seemed deliberately to circumvent the process of formal education. It relies, instead, on avenues of purely political training, i.e., the Party and its youth affiliate. This practice inevitably favors the working class. Its effect has been to give the top leadership—or, perhaps more precisely and at the same time more broadly, the professional Party officials—a noticeable proletarian character, certainly as compared with the professional elite of the society as a whole.

All such measures of recruitment can drain off only a small proportion of the workers; they leave the vast majority unaffected —all the more so because, in line with the feverish urgency of the effort toward industrialization, the conditions of life and work imposed on the industrial labor force have been most stringent. The average worker in the USSR has been so preoccupied with these conditions that he has had little opportunity to escape into a different social stratum. To put it another way, the working class as a whole has developed only fairly modest aspirations and expectations concerning upward social mobility. In this, it appears to be similar to the industrial working class of the United States and other Western countries.[9]

If we look at the workers' situation from the point of view of the group's social prestige, in its own eyes as well as in the eyes of others, the image is rather contradictory. On the one hand, official ideology never tires of pointing out that the workers are the dominant class. This notion is complemented by the egalitarian rhetoric which assures all Soviet citizens (and makes them assure themselves) that all are equal, that each type of toiler can and must be proud of the specific contribution he makes toward the growth

[9] According to Robert Lane, the freedoms in which American workers appear to be most interested are (a) freedom to criticize the heterodox; (b) freedom to say conventional things; (c) industrial freedoms, such as job mobility, freedom to be late for work, coffee breaks, and the like; and (d) freedom of consumption. See his *Political Ideology* (Glencoe, Ill.: The Free Press, 1962).

and prosperity of Soviet socialist society. Daily life in Soviet society indeed manages to blur sharp distinctions of rank by throwing workers together with professionals in a great variety of activities. This, too, furnishes many occasions for confirming the feeling that all are equal or that all accept each other regardless of rank and position. Yet despite the egalitarian rhetoric, the typical Soviet worker seems pretty sharply conscious of having lower-class status, both in his own estimation and in the estimation of the professional elite.

To some extent, this attribution of lower-class status to workers can be explained by the preoccupation of the Soviet political system (both those who dominate it and those who are its subjects) with what is called culture (*kul'tura*) or culturedness (*kul'turnost*). These terms, in Soviet parlance, denote the mastery of all the techniques required to cope with life in the industrial age. To have culture, or to be cultured, therefore means to be literate, to have an up-to-date general education—to be interested in and have knowledge of public affairs and modern science, as well as art and literature. It also means to have developed the habits of daily life which enable the individual to get along with the complexities of large bureaucratic organizations, modern machinery, and big-city life. At times, Soviet citizens are prone to measure the degree of a person's "culturedness" by petty externals, such as table manners, style of dress, or cultural interests and attainments. It is "cultured" to wear a necktie or go to a symphony concert; it is uncultured to spit on the floor, get drunk in public, or openly manifest amorous affection for a member of the opposite sex. The intense preoccupation of the regime and its citizens with culture, defined in such a fashion, can be explained as part of the system's gigantic and feverish effort to modernize a backward society. In this effort, it is at times difficult to distinguish the petty externals from the intrinsic attainments. Even Peter the Great had had difficulty distinguishing one from the other. Hence in his attempt to Westernize his empire he wasted time putting his aristocrats into Western clothing, demanding that they shave off their beards, and forcing them to take up pipe-smoking. Similarly, in trying to replace the peasant way of life with the industrial age, many in the Soviet regime concentrate on external manners and middle-class values. Quite likely this tendency is enforced by the inevitable snobbishness of the educated elite, threatened as it is by the proletarian character of the political elite and by its own recent rise to higher status. Finally, emphasis on the spit-and-polish and sophistication of urban life is enforced by the latent but strong inferiority complex that Russians have had for centuries in the face of Western Europe, and which makes them painfully self-conscious whenever Western observers have a chance to witness "uncultured" behavior or "uncultured" features of the Soviet way of life.

The life and work of the proletariat, however, is rough. The workers' training and labor stresses physical rather than intellectual accomplishments. The factory is dirty, stinking, and noisy. Squeamishness, fastidiousness, and aesthetic refinement are highly dysfunctional in the worker and therefore have little chance to develop. The workers' ties to the peasant way of life are still quite strong; and one of the features of this way of life is a direct, spontaneous, and uncomplicated attitude to such facts of life as digestion and sex, matters on which "cultured" conversation and behavior have placed a strong taboo. It is reasonable to assume that the persistence of "uncultured" behavior, seen in this light, is often a subtle form of rebellion or defiance; in fact, Western observers seem to feel that the typical Russian worker reciprocates the antagonistic feelings of the educated toward him. He, too, seems to be affected by an inferiority complex vis-à-vis the West, but in his case the more normal reaction appears to be neither groveling admiration of the West nor self-conscious denigration of everything Russian, but rather a strengthening of his feelings of nationalism, and therefore a strong tendency to give aggressive support to his government's foreign policy.

At the same time, the persistence of "uncultured" behavior on the part of the workers may be more than defiant self-assertion against the educated elite. Some of it undoubtedly is also a token of rebellion against the industrial way of life itself and the demands it makes on the workers. It is a revolt against punctuality, orderliness, and industrial discipline; against the authority and command of planners and managers; against the regime of economic and psychological austerity that accompanies the industrialization effort. The forms this rebellion can take are part of the phenomenon called "lack of culture" in Soviet parlance. Uncultured behavior therefore includes voluntary and unauthorized job mobility, lateness, absenteeism, malingering, and other devices for shirking work assignments; and to these devices Soviet workers have resorted again and again, in defiance of the goals of the elite. At the same time, the workers' self-assertion at times takes the form of militant egalitarianism, to which we referred earlier. This may appear as open envy of everyone who is better off materially; or it may manifest itself in a remarkably virulent xenophobia, a suspicion of anyone who is different or who exhibits individuality. From time to time, the ruling party has found it useful to exploit this levelers' attitude of the workers, which can be directed most easily against the professional and intellectual elite. When used against them, it can be a potent weapon because the substantial advantage this elite enjoys puts them forever on the defensive in a society with a certain egalitarian bias.[10]

The image we are here presenting of the Soviet working class and its relation to the political system must be supplemented by the observation that the Soviet proletariat is probably far more heterogeneous than the peasantry, and therefore presents a somewhat less formidable obstacle to the policies of the regime. To be sure, among collective farms are significant differences in technological advance, educational level, living standards, and even social prestige. But the range of outlooks as well as levels of status and prosperity among the workers appears much wider; it depends not only on level of education and skill, but also on the industry employing the worker.

White-Collar Workers and the Intelligentsia. Soviet ideology main-

[10] The petty tyranny of the lowest common denominator which the creative non-conformist is likely to face in many Western societies or sub-cultures is our own equivalent of this phenomenon. Such tyranny may take the form of consumption patterns which through consumer sovereignty lead to the production and marketing of articles in poor taste. Or it may manifest itself as subtle but insistent peer group pressure in a host of different life situations.

tains that the society of the USSR is composed of two classes, workers and peasants, plus one "stratum": the intelligentsia. This last term denotes the large number of professional experts and managers in politics, industry, communications, education, science, art, and entertainment—in short, people with higher education of all sorts who are clearly neither workers nor peasants. Such a classification seems to leave out lower white-collar workers such as secretaries, bookkeepers, and the like. Some of these may be classified as workers, but many are considered members of the intelligentsia. This category thus includes virtually everyone who does not work with his hands, from cabinet ministers, engineers, and teachers to clerks and salesmen; consequently "intelligentsia" has become an almost meaningless statistical term, even for Soviet purposes.[11]

Obviously, no simple classification scheme can adequately portray the complex professional structure of an industrial society. At the same time, the general pattern of this structure in the USSR is dictated by both the level of industrialization and the peculiarities of the Soviet social system. The peculiarities most directly affecting the professional structure are, first, the elimination of free enterprise, which brings with it the disappearance of the independent businessman; second, the tendency to neglect those branches of production and services that directly benefit the consumer decreases the proportion of persons occupied in such pursuits; finally, the pressure on women to supplement the household budget by seeking outside employment is much greater in the USSR than in the United States, and women therefore make up significant portions of many occupations into which they would venture much less often in America. For various reasons this is so not only in some highly skilled professions such as medicine, but also in jobs requiring hard physical labor, such as farming, where the war and other factors have caused a chronic shortage of manpower.

In any analysis of the political system, the white-collar profes-

[11] See M. N. Rumkevich, "Stiranie klassovykh razlichii i mesto intelligenstii v sotsial'noi strukture sovetskogo obshchestva," in *Filosofskie Nauki,* No. 5 (Moscow, 1963).

sions must be viewed with considerable care. In particular, we must distinguish between its upper and lower strata. It seems, for instance, that as a political force the lower levels of the white-collar class must be discounted. In no modern society have the members of such a stratum, however numerous, developed strong organization or feelings of solidarity. Nor has any political system felt the compulsion to give much consideration to the opinions, aspirations, or fears of this group. As a political force, therefore, the lower white-collar group is relatively unimportant. True, political sociologists have pointed out that such movements or currents as Populism, McCarthyism, National Socialism, Poujadism, and comparable movements in tsarist Russia gained strength by virtue of lower-middle-class support. The concept of the "lower middle class," however, is too vague, since it comprises two very different groups, only one of which has been of great political significance; this is the group of small independent producers and traders, a class that was once dominant but is rapidly being displaced by the machine age. In Russia this preindustrial middle class was never strong and was wiped out by the revolution. In contrast, the "new lower middle class," which fulfills vital, albeit menial, functions in the age of industry and giant organization, has so far shown little capacity for playing a major political role.

The situation is different for the upper layer of the white-collar population. As a matter of fact, the educated elite, the intelligentsia in the narrower sense, is of salient importance in all political systems, including the Soviet. Both before and since the revolution of 1917, this stratum has been far more important than its size would indicate; and it has always been a rather separate and self-conscious group. In tsarist Russia, this self-consciousness may have been partly the result of its small size. Anyone with formal (or even informal) higher education was thereby distinguished from the gray mass of the population. Moreover, in underdeveloped countries more than elsewhere, education and professional status are seen as valid reasons for claiming a right to rule—the professional elite likes to think of itself as *the* elite. If, as in tsarist and Soviet Russia, this claim is not honored, the intelligentsia tends to oppose the prevailing political system. Its members become critics and spokesmen of reform.

The fact that in the Soviet Union the intelligentsia enjoys far greater material comforts than the average citizen does not necessarily alleviate this tendency. True, this difference in living standard gives many members a stake in the existing system and discourages them from challenging or questioning it, lest they lose their status advantages. But some members of the intelligentsia are made to feel uneasy about their advantages, and thus come to regard themselves as parasites, as beneficiaries of injustice and exploitation. Their self-consciousness as members of the educated elite turns into a guilty conscience. The resultant self-torture of the educated was a recurrent phenomenon under tsarism; it may still, or again, be operative in Soviet society, although to estimate the extent of such feelings would be impossible.

Troubled or not by such doubts, the educated elite easily loses its feeling of identity with the masses, and, at times, even with the nation and the political system. Education tends to elevate at least some people above narrow national horizons. It gives a world perspective to at least a few. It declasses some of its recipients and often corrodes their identification with, or loyalty to, primary groups from which they have sprung. It sometimes destroys for the student his whole world of values, attitudes, and preconceptions. Without doubt, some of this impact of higher education is felt by some members of the present-day Soviet intelligentsia.

We shall see later in this book that the Soviet regime makes use of a wide range of effective devices to check such critical tendencies and to inculcate in the intelligentsia more positive attitudes of acceptance, collaboration, and identification with the system. Its success should not by any means be underestimated, for it is very great. Some of this success can be explained by the very process of alienation we have described: in some members of the intelligentsia, the feeling of being different from the masses leads to identification with the Soviet system. The higher education they have received makes them aware of the backwardness and the "unculturedness" of their own country and gives them a painful consciousness of the primitive brutality of its political elite. They develop a strong feeling of Russia's inferiority to the West, and hence a compelling urge to help in leading their nation out of this deplorable state. However profound their contempt for their own rulers and their yearning for greater autonomy, some of these members of the intelligentsia seem to have persuaded themselves that the Communist regime which they hate is necessary so that Russia may rapidly join the ranks of the civilized nations. Their alienation from their own society thus leads them to accept the system as a necessary evil.[12]

At the same time a certain penchant for criticism of the political system persists among the educated. But they cannot translate it into political action, and even expressing such sentiments carries inordinate risks. Hence, those with such an attitude are likely to repress it or find safe and acceptable outlets for it. Stoical or cynical acceptance of the system is one typical stance resulting from such repression. The so-called "inner emigration" is another: an attempt to flee into the esoteric world of professionalism, in the hope that professional matters can be kept out of politics and politics out of professional matters. In many cases, such a devotion to professional goals may be seen not only as a personal escape from public affairs, but as devoted service to the people or the nation. Underpaid and overworked, the Soviet medical profession seems to be composed very largely of persons (primarily women) who see themselves as self-sacrificing benefactors of the people, as distinct from the regime; and many teachers apparently define their roles in similar fashion.

Another road to "inner emigration" seems to be the attempt of educated Russians to maintain or seek some sort of spiritual autonomy or simply a preoccupation with the spiritual or emotional life. According to many students of Russian society, this is a persistently recurrent trait of the Russian national character, linked perhaps to the profoundly mystical and emotional quality of Eastern Orthodox religiousness—a quality which anyone who visits a Russian church service feels at once. Religiousness is one of the forms that inner emigration into the emotional life may take;

[12] A. Zr., "Soviet Satire and Soviet Life," *Problems of Communism*, X, 5 (September–October, 1961), 22 ff.

but quite apart from the militant atheism of the regime, the Soviet intelligentsia as a whole seems to have a pronounced secular orientation, which bars the road of religiousness to all but a minority. On the other hand, literature, the theater, and music are apparently much more important to the educated Russian than to the educated American. These arts are, in all seriousness, a realm of existence, a universe of meaningful discourse within which the members of the Soviet intelligentsia move with easy familiarity, and in which they can indulge, more than in the everyday life of work, their imagination and their lyrical emotions. Yet another path of inner emigration is to make family life a refuge from ever-encroaching public life. This path, however, is extremely difficult, owing to overcrowded housing, the large-scale employment of women, and other factors in Soviet life. Finally, the Soviet intelligentsia has often shown a remarkably strong yearning for emotional spontaneity, for directness and sincerity, for elimination of the dualism between human and civilized behavior. Employing the term very loosely, we might call this the romantic urge in the national character of educated Russians. It has often been observed, but is difficult to describe. At times it has manifested itself in a defiance of accepted moral codes, especially those governing the relations between the sexes. But what to the Western puritan may look like irresponsible hedonism or prurient libertinism may, in the case of the Russian intelligentsia, be a much more innocent and earnest attempt to raise human relations to a higher level by eliminating repressive, stuffy, and artificial norms of behavior. Thus the advocacy or practice of "free love" may be entirely compatible with the intelligentsia's bias against frivolity and naked hedonism.[13]

This is not to imply that the Soviet intelligentsia is without those

[13] The whole gamut of romantic urges summarized here has manifested itself so persistently in the Russian intelligentsia in the last 150 years or so that many writers would describe it as a typically Russian phenomenon. Yet romanticism in all its variations is a generally Western rather than a Russian mood; and Richard Pipes undoubtedly is right in regarding its many manifestations as expressions of the yearning for privacy that modern commercialism and industrialism have engendered everywhere. See Richard Pipes, "The Historical Evolution of the Russian Intelligentsia," in Pipes, ed., *The Russian Intelligentsia* (New York: Columbia University Press, 1961), pp. 47–61.

who try to escape from boredom or hard work in more down-to-earth fashion such as alcoholism, an unrestrained and irresponsible sex life, conspicuous consumption, addiction to the drug of the entertainment media, delinquency, or suicide. Regarding some of these escapes, we have little or no information. For instance, data concerning suicides are carefully withheld from the public by Soviet authorities; only very selective aspects of criminality and delinquency are reported. On the other hand, the craving for vodka can be freely observed by any foreign visitor in the dining rooms of Soviet hotels; it seems to be a persistent problem affecting all classes and layers of the population. Delinquency and fascination with what we might call the "beatnik" life seem to be as rife in Soviet society as in our own, and some of its practitioners obviously are members of the *jeunesse dorée*—sons and daughters of the political and professional elites.

In order to portray the status and the muted interests of the Soviet intelligentsia more precisely, one must summarize its ambiguous relations to the Communist Party. At the time of the revolution, the Party had been created and was led primarily by members of the intelligentsia, even though they asserted that they were speaking in the name of the industrial proletariat. Even at that time, however, the Party manifested a certain bias against the intelligentsia which it has never shed. This bias showed itself in the persistent desire to recruit workers for membership and promote them to high positions; in the Party's impatience with free and open debate; and, later, in the wholesale extermination of the Old Bolsheviks during the Great Purge of 1936–1938. Moreover, the Party's claim to total control of all human endeavors comes into conflict with the professional experts' desire for professional autonomy, just as the notion of an official ideology valid for all branches of human knowledge clashes with the experts' claims to specialized wisdom. In all complex societies we frequently observe conflicts between technical or professional and political considerations. In the USSR, such conflicts are likely to take the form of tension between the Communist Party and the intelligentsia.

Matters are complicated by the fact that in the first decades of the Soviet regime the members of the professional elite (as distinguished from the intellectuals occupying high Party positions) were justly considered great loyalty and security risks. The people with higher education had, after all, been trained under tsarism and were considered part of the formerly privileged class. They were suspect and—politically and socially as well as economically —the revolutionary regime sought to eliminate them. Many communists thought that the USSR could dispense with their services. They thought that the days were over when the common man had to take orders from a small upper stratum. In the early days of the revolution, this idea apparently was widespread among the working classes as well. Yet soon after the revolution the Soviet regime realized that it could not dispense with the services of the intelligentsia, at least not for the time being. The old professional elite was therefore called back and placed in positions of responsibility and authority. Members of that elite remained suspect; their activities were controlled, supervised, and hampered in many ways, as we shall see; and when things went wrong, they became convenient scapegoats. At the same time, the rewards they received were high enough to arouse the indignation and envy of many people from the lower classes. In short, the Soviet political system has both harassed and pampered the intelligentsia.

Meanwhile, a new Soviet intelligentsia has been reared, which may be considered less of a loyalty and security risk. Yet, as we have seen already, status advantages have shown a surprising persistence, in that a large proportion of the new Soviet intelligentsia has come from old-intelligentsia families. The resulting continuity may have been reinforced somewhat by the transfer to the new intelligentsia of views and attitudes held by the educated elite under tsarism. A possible indication of such a transfer of values from one generation to the next is the occasional recurrence of "typically Russian" themes in the intellectual life of the present generation.

By mentioning the difference between the old and the new intelligentsia, we have touched upon a much broader conflict between generations that pervades all of Soviet society and complicates its political culture.[14] Here, once again, the Soviet system conforms generally to the pattern of all industrial countries, caught as they are in a process of rapid and perpetual technological change and corresponding social upheaval. Under such conditions it is inevitable that outlooks, expectations, and patterns of living within the system change from one generation to the next. The younger people, not having experienced the problems of the past, are likely to live more exclusively in the present. Where changes have been rapid and profound, this ignorance of the past creates great differences in attitudes. In recent decades, Soviet society has gone through severe hardships, which are now yielding impressive results. Many observers feel that the older generation which has lived through the hard decades of construction tends to be impressed by these results and grateful for what it now receives, whereas the young more often are restless and dissatisfied, ignorant of the price that has been paid for the present-day level of comfort. If this observation is correct, it is somewhat ironic; for the older generation, which having gone through the purgatory of Stalinism is now making no further demands, includes the age group which grew up before the revolution and accepted the Communist regime itself only with great difficulty and reluctance. In contrast, the younger generation has experienced no other system and has in fact internalized communist doctrine in very thorough measure. Nonetheless, it is these products of Communist socialization who seem to be more restless. At the same time, it would be as foolhardy to generalize about this as about any other group in Soviet society. No one set of attitudes is shared by the young; instead, the values and views of peasants and workers, intellectuals, managers, and politicians, of believers and

[14] In Russian intellectual discourse, the conflict of generations is referred to as the problem of "fathers and sons," in allusion to Turgenev's novel. Soviet ideology denies the existence of such a problem in its own society, but recent Soviet discussions of cultural and political issues have nonetheless focused on it. Much of the heated debate concerning the form and content of art and literature had to refer to it again and again; and so have the discussions over Stalinism and destalinization. See, for instance, Priscilla Johnson, "The Regime and the Intellectuals," Special Supplement to *Problems of Communism*, XII, No. 4 (July–August, 1963), i–xxvii.

atheists, and the many other groups in Soviet society must, somehow, be echoed within each generation.

Even a sketchy survey of group values in Soviet society would not be complete without some mention of the interests of national minorities. We have already described the Great Russians as the Soviet equivalent of white Protestant Anglo-Saxons in the United States. All this comparison is meant to convey is that, other conditions being equal, the non-Russian is likely to have less chance of advancement in Soviet society as a whole. The reasons for this situation will be discussed in a later chapter dealing with Soviet minority policy. At this point we only wish to call attention to the complexity which the national problem adds to the Soviet social structure. It does so because this society, in which Great Russians form a large plurality and the Slavs constitute a sizable majority, contains national minorities of widely varying backgrounds and levels of civilization. They include the Baltic peoples, who are proud of their historic ties to the West and at times have difficulty repressing their contempt for (or hatred of) the Russians. There is a congeries of tribes and nations on both sides of the Caucasus range, among them peoples like the Armenians and Georgians who look back to centuries of independent culture, and whose past relations with Russia, as well as with each other, have been highly ambivalent. Both the Baltic area and the Caucasus were trouble spots of revolutionary nationalism in tsarist times, and in the Communist Party some of these nationalities were very strongly represented. In fact, while Stalin was in power, his native nationality group, the Georgians, seemed to occupy a privileged position equal to that of the Russians. The Westerner visiting Georgia feels at once that he is among a nationality very conscious of being different from the Russians.

The Soviet melting pot also includes millions of Central Asian Moslems, whose way of life until a few decades ago conformed to the medieval pattern of the Islamic world. Furthermore, sizable minorities of Mongols, Koreans, Tatars, Finns, not to mention Eskimos and numerous other tribes existing on very primitive levels of civilization, are scattered over many parts of the USSR.

The relationship of these various nationalities to the regime has been complicated, and their attitude can therefore be expected to be ambivalent. On the one hand, the industrialization and modernization promoted by the system have had the effect of corroding and changing their old way of life. Hence the efforts of the Party to bring its conception of "culture" to these native populations has inevitably engendered traditionalist resistance forces; and these in turn have strengthened the rulers' readiness to use violent means to change these nations in the Soviet image. On the other hand, industrialization has also brought blessings. While it may not have raised living standards very noticeably for the nationalities affected, the regime has attempted to raise to twentieth-century levels the literacy, education, and acculturation of such national groups. There is no doubt that this effort has stirred the imagination and enthusiasm of the younger generations of the more underdeveloped nationalities. Among many members of this generation there must be a tremendous feeling of indebtedness to the Soviet political system. Yet this gratitude may be tempered as a result of the fury with which frequent purges have decimated the ranks of national leaders and by the strict check which the regime puts on even the slightest manifestations of a spirit of national independence or autonomy.

If there is one point this sketchy survey of group values in the USSR was designed to bring out, it is that facile generalizations about a Russian national character cannot be made. Many mutually contradictory interests and behavior traits are distributed, in widely divergent fashion, among different groups of the population.

GOALS OF THE POLITICAL ELITE

The values of the different groups comprising Soviet society have been summarized because any political system must feel the impact of such values in its structure and functioning. The next step in any discussion of Soviet politics would be to examine how different group interests can be, and are, formed and expressed; how they confront each other, and how such a confrontation can lead to resolutions. This book may be able to shed a little dim light on this matter, but no more than that, because the Soviet political system is not designed to provide a free play for conflicting group interests. Instead, it is a machinery for decision-making which is clearly dominated by a comparatively small ruling group, an oligarchy or power elite which has persistently sought to repress and suppress all conflicting interests and to impose its own values on the entire system. Again, we shall have to examine in detail the institutions and practices through which this imposition and trans-formation of values is carried on. But first we must examine the goals and values that can be attributed to the elite. What, in other words, are the aims guiding the Communist Party in its management of the Soviet political system?

The answer to this question will be complicated, for the following reasons: First of all, it is necessary to distinguish between articulated and esoteric values, between actual interests and rhetoric. At the same time, the difference between these two sets of values must not be overestimated; indeed, to a considerable extent they may coincide. Finally, it will become apparent that both the publicly stated values and the real interests of the Soviet elite have undergone transformations and may still today be in the process of change.

Socialism.   Great revolutions typically are made in the name of lofty ideals concerning the improvement of man's well-being and his relationship to his fellow-men. Now the doctrines of political philosophers and prophets are always subject to interpretation, and any attempt to measure an actual political system against the values voiced at the time of its birth is therefore a highly controversial undertaking. Nonetheless it seems safe to observe that no political system has ever completely fulfilled the expectations generated at the time it arose. Hence any comparisons between actuality and professed values, between promise and fulfilment, will inevitably prove to be embarrassing to the system examined. If at this point we propose to examine the goals of the men who made the October Revolution and instituted the Soviet regime, it is not merely for the purpose of demonstrating the extent to which actual developments have frustrated these goals, but also simply to narrate the aims and expectations of the Soviet Founding Fathers. We shall have to investigate to what extent these ideals are still part of the goals, either of the elite or of some other groups, and we shall see at the same time how the emergence of other problems claiming priority led to the modification of the original goals.

The communists came to power with the help of promises and slogans that appealed to the impatient radicalism of the poor and underprivileged. They promised peace with the Germans, land to the peasants, control of the factories to the workers, national self-determination to the minorities, and political power to the broad masses of the population. But these were promises of the moment. Beyond them, the leaders of the Communist Party had very definite ideas of what Russia under communist rule would look like. These ideas can be found in their speeches and writings around the time of the October Revolution. The most famous of these writings is V. I. Lenin's book, *The State and Revolution,* written in the late summer of 1917.

In this book, the leader of the Communist Party asserted that the coming revolution would bring to the Russian people the following benefits—and bring them at once:

1. The rule of the people and the abolition of classes. No longer would the people be divided into rulers and ruled, exploiters and exploited. No longer would there be social inequality. Instead, all Russians would henceforth be equals not only under law, but also in fact.

2. The withering away of government. The rule of men over men through laws, courts, bureaucratic hierarchies, police forces, and other means of coercion was necessary, in Lenin's view, only when society was divided into classes. Once classes were abolished, government would no longer be required. All that would be needed would be an administrative apparatus to run the national economy, keep accounts and control operations. In a modern society, these functions would be so simple that every citizen could perform them. No longer, therefore, would society need specialists in government

who could turn into arrogant, oppressive bureaucrats; instead, everyone would be able to get a turn at running the administration. Similarly, every citizen would spontaneously and joyously help enforce collective discipline and defend the country from outside attack. For this reason, the new communist society could dispense also with standing armies and police forces.

3. An unstated precondition of such a society was the assumption that Russia could produce enough for all its citizens, that scarcity of any of life's necessities would be a thing of the past. Lenin made this assumption because he thought that the machine age had made economic abundance possible, and that the working class would cheerfully give of its labor for the common good without having to be coerced or bribed.

4. Finally, Lenin and his comrades thought that the coming of such an ideal society was guaranteed by the spread of the revolution over the entire civilized world. He often said that Russia alone would never be able to realize socialism, but he was confident that the Russian revolution would not remain isolated. On the contrary, he firmly believed (and demanded a like faith from his followers) that the communist revolution in Russia would inevitably be the signal for the workers of the entire world to rise up in revolt against their own ruling classes. All of Europe would then turn socialist, and, united with a socialist Europe, Russia would at once become a socialist society.

Power. Why the doctrines of socialism could become popular among radical Russian intellectuals is an intriguing question with which this book cannot deal. Suffice it to say that peculiarities of Russian society and government forced these converts to modify the ideas they had accepted. The need to adapt Marxism to Russian conditions, which became the occasion for bitter disputes and chronic disagreements among the followers of that doctrine, led to the rise of two distinct parties, both claiming to represent the Russian workers, both asserting that their program and manner of operating were faithful to Marxist holy writ. Again, this is not the place to present the main differences between these two wings of

Russian Marxism. Here we can only summarize the thoughts and policies of Lenin, creator of the Bolshevik faction which seized power in the October Revolution.

Lenin and his followers were among the more radical thinkers within the Marxist camp. They were ever conscious of the final goal to be reached and highly impatient to attain it. They were obsessed with the need to act, to overcome obstacles, to swim against the current, to outmaneuver the forces of history in order to bring about a better society. Perhaps because of this impatience, Lenin was also ruthless. He insisted that a true revolutionary must be ready to use any and all means for his purposes. Authority requires toughness. "Whoever has power and does not know how to use it for the good of the people is worthless," as Khrushchev said recently.[15] At the same time, the revolutionary leader must not make himself a slave of his means; on the contrary, he must be flexible and ready at any moment to discard past methods in favor of new ones more likely to further his cause under different circumstances.

Lenin, even while he professed faith that history was in his favor, secretly feared that time might be running out and that circumstances favored the enemies of the working class. He was impatient with those who thought that the fall of capitalism and the coming of the proletarian revolution were inevitable. He had great respect for the cunning of the capitalists and limited faith in the working class. About his own opinions he was dogmatic, and he transferred this high opinion of his own powers of discernment to his organization, the Communist Party. In this manner, something resembling infallibility was attributed to the Party and to those who led it.

Lenin was obsessed with problems of organization and control. Distrustful of the forces in the society in which he lived, he sought to extend principles of scientific management to politics—and even to the most chaotic task in politics, making revolution. His aim was, through organization, control, and rational management, to manipulate individuals, groups, and classes so that they would work for his revolutionary purposes even though such effort might be against their own intent. Soviet ideology echoes these ideas of Lenin

[15] *Izvestiia* (April 26, 1963).

by boasting forever that its political system has subjected social life to the conscious control of man (a formula familiar to many Western social scientists, because such an aim is for them the goal of all bureaucracy). The instrument through which Lenin sought to effect this manipulation of men was the Communist Party. To Lenin, it was the organization of class-conscious professional revolutionaries who would act as the general staff of the world revolution. The problem of devising a Party organization which would assure that correct decisions would always be made by the leaders and carried out by the followers was always foremost in Lenin's mind. Whether he succeeded in devising such an ideal organization is highly doubtful. In any event, we should note that the principles by which communist parties everywhere organize themselves today and the methods by which they formulate decisions were first laid down by Lenin.

As for the program of action the Party was to follow, Lenin tried to adapt it to the circumstances of the given moment. Throughout the years preceding the October Revolution, he argued that Russia, a backward country, had to go through two revolutions instead of the one demanded by Marx: a bourgeois revolution to destroy tsarism and transform Russia into a capitalist society, and a proletarian revolution to overthrow capitalism and usher in socialism. The timing of these two revolutions remained a matter of controversy, with Lenin himself changing his mind several times. After the overthrow of tsarism he asserted that the two revolutions might merge or telescope into one another, so that the dictatorship of the proletariat might be established at once after the fall of the old regime. We have already briefly discussed the benefits he expected from such a proletarian dictatorship.

Industrialization and its Social Cost.   Lenin has been dead for over forty years and many of the details of his program have been abandoned by the party he founded, yet the Soviet political system and its rulers still voice their assent to the broad goals of 1917 and maintain that they are faithful to the ideas of *The State and Revolution.* At the same time, it is obvious that shorter-range goals have been developed by the Soviet elite, who have pushed the fulfilment of the revolutionary ethos more and more *ad calendas Graecas.* Moreover, these more immediate goals of the elite have undergone repeated changes. In theory, they always serve to bring about long-range ideals; whether or not this assumption is valid remains controversial. In any event, primary attention must always be given to the short-range aims; and in fact the Communist Party has always sought to bring about a total commitment of the entire political system to whatever goals of the moment claimed paramount effort. The principal ideological textbook of the Communist Party has this to say about the central importance of the industrialization program: "Historical conditions developed in such a way that the first countries to take the path of socialism were those with a comparatively backward economy and culture. In the course of socialist construction the peoples of these countries have had to complete the work that was left undone by capitalism—create modern industries, overcome survivals of pre-capitalist formations in economy and culture, and in people's minds. All this demanded additional effort and sacrifice. . . ."[16] In view of this pragmatic orientation, the entire history of the Soviet political system can be seen as a series of adjustments to changes in elite values and preoccupations. Chapter II tried to make this clear already. It showed that the Party's preoccupations changed as follows: In 1917, the major goal was the seizure of power. Once this had been achieved, the problem of winning the civil war loomed above all other interests and goals. This, in turn, was superseded by an ideological interregnum, a period of consolidation, reconstruction, political wrangling, and intellectual stocktaking. Finally, the era of industrialization began, during which the overriding goal of all Soviet policy was the most rapid possible transformation of the country into a powerful modern industrial nation. Since this is still the major interest of the Soviet political elite, we must spell out in some detail the implications of this tendency to give priority to the exigencies of rapid economic growth. At the same time, we shall see later on that a number of additional interests of the elite must

[16] *Fundamentals of Marxism–Leninism*, p. 202.

be taken into consideration, which makes the task of outlining the motives of the Communist Party quite complicated.

The reasons that compelled Stalin and his Party comrades to commit the total resources of Russian society to a crash program of industrialization are difficult to reconstruct. Marxist dogma and Russia's weakness in the face of the Western world are the two most obvious motives. Many authors subordinate both of them to Stalin's personal ambitions or to the Party's desire to stay in power. Undoubtedly all these facts were of great importance; but the Party's drive to maintain control over Soviet society was as much jeopardized as aided by the excesses of the first five-year plans. Whatever the reasons, Soviet industrialization, ever since the period around 1930, has been marked by feverish haste and ruthless determination. Clearly, no other interests or considerations were to interfere with the single-minded pursuit of this goal. In terms of elite interests, this means that the inevitable economic hardships engendered by any effort to build up industry in an underdeveloped, understaffed, undertrained country have not greatly troubled the architects of the program. Only the minimal resources were committed to satisfy the most urgent consumer needs. In its economic treatment of the Soviet population, therefore, the political elite has acted as if it wished to live by the code of behavior which Marx attributed to capitalist exploiters. In both cases, this code of behavior follows logically from the overriding priority given to the urge to accumulate. The analogy can easily be extended to broader patterns of social relations in Western and Soviet eras of early industrialism. Both England in the middle of the nineteenth century and Soviet Russia a hundred years later subjected their working classes to barbarous conditions of life and work. In both societies, the lower classes were (in practice, if not in theory) disenfranchised; both systems were dictatorial, even though oligarchic rule was hidden behind the cloak of liberal rhetoric. In both societies, moreover, the elite interests' concentration on economic growth and accumulation meant exclusion of all other values and interests. One might go so far as to say that accumulation was the religion; and it was pursued with religious earnestness, with utterly unhumorous devotion that left little room for frills, frivolity, play, or other hedonistic preoccupations. Victorian stuffiness and pompousness is the mark of these preeminently repressive societies.

In turn, the resolve to impose strict economic and personal austerity upon the population must have reinforced the already strong bias of the Soviet elite toward tight centralization of planning and dictatorial methods of government. This bias was strengthened even more by the realization that a twentieth-century society could not be made viable so long as preindustrial habits of thought and life had not been eliminated in the population. Industrialization, the Party came to realize, requires a people trained in handling modern tools, and such training must be given not only to scientists and engineers, but to the entire population; for the transformation of an agrarian country into a land of machines and cities means a thorough change in the whole way of life, the transformation of a people from rural into city folk. This training has been going on in the Western world since the beginning of the industrial revolution. Even when it is slow and spontaneous, it is a painful process during which people rooted in old habits, traditions, and values are hammered into different shapes by the changing needs of modern life, while those who are unwilling to give up their accustomed way of life are cast aside in the grim struggle for success and recognition. But when this process (which Lenin called a "cultural revolution") is pressed into a short span of years and is promoted vigorously by governmental policy, the suffering it produces is multiplied. This is happening in the USSR today.

The aim of the "cultural revolution" is to eliminate all those habits and traditions that prevent former peasants from adjusting to the rhythm of the machine, from becoming literate city dwellers skilled in handling and servicing the complicated tools and gadgets of modern civilization.[17] We shall later examine the manner in which educational institutions as well as other parts of the Soviet political system are geared to carry out this process of training,

[17] A recent Soviet text defines the cultural revolution as "a process in which the broad masses of the toilers come to dispose of all the blessings of culture which previously were a monopoly of the exploiter classes." P. I. Nikitin, *Osnovy politicheskoi ekonomii* (Moscow, 1962), p. 216.

education, indoctrination, and socialization. But we should be aware also that manipulation has been a method at least as important as education and indoctrination. The manner in which the Soviet regime has sought to manipulate its citizens so as to make them change their way of life has been a characteristic application of Leninist principles of organization. He had been obsessed with problems of organization because he had seen in organization a potential tool of unequaled importance. To him it was a means by which men could be manipulated and history made. In it he saw the secret of political rule; for organization could become the transmission belt through which the leader's will and ideas could be transferred to individuals, groups, and classes.

Soviet ideology ambitiously states the goal of its political system to be not merely manipulation of men, but a change in human nature; it boasts of significant success in this effort: "The remoulding of human consciousness in the course of the socialist revolution in the U.S.S.R. and the People's Democracies, the appearance of new spiritual traits (collectivism, for example, as opposed to bourgeois individualism) convincingly refute the bourgeois sociologists' assertion that human nature cannot be changed."[18] The cultural revolution therefore can be redefined as an attempt to change men through reorganization. A double strategy was used by the communist regime for this purpose. The first step was an attempt to destroy the entire network of organizations and associations that had characterized Old Russia's society. The most important targets were those informal, traditional, natural (or primary) associations in which men grow up: family, church, nationality, and peasant community. In the first phases of the Russian revolution all but the last of these came under heavy pressure; the peasant community was uprooted at the time of the collectivization. By every means at its disposal the regime showed its hostility to these primary associations and to men who remained rooted in them. Whoever remained loyal to the ties of family, religion, nationality, and community was suspect and risked severe sanctions. In severing men from these ties, the Soviet regime attempted to reach the first goal

18 *Fundamentals of Marxism–Leninism*, p. 144.

of the cultural revolution—the transformation of men having some security within these bounds into helpless, rootless, isolated social atoms.

While this process of atomization was going on, the second phase of the cultural revolution began: the erection of a new network of primary and secondary ties, of those associations and organizations without which no society can function. But this new network of human organization was entirely the creation of the Communist Party and in this way became part of the machinery of government. By using all parts of this more and more complicated machinery, the elite hoped to subject the individual to its will at every moment of his life, in every activity he undertook, through every group to which he belonged, even if it were as small as the monogamous family. Indeed, even in this most personal realm the elite has tried to interfere by placing the family in a service role so that it might help in the five-year plans and in the defense of the USSR. As we shall see, the elite has by no means succeeded in making its political and social controls as effective and thoroughgoing as it desired. But it nonetheless managed to devise a system of deliberate social control as far-reaching and effective as any social system of the past for shaping the activities, the minds, and even the emotions of its citizens.

The cultural revolution, which was at least one of the reasons for this total restructuring of society, is an attempt to fit Soviet citizens into the machine age; and its pursuit was a logical corollary of the elite's preoccupation with economic growth. Several additional goals of the elite must also be seen as part of this effort. One of these is the creation and maintenance of an incentive system designed to make individuals give their best in effort and talent to the goal of industrialization. The need for incentives had not been foreseen by the elite, who had counted on the revolutionary enthusiasm of the population and believed that once the exploiters had been replaced all citizens would cheerfully and voluntarily contribute to the best of their ability. When this expectation turned out to be utopian, the communist rulers decided that a competitive system of differentiated rewards had to be created to make it worthwhile for all citizens to work earnestly and hard. At first the regime was apologetic about this turn away from its earlier egalitarian dreams; however, the maintenance of a social system marked by great differences in status, rank, and material welfare was so important that, in time, it became part of the value system guiding the elite, and to some extent it still is today.

Another inevitable accompaniment of the drive to industrialize is the need to organize the entire society according to principles of rational management. We have already related this interest to the centralist biases of the communist movement as well as to the needs of the cultural revolution. It should be understood, however, that— these motives apart—the tendency to organize society in such fashion is inherent in the industrial way of life itself. The machine age intensifies the differentiation of functions far beyond anything previous societies might have imagined. It therefore tends to give more and more authority to experts in various fields, while at the same time making all the various operations more and more dependent on each other. The entire social fabric becomes more complicated and more dependent on a fine adjustment of all parts to each other; this, in turn, strengthens inherent tendencies toward the development of hierarchic command structures. In short, the industrial way of life has an inherent bias in favor of the bureaucratization of society; in the case of the Soviet elite it therefore reinforced values already strongly held.

Furthermore, the Soviet elite is strongly preoccupied with the indoctrination of its citizenry. We have above linked this interest with the pursuit of the cultural revolution; in fact, the motives for the urge to indoctrinate are broader. Beyond the need to re-educate peasants, nomads, and other members of preindustrial cultures for life in the machine age, indoctrination aims at making the citizens identify with the goals of the elite and at legitimizing its rule. No political systems can afford to neglect these aims, and the devices by which such indoctrination is furthered are fairly common to all. The difference in method between the USSR and other political systems is primarily that the USSR has a highly centralized system of indoctrination and an official ideology which takes the form of a rather rigid political catechism. By indoctrination the regime tries to convince the citizens that they are living in the best of all possible social systems, partly by linking the political system and its elite with the ethos of the revolution. In this fashion it seeks to establish the dogma of the legitimate succession of the present elite to the ideological heritage of Marx and Lenin. At the same time, it also seeks to link the system with the ethos of Old Russia and thus tries to establish the dogma of the legitimate succession of the present elite to all that was valuable in tsarist times. To strengthen further the citizens' commitment to the system, it denigrates all other systems and attempts to eliminate even the possibility of the citizens' thinking about alternatives to the Soviet way of life. The result of these strivings is the emergence of an apologetic theory of state as the official, elite-approved and elite-propagated, ideology—a set of dogmas conservative in their implications and traditionalist in their manner of arguing, an ideology in basic contradiction to the spirit, if not the letter, of Marxist doctrines. In developing its apologetic theory of state, the Soviet political elite denied the Marxist hope for a society without domination, suppression, and exploitation; it regards the very yearning for such a society as something disruptive and subversive. To be sure, Marxist doctrines and words were twisted in such a fashion as to create the impression that a major portion of the dreams of Marx and Engels had come true. But this only illustrates other violations of the spirit of Marx. First of all, it means a denial of the critical attitude which is the moral foundation of Marxist doctrines. Marx had written that "the highest being for man is man himself"; from this he had derived the moral command to destroy all social institutions in which man is oppressed, degraded, dominated, or exploited by his fellow-man. In contrast, the ideology of the Soviet elite sharply discourages all radical, fundamental criticism of the Soviet political system. Second, the Marxist commitment to a scientific attitude in the exploration of human society has been abandoned. In its place, the Soviet elite has placed insistence on partisanship in all fields of knowledge. According to the principles of partisanship, facts are relevant only if they fit into a preconceived scheme of explanations; scientific conclusions are valid only if they do not conflict with the dogmas of the party. From the point of view of the outsider, however, these dogmas which constitute the official doctrine of the elite can only be described, to put it bluntly, as a web of half-truths and outright fabrications hedged in by strong intellectual taboos.

Theory of the State.   According to official Soviet doctrine,[19] the USSR is a socialist state, a government of the toilers, for the toilers, and (with limitations) by the toilers—"toilers" being all people who work for a living rather than live by exploiting the labor of others. By definition, all Soviet citizens are toilers because private property in the means of production (which leads to exploitation) has been abolished; all means of production are in the hands of the people, either as cooperative property or as government property. "The state," says the 1961 platform of the Communist Party (Part Two, section III), "which arose as a state of the dictatorship of the proletariat, has become, in the new contemporary period, a state of the entire people, an organ expressing the interests and will of the people as a whole." By definition, therefore, there can be neither exploitation nor class struggle. In the words of the basic ideological textbook, "The state ceases to be a class state in as much as it becomes the expression of the will and interests of the whole people . . . the state *loses its age-old characteristic of being an instrument of class suppression.*"[20] Nor can there be any major conflict between the interests of individuals, groups, or classes and those of the community as a whole. Moreover, since the Party represents the interests of all the toilers, no one in his right mind can possibly oppose the policies and pronouncements of the party; anyone doing so places himself outside the political community and must be

[19] The basic text in which the Soviet regime expounds its self-image is *Osnovy Marksizma–Leninizma,* which is available in English translation (*Fundamentals of Marxism–Leninism*). The theory of the state, more strictly speaking, can be found explained in law texts such as N. G. Aleksandrov and A. I. Lepeshkin, eds., *Osnovy Sovetskogo Gosudarstva i Prava* (Moscow, 1962); or P. S. Romashkin *et al., Teoriia Gosudarstva i Prava* (Moscow, 1960); or A. Denisov and M. Kirichenko, *Soviet State Law* (Moscow, 1960).

[20] *Fundamentals of Marxism–Leninism,* pp. 595–596.

punished.[21] Just because no individual is allowed to oppose the interests of the toilers (as defined by the Party), government in the Soviet Union is more truly representative and more truly democratic than any other government, and the rights of the citizens are guaranteed more meaningfully than anywhere else. By implication, the state is the highest embodiment of the people's interests, regardless of its form or its manner of operation. Indeed, dictatorial government, because it rules in the interest of all, is fully compatible with democratic principles. Soviet ideology repudiates the liberal idea that individuals and groups should be protected against their government.

Within the state, the Party commands because it knows the interests of the toilers. Its membership is defined as the most progressive and enlightened segment of the population, the vanguard of the citizenry. The right to rule is theirs by ascription. This assumption that the Party represents the people is the cornerstone of all Soviet ideology and is not subject to challenge. It is the essence of *partiinost*—that axiomatic truth of all Party dogma against which all rational findings must be measured.[22] In analysis of the political system of the USSR, one implication hidden in the concept of *partiinost* is of particular importance to us. That is the fact that there can be no social science, in the Western sense of the word, in the Soviet Union. There can be no open-minded inquiry into the history, structure, and functioning of social and political institutions, nor, indeed, any closed-minded or biased inquiry, unless the bias is that of accepting from the very beginning the

[21] Although Western sociology, in its models of the social structure, eschews the vindictive or punitive implications that Soviet spokesmen do not hesitate to draw, its image of the deviant person as a dysfunctional and, in a sense, unexplainable phenomenon at times comes surprisingly close to the Soviet view. For a critique of this trend, see Ralf Dahrendorf, *Gesellschaft und Freiheit* (München: Piper Verlag, 1963), especially Chapters 4, 5, and 9.

[22] *Partiinost* might be seen as a perverted form of pragmatism, and we might fruitfully apply to it the critical comments of communist spokesmen on pragmatism. "By its failure to recognize the objective difference between truth and falsehood and by identifying truth and utility," writes a Soviet textbook, "pragmatism encourages unprincipledness and enables the ideologist of the ruling class to justify every profitable lie and every criminal act." *Fundamentals of Marxism–Leninism,* p. 113.

axioms of Soviet ideology. And, since all so-called social science in the USSR must serve the purpose of proving these same axioms all over again, Soviet social science cannot but move in an eternal circle, trying to demonstrate the assumptions which underlie its own arguments. Thus, the development of sharp and meaningful tools of inquiry is prevented, because they might show the shakiness of the basic presuppositions. Instead, social science in the USSR is reduced to a system of apologetics, serving the purpose of demonstrating that the Soviet Union is the best of all possible worlds. Socialism has been established; the class struggle has been abolished; and communism is just around the corner.

In claiming that socialism was achieved a quarter of a century ago, Soviet doctrine has developed its very own definition of socialism. In Soviet terms, socialism is attained once the last capitalists have been expropriated, and all means of production are in public possession. Public ownership of the means of production thus is the essence of socialism as defined in the USSR. It follows that some other features, which in different definitions might be considered essential to socialism, are not included. Socialism, as defined by Soviet doctrine, does not mean abundance; on the contrary, it is defined as that society which devotes all its efforts to the promotion of economic growth so that abundance—and with it communism—can at last be attained. Nor does socialism imply social equality; on the contrary, since voluntary work for the common good has not yet become the habit of every citizen, incentives are still required to make people work, and incentives imply a system of managed inequality, in which the exact amount of rewards is to be determined by the individual's performance or his value to the community. Socialism therefore is defined as that system which functions according to the principle, "From each according to his ability; to each according to his work." And this motto is supplemented by the stern warning, contained in Article 12 of the 1936 Constitution, "He who does not work, neither shall he eat."

Soviet ideology is not quite consistent on this point, although the inconsistency must not be revealed. Even though it affirms the necessity for rewards and sanctions, for organized competition and managed inequality, it claims at the same time that inequality and competition under Soviet socialism are different from analogous features under capitalism. They are more benign because they are freely accepted by the people (as represented by the Communist Party). This assertion, in turn, is part of a broader set of ideas which stress the benign character of those features which socialism shares with capitalism. Among them is the notion that the class struggle has been abolished even though classes still exist; the existing classes simply are declared to be no longer antagonistic to each other; hence, there is class cooperation instead. Again, individual interests still do not altogether coincide with the public interest, but the conflict between them is no longer sharp. Moreover, while there remains a need for rewards and sanctions to make the citizens work for the regime, this insight is matched by a theory which imputes enlightened self-interest to all the citizens. Even though there is competition, Soviet theory claims, the principal incentive is not the desire to best one's fellow-citizen, but the wish to contribute to Soviet economic development and to personal growth. Soviet citizens compete with each other not for the purpose of cutting each other's throats but in order to become more useful and productive citizens. Soviet theory thus assumes a considerable amount of altruism and is prone to explain it as enlightened self-interest, since, after all, every Soviet citizen, in working for the state, is working for himself because the state promotes his interests. In fact, the harder he works and the less reward he receives, the more quickly will he benefit from the general economic growth resulting from his and his fellow-citizens' labor and deprivation. The realization that incentives are required is thus balanced by the expectation that the citizens will wish to postpone gratification of their material needs for the sake of raising the common level of production.

Thus the Soviet political ethos today looks with favor upon a system of managed inequality, after indulging, for a decade or more, in radical egalitarianism—inequality not only in material reward, but also in degree of public authority. Lenin's statement that after the revolution any kitchen help could have a turn at running the government was abandoned very quickly. But, together with the continuing cult of equality in Soviet doctrine, the regime fostered a distrust of authority and rank and repudiated the rank-consciousness which had been so characteristic of tsarist bureaucratic and militarist society. Public management by committees, a feature of early Soviet administration, was a token of this revulsion against authority as such. This, too, has given way to the authoritarian principle of "one-man-command" (*edinonachalie*), which was made part of the definition of socialism.

As for the nature of communism, that era which Soviet society is asserted to be entering at the present time, official doctrine is still in the process of defining it. From the Party platform adopted at the Twenty-second Congress in 1961 it is clear that the communist society is supposed to be one in which the economy has been developed to such a state that minimal standards of material comfort and security can be provided for all citizens. At the same time, the reader of the platform is left to understand that, at least in the first phases of communism, a system of managed incentives will remain in operation and, with it, inequalities of reward and status. Furthermore, communism, as visualized by present Soviet doctrine, foresees a growth of communal at the expense of individual and family life. Children will be educated in boarding schools, so that the role of the parents will be curtailed. The household chore of preparing daily meals will be eliminated by the provision of free meals for all in communal kitchens and dining facilities. Leisure-time activities will be organized more and more by the community. In addition, the definition of communism specifies that further inroads will be made into the peasant way of life; the regime and its ideological spokesmen foresee a gradual transformation of the collective farm system and a significant lessening of the difference between city and country. Finally, the definition of communism specifies that government functions will be transferred to local and communal organizations. Greater reliance is to be placed on grass-roots organizations, especially among workers and the young, for enforcing conformity and ferreting out deviancy. At the same time, all current definitions of communism insist on the continued sovereignty of the present political elite: the "state" may begin to wither away, but the Communist Party, as the institutional expression of the general will, will remain in control. Altogether, the doctrinal pronouncements dealing with this vision of the foreseeable future are marked by caution and timidity. They betray a firm resolve not to shake the foundations of the present political system.[23]

Having defined Soviet society as the best of all possible societies, as a world of harmony and cheerful collaboration, the official doctrine has created one great difficulty for itself: it has closed the door to any searching explanation of mistakes in policy, major disagreements, the persistence of serious social grievances, and deviations from officially accepted standards of thought and behavior. Mistakes cannot by definition be due to structural deficiencies in the social system, because the system is defined as perfect, at least in design. Disagreements cannot be accommodated, because the monolithic image of a brotherly Soviet society does not account for a profound clash of interests. Nor can individual deviance be explained by reference to any features of the social system. Instead, it must lamely be blamed on evil influences from outside the system or laid to moral or physiological flaws in the deviant individual.

Nor can the doctrine allow any thorough and dispassionate investigation of how the system in fact functions, how decisions are made, what motivations activate them, what the levers of power

[23] From the flood of literature dealing with the transition to communism which is now being published in the USSR, the following can be cited as representative samples: Akademiia Nauk SSSR, *Stroitel'stvo kommunizma i obshchestvennye nauki;* materialy sessii obshchego sobraniia Akademii Nauk SSSR, 19–20 oktiabria 1962 g. (Moscow, 1962); S. G. Strumilin, *Problemy sotsializma i kommunizma v SSSR* (Moscow, 1961); P. I. Nikitin, *Chto takoe kommunizm?* (Moscow, 1961); S. P. Pervushin, *Nekotorye problemy perekhoda ot sotsializma k kommunizmu* (Moscow, 1960); B. S. Ukraintsev et al., *Dialektika pererastaniia sotsializma v kommunizm* (Moscow, 1963); Akademiia Nauk SSSR, *Ot sotsialisticheskoi gosudarstvennosti k kommunisticheskomy obshchestvennomu samoupravleniiu* (Moscow, 1961).

This list could be multiplied by adding books, monographs, brochures, and articles dealing with the implementation of the transition to communism in a host of specific areas—art, education, penology, agriculture, daily living, wage policy, and many others.

are, and who wields them. Such an analysis cannot be tolerated because it might yield a picture very much at variance with the idyllic image of a cheerful socialist commonwealth. Soviet ideology thus makes it impossible to criticize or even to describe the society and the political system.

One other consequence of Soviet ideology should be noted in passing: the all-pervasiveness of the axioms on which it is based. Not only do the pursuits of social scientists revolve around the task of demonstrating, over and over again, the truth of the dogma; the same dogmas become the principal contents also of the arts, the entertainment media, and all the humanist endeavors of philosophy and criticism. They have managed to intrude even into the biological and physical sciences. The indoctrination of society with the official theory of state was to be total.

It was to be, but is not. Although the academic disciplines of social science have tended to conform faithfully to Party dogma, much factual, realistic, and interesting work is nonetheless produced. Outside the universities and academies, it is the practical administrator and the expert in actual problems of material and human engineering who often break through the smokescreen of ideology. Much of Soviet life and Soviet problems are examined by such people in useful businesslike fashion. Similarly, art and literature have shown increasing tendencies to break out of the hard varnishlike crust of bland, rosy-hued conformism and deal realistically, bluntly, and courageously with many facts of Soviet life.

In referring to Soviet ideology as a deceptive smokescreen, I do not mean to infer, self-righteously, that a similar conflict between science and ideology is not raging in the West. Here, too, trenchant criticism and a detached, thoroughgoing analysis of how the society actually functions must struggle continually against many ideological stereotypes.

Other Elite Interests.   To all the above values and interests—the cultural revolution and the competitive rat race, organization and total control, bureaucratic management and indoctrination—the Soviet elite is very firmly committed. Most of the tasks designed

to implement these aims have been pursued with haste and ruthlessness and in a spirit of self-righteousness. The elite has always
identified itself with the entire society and its interests (one might
almost imagine a communist saying that "what is good for the
Party is good for Soviet Russia"); hence, anyone not in agreement
with the elite was by definition outside society, a traitor, an enemy.
The rulers have shown furious impatience not only with the peasant
way of life, but with all group interests not in tune with their own
priorities and with anything standing in their way. Convinced that
their aims could be fulfilled only if all obstacles and adversaries
were eliminated, they have been grimly aware of the tremendous
resistance latent in many groups of the population. At the same
time, too stubborn to understand the stubbornness of others, they
have shown themselves unable to comprehend these primary group
interests. The resulting state of mind of the elite has been something akin to paranoia. There has been a tendency to look for
enemies where none existed and a penchant for blaming the ill
will and criminality of hostile elements for the many inefficiencies,
mistakes, bottlenecks, and failures accompanying the regime's program. The elite has been prone to lash out wildly, to engage in
witch hunts, to kill or jail many innocent and useful citizens so as
not to let a single enemy escape.

Up to this point, we have derived a complex syndrome of goals
and values from the elite's commitment to the most rapid industrialization and to operational traditions of the communist movement.
In perhaps a perverted fashion, these culture traits were symbolized
by the personality of Josef Stalin, whose character seems to have
been suspicious and vindictive, cunning and ruthless beyond limit,
and whose paranoiac tendencies imprinted themselves inevitably
on all Soviet institutions and behavior—including, perhaps, the
men with whom he surrounded himself and who struggled with
each other after he died. In a certain way, everyone in the USSR
who was endowed with any authority might be said to have been
a miniature Stalin; and although Stalin has been dead for almost
a decade, many of these little Stalins are still in positions of authority.

But even though the Stalinist syndrome of attitudes and values can be derived from the resolve to industrialize as rapidly as possible, other interests have contributed to the outlook of the Soviet political elite. One is the result of the impact of world affairs on the Soviet system. Like the political elites of all other systems, the Soviet rulers have felt compelled to maintain and strengthen their own political regime in a world of strong and hostile rival systems. This aim has forced them to commit precious human and material resources to such expensive pursuits as modern armament, military and political intelligence, support of communist movements all over the world, publicity, and, in more recent years, substantial economic aid to indigent countries. The elite's perception of the country's interests has always been determined by a number of factors, including principally, (1) Marxist–Leninist views on the nature of the contemporary world; (2) the regime's experience in dealing with other governments; (3) the ups and downs of the Soviet citizens' morale; (4) estimates of the political and military strength of the USSR; and (5) the development of modern weapons and technology. Obviously, these and various additional questions that enter into consideration of foreign policy are highly controversial and subject to different interpretations. Moreover, it seems clear that undue emphasis on one or a few sources of information must lead to different conclusions about the national interest of the USSR. In any event, there has often been sharp controversy within the Soviet political elite over fundamental issues of foreign policy. Even the broadest outlines of the national interest, which might be assumed to be self-evident, are in fact subject to conflicting interpretations. For instance, although every member of the political elite would agree that the enemies of the USSR must be kept at bay, the nature of the enemy, the degree of immediacy of his threat, the clearness of the danger he poses have always been rather controversial questions. All we can say, therefore, is that the Soviet political elite has always tended to be apprehensive about dangers lurking on the international scene, and that this latent fear has markedly increased its sense of urgency for speeding the process of industrialization. At the same time, the alleged danger posed by foreign enemies has often been used to justify this very urgency and the harsh measures adopted to implement a crash program of economic development. Foreign dangers have been used to mobilize the citizens, to instil in them a sense of perpetual emergency, and to rally them around the regime. In short, world tensions (real or imagined) have been used to justify the dictatorship. Those among the elite who, for whatever reasons, have wished to promote a more relaxed regime have always had the burden of proving that the USSR could afford to relax its vigilance and its frantic build-up in the face of the enemy. The official doctrine today maintains that the danger has lessened appreciably. The enemy still threatens, but he is no longer an overwhelming foe, since the grip of encirclement with which he once enveloped the Soviet Union has been broken. Nonetheless, world affairs still demand the careful attention of the leadership.

In addition, domestic considerations beyond those we have discussed so far must come into the purview of Soviet policy-makers. Some of these are so vague and are so common to all political elites that they need hardly be mentioned; others are special problems faced only by Soviet leaders. The most fundamental of the former problems is that of staying in power and perpetuating the present political system. But, again, while staying in power might be considered synonymous with preservation of the system, the two goals might also be seen as conflicting. In a rapidly changing world, it might be argued, a political elite can hope to preserve its power only if it succeeds in promoting peaceful change which adjusts the entire system to profound social and technological transformations. One of the special problems of leaders in the USSR is the perennial task of using limited and inefficient agricultural resources so as to provide adequate food supplies to a steadily growing population. This critical food problem is part of a more general pressure of rising expectations in regard to living standards as a whole.

Very closely related to both these aims is that of mitigating possible conflicts by integrating the various interests of the elite—and, indeed, of the entire society. Integrating the many conflicting interests of the Soviet political system is not merely an ideological problem to be resolved by purely verbal solutions, by formulas. It is also a political problem, because each of the many goals enumerated in the preceding pages, and many others, is likely to have its special spokesmen within the political elite and thus can be seen as a special interest within the complexity of elite values. In other words, even though the Soviet elite may present a common front against the interests and values of groups outside the Party, it is growing more and more heterogeneous within; and this trend toward diversity of interests within the elite is likely to increase with the further development of the USSR into a mature industrial society. If this diagnosis is correct, the elite goal of ensuring the continual integration of elite values will grow in relative importance, and the leaders of the USSR will be able to pay more and more attention to it precisely because their goal of industrializing the country will have been attained.

Let us end this section by returning to the masses of the citizenry. In the preceding pages we have contrasted popular interests with elite interests. This confrontation doubtless has given the impression of irreconcilable hostility between the two sets of goals. Indeed, many Western observers of Soviet society have portrayed its system of government as a perpetual civil war of the Party against the masses, the Kremlin against the people. To a limited degree, this image of the system is still correct. But we must be aware also that the political elite has succeeded, after decades of frantic indoctrination, in implanting at least some of its values in the minds of vast numbers of citizens. It has, first of all, given them their general frame of reference, a language of communication, a standard set of views on world affairs and different social systems which has led the average man in the USSR to take many aspects of Soviet socialism for granted. Furthermore, the vast majority of the people appear to be committed to the goal of accumulation. To this end, they also seem to have accepted the competitive society of unequals. The number of citizens who identify with the elite by internalizing its values seems to be growing rapidly, and we can expect this growth to continue so long as the leaders can satisfy some of the most pressing interests of the masses.

THE CONSTITUTION OF 1936

At the beginning of this discussion of the political culture in the USSR we pointed out, in passing, that it might be useful to differentiate between implicit and explicit values, between actual motives and a professed ethos. It is, of course, not always easy to classify any specific element of the elite culture as either implicit or explicit. For instance, the socialist rhetoric is an obvious part of the explicit or manifest value system; to what extent it should also be regarded as an actual motive force for any group within the Soviet political system is very difficult to say. How meaningful as guides to action are Sunday sermons to those who listen to them devoutly —or even to those who preach them fervently—once a week?

In the case of the Constitution of the USSR (and the constitutions of its constituent republics) the decision seems much easier. In the eyes of the Western observer, at least, these constitutions are much more explicit, rather than implicit, political culture. To express this more forthrightly: the Soviet Constitution seems to be window-dressing that has little relation to the actual workings of the political system. However, even as window-dressing, the constitution is part of the political culture.

All constitutions become part of the ethos of a political system. Ostensibly (and often quite genuinely) they establish rules of behavior for the political system and give a sacrosanct character to these rules. These rules may spell out the kinds of decisions the government may make that are binding for the citizens; the forms these decisions should take; the procedures by which they are to be formulated; the agencies and institutions with authority to make such decisions; and, perhaps, the sanctions that may be applied to enforce them. Constitutions may establish jurisdictions for different organs of government and may provide avenues of access to the decision-makers for various groups of the population. Finally, constitutions may determine conditions under which public authorities may not be authorized to interfere with the lives of individuals or groups. Whatever rules they establish, constitutions limit the authority and freedom of action of authorities, if only by the fact of specifying such authority. Any constitution that is actually in use cannot but limit the authority of political institutions. For this reason, constitutions reflect a certain antiauthoritarian bias, and constitution-writing was fiercely resisted by the absolute princes of the eighteenth century, even though the constitution might re-affirm their right to absolute rule. The hidden implication of any constitution is that the citizens as well as existing institutions are things to be protected from governmental arbitrariness.

Constitutions are almost inevitably the product of revolutions. At least they represent a new consensus, and hence a fundamental change in the political system, however it may have been brought about. By that very token these products of significant change are also conservative documents. They attempt to make the newly at-tained order permanent by codifying it into ground rules of po-litical behavior.

Superficially, the Constitution of the USSR, adopted in Decem-ber of 1936, fits all these generalizations. It marked the end of a period of violent upheaval—that "revolution from above" which saw the destruction of the independent peasantry and merchant class and the serious beginning of Russia's industrialization. At the same time, it was hailed as a codification of the newly attained order of socialism, a social system which allegedly had the backing of the entire Soviet population. And because it supposedly had this backing, certain restrictions and discriminatory clauses that in previous Soviet constitutions had favored the working class could now be removed. The words of the new Constitution breathed a certain liberal spirit. The assumption that the people of the Soviet Union had accepted the new order with all their hearts was made the premise on which the entire Constitution is based. But the premise was false. The population had by no means been won over; and the Party was fully aware of this, as manifest by its strict police regime. Moreover, the writing and adoption of the Constitu-tion coincided with the beginning of the Great Purges, that orgy of police terror which profoundly shook the entire political system. The Constitution was adopted during a period when the spirit of civil war rather than that of democracy ruled in the USSR. Perhaps this crisis explains the regime's eagerness for the Constitution: At this turbulent juncture they wished to plant upon a pedestal a document that presented the image of an ideal socialist commonwealth. Perhaps this image was to deflect the citizens' (or the foreign observers') attention from the totalitarian features of actual Soviet rule. Perhaps it was to fulfill a magic function: if the image of a well-integrated society in basic consensus could be invoked often enough, these incantations might speed the development of such consensus.

The Constitution of 1936 has been amended frequently, but its basic features have remained virtually unchanged. Its first chapter defines the USSR as a socialist state of workers and peasants, presents the doctrine of the society's class structure, and outlines the types of property recognized in the society. It also establishes the binding authority of the national economic plan. Adherence to this plan of production is thus established as a constitutional duty. Chapter Two defines the Union of Socialist Soviet Republics as a federation of sovereign republics and spells out in considerable detail the rights of the federal units. These include the right to secede from the Union, the right to conduct foreign relations and maintain armed forces, and the right to veto any changes of their boundaries enacted by the Union.

Chapters Three and Four discuss the elective representative institutions, designated as "organs of state power." These are, of course, the soviets. On a Union level, according to the Constitution, the bicameral Supreme Soviet is the source of all authority. It is sovereign. It has the exclusive power to enact laws, and thus appears to constitute the legislative branch of the government. It makes decisions by majority rule; larger majorities are required for such fundamental decisions as constitutional amendments; and the Constitution specifies how frequently it is to meet. In addition to being the exclusive source of legislation, the Supreme Soviet also is the ultimate source of all administrative authority, because it appoints the two principal administrative agencies—the Presidium of the Supreme Soviet and the government proper, which is the Council of Ministers. Both of these bodies are responsible and accountable to the Supreme Soviet.

The structure of authority is analogous on lower levels of the political system, from Union Republics down to villages. On all these levels, the Constitution provides for elected representative soviets which function as the source of all laws and administrative agencies. In providing for direct elections to soviets on all levels of the system, the 1936 Constitution departed significantly from the previous two constitutions of the Soviet regime; according to these previous arrangements, direct elections by the population created only the lowest tier or representative institutions, the local and village soviets. All higher bodies, governing larger units of territory, were composed of delegates picked by the next lower assembly, so that the nation-wide gathering of representatives, then called Congress of Soviets, was the product of a multiple screening process through various levels of administration.

The fifth chapter of the 1936 Constitution provides the blueprint for the executive or administrative machinery, the "organs of state administration." This is the Council of Ministers; and the Constitution, while making it responsible to the Supreme Soviet, assigns extensive authority to the Council in virtually every imaginable area of jurisdiction, including the authority to override the decisions of the governments in the Union Republics. Subsequent chapters provide for analogous organizations for the executive in the constituent republics and all lower levels of the system. Chapter Nine provides for a judicial organization which includes the guarantee of judges' independence.

Chapter Ten deals with the rights and duties of citizens. Here are listed all the customary liberties granted by modern constitutions—freedom of speech, freedom of the press, freedom of assembly; also freedom of organization and freedom of religious conscience. There are provisions granting freedom from arbitrary arrest, establishing the inviolability of the home, the privacy of personal correspondence, the right of asylum for "foreign citizens persecuted for defending the interests of the toilers, or for scientific activities, or for struggling for national liberation." Equal treatment for both sexes and for persons of different racial or national origins is guaranteed. So are the somewhat less customary rights to remunerative employment, the right to rest and leisure, the right to social security for the sick, the aged, and the disabled, and the right to an education.

Chapter Eleven deals with the electoral system. Deputies to all soviets are to be chosen on the basis of universal, equal, and direct suffrage, and by secret ballot—the traditional demand of radical democrats throughout the nineteenth century. All citizens eighteen years or older are entitled to vote; the minimum age at which a citizen may serve as Deputy to the Supreme Soviet is twenty-three. Candidates are to be nominated—and here, suddenly, realism creeps into the Constitution—by "public organizations and societies of the toilers" such as the Communist Party, trade unions, cooperatives, the Party's youth affiliate, and "cultural societies." Once elected, deputies are accountable to their constituents and may be recalled at any time by a majority of the voters.

The last few articles of the Constitution describe the flag and the coat of arms of the USSR and establish the city of Moscow as its capital. The coat of arms includes the familiar hammer and sickle, symbolizing the brotherly union of factory workers and peasants that supposedly forms the constituency of the Soviet state. The tools chosen for inclusion in this symbol of Soviet sovereignty unwittingly reflect the low level of technological development of the society at the time the Soviet political system was formed.

Finally, Article 146 specifies that amendments to the constitution may be made by a majority of two thirds in both chambers of the Supreme Soviet.

The Soviet Constitution departs in two ways from the models established by constitutions operative in other parts of the world. One of these departures is to list not only rights, but also duties of citizens. Some of these duties are so obvious that it is not clear why they are stated at all. For instance, it ought to be understood as a matter of course that the constitution and the laws should be obeyed—even though, as we shall find, in practice the Constitution of the USSR is disregarded in many essential aspects. The Constitution also makes it the citizens' duty to maintain labor discipline, perform public duties honestly, and respect the rules of socialist behavior. This last duty is so general that it seems to include any standard of conduct the Party may desire and sanction at any particular time. Furthermore, the Constitution establishes universal military service and singles out two crimes as particularly repugnant. One of these is any offense against public property; persons committing such offenses are branded as "enemies of the people." The other crime, declared to be the most heinous of all, is treason; the Constitution defines it in very general terms, including the catchall phrase, "impairing the military power of the state."

The other departure from customary patterns is a bit more unique: the Soviet Constitution not only lists the rights of the citizens, but also indicates how these rights are implemented and guaranteed. This inclusion can be explained as a direct outgrowth of Marxist–Leninist theory concerning liberal-democratic governments or, to use the Soviet term, bourgeois democracy. Bourgeois democracy, Soviet ideologists claim, prides itself on having extended full civil and political rights to all citizens regardless of class. But this pride is unfounded, because in reality these rights are meaningless, and extending them is an act of hypocrisy, for, so long as capitalism prevails, civil rights will benefit primarily the rich. What good is freedom of assembly to the poor classes who cannot hire a meeting hall? How unfair in its actual operation is the freedom of the press, so long as the publication of books and papers requires money that only the wealthy can provide! Therefore, the Soviet Constitution tries to demonstrate the meaningfulness of civil rights under socialism. Accordingly, it asserts that the right to remunerative work is guaranteed by the very establishment of the socialist system; the right to leisure, by legal limits on the work day; the right to a vacation, by laws providing paid annual vacation to urban workers and employees, and so forth. Finally, the customary freedoms of speech, press, and assembly are said to be guaranteed by the fact that the facilities essential to the exercise of these rights are placed "at the disposal of the toilers and their organizations." Article 126 then lists the public organizations. They include trade unions, cooperative societies, youth organizations, and others—but, foremost, the Communist Party, "the leading core of all organizations of the toilers." In plain words, therefore, civil rights are guaranteed by placing all facilities essential for their exercise into the hands of the Party and its daughter organizations. This can be regarded as a guarantee of rights only by those who accept the dogma that the Party represents the interests of all the citizens. To anyone not accepting this dogma, the civil rights provided by the Constitution must appear fraudulent and inoperative.

In fact, the entire Constitution is largely inoperative, not to say fraudulent; at best, it does not give an adequate picture of the actual political system. It is not even a useful guide to lawyers or administrators within the system who might wish to orient themselves in it. More than in many other political systems, the real constitution of the USSR remains unwritten.

The unrealism of the Constitution can be traced through many of its provisions. One of them is Soviet federalism. Some of the articles pertaining to federalism have actually been declared to be inoperative, for instance, the right of Union Republics to secede. Any attempt to exercise this right would be considered a crime. Other provisions have been violated in fact, for instance, the one which specifies that no changes of Union Republic boundaries must be made without prior consent of the republics concerned. Similarly, the right to maintain armies and conduct foreign relations has remained meaningless, except for giving United Nations seats to the Ukrainian and Belorussian Socialist Soviet Republics.

The declaration that sovereignty resides in the "organs of state power" is specious. The exclusive right of the Supreme Soviet to make laws becomes meaningless when we realize that many binding decisions do not take the form of laws—edicts issued by the Presidium of the Supreme Soviet; decrees published by the Council of Ministers; resolutions of the Central Committee of the Communist Party; and a host of other regulations of which the Constitution makes no mention. Only a minute portion of authoritative decisions in the USSR take the form of laws. The majority rule which supposedly governs the deliberations of the Supreme Soviet is a fiction, since nothing has ever been decided by this body except unanimously. As we shall see later, the distinction between elective-representative institutions and administrative agencies is also ficti-tious; in actual fact, election and recall procedures conceal an appointment process which governs both the soviets and the execu-tive bodies. For this and other reasons, therefore, the dependence of the Council of Ministers on the Supreme Soviet is also a fiction.

The independence of judges is stated but not guaranteed by the Constitution, and there is no indication that the statement is honored in practice. There is no provision for judicial review or any other interpretative procedure. Hence any interpretation of the Constitution is made by the administration itself or by the constitutional lawyers it appoints. There are, furthermore, no pro-visions concerning enforcement of observance of the Constitution or providing recourse for those who might feel their constitutional rights abridged. In fact, it is generally understood by the people that the Constitution must not be used for any purposes that are opposed by the regime in power. The Constitution does not there-fore protect anyone against governmental arbitrariness; instead, it codifies such arbitrariness.

The question of why it was adopted at all remains something of a puzzle. Undoubtedly, it fitted in with the ideological claims of the regime, according to which socialism had been achieved. The Constitution was to be a symbol of this achievement, both for the Soviet citizenry and for the outside world. It is little more than that—an ideological device which, unlike the Constitution of the United States, commands very little passion and cannot be con-sidered a potent political force. Some day, perhaps, in a period of greater political fluidity, it may be taken more seriously by those who today go through the motions of observing it. Some day, a group of deputies in the Soviet system may appeal to the Con-stitution in an effort to make the government responsible in fact to the elected representatives. Some day a Soviet court may declare itself competent to interpret the Constitution in a manner which diverges from prevailing dogma. If ever such a challenge be raised, the Constitution will change from mere window-dressing into an actual political force.

Part Two

The Rulers

Chapter IV
The Party in the Political System

If we were to single out one central point on which the Constitution of the USSR presents an unrealistic image of the political system, it might be its failure to account for the role of the Communist Party and its relations with the formal or "constitutional" government structure. The Constitution, in all its 146 Articles, mentions the Party but once, almost as an afterthought, in Chapter X, dealing with the rights and duties of citizens. Article 126 in this chapter reads as follows:

> In conformity with the interests of the working people, and in order to develop the organizational initiative and political activity of the masses of the people, the citizens of the USSR are guaranteed the right to unite in public organizations: trade unions, cooperative societies, youth organizations, sport and defense organizations, cultural, technical, and scientific societies; and the most active and politically conscious citizens in the ranks of the working class, working peasants, and working intelligentsia voluntarily unite in the Communist Party of the Soviet Union, which is the vanguard of the working people in their struggle to build a communist society and is the leading core of all organizations of the working people, both societal and governmental.

The Constitution thus recognizes the Party as the "leading core" of the political system and in this fashion summarizes the work of over 9 million people in a vast and all-embracing web of organizations, engaged in as broad a range of activities as any government

of a large modern state. Even the formal participation of the Party
in the governmental process cannot be summed up in such laconic
fashion. From reading the Constitution, one could never guess, for
instance, that decrees or regulations issued by the Party have the
force of law within the entire society, or that Party agencies play
a decisive role in the recruitment of personnel on all levels of the
political system, from the highest to the lowest, whether the office
be elective or appointive. Nor would one guess that discussion of
public issues takes place almost exclusively within the confines
of the Party structure, and that the policies and administrative decisions derived from this discussion are formulated by the Party
rather than the "constitutional" government. In fact, from reading
the Constitution alone one would not guess that the Soviet political
system is governed by the Party far more than by the government
itself.

The question has at times been asked, not indeed why a Constitution should have been written which so much distorts actual
political relationships within the government, but rather why the
Party, which governs the USSR, has troubled to create, in addition
to its own sprawling political machine, a separate governmental
structure no less sprawling and no less complicated. From all this
it is obvious that we shall have to go far beyond the Soviet Constitution to examine the place of the Communist Party within the
political system and its precise relations to the formal governmental apparatus.

In beginning with this attempt to place the Party within the
total political system, we are reversing the order of presentation
customarily observed in books on Soviet government. Usually,
authors begin by outlining the history of the Party and then proceed to present its formal structure; only after this do they get
around to a discussion of the way in which this structure meshes
with the larger social organization and the functions of the Party
within the total system. By reversing this order, the present
book may seem to violate the logic of historical presentation, but may add clarity to the reader's understanding of the
larger whole within which the Party operates.

FUNCTIONS OF THE PARTY

We began by criticizing the Soviet Constitution for neglecting to account sufficiently for the Party. It might be well to remember at this point that the Constitution of the United States also does not mention parties. Yet it is not too difficult to make statements about the role of parties in the American political process; in fact, there is a wealth of literature on the subject. Many political scientists describe the American parties as machinery for the purpose of electing Presidents, or, more generally, as vote-getting organizations. In other words, parties are seen as instruments for obtaining that political power which is available by virtue of holding elective office. At the same time, the elected officeholders often can reward their party followers with appointive offices and other forms of political power. From the point of view of the entire political system, the parties therefore serve as recruitment agencies which provide the system with leaders. Some or all of the political elite are chosen through or by or with the participation of the parties.

Furthermore, parties raise issues and, in doing so, represent various community interests. In multiparty systems, the parties often serve to articulate the interests of specific groups; in systems where the various pressure groups speak for themselves or where there are only two major parties, the parties function as the aggregators and integrators of conflicting interests. In all political systems, biparty or multiparty, the parties formulate programs, platforms, and policy proposals.

Does any of this apply to the Communist Party of the Soviet Union? Obviously, it is not a vote-getting machine. The struggle for power in the USSR was decided decades ago; government is now firmly in the Party's hands; its leaders automatically rise to top positions within the political system. From the point of view of the power struggle, therefore, the CPSU might just as well dissolve itself. But by the very token of having the monopoly of political power it is fulfilling a familiar function of parties everywhere: through it the system recruits its political elite. Having no rivals in the form of other parties, the CPSU may, indeed, perform this function very differently, as we shall see in due time; but perform it it does.

Similarly, we shall see that in the play of conflicting interests the Communist Party functions much as do parties in other political systems. It too serves as the agency of aggregation and integration, as the agency from which emerge programs and platforms, ideological positions and policies. Hence it must also serve as the arena for political conflict. Policy formation is the result of a deliberation process in which problems are appraised, priorities established, solutions proposed, and alternative policies considered. In the Soviet political system, all these stages of policy formation take place within the framework of the Party. We have no information about the form these processes take. We know next to nothing about the procedures established for bringing problems to the Party's attention, and nothing at all about the rules governing the subsequent steps. Only one thing is clear: In a society as complex as the USSR, it is inevitable that there is a never-ending need for authoritative public policy regarding a myriad of problems. Every such problem can be seen as a clash of interests and must be decided on the basis of the Party's values and priorities. A decision is therefore the result of weighing the Party's values and the interests of various groups, both within the Party and outside, which have a stake in the decision. Because this process is carried on within the confines of the Party, the Party must be seen as the arena within which occur all conflicts of interest in the Soviet political system. The Party thus serves the function of professional politicians whose task it is to formulate policies that will not disrupt the political system itself, and whose skill consists in steering carefully among conflicting interests, whether they emanate from broad classes, groups of professional experts, or self-appointed guardians of political orthodoxy. The CPSU shares this function with professional politicians in other political systems. The difference between them is not the function they serve but the fact that the decisions made by the Communist Party become binding on the political system.

Parties in multiparty systems, by articulating or aggregating interests emanating from the constituents, also fulfill the function of representation. Can we say the same thing about the CPSU? The Party's own spokesmen would give a positive answer to this question. They would say that the Communist Party knows the interests of the working class and all the toilers, that it articulates and promotes these interests, and that in formulating authoritative policies it acts in their behalf. The Party thus claims to be the one and only true representative of all the people in the Soviet Union. Government in the USSR therefore might be defined as government of the people, for the people, by the Party. But these claims to represent the people's interests are not verifiable, because the Soviet political system contains no elaborate machinery for guaranteeing the representative nature of the Party, no constitutional devices which might compel the Party to be responsive to the wishes of the constituents. To be sure, the Party makes use of various methods of probing into public opinion. Moreover, Party leaders have shown an awareness of various group interests in Soviet society, may have taken these interests into serious consideration, and have occasionally attempted to make the Party itself representative by recruiting members from various groups and strata of the population. But at the same time the Party's spokesmen openly concede that these measures do not count very heavily in policy formulation. The public interest is defined by the Party primarily according to its own doctrines. The representatives of the public are either self-appointed or co-opted by an established oligarchy, which therefore decides for itself who is and who is not truly representative. Hence all the claims of the Party to be representative are tautologies, depending altogether on definition. In the Soviet political system, therefore, Burke's theory of virtual representation is carried to its logical conclusion: the constituency not only has no influence over its elected representatives; it does not even elect them.

The only observation we might add to this would be that a party congress, at which all delegates unanimously applaud the speeches of the leaders and approve their acts, is fulfilling a representative function: By demonstrating their political passivity and helplessness, the delegates who thus pay their obeisances before the leaders effectively represent the helplessness and passivity of all the constituents within the political system.

Most readers doubtless recoil from the notion of attributing representative functions to the Communist Party. What causes them to recoil is probably the fact that the Party takes account of the views of the constituents only at its pleasure, and that the system provides no alternative, no opposition party. In other words, we refuse to accept the idea that a heterogeneous society could be effectively represented by a single, highly centralized organization.

At this point it becomes pointless to make further comparisons with political systems that incorporate representative institutions in which several parties compete with each other. Instead, the place of the Communist Party of the Soviet Union within the total political system may be understood more easily if we compare the structure of the USSR to that of a giant Western business corporation. The similarities between these two structures are striking, as scholars are beginning to observe with increased frequency. They go beyond the organizational forms, the absence of truly representative institutions or effectively enforced responsibility to a broad constituency in decision-making; they include the thorough bureaucratization of management on all levels—and we shall see that the position of the lower- and middle-level administrator in the USSR is analogous in many respects to that of his colleagues in the Western business bureaucracy. Similarities even include the broad aims of the organizations, which in the cases of both the Soviet Union and the giant corporation are best described as the accumulation of wealth and power and the preservation of the enterprise.

We shall return to these and other similarities at appropriate points. Here we are interested in the place of the Party within the entire political system. Expressing it in terms of the modern corporation, we should then say that the position of the CPSU becomes closely analogous to that of the stockholders. The Party owns the Soviet Union. It does not, of course, have legal title to the country and does not claim it. But it acts as if it owned it; and since it gets away with acting in this fashion, it does in fact own it. Or perhaps it would be more appropriate to use the term which political scientists use in lieu of ownership—sovereignty. The terms are anyway virtually interchangeable.

The Communist Party, then, is sovereign in the USSR, just as the stockholders are sovereign within their corporation. Like the stockholders' meeting, the Party is not a group of equals, and the individual quality of ownership, the nature of sovereign rights, varies with the quantity of controlling shares held. The individual stockholder has as little control over the enterprise as the rank-and-file party member has over Soviet government. The men who run the concern are the major shareholders who sit on the Board of Directors; in the USSR they are the men who are in command of the Communist Party, so that the party's Central Committee and that Committee's Presidium, together with the Secretariat, must be seen as agencies which, together, fulfill the function of the Board of Directors.

A precise definition of the sovereign owners is made quite difficult by the remarkable fuzziness of the boundaries between owners and managers. The two groups overlap to a considerable extent, and therefore students of Western corporations have tried to demonstrate that the managerial revolution has done away with the ownership function altogether. Similarly, the overlap between Communist Party and government in the Soviet Union has created difficulties for outside observers. Indeed, there have been periods in the history of the USSR during which the merger of the two structures was so intimate that it would have been difficult to assign functions to one which the other did not also serve. For this reason, Western scholars sometimes wondered why the Party continued to exist at all, and some, applying concepts analogous to that of the managerial revolution, forecast its disappearance. Most observers today would doubtless acknowledge that the Party has re-emerged as a distinct structure within the Soviet political system; and yet the boundaries continue to be very obscure. Career lines in the Party and in other hierarchies cross more frequently, perhaps, than corporate, governmental, legal, political, and military careers in the United States. As in the Western corporation, members of the "Board of Directors" appoint themselves to managerial positions, while successful managers in production, administration, or public relations rise to positions of ownership. And yet, despite this confusion, it is as legitimate as it is useful to distinguish between ownership functions and management functions and to realize that, in the Soviet political system, the former are performed by the Party.

As sovereign of the Soviet Union, the Party (that is, its highest decision-making organizations) not only determines basic policies and thus defines the goals of the entire system. It also shapes the structure within which the goals are to be attained and the policies carried out. In other words, the Party organizes and reorganizes the government, the administration, the entire associational life of the society; it does so in sovereign fashion, unencumbered by any fundamental respect for the institutions it has itself created. This, of course, is a sharp negation of the very notion of constitutionalism. A constitution establishes rules of the game for the political process and creates certain structures which it endows with authority. In the USSR, all governmental authority is derived from the Party, and the Party can take it away; the Party also can change the rules of the game.

Just as the Board of Directors (with the approval of the stockholders) appoints the officers of corporations, so the Party has the power of hiring and firing managerial personnel, from the very top on down. Political scientists would express this today by saying that the Party recruits the political elite in the Soviet political system, or at least plays a major role in the process of elite recruitment. Here too it acts with the liberty of the sovereign, hiring and firing at will. The Party leaders may appoint themselves to top positions in the government or they may choose people they expect to carry out their policies. In any event, it is obvious that reorganizations and reassignments in the formal governmental structure are related to personality clashes or policy disputes within the party leadership, just as proxy fights in a corporation may lead to managerial shakeups.

In demonstrating similarities it is important to draw attention to dissimilarities as well. At some point, all analogies become misleading; so also the comparison between the CPSU and corporation shareholders. For one thing, Party members on lower levels of the political system are infinitely more active in the enterprise than stockholders of corporations, who as a rule are passive, if not entirely disinterested in "their" corporation's activities. The Party member, in contrast, takes an active interest in the conduct of public business. His concern is with regular and careful supervision of the way the policies of the Party are being carried out. This task of supervision, on all levels of political activities down to the very grass roots, must therefore be added to the functions of the Communist Party.

Yet another Party function might be described as political communication. Two very different, albeit related, tasks are involved here. One is that of political intelligence: the Party must keep itself informed about all developments within the entire system that might affect the success or failure of its goals and policies. In having its members and intermediary agencies supervise the execution of policies, the Party can be expected to gather much of the information it needs. In that sense, the tasks of supervision and intelligence-gathering overlap or coincide. But the Party also wants to have information about the needs or interests of the various groups composing Soviet society. Political intelligence thus includes the problem of gauging public opinion, or the moods of the masses. For our purpose, which is to survey the various functions carried out by the Party, it does not matter whether or not these opinions or needs are taken into serious consideration when policies are actually made. The fact remains that the Party does function as a channel of communication for making public opinion and group interests known to the policy-makers. In this particular instance, we can, once again, see analogies with the functions of parties in other political systems.

The second task inherent in the Party's communication functions is that of political socialization. By this we mean the process of training the citizens for their roles in the political system. Political socialization involves not only continuous effort to make the citizens accept the structure of the system as legitimate, but also the attempt to make them internalize the goals of the Party and accept them as their own. As a result of socialization the constituents identify with the system so that their personal interests coincide with the goals of the rulers. In short, the Party seeks to mobilize the citizens by indoctrinating them, as well as to give them high morale and *esprit de corps*.

THE PARTY AT THE NATIONAL LEVEL

A survey of the functions of the Communist Party within the Soviet political system would not be complete without a description of the manner in which the organization of this sovereign elite meshes with the entire complex structure of Soviet society. Examination of this relationship will at the same time enable us to see how the Party performs different tasks at different levels of the Soviet system.

We have already stated that the topmost agencies of the Party, at the national level, assume command over the entire society, formulating programs of action binding on all citizens. The priorities and goals the Party establishes become the goals and priorities of all, because, as we shall see, the Party has at its disposal an elaborate set of rewards for those who conform to its ideas and sanctions for those who do not. The range of decisions made by the Party on the national level includes not only programs and policies, but also the organization of government and the recruitment of the elite. The Party high command has the power to create and abolish all and any agencies within the political system, from the lowest on up to cabinet ministries and Union Republics. The Party also appoints and dismisses the highest office holders, from the President of the Republic (or its Soviet equivalent) on down.

The forms in which decisions on these matters are transmitted to the agencies and persons concerned vary considerably. From the scant information we have it seems evident that there is a steady flow of directives from central Party agencies to governmental and societal organizations, directives and orders which are not published and may in fact be strictly classified. Such directives may take many forms, from guidelines sent by some division within the Party's Central Committee to formal decrees of the Central Committee Presidium. Party policy pronouncements may even be made in the form of seemingly casual pronouncements by one of the highest Party leaders, or they may be issued as editorials or articles in the daily newspaper *Pravda,* the journal *Kommunist,* or some other organ of the national Party headquarters. In elite recruitment for non-Party organizations, the Party may reserve the right to select an officeholder or may, in less important cases, retain the right of confirmation. Here too the decision may be transmitted in formal or very informal fashion. But, so long as the Party command is itself unanimous, the managers are never left in doubt concerning the will of the sovereign. At the same time, however, the informality of the process, the lack of publicity and codification, do give administrators a good deal of uncertainty. Since, moreover, directives reach the top managers from a variety of high Party agencies and personalities, and may, in fact, reflect differences of opinion within the highest command of the Party, the highest agencies of management in the USSR often find themselves facing contradictory instructions. In such situations, as we shall see, the managers must be guided by their understanding of the weight which Party superiors ascribe to different goals and also by their perception of the ups and downs of the struggle for power within the highest command of the Party.

The Party's control over the recruitment of top personnel in non-Party agencies is marked by the frequency with which the lines between the Party and other structures are crossed. Experience in highest Party offices often leads to assignment to highest government offices; likewise, after filling a very high office in a non-Party institution, a Party member may be assigned to a full-time Party job. Frequently, those who hold high governmental positions simultaneously occupy some party office of national importance; and at all times everyone holding any kind of office of great authority on the national level can be assumed to be a member of the Party.

A brief survey of the manner in which the highest executive agency of the Soviet government has been staffed in the past will illustrate the point and will at the same time show subtle changes in the pattern of elite recruitment. This agency is the Soviet cabinet, called the Council of Ministers (until the early 1940s it was called the Council of People's Commissars or Sovnarkom). Of the fifteen members who formed the first cabinet in October 1917, six were members and one a candidate member of the Party's Central Committee, which at that time numbered 21 members and 10 alternates and included the most prominent Bolsheviks, Lenin's most trusted or most valuable advisers—in short, the top elite of the party. Obviously, only a minority of these men and women were given cabinet appointments, and many of them had no official connection with any governmental structure; some cabinet posts were given to persons of far lesser rank in the Party. The commissariats headed by Central Committee members included the following: Chairman (Lenin), Interior (Rykov), Agriculture (Miliutin), Trade and Industry (Nogin), Foreign Affairs (Trotsky), Nationalities (Stalin), and Justice (Lomov, a candidate member). The commissariats of Labor, Defense, Education, Finance, Food, and Post & Telegraph were in the hands of nonmembers of the Central Committee, but all of them were sufficiently authoritative figures within the Party; indeed, the Commissar for Education, Lunacharsky, was one of the most prominent personalities of the Russian Marxist movement, and was much better known to rank-and-file Party members, as well as to outsiders, than were some of the Central Committee members.

If we go higher yet in the Party hierarchy and examine the Political Bureau (Politburo) created in 1919, we shall find again that a minority of its members were associated, officially, with the Council of People's Commissars, whereas the majority of Politburo members and candidates held no government appointment. And if we wish to go higher yet, we shall have to look at the triumvirate that governed the Party during Lenin's last illness and after his death. Of these three men, Zinoviev, Kamenev, and Stalin, only the last was also a member of the Sovnarkom.

After Stalin's victory over his rivals within the Party, even the highest political offices were at times given to people of lesser importance within the Party. Rykov, who succeeded Lenin as Chairman of the Sovnarkom, was a compromise candidate for that job; he held on to it for a long time, even though his political star was beginning to decline. Chicherin, who succeeded Trotsky as Commissar for Foreign Affairs in early 1918, was never important in the Party. He became a member only at the time of his cabinet appointment, and was added to the Central Committee only in 1925, when the importance of that body had already declined somewhat—if only because its number had swelled to 63 members and 43 alternates. Here we obviously have an example of reverse recruitment: co-option to the Party following appointment to high governmental office. As the Stalin dictatorship entrenched itself more and more, the prominent Old Bolsheviks were replaced by men who might be described as Stalin's creatures; again, the impression is that the members of the Council of People's Commissars were, with few exceptions, people of secondary rank within the Party. Appearances may have been deceptive in the troubled period of the Great Purge, during which about 50 of the 71 full Central Committee members elected in 1934 were eliminated (as was an ever greater proportion of the candidate members). At that time the turnover of personnel in governmental organizations was similarly rapid, and persons were appointed to very high posts without having high formal status in the Party. For instance, neither Ezhëv (People's Commissar for the Interior) nor Vyshinski (Prosecutor General) held membership or even candidate membership in the Central Committee at the time he was appointed to his all-important cabinet post. Ezhëv was eliminated before the next Party congress could elect a new Central Committee, so that he, perhaps the most powerful government official for a year or two, never attained even this diluted honor, to say nothing of membership in the Politburo. His case is an illustration of the Party's loss of sovereignty during Stalin's rule. Because of it a man could become powerful even without having high Party rank, so long as he was a member of Stalin's personal secretariat. Perhaps Stalin's decision, at the beginning of World War II, to assume the Chairmanship of the Sovnarkom, may be interpreted as yet another symptom of the same downgrading of the Party: obviously he felt that it was insufficient for him to govern the country from his all-powerful position as the Party's General Secretary and chairman of its Politburo.

At the same time, there were signs pointing in the other direction. One that interests us in the context of this discussion is the phenomenon of the so-called Politburo ministries. A number of Politburo members always had cabinet appointments, and as a rule they held the most important or sensitive cabinet posts, such as Interior, Foreign Affairs, Commerce, Heavy Industry, and the Chairmanship. By virtue of their conspicuous Party rank these People's Commissars or Ministers undoubtedly far outranked their fellow Ministers in prestige as well as power. At the same time, the control these Ministers had over important branches of the government service may have provided them with political strength within the Party that they might not otherwise have possessed. One might doubt the value of such strength so long as Stalin was still in command, but it might have been considered indispensable in the inevitable struggle for power that would ensue after his death. It is therefore interesting to note that Stalin, in his obvious attempt to arrange for a more orderly succession, during the last months of his life abolished the Politburo ministries. Six months before his death, at the Nineteenth Congress of the Party, all the Politburo Ministers were promoted to Deputy Chairmen of the Council of Ministers; their portfolios were handed to men of secondary rank in the Party. In the light of our observations, these promotions may have been a device to deprive them of their power bases within the governmental structure; that, in fact, the men concerned did not cherish their promotions is confirmed by the eagerness with which, immediately after Stalin's death, they resumed control of their former ministries.

Since 1953 the pattern of recruitment for highest governmental office has been no less confusing. For instance, in the summer of 1961 the highest decision-making organ of the Party, the Presidium of the Central Committee (formerly called the Politburo), contained fourteen full members, of whom only five had cabinet appointments; one held the ceremonial office of Chairman of the Presidium of the Supreme Soviet, making him formally the head of the state. The full Central Committee contained 133 members, of whom 15 held cabinet posts in the Council of Ministers. The Council of Ministers, in turn, was composed of the following: 1 Chairman, 2 First Deputy Chairmen, 4 Deputy Chairmen, 15 Ministers, and 21 Chairmen of departments at the ministerial level—a total of 43 members, of whom, as we just stated, only 15 were full members of the Party's Central Committee; and even among these there were some who had obviously risen in the government service and only as a result of attaining high government office had been co-opted into the highest ranks of the Party. Certainly this is true of the Minister of Foreign Affairs, Mr. Gromyko. Most astonishing, even of the four Deputy Chairmen of the Council of Ministers, only two are full members of the Central Committee. Of the two Deputy Chairmen who do not hold such high Party rank, one is also the Chairman of the State Planning Commission, and the other chairs the State Scientific and Economic Council. It is fair to surmise that both of them rose as experts in management and planning.

A brief look at the ministries and departments headed by full members of the Central Committee will round out the picture:

*Ministries and Departments headed by full members
of the Central Committee, July 1961:*

Foreign Trade
Railroad Communications
Ministry Without Portfolio
Foreign Affairs
Defense
Culture

Committee for Aviation Technology
Committee for Questions of Labor and Wages
Control Commission
Committee for State Security
Committee for State Purchases

*Ministries and Departments headed by persons
not full members of the Central Committee:*

Transport Construction
Merchant Marine
Electric Power Station Construction
Finance
Postal Service and Telecommunication
Geology and Mineral Resource Conservation
Health
Agriculture
Higher Education
Committee for Automation and Machine Building
Scientific and Economic Council
Committee for Foreign Economic Relations
Committee for Defense Technology
Committee for Radio and Electronics
Committee for Shipbuilding
Committee for Chemistry
Board of the State Bank
Committee for Cultural Ties with Foreign Countries
Committee for Sound and Television Broadcasting
Committee for the Use of Atomic Energy
Committee for Coordination of Scientific Research Work
Committee for Building Affairs
Committee for Vocational and Technical Training
Central Statistical Administration

Perhaps the only item in this chart that ought to evoke our surprise
is the fact that the Ministers of Agriculture and Higher Education
are not members of the Central Committee.

Detailed information concerning the careers of each of the above officeholders would confuse the picture further. For instance, concerning the two First Deputy Chairmen of the Council of Ministers, it would be difficult to say whether they made their careers in the Party or in the government. Both held highest ranks in both organizations for decades. A more puzzling case is that of Nikolai G. Ignatov, one of the four Deputy Chairmen. A Red Army volunteer in the civil war, a Party member since 1924, he rose in the Party and held many important assignments. Governmental office did not come to him until 1960; and there are indications that his appointment coincided with a political shift in the Party in which he lost status. His designation as a Deputy Chairman of the Council of Ministers might therefore have been some sort of honorable demotion or retirement, an appointment as Elder Statesman.

THE PARTY AT THE TERRITORIAL LEVEL

Let us now turn to lower-level Party organizations to study further how the Party organization meshes with the governmental structure. The Party has territorial organizations corresponding to the administrative subdivisions of the entire country—Union Republics and Autonomous Republics, regions, provinces, and so forth. The Party is organized as a command structure in which information moves up while policies and directives are handed down. At the very top of this hierarchy, the command center is difficult to define, because a number of agencies have at times competed with each other—for example, the Secretariat and the Central Committee, as well as the executive agencies of the latter, formerly known as the Politburo and now called the Presidium. Indeed, under Stalin, the center of authority, as we have pointed out repeatedly, may have been a non-party organization, that is Stalin's personal secretariat.

In the subordinate Party organizations, let us say at the level of the province, (*oblast*), the center of authority is perhaps a little easier to define. All the evidence we have leads us to assume that on this level the decision-making organ of the party is the Bureau

of the provincial Party committee, known as the *Obkomburo*.[1]
It usually includes the provincial Party Secretaries, some division
chiefs of the Secretariat, the Chairman of the provincial government executive (*Obispolkom*), and possibly such people as the
provincial Komsomol (Young Communist League) secretary, the
head of the provincial police department, perhaps the district military commander, and, quite probably, the chairman of the provincial Economic Council. This group of Party members effectively
governs the provincial Party organization and, through it, the entire
life of the province. Its principal activities toward this end may be
summarized as follows.

First of all, the *Obkomburo* is concerned with the personnel
and its recruitment, training, and assignment in all party organizations subordinate to it. It supervises all their activities, assists them
with material, personnel, or advice, when necessary, and adjudi-
cates any complaints or conflicts reaching it from these lower
organizations.

Further, the provincial Party organization concerns itself with
the entire economy of the territory within its jurisdiction. Directly,
as well as through subordinate Party organizations, the *Obkomburo*
will convey to factories, farms, and other producers the pressure
to meet established production goals. It also takes an active part
in such economic activities as the securing of supplies and the
allocation of material and human resources. It closely examines
and helps to formulate the production plans that are to be submitted for approval to higher authorities; it establishes deadlines,
inspects premises and finished products, and evaluates the performance of the many agencies and organizations that participate
in the economy. In discussing this work of the *Obkomburo,* Fainsod
speaks of its "round-the-clock concern" with the task of fulfilling
the goals that have been set by Moscow. In short, the provincial
Party organization, working within the broad limits established

---

[1] As we shall see, during a comparatively brief period from 1962 to 1964
there were two *obkomburos* in each *oblast,* because in these two years the
entire Party organization, from the Secretariat down to the primary organizations, was divided into two branches, one for the agricultural or rural and
another for urban and industrial affairs. This rather startling experiment was
ended in November 1964.

by the national plan and national laws and regulations, maintains continual close supervision over the provincial economy, leaving no doubt as to who is sovereign in all matters that require authoritative decisions.

Similar supremacy is wielded by the Party over the provincial government executive (the *Obispolkom*), over education, entertainment, culture—in fact, over all other organizations and associations that are active within the province. "With the possible exception of the army and the NKVD," writes Fainsod, speaking about the Smolensk *Obkomburo* in the 1930s, "there was no organized activity in the oblast which was free from the bureau's guidance and direction."[2]

In wielding this supremacy, the *Obkomburo* not only relays the commands that are passed down to it from higher organizations; it also makes policies of its own, which may be thought of as implementations of the commands from above. In other words, the *Obkomburo* takes a decisive and authoritative part in translating the demands and commands of the regime into actual organization and activity. In doing this, it sets the pace of work for all the various structures under its supervision. Whether all this activity by the *Obkomburo* should be classified as policy-making or as administration depends primarily on the observer's point of view. For the national offices of the Party, the network of territorial organizations is a set of executive or administrative agencies—"the field," as American administrators would say. But in the eyes of the citizens and officials, the agencies and associations within the confines of a given territory, the *Obkomburo* is the sovereign policy-maker.

One of the most crucial among the *Obkomburo's* activities is the recruitment of personnel for the many agencies under its supervision. In the USSR, all offices are public offices, all appointments to public office are political appointments, even though the degree of political control varies. Control is stricter over positions of greater authority or responsibility. The precise nature of the Party's

[2] Merle Fainsod, *Smolensk Under Soviet Rule* (Cambridge: Harvard University Press, 1958), p. 73.

control over appointments is spelled out in a set of regulations which specifies the range and nature of supervision to be exercised by any given Party organization. This set of rules, which is subject to change, is called the *nomenklatura*. The *nomenklatura* is a list of persons and positions of authority over which a given Party agency is expected and authorized to maintain control. It is divided into two rubrics: the basic nomenclature is a list of those posts which can be filled only by the Party, whereas the supervision nomenclature lists those appointments which can be filled only *in consultation with* the Party. In the latter case, the precise nature of the consultation is not spelled out; there has been considerable variation in practice, from active interference in the appointment-making process to the granting of routine approvals. The *nomenklatura* is, as mentioned, subject to change by order of higher Party agencies. Items may be deleted or added, and they may be transferred to the nomenclature of a higher or lower party organization.

The nomenclature provides a good illustration of the manner in which the Party pervades and dominates institutions which, on paper, possess administrative or constitutional autonomy. According to law, chairmen of collective farms, secretaries of trade unions, and executive officers of many other associations of various kinds are to be elected by all the members of the organization. This applies also to elected delegates in local, regional, or national assemblies (soviets), as well as to the executive officers picked by those soviets to function as day-to-day government officials. In the prevailing practice, however, a Party representative from the bureau which has the particular office in its nomenclature makes the nomination (*rekomendatsia*) during a meeting of the collective farm, trade union, soviet, or whatever. The farcical nature of the presumably democratic election process becomes apparent when we realize that frequently people are nominated who are unknown in the collective farm, trade union, or other agency concerned. Although there have been instances of grass-roots rebellion, according to the Soviet press, such nominations are very rarely disregarded. In short, wherever elective offices are at stake, the Party selects the candidates so that the election itself is no more than a (virtually automatic) confirmation. That the same Party influence is wielded in picking candidates for appointive office should have become quite clear.

The recruitment of personnel for all responsible positions within the entire society is a formidable task. As stated already, it can be pursued with all seriousness or can become an empty routine. From the point of view of the Party leadership it is, of course, a very vital concern, and the Central Committee has made it clear that it expects territorial organizations to make nominations only on the basis of personal acquaintance with the nominees.[3] The Party command, at all levels of the political system, is therefore obliged to cultivate personal acquaintance with the leading personalities in all fields of endeavor; familiarity with their record of achievements apparently is not deemed sufficient ground for recommending them. As a result of this obligation, the fabric of high society in the USSR is very close knit. At any one of the various levels of the political system, there is a managerial set somewhat analogous to the country club set in the United States, where the leading citizens from various professions mingle and become acquainted with each other. The analogy should be applied with caution, as it has many limitations; perhaps the most important feature of the Soviet managerial set is the wide power the Party has in co-opting, blackballing, and ejecting personnel. Despite these reservations, however, we shall return to the analogy between the Soviet managerial elite and the American country club set.

We need not at this point go into details concerning the work of the territorial Party organization in the field of socialization and indoctrination. It is obvious from what has been said that its control over media of mass communication, over the school system, over entertainment and other cultural activities, is exercised in the same fashion as its control over administration, production, and personnel. Here, too, in consonance with directives from higher Party headquarters, the territorial organization determines policies,

[3] Borys Lewytzkij, "Die Nomenklatur," *Osteuropa,* XI, 6 (June, 1961), 410.

provides blueprints for organization, recruits personnel, supervises operations, and reserves the right to participate, in some form, in all major decisions. In addition, the Party maintains its own agencies of socialization and indoctrination, under the supervision of the ideological section known until recently as section for Agitation and Propaganda (Agitprop). Some of the activities undertaken for these purposes are intended strictly for intramural use. These include Party schools and training courses, lectures and seminars, as well as the distribution of orientation material among Party members. Even the newspaper published by a territorial Party organization falls within this category, for though anyone is free to buy it at the newsstands, it can be assumed that few but Party members will become regular subscribers; this is even truer of other periodical literature published directly by the Party. Other indoctrinational and educational activities undertaken by the Party are aimed primarily at the general public. Here, too, the printed as well as the spoken word is used in lectures and rallies, posters and displays, newspapers, periodicals, brochures, and books. Finally, there are the ubiquitous information centers maintained by local and regional party agencies for the purpose of guiding and informing any citizen who wishes to be enlightened on any current issue. Such a center is called an Agitation Point (*agitpunkt*). It may occupy a spacious office or be no more than a booth containing a party information officer (*agitator*) provided with a selection of printed handouts dealing with current issues. At times of major political or ideological changes, when the public can be expected to be especially eager for enlightenment, special *agitpunkty* may be set up in public squares, parks, or other places to handle the crowds of enquirers.

Agitators, it should be noted, act not only as information and education officers for the population, but also as collectors of political intelligence. The very questions the public asks them must be of great interest to the Party as indicators of the mood of the masses. In most recent years, the Party has, indeed, begun to survey public sentiment by opinion polls. But in the Soviet Union the use of this device is obviously still in its trial stage, and for the time being the *agitator* remains one of the most important sources of this kind of information.

The *obkomburo* itself receives a great deal of intelligence directly. In the eyes of the citizens, the Party leadership at its various levels is often regarded as a court of last resort, a ready recipient of complaints or petitions from anyone who may either feel that he has been wronged by an official agency or who wishes to call alleged mismanagement or evil-doing to the Party's attention. From the evidence we have it seems that the Party leadership treats such information, allegations, and complaints quite seriously. They are a vital link between the leaders and their constituents, precisely because they circumvent the ordinary channels of communication.

Finally, we see in the provincial Party headquarters a bargaining agency between the local administration and the highest leadership. On the one hand, we have seen that the territorial leaders channel commands and expectations down to the producers and administrators at the grass roots, and they take a most active interest in enforcing their fulfillment. At the same time, the leaders are interested in receiving commands that can in fact be carried out, objectives and expectations that are consonant with the capabilities of the local constituency. Hence they will continually seek to scale down the demands so as to maintain a consistent record, for their region, of attaining set objectives. For it is the Party leadership, as much as anyone else, that receives credit for the fulfillment of plans within the territory of its jurisdiction; it is the party leadership which must expect censure, demotion, or other sanctions if the many different activities within its area are found to be deserving of criticism. The Party leaders within any given territory are in command, and they are held responsible for performance.

It is thus apparent that, despite persistent centralist trends in the Soviet political system, a considerable portion of the sovereignty we have attributed to the Party's highest command is passed down to regional Party headquarters. Within the *oblast,* the First Secretary is the leading citizen. His *Obkomburo* is a gathering of the ten or fifteen most authoritative individuals of the province. The broad framework of policy directives and organizational forms comes from above, but within this framework the regional Party leaders have a great deal of authority, autonomy, and latitude. They act as a territorial board of directors. Because of this, the character of regional and local government, administration, and personnel is deeply affected by the character of the small oligarchy in charge of the territorial Party organization. Because of this, also, regionalism and conservatism can be expected to develop, and have developed repeatedly within the Soviet political system. At the same time, we can understand more clearly why it is imperative that any change of policy or personnel at the center must be followed by sweeping shakeups in the regional Party administration before they can become effective.

This exceedingly close identification of the Party with the various governmental agencies and social organizations under its control has led to the emergence of a perennial problem: The Party has never been able to determine with sufficient preciseness how much control was desirable or fruitful. On the one hand, as we have seen, its leaders were obsessed with the need for controlling all human behavior within Soviet society and to allow no autonomy whatsoever to groups or organizations. But if this principle were carried to its logical conclusion it would lead to the abolition of all organizations outside the Party and to a complete identification of the Party with the government. Yet this has never been the intention of the command; and because Party officials nonetheless show persistent tendencies to extend their control over non-Party organizations, the complaint against undue meddling and interference is equally perennial. Instead of managing these non-Party agencies the Party is only to guide them—indeed, it is to enforce managerial responsibility and prevent the buck of decision-making from being passed to the Party. At the same time, insistence on promoting and enforcing managerial responsibility must not lead to excessive managerial autonomy. Hence Party leaders in lower-level organizations are criticized as often for being passive and permissive—if not apathetic—as for undue interference with the work of the managers. In theory, the Party is to steer a careful middle course between these two extremes, a course which combines close interaction with a clear division of functions, in which the agency being supervised is responsible for carrying out all orders and attaining all set objectives, while the Party helps to clarify the various directives and aims, gives advice, integrates the many conflicts of goals, and helps smooth the thorny paths the agency has to travel through the complex bureaucratic jungle.

This close relationship, however, gives rise to one great difficulty: It becomes almost impossible to fix responsibility for successes and failures. The gears of Party and society mesh so closely that credit or blame cannot be placed clearly on any agency involved in the business of carrying out the directives flowing from above. Party leaders have always been troubled by this and have condemned subordinates for indulging in excessively close relations with the bureaucrats they were supposed to supervise and advise. Official Soviet slang refers to such closeness as "family relations" and condemns them as a perversion of proper procedure. Obviously, family relations are a protective alliance between the Party and the agency it supervises. It is of great benefit to both. Although the agency must share credit and rewards for its successes with its Party secretary and his staff, it also receives valuable aid and protection. Similarly, there are benefits for the Party leader. He must identify with the agency under his supervision and must work hard to protect and further it. He must bargain in its behalf and secure for it benefits to which, according to laws or plans, it may not really be entitled. In short, he must make an all-out effort to "go to bat" for the agency he is to supervise, so as to ensure that it will make an outstanding performance record. For this outstanding record he will then be able to take credit. In a well-organized "family relationship" there may be an elaborate conspiracy and complicity to cut corners, break laws and regulations, defraud higher supervisory organization, and in other ways violate the rules of Soviet behavior. "Family relations" thus are strong and viable informal organization patterns that cut across the well-constructed lines of command and supervision of the Soviet bureaucratic structure.

THE PRIMARY ORGANIZATION OF THE PARTY

On the local level, in the *raion* (district) and the town, the pattern of Party activity is analogous to that just described. Only at the grass-roots level do the structure and functioning of the Party undergo some changes, principally because at this level the organization of the CPSU is functional rather than territorial. Within each organization of the Soviet government—an economic enterprise or workshop, an army unit or the regional field office of a ministry—in short, within any organization or agency employing a substantial number of individuals, all those employees who are members (or candidate members) of the Communist Party will form a primary organization headed by a Secretary. These primary organizations constitute the lowest level of the vast machinery of the CPSU. Their work is geared to the performance of the Party's functions at the grass roots.

The primary organization is an adaptation of the conspiratorial cell. Under the tsarist government, all political activity was subversive; hence, all those engaged in it sought protection against the police. They found some of this protection by organizing into very small groups connected to other such groups (and to the higher Party organizations) only by one contact man. Keeping contacts between the different cells to a minimum made the Party less vulnerable to mass arrests and lessened the danger of betrayal. No individual police informer could obtain information about more than a handful of Party members. Curiously, this organization, so uniquely fit for conspiratorial work, has also turned out to be very suitable for the purposes of a ruling party. It helps the CPSU to penetrate very deeply into the fabric of the entire society.

As we shall see, the Soviet political system is a complex structure composed of many different authoritative hierarchies. On intermediate and lower levels, each individual agency of this political machinery is subjected to commands, regulations, and controls from a multiplicity of superior organizations; consequently, the numerous obligations imposed on the agency are, as a rule, contradictory or inconsistent. To be sure, in the final analysis all the command or control bodies are directly or indirectly following the directives of the Communist Party; hence, all the different goals and standards of performance they impose on subordinate agencies ultimately come from the same source. But the inconsistency of the orders received by the lower levels should not astonish us, since we have already seen that the interests of the Party elite themselves are complex. Moreover, for the purpose of realizing one clearly defined objective in a concrete situation many different methods will be used or will be tried out; in this connection we have seen that lower-level Party organizations appear to have wide latitude in using different methods for implementing goals handed them by the Party command. To be faced with a bewildering complexity of tasks is the normal situation for any low-level agency in Soviet society, as it is for individuals and groups in Western societies.

One major function of the Party's primary organization undoubtedly is to help those in command of primary agencies to find their way through the multiplicity of obligations by adjusting, weighing, or reconciling seemingly contradictory instructions and establishing a system of priorities, a hierarchy of values that attempts to relate the different objectives to each other. In helping the agency to accomplish this job of self-orientation, the primary organization will itself be guided by current Party directives as well as by its less formal perception of the general drift of opinion among the top leaders. In conveying an awareness of this political climate to the organization within which it exists, the primary organization performs the same function of interest aggregation that the Party's high command performs on a national level. In addition, by thus acting as the agency's policy planning staff, the primary organization effectively represents the stockholders of "USSR, Inc." within each administrative subunit in the field. That the members of the primary organization actually develop a sense of ownership and sovereignty is attested to by their habit of referring to the agency within which they exist as "their" factory, regiment, college, state farm, or whatever it may be. As with the *oblast* committee, the sense of ownership may be the result of the responsibility the primary organization is given for the over-all performance of "its" agency.

In addition to its policy-planning function, the primary organization carries out the many other tasks we have attributed to the Party. At the grass-roots level, the objectives that may demand most time and attention are those of political socialization and intelligence-gathering.

If our analogy between the USSR and Western corporations makes sense, then the Party owns the Soviet Union and directs all its public activities. We should then be correct in stating that all other formal organizations within the Soviet political system are creations and agents of the CPSU, that the whole of the USSR is one vast and complicated fabric of Party-front organizations. Furthermore, all the policies carried out by those many organizations would be executions of Party policies and directives. We may find that this machinery has a persistent tendency to get out of control and assume interests of its own; we may find also, perhaps in connection with this, that the Party itself is rapidly growing more heterogeneous in composition and interests. But despite these serious qualifications, the above image of the entire political system as a creation of the Communist Party still is true, and this entire book therefore is a study of the ways in which the Party carries out its various policies. Before we continue this study, however, we shall have to become far better acquainted with the composition and structure of the Party itself.

Chapter V
Membership

In discussing the composition of the CPSU it is essential to distinquish between two basic types of members, the rank-and-file and the *aktiv*. Rank-and-file members are those whose activities as Party members are part-time only, because they earn their living by holding jobs in some non-Party agency. They are thus performing their Party work in addition to their more regular duties. The *aktiv*, in contrast, comprises those people whose employer is the Party and who are therefore full-time Party officials —professional communists, as it were. In this brief survey of the Party membership, we shall begin by talking about the Communist Party as a whole, and then go into some detail first with regard to rank-and-file members, then move up to the *aktiv* and through them to the very top of the party elite.

At its twenty-second Congress in 1961, the Communist Party of the Soviet Union announced that it had roughly 8.9 million members and about 840,000 candidate members. In April of 1963, Mr. Khrushchev announced that the total number of members and candidates had come to exceed ten million.[1] To this number it might be useful, at least for certain purposes, to add the 19 million members of the Party's youth affiliate, the All-Union Leninist Communist Union of Youth (VLKSM or Komsomol).[2]

[1] *Izvestiia*, 26 April 1963.
[2] For recent statistics regarding the numbers and distribution of Party members as regards locality, nationality, profession, and the like, see "KPSS v tsifrakh, 1956–1961 gg.," *Partiinaia Zhizn*, No. 1 (1962); also "Kommunisticheskaia Partiia Sovetskogo Soiuza," *Politicheskoe Samoobrazovanie*, No. 7 (1963).

The Party might be described as a "cadre" party with a generous sprinkling of industrial workers and a very small peasant component. Whereas some of the working-class members might be actual workers at the bench, the relatively few collective farmers within the ranks of the Party are very likely to hold some leadership position, such as team foreman or farm chairman. The term "cadre" in Soviet parlance is synonymous with "elite" as used by Western social scientists. It denotes the leading personnel of any organization or group, the commanders and their essential staffs. The definition of the CPSU as a cadre party therefore means that its leaders have sought to recruit into its ranks the leading citizens of the Soviet Union, those men and women who hold positions of authority, responsibility, and prestige, those who by virtue of their status within the community are opinion-makers or -manipulators. If we knew the social composition of the Party membership more precisely, we would therefore also have a fairly sensitive gauge of the importance Party leaders attach to various positions within society. As it is, the statistical information we do possess is too vague to be of much use, and we therefore complement our insufficient factual knowledge with unreliable impressions. According to these impressions, the peasantry is vastly underrepresented in contrast to, for example, the engineering profession which sends a sizable portion of its numbers into the Party. The most general observation would be that the higher a person's rank within his profession, the more likely will he be a Party member. Given equal rank, a person holding a line job is a more likely recruit than one holding a staff job—that is, an administrator more likely than a professional expert. Thus physicians or professors are far less likely to be Party members than hospital administrators and deans; statisticians, attorneys, or lathe operators less likely than factory managers, judges, or shop foremen. Many responsible positions or ranks within the society can be expected to be held only by Party members. These would probably include generals in the armed forces, police officers of field grade, public prosecutors, federal or republican cabinet ministers, and perhaps many other categories. Again we have no precise information, and surprises may be in store for whoever is in a position to take a close look.

One of the most puzzling questions concerns the proportion of workers in the Party. The leadership repeatedly stresses the need for recruiting workers, and in the West this is usually taken as an indication of failure to recruit sufficient numbers of them. In the occasional statistics that are published, no distinction is made between actual workers and foremen or trade union officials. Nor can we be very sure as to the accuracy of our vague impression that workers are given a disproportionate chance to rise to leadership rank within the Party. We *can* say with a fair amount of assurance that there seem to be more workers in the political elite than in the professional elite; and this really means no more than that the general educational level of the Party is lower than that of the professional elite. To be sure, the Party *aktiv* contains an ever-growing number of people with university training, but formal education is not as essential a prerequisite for advancement in the party as in the professional elite. In this, the Soviet political leadership is comparable to the politicians (as well as to an older generation of business executives) in the United States. Speaking to the Eighth Congress of Soviets, in December 1920, Lenin predicted that in the society he and his party hoped to build professional politicians would become superfluous and would be replaced by economic managers. "It will be not only politicians and administrators who will henceforth mount the rostrum at all-Russian Congresses, but also engineers and agronomists. This marks the beginning of that very happy era when politicians will grow ever fewer in number, when people will speak of politics more rarely, and at less length, and when *engineers* and agronomists will do most of the talking."[3] But the very existence and functioning of the Party, as well as the character of its leading members, proves that Lenin's dream has not yet come true, though it has doubtless become somewhat more realistic.

A few highlights about the growth and changing composition

[3] Quoted in James H. Meisel and Edward S. Kozera, *Materials for the Study of the Soviet System* (Ann Arbor: George Wahr, 1953), p. 123.

of the Party since 1917 should be given. At the time of the October Revolution, Communist Party membership numbered about 240,000; these members were mostly industrial workers or rebellious intellectuals, with a substantial over-representation of Russia's national minorities, especially from the Caucasus and the Western borderlands. During the civil war, their numbers were swelled by a considerable influx of predominantly younger people caught by revolutionary enthusiasm. Although the Party leadership occasionally complained that careerists and bandwagon-jumpers had joined the Party, they should not, perhaps, be taken too much at their word, because, on the whole, joining the Communist Party or the Red Army during this particular period was an act of self-sacrifice or at least, in political terms, a gamble. The Red Army, incidentally, was during the period the most obvious group from which new Party members could be recruited; another such group was the Cheka (political police). At the same time, the broad masses of the very poor, workers as well as peasants, were urged to become members, because the Communist Party in the first years of its rule had a virtually limitless need for members who might help manage the newly conquered society or supervise the old managerial elite drafted into continued collaboration with the new regime. In thus trying, by necessity, to expand the membership rapidly, the Party leadership could not afford to apply exceedingly demanding standards of evaluation. Throughout its history as a ruling elite, the Party has measured prospective members by two basic criteria—competence and loyalty. And, at least in the early decades of Soviet rule, the handiest—albeit, crudest—indicators of these two qualities were education and lower-class origin. The higher a person's education, the more useful would he be for a regime trying to reconstruct and manage a vast country disturbed by war, revolution, and the hostility of the upper classes. The poorer a person, the more probably would he be in sympathy with bolshevism or, at least, with the revolution. It is immediately apparent that the two standards of evaluating prospective members excluded each other, and that the Party had to make a choice. It emphatically chose loyalty rather than competence, at least in the short run; for many years after the revolution the party by-laws favored workers over peasants and lower-class people over middle- and upper-class people as applicants for membership. Meanwhile, the Party attempted to give its lower-class recruits competence by organizing adult training courses for them in a great variety of pursuits. In the long run, the problem would, of course, solve itself as soon as a new generation of Soviet intellectuals and professionals had been reared, from among whom the most loyal could then be recruited into the Party. This has more and more become the prevailing pattern, and that is precisely why the rank-and-file membership can now be characterized as the cadre of Soviet society. To return to an analogy made earlier, we might once more describe the CPSU as the country club of the Soviet Union, because it includes those "civic leaders" and executives who in the United States would likely be members of country clubs.

Entry into the Party is essentially a process of co-option, in which the Party rather than the prospective member takes the initiative. Application for membership is usually made at the suggestion of the primary organization. An applicant must be recommended or sponsored by three members who have been in the Party for three years and have known him for at least one year; or, if the applicant has been a member of the Party's youth affiliate, his Komsomol unit may be used in place of one of the references. Sponsors have always been held responsible for the performance of the members they have recommended; hence any such recommendation is a weighty matter. Once an applicant has been admitted into a primary organization, he remains a probationary member (candidate) for one year or for a longer period if the organization decides to postpone granting full membership. In exceptional cases, the highest leaders have been known to shorten the probationary period. These basic rules, which have governed recruitment procedures since before the revolution, were complicated in the early decades of the regime; various procedures made entry into the Party easier for workers by imposing on peasants, white-collar employees, and professionals more stringent conditions regarding sponsorship and probationary service.

The duties of a Party member may be summarized as follows. First, he is to provide to the individual citizens outside the Party all those services and all that guidance which Party organizations render to organizations and agencies throughout the Soviet political system. In order to be equipped for rendering this service, the Party member must unceasingly educate himself in at least two ways. First, he must become familiar with the Party's general ideology, including knowledge not only of its broad goals, but also of its history, institutions, and procedures, down to the very language spoken by initiates. Second, he must keep himself informed as intimately as possible about current public issues, policies, and goal priorities. The Party member must be both indoctrinated and a well-informed citizen. The member attains this knowledge through a variety of means. He may receive formal schooling in Party schools, ranging from top leadership academies to lectures and discussions organized by primary organizations. More informally, members gain information through contact with their primary organizations, through the media of communications—even through the rumor mill, that most informal but effective educational institution which seems to play an important role in the Soviet political system. As any reader who attempts to keep himself informed in a complex world knows, the urge toward self-education is a tremendous burden on any individual, and it is an almost Sisyphean labor, because one can never learn enough. But in addition, the CPSU member is expected to be an activist and model citizen. "Activism," in this context, means serving in a great variety of civic duties, such as election campaigns, civil defense work, or promotions of special projects; the activist might be described as a pace-setter in civic volunteer work. And, more broadly, as a model citizen the Party member is expected to lead a life above reproach. Party members are presumed to be more informed, more intelligent, more self-disciplined, moral, and law-abiding than the general citizenry. It may be argued that they have more ample opportunity to conceal their lapses from moral standards, less need to violate many laws, and a good deal of protection, through their political contacts, when they get into trouble. But at the same time courts and other authorities deal more severely with offenders who are in the Party than with those who are not for, they argue, Party members must live up to a higher standard of expectations.

From all this it must be plain that Party membership is a formidable responsibility which a Soviet citizen is not likely to undertake light-heartedly or on the spur of the moment. Obviously, it carries with it a great deal of extra work and extra worry. Moreover, it places the individual in a far more exposed position from that of the ordinary citizen. As his status rises to that of an acknowledged civic leader, his responsibilities also increase, and with them the possibilities of being criticized, censured, demoted, and punished. The high and mighty fall harder than the meek and low. The party can be a hard taskmaster, and its severest sanction —expulusion—is difficult to bear. No one leaves the Party voluntarily; hence, to be a former Party member probably is worse than never having been a member at all. An expelled member must feel like an outcast. His status in the Soviet system is analogous to that of a defrocked priest among believers.[4] To these disadvantages of membership one other should perhaps be added: the negative deference which broad strata of the population have given in the past, and may still be giving today, to Party members. Certainly, up to the time of World War II considerable portions of the population, especially among the peasantry and national minorities, looked upon the Party with hatred and contempt. Membership therefore had the effect of alienating the individual from the people, of erecting a wall of hostility between members and nonmembers. This predisposition, however, may be disappearing; our evidence about it is somewhat dated.

And the advantages of being a member? They are numerous and considerable. Being a member of the country club set gives the member easier access to the decision-makers, thus increasing his own influence and power. This accretion of power is aided, furthermore, by the fact that Party membership gives easier access to

[4] The rate of expulsions has been declining rapidly, so that Party membership has tended more to turn into a privilege. For figures see "KPSS v tsifrakh, 1956–1961 gg.," *Partiinaia Zhizn*, No. 1 (1962).

political information. Members can be expected to feel that they are on the inside track in Soviet politics, that they have more of the inside dope than those outside the Party. They may take considerable pride in belonging to the country's political elite, to the decision-makers, to the soldiers of the revolution, to a secular order which is reshaping the world in sovereign fashion.

Membership in the Party may thus appeal to a person's pride as well to his loftiest instincts as a servant of his society. It may, at the same time, gratify his personal ambitions. The power and influence accruing from access to the circle of the initiates makes itself felt in each member's professional and personal life. Within his profession, he can move higher and more rapidly, because Party members, as we have seen, are more eligible for advanced assignments. Moreover, a Party member can deal more firmly and more securely with the many bureaucratic agencies of the government and, with the help of the Party, he can at times cut corners or evade normal channels more readily than a nonmember. Many of these advantages may also be used to ease the path of advancement or the professional work of a member's family and friends. In short, Party membership may be an important means of securing (though not guaranteeing) an individual's professional and personal success. It is therefore likely also to add, however indirectly, to his and his family's material well-being. Perhaps it would be an overgeneralization to say that in the United States the possession of money gives a person power; but it is certainly no more oversimplification to say that in the USSR the possession of power gives one money; hence, since Party membership adds to an individual's power, it may well add to his money.[5] At the highest level of Party leadership this is certainly true. We know very little about the lives of the most powerful men in the CPSU, but the scanty gossip that seeps out occasionally indicates that they live a life of material ease, and often of luxury or even revelry. Like the ruling oligarchy in other societies, including our own, the Party leaders are secure from public scrutiny of their private lives, and

[5] Similarly, Oswald Spengler distinguished between the English class structure (based on differences in wealth) and the society of Prussia, which he said was divided into those who command and those who obey.

some of them seem to feel that they are above morality—that morality is for the masses.

By now we are already talking about the *aktiv* rather than the rank-and-file membership. Although we are making a clear distinction between these two groups, it is impossible to draw the line between them exactly. The *aktiv* was defined as those people whose full-time work is in the Party. But individuals may move easily from Party work to non-Party work or vice versa, and may do so repeatedly. In principle, every member is forever at the disposal of the Party; and whatever his professional preparation, he may at any moment be assigned to full-time Party work and then reassigned to a professional job in the line of his training and experience. In short, the transition from any number of professional roles to that of a professional politician, or vice versa, seems no more extraordinary in the USSR than it is in the United States. Even so, in both societies we can distinguish a political elite. We might restrict the definition of such an elite to those who have spent the greater part of their adult lives in full-time political work, or whose careers, after hesitating between political and nonpolitical assignment, come to rest in the political line. The *aktiv* would thus consist of those whose (most recent) professional assignments have been predominantly in the Party.

One problem to which we have already alluded may, in the long run, serve to emphasize the difference between the professional and the political elites; that is the magnitude of the task of remaining a competent generalist. As we saw, being a Party member is a very formidable task, because so much general knowledge about current events is required of a *good* Party member. For a person fully engaged in his own profession, the cultivation of such general information becomes more and more difficult; he simply has no time to be a good Party member, unless he is ready to neglect his professional job. People in various professional lines are thus forced, as they are in other societies, to make a choice between devotion to their specialty and devotion to a career as an operator, manipulator, and organization man. Devotion to the specialty makes the person unavailable or unsuitable for political assignments; devotion to professional politics gradually alienates him from his profession and makes him eligible for a career of professional politics. Thus, the gulf between the professional elite and the political elite tends to widen.

We have only the sketchiest knowledge about the actual process of recruitment from rank-and-file Party membership into the *aktiv*. It seems to involve several steps, or possible lines of advancement, all of them related to either loyalty or competence, the two major criteria for recruitment of Party members ever since 1917. Among the skills and competences that lead to advancement into the *aktiv,* the most important appears to be managerial success. Directors of economic enterprises who consistently succeed in attaining their production goals; collective farm chairmen who have demonstrated their ability to rouse the energies of the peasants and harness them to the purposes of the regime; production engineers who have shown themselves inventive and forceful in raising the efficiency of their plants; trade union officials who by their personality, bargaining skills, or organizational talent manage to contribute to a rise in the productivity of labor—people with these and similar talents the Party seeks for its own leadership. The skills the Party needs, in short, are competence in the manipulation of men, and the ability to make people identify with the Party's goals and successfully to attain them.

By themselves, however, such skills are insufficient prerequisites for co-option into the Party *aktiv*. They must be supplemented by something we have called political loyalty, but which might more aptly be described as political sensitivity. Let us note first of all that this sensitivity is intimately related to the productive and administrative skills the Party seeks. For one thing, political sensitivity is itself one of the indispensable items in the equipment of the capable administrator, manipulator, or producer; conversely, the shrewd organization man who possesses these various talents soon learns that he will succeed only if he shows himself to be in tune with the prevailing political climate. Lasting success in the

Soviet political system can come only to those who show both competence and political sensitivity.

To describe this sensitivity we might break it down into a number of components. Perhaps the most basic element is unquestioning acceptance of the political system, a fundamental conformism or conservatism and a concomitant readiness to adjust one's behavior, goals, and personality to prevailing patterns—the frame of mind David Riesman has called "other-directedness." Beyond this, however, those who wish to advance in the Party must manifest doctrinal soundness by being able to demonstrate substantial knowledge of the Party's history and sacred writings and by mastering the Party jargon. The aspirant to higher office must be able to express all problems, issues, policies, and events in approved terms and must be able to understand the Party's esoteric code of communication. These aptitudes, in turn, will give him another element of political sensitivity, namely the ability to sense the ever-changing hierarchy of values, standards, and priorities of the top leadership. Political sensitivity is both manifested and improved by a man's loyalty to those top commanders who win—and if he does not have such loyalty, he must at least seem to have it.

The personality syndrome of people who present this kind of image to the Party leadership is that complicated and contradictory mixture of traits that has been dubbed "organization man," a personality type with whom, supposedly, the commanding heights of our governmental, educational, and corporate bureaucracies abound. It is a strange mixture of ruthlessness and subservience, deviousness and sheer hard work; it combines timidity with inventiveness, imagination, and the daring to experiment; high regard for regular procedure, conformity, and fear of responsibility. Moreover, while it presupposes intelligence, it discourages narrow expertise: the professional politician must be a generalist, able to ask questions, to pick brains, to make use of his staff, but not unduly burdened by special knowledge, with the versatility of the dilettante where public issues are concerned.

An attempt to refine this vague image would be intriguing, but it is doubtful whether we have impressions sufficient even for making informed guesses. Among the questions it would be useful to investigate would be, for example, the importance of camaraderie and social contacts within the Soviet political elite. How important a method is it for those who wish to gain entrance into the *aktiv?* A much more complicated and controversial problem would be to compare more carefully the successful professional politician in the USSR with the successful executive in the United States. To be sure, we have pointed out broad similarities of personality requirements, but within these requirements there doubtless are subtle or not-so-subtle differences. The prevalence in the USSR of a formal doctrine, an elaborate official ideology that must be mastered, is one obvious difference. Another seems to be the continued preference of the Party *aktiv* for production engineers, as against the growing predominance of marketing and public relations specialists in the American corporate elite, and lawyers in the political one. Furthermore, it would be interesting to substantiate the persistent impression that the Soviet political elite recruits people of more openly ruthless and violent disposition, persons who are less open-minded and more authoritarian than corporate executives in the United States. Even if these impressions could be substantiated, the findings might have no more than ephemeral validity, if it is assumed that, with its growing heterogeneity and maturity, the Soviet political system too will have increasing need for negotiators and bargainers, for urbane and bland manipulators and persuaders rather than local and provincial replicas of the despotic man of steel who imposed his will on a reluctant and recalcitrant peasant population.

Just as there is no hard-and-fast difference between rank-and-file Party members and the *aktiv,* so the latter very gradually shades into the top leadership. What proportion of the 9 million members are full-time Party officials we do not know. How many of these officials should be considered part of the top elite is a matter of definition. The 4000 or so delegates to the Twenty-second Party Congress of 1961 obviously represent one top layer that is easily identified. A narrower peak of the pyramid is scaled when we take the approximately 200 members of the Central Committee. About the same number, but a slightly different selection, is obtained by regarding as the top elite all provincial and Union Republic First Secretaries, in other words, all the highest field commanders, the *Gauleiters* of the CPSU. And, finally, the very tip of the Party's power pyramid can be narrowed to the twelve members and six alternates (candidate members) of the Presidium of the Central Committee. The only step that then remains is to narrow the leadership to the Party's First Secretary. Let us agree on identifying the top leadership as comprising all the members of the Central Committee, together with all *oblast* and Union Republic First Secretaries. Even then, however, this top leadership will be difficult to describe, for two reasons: one is the scantiness of information available about the individuals in this group; the other is the astonishingly rapid turnover of personnel in these higher ranks of the Party. Although at the very tip of the pyramid there may be prolonged periods of stability, there is much less stability among the ranks of the highest field commanders or within the national command. Instead, the turnover of leaders is very fast, the average tenure of office for *Obkom* First Secretaries being less than three years. *Oblast* secretaries may be taken from one province and assigned to another; they may be given some staff duty with the Central Committee or the Secretariat; indeed, they may be given a full-time assignment in a non-Party agency, as cabinet ministers, factory directors, mayors, or in a great variety of other more or less exalted posts. The personnel of the top Party elite is thus unstable in two ways: on the one hand, assignments within the elite change hands frequently through shakeups which do not change the composition of the entire elite; on the other hand, there is a great deal of mobility into and out of this top elite, some sort of metabolism of personnel between the Party leadership and the top ranks of the professional elite. Hence the very composition of the Party leadership corps is in continual flux. In any particular case, it is often impossible for the outsider to determine whether a person's reassignment represents a move up, down, or laterally within the complex structure of the political system.

Western scholars attempting to explain the rapid turnover of personnel in the Party elite have been tempted to argue that the top command keeps reassigning and shifting its chief lieutenants so as to protect itself against them. Keeping the provincial satraps on the move, so the argument goes, prevents them from consolidating their power within their territory and acquiring too much political strength. Equally important, it prevents them from establishing a smoothly working relationship with the entire political machinery of the territory. By forestalling the formation of such a well-integrated local administration, the Party prevents centrifugal tendencies of localism and regionalism from making themselves felt as a challenge to the centralist bias of the system. Undoubtedly this analysis is correct, although the alleged danger of the local chiefs' acquiring too much political strength may be vastly overrated by the Western observers and by the top Party leadership. Moreover, the analysis overlooks the fact that the frequent rotation of executive personnel is a routine in many other bureaucratic structures, in which paranoid suspicion of underlings is not necessarily attributed to the top leaders. This policy of regular reassignment is practiced in the armed forces of the United States, as well as in many business corporations and government agencies. In most cases it is explained less by centralist urges than by the effort to give aspirants for highest office the greatest possible variety of experience and as much chance as possible to prove their worth. It is a training and recruitment device for screening national leaders, even though it may also be part of political maneuvering and power plays.

From the point of view of the individual leader, this rapid turnover of high command and staff positions in the Party is part of a fierce competitive struggle between all those Party members of more or less equal rank. The higher one rises in the Party the less chance he has of further promotion, because status pyramids get narrower and narrower toward the top. Every army lieutenant can figure out what mathematical chance he has to become a colonel or a lieutenant-general. Similarly, the members of the party *aktiv* are aware of the great number of colleagues who compete with them for higher assignments. Since those who are closer to the top may have risen as far as they have because, among other things, they have a more highly developed competitive instinct, it may well be that the competition increases in bitterness in the highest ranks; but this is speculation. What can be stated with assurance is that to survive and succeed in this rat race requires a consistently excellent performance record, also, probably, good connections, and certainly that mysterious combination of personal qualities which appeals to the highest Party personalities.

In short, the highest Party leaders are people who have been successful in several lines. First, they are experienced and highly recognized politicians, administrators, engineers, leaders of men, or masters of bureaucratic machines. Second, they are survivors of a never-ending bitter struggle among competitors in a vast political jungle where everyone is everybody else's rival. Finally, we can take it for granted that they have been members of the Party for all their adult lives. This last observation was not always true. During a brief period in the middle of the 1930s, when the USSR was settling down to its present system of government, it was disadvantageous to be a veteran Party member. At that time, an entire generation of experienced Party leaders was eliminated, and a new set of younger men came to the fore. One reason for this change of the guard was undoubtedly that the qualities required of a professional revolutionary are quite different from those that enable a man to function well as a government bureaucrat. A second reason was that Josef Stalin appears to have regarded the leading representatives of this generation of Party officials as dangerous rivals.

This observation leads us to realize that there is one more essential qualification for those who are destined to rise to the top ranks of the Party elite: these veteran professional politicians have to be regarded as valuable, if not indispensable, lieutenants by the Number One man in the Party. At least until 1953 all recruitment to the very top was, in the final analysis, selection by Stalin. Matters may have changed significantly since his death. But, even if only in order to register the changes that have taken place, we shall have to examine the person of the dictator in the Soviet political system carefully. Perhaps we should refer not to the person, but to the institution of the dictator,[6] for one might say with justification that in the USSR he is an institution. Whatever he may be called, however, his recruitment and functions are so intimately linked with the internal organization of the Party that it might be best to view him as part of this general organization. Hence, in order to understand the position of the Number One man in the Communist Party, we shall now turn to its internal organization and decision-making processes.

[6] For an elaboration of this point, see pp. 176 ff.

Chapter VI
Organization

The Marxist theory of revolution is based on the assumption of working-class rationality. Capitalism, says Marx, so exploits, degrades, and dehumanizes the workers that they are pushed into a consciousness of their misery and of the social relationships that cause it. The class consciousness of the proletariat is thus a full understanding of contemporary society and of the means by which it can be overthrown. In the writings of Marx and Engels, this class consciousness is the essential precondition and driving force of the social revolution.

This was precisely one of the points on which Lenin departed from Marx. Marx seems to have assumed that class consciousness would develop spontaneously within the working class, though intellectuals, by articulating it in systematic form, might help to promote or speed up this spontaneous process. Lenin, in contrast, did not believe in the spontaneous and inevitable growth of proletarian class consciousness, certainly not among the workers. Instead, he argued that this consciousness would have to be inculcated into them from the outside, and that it would develop by itself only in a small elite of enlightened intellectuals from the upper classes. By themselves, the workers would be able to develop only false, illusory consciousness. Spontaneous developments, thus, would bring damnation rather than salvation. Spontaneity would therefore have to be curbed and controlled—a strange conclusion for a politician committed to what seemed to be a highly deterministic theory.

The agency for controlling spontaneity in historical development was to be the Communist Party. As Lenin saw it, it was to be the institutionalization of consciousness—a small elite of enlightened men and women devoting their lives to the cause of the proletarian revolution, bound to each other by ties of discipline and loyalty. This small group of professional revolutionaries would serve as the general staff of the working-class movement and its revolution. It was to lead the proletariat in all its political activities, controlling spontaneity, guiding it into the correct channels, educating the workers to consciousness, goading them into rebellion, and manipulating them so as to help promote the revolution. In reading Marx, we get the impression that he thought of the working class as the Chosen People who would inevitably lead the rest of mankind out of the Egypt of capitalism into the socialist Promised Land. Reading Lenin, we feel that for him the proletariat was the given historical force which best lent itself to use by a politically sophisticated band of conspirators. For Marx the proletariat was the life force; for Lenin, it was the raw material of history.

In its theory of revolution, Marxism lays as much stress on theory as on action, on consciousness as on power. Both are essential to the consummation of what Marx thought were inevitable trends. In the original theory, both reside in the working class; but in Lenin's version of Marxism they are separated. In the latter's theory, power lies with the masses; for neither ideas nor intellectuals nor any small leadership can make history. But whereas power lies with the masses, consciousness resides in the elite. The problem for Lenin was how to combine the two in inseparable unity. To solve this problem was the function of the Party as he saw it.

The Party's task is thus manifold. First of all, it is to instill consciousness into the workers through a process of education, propagating Marxist doctrines as quickly and as intensively as possible, for only consciousness can truly bring salvation. At the same time, the Party's propaganda activities serve another purpose, namely, that of selling the Party to the masses, tying the workers to the Party even though they may not yet be fully class conscious. Party publicity thus serves two purposes: a long-range task of rational education, and a short-range objective of salesmanship.

In the Party's own opinion, these two efforts overlap: the Party attracts followers precisely because it voices their unconscious interests. But, in fact, the following the Party wishes to attract has often transcended the limits of the industrial working class; for many purposes, the Party wishes to attract broader masses. Hence, it must appeal to interests other than purely proletarian ones. There is therefore the possibility of conflict between the purposes of instilling consciousness and attracting a mass following.

Behind the urge to attract the masses is the need to manipulate them. The Party wishes to change the world. It can do so only by causing the masses to act. In the ideal situation, the masses would act because they have been made class conscious. In the real world, they act because they have attached themselves to the Party and allow the Party to lead them and to manipulate them. They may have been attracted to the Party on the basis of its publicity, but they are tied to it by organizational links. In Lenin's eyes, organization was the most important secret of political power. Whatever you could organize you would dominate. His aim therefore was to manipulate his contemporary society by organizing as many of its various groups as possible. Lenin was aware that most human activities are carried out in or through various organizations and associations. From this he concluded that the Party would be able to dominate these human activities if it could dominate the organizations and associations through which they were carried out. In this case, the organizations would become transmission belts by which the interests and policies of the Party could be transferred to the masses, to groups, and to individuals. Thus the Party, in the larger sense, would be far more than a small general staff of the revolution; it would be complete only if a whole cluster of mass organizations were made to follow the directions this general staff would give.

At the same time, the general staff must not only give orders but also respond to the initiative of the masses. Consciousness must maintain sovereignty over spontaneity (to use communist terminology); but it must also be sensitive to it so as to be able to channel this elemental energy in the proper direction. It should once again be clear to the reader that, at least potentially, this response to the wishes of its followers may conflict with the Party's urge to impose its goals on the masses through organization.

These contradictions are symbolized by, or related to, the conflict in principles that governed the Party's decision-making processes. On the one hand, the Party considered itself the infallible conscience of the proletariat; on the other hand, it was ever mindful of the need to remain sensitive and responsive to the opinions of the masses. Again, as a militant striking force, it had to centralize its organization and activities so as to subject all members and followers to the strictest conspiratorial discipline. The Party could not afford wavering, doubt, or discussion in the midst of its never-ending battle. Yet, on the other hand, the membership was defined as the conscious elite; and democratic traditions were strong within the socialist movement. Hence the Party was committed to decision-making procedures that gave a free and equal voice to all members, either directly or through representative institutions. In a society of the elect, every member's opinion should be heard carefully, and general participation in decision-making should be encouraged.

The resulting conflict between democratic and bureaucratic principles is reflected in the formula Lenin used to describe Party organization. This term, "democratic centralism," is still accepted today as the principle governing decision-making in the Party. Lenin defined it as a combination of freedom to criticize Party policies with unity and discipline in action. Criticism and free discussion were admissible only so long as they did not disrupt Party unity in carrying out policies already agreed upon. Once it was committed to any line of action, the Party could not tolerate dissent or debate. In this sense, all decisions were, almost by definition, unanimous. The Party statutes make this policy explicit by interpreting the principle of majority rule so as to make it majority dictatorship. The minority must submit, and by submitting make any decision unanimous. But once a decision has been adopted unanimously, it becomes difficult even to question the manner in which it is being carried out, because every such discussion comes close to interpreting the unanimous decision itself, if only by seeking to interpret it. Theory and practice, decision and execution are so closely linked that insistence on unanimity and loyalty virtually prohibits all discussion. More particularly, it becomes impossible for individual members or groups of members —or, indeed, for entire subordinate organizations—to argue that a decision or policy should be reexamined because, possibly, it may have outlived its usefulness. In effect, therefore, the will of the membership cannot even place something on the agenda for discussion. *Roma locuta causa finita.* Only the Party's highest leaders can decide that a given issue is open for discussion.

The party's by-laws thus reflect a very strong centralist bias. Moreover, they openly admit grave reservations about intraparty democracy, lest the freedom it gives be abused by "anti-Party elements." What is dangerous in democracy is the disunity it brings to a supposedly monolithic striking organization; equally dangerous, from the point of view of the leaders, seems to be the semblance of disunity created when disputes and discussions go on in public. The greatest concern of the leaders, however, seems to be that a party which is given some internal freedom of debate and criticism cannot be managed and controlled; it gets out of hand and therefore loses its effectiveness as a political tool.

Democracy became a problem for Lenin because of the growth of tension and disorganization within the Party. This, in turn, was a function of the rapid increase of its membership, as well as the seemingly unsurmountable problems it faced during the first years of its rule.

During 1917 the Russian Communist Party (of Bolsheviks), as it called itself from 1918 to 1924, increased its membership from less than 24,000 in January to more than 200,000 at the time of the October Revolution. Although a substantial portion of the rank-and-file membership seems to have been factory workers, the national leaders as well as many local organizers and other members were educated people from the upper classes.[1] Members of minorities, such as Letts, Jews, Georgians, and Poles, constituted more

[1] Leonard Schapiro, *The Communist Party of the Soviet Union* (New York: Random House, 1959), pp. 171–172.

than ten percent of the membership. At the beginning of the Revolution, the Party had considerable homogeneity, but its growth brought greater variety in background and views of the members. The small band of men constituting the Bolshevik faction at the beginning of 1917 were primarily those "hard" Leninists who had stuck by their leader in the years preceding World War I when he was preoccupied with the task of setting up the Bolshevik wing as the one and only Marxist workers' party of the Russian Empire. They had remained loyal to Lenin, presumably, because they shared his views—which means that they were preoccupied with problems of Party organization and tended to be ruthless and unsentimental concerning the use of methods in political warfare. During the war, the hard core of old-time Leninist organization men was swelled by the addition of those who so fervently agreed with Lenin's views on the war and on the strategies to be pursued by the revolutionary proletariat that they could no longer collaborate with the moderate leaders of the Second International. But the fact that they agreed with Lenin on this issue did not necessarily imply that they shared other typical Leninist views. The resulting heterogeneity of outlook was multiplied when in the spring of 1917 Lenin's ultra-radical April program attracted all those former anti-Bolsheviks who liked the boldness with which he proposed to ride the elements that the Revolution had freed and who were inebriated by the millennial prospect opened up by this program of an immediate leap into communism. Finally, during the civil war, membership expanded almost explosively, as hundreds of thousands entered the ranks of the Party, most of them in a burst of crusading enthusiasm. Joining the Party at that time cannot be explained by careerist motives, because Party membership during the civil war meant self-sacrifice and heroism, even though it did bring privileges with it. Whatever the motives of those who joined, the Party welcomed new members, and, by the end of the civil war, had grown to almost 750,000, despite obviously heavy losses due to the civil war.[2]

In the early years of the Bolshevik regime, the Party organiza-

[2] *Ibid.*, p. 231.

tion, too, was relatively unstable. Before the war, Lenin's small band of devoted followers and organization men had been homogenous, loyal, obedient. The political machine which during the civil war multiplied its size many times quickly became heterogeneous, unwieldy, and racked by deep dissent. Local committees often were left without guidance or coordination for prolonged periods and had to improvise policies by themselves. This, however, was difficult, because Party traditions and Party ideology provided little guidance for solving the problems of government and management facing the regime. Moreover, the perpetual emergency created by the civil war, economic ruin, and social dislocation necessitated drastic action. Under these circumstances sharp disputes were bound to arise. Without going into detail, we might characterize these issues in the following fashion. First, the emergency measures of the civil war period engendered sharp conflicts of conscience in the minds of the trained Marxists heading the Party because many of these measures, though obviously expedient, violated principles or assumptions that had hitherto been considered essential elements of socialist doctrine. To express it differently, many principles of socialist behavior, hitherto accepted implicitly, turned out to be a hindrance to the vigorous pursuit of the struggle for power and for governmental control. Outstanding among these assumptions was the widespread belief that scrupulous adherence to the rules of democracy in government, management, military leadership, and party life was an integral element of socialist behavior, and that dictatorship, hierarchical organization, bureaucratic management—not to mention the hiring of former tsarist officers, civil servants, and professional men—violated principles of socialism. At many points, the conflict between expediency and revolutionary purism was linked with the clash of special interests or the fear of special groups that the Bolshevik regime was about to rob them of the gains they had made in the revolution. Finally, as is inevitable in a rapidly expanding institution, conflicts between personalities and cliques did their share to exacerbate an already very tense situation within the Party.

From the point of view of the Party leadership, and indeed from

the point of view of any Party member, this factional strife and
lack of organization were deplorable and untenable, especially in
view of Lenin's preoccupation with discipline and organizational
efficiency. Throughout the period of the civil war, therefore, he
made strenuous efforts to cope with dissident and centrifugal forces.
A broad range of devices could be applied for this purpose. One
of them was compromise. Lenin was of extremely dogmatic inclina-
tion; whenever he had worked out a solution to any problem he
knew that he was right and that all other solutions were wrong.
And yet, in this period of permanent emergency and perpetual
experimentation, there were issues on which he yielded to overwhelming majorities in the Central Committee, because he wished
to preserve the unity of the Party. At the same time, even when
he stood alone against all or most of his comrades, Lenin often
could afford not to yield, because his prestige as the undisputed
leader of the Party was extremely high. This prestige was based on
a number of personality traits that made him outstanding among
professional revolutionary Marxists at the time. He was a man of
very high intelligence, tremendous erudition within an ideologically
restricted field, and great persuasive powers, both in the committee
room and before mass audiences. He combined an almost wild
romantic sweep with uncanny political horse sense—revolutionary
maximalism with the prudence and flexibility of an experienced
politician. Foremost, however, he was the master of a political
machine who knew how to cash in shrewdly on his own indis-
pensability. His opinion carried more weight than that of anyone
else, and a threat on his part to resign was sufficient in some cases
of extraordinary importance to bring the Central Committee in
line. The Party was Lenin, and Lenin was the Party. He had built
it, almost single-handed, it seemed; and his lieutenants obviously
could not even imagine carrying on the business of the revolution
without him. His illness and death therefore dealt a very serious
blow to the party.[3]

Theoretically, the by-laws of the Party, particularly the rules of

[3] Lenin had his first serious stroke in 1922, recovered for a brief period
late that year, had another paralyzing stroke in 1923, and died on January
21, 1924.

democratic centralism, should have curbed excesses of Party strife, but during the civil war these rules seemed to be largely in abeyance. Although disciplinary measures, including expulsion, were at the disposal of the Party leaders, they were not used and probably could not have been used at the time without reducing the Party to an impotent small clique. Although all members were, according to the statutes, expected to submit to all Party directives, this provision simply could not always be enforced. In fact, it was often difficult to acquaint local and regional organizations with current Party policies, although there was, of course, a central Party press accessible to all organizations. The importance of the press in giving unity to the sprawling organization therefore was considerable. But the most effective instrument for curbing dissent and disorganization in the Party was its growing bureaucratization. By this term we mean the increasing weight that accrued to administrative (as against representative) agencies within the Party. These administrative agencies included permanent commissions as well as special agents sent into the field as inspectors, troubleshooters, and arbitrators. But increasingly the function of centralization and control was carried out by the Party Secretariat and its field organizations, its main weapon being personnel policy.

This rapid bureaucratization of the Party was most effective in curbing the independence of subordinate organizations and of the rank-and-file membership. But because it could not have the same efficacy in the highest ranks of the Party, at least not so quickly, Lenin took one more drastic step to force unity and discipline upon the Party. At the Tenth Party Congress, in early 1921, he suggested and vigorously lobbied for the adoption of a rule against "factionalism." This took the form of a resolution, "On the Unity of the Party," which made the formation of any factions within the Party a breach of discipline punishable by expulsion. In practice, this meant that Party members henceforth were forbidden to get together in informal groups for the purpose of discussing policy, personnel, or any other Party matters. Any such informal gathering could be interpreted as the formation of a faction, and the only permissible forum for debate was the regular membership meeting, the Conference, the Congress, the bureaus, or other formally established committees. Political opinion within the Party was thus effectively atomized and prevented from congealing into a formidable movement. Each member, with his views, was left alone face to face with well-prepared views and policies of the Party leaders. The individual was deprived of any legal method of determining whether or not there might be support for his own views among his comrades. Any dissent, even on slight matters, meant opposing the solid bloc of the entire membership. The resolution "On the Unity of the Party" could not, it is true, be fully enforced for a number of years.[4] But when it finally could be made effective, Party democracy, for all but the pretense, was at an end.

In the organization of the Party as a decision-making machine, the formula of democratic centralism was reflected in a seeming balance between representative institutions and subordination to executive orders—a synthesis of Party democracy with a quasi-military command structure. And, just as in practice centralist tendencies were given preference over democratic ones, so on the organization of the Party and in the actual functioning of its institutions the command structure dominated the supposedly representative institutions.

In theory, and according to the Party's by-laws, all authority within the Party is derived from the membership, and this sovereignty of the members is reflected in the organization of all its institutions, from the lowest to the highest.[5] At the lowest level of the Party, in the primary organization, authority supposedly rests in the meeting of all the members, which is to be held at least once a month. Executive powers are delegated by the members to an executive committee, called the *bureau,* the size of which

[4] At the same time, the Tenth Congress was the occasion for launching the first major purge of the Party. Almost a third of the members were expelled in 1921.

[5] For Soviet discussions of Party organization, see L. Slepov, *Vysshie i mestnye organy partii* (Moscow: Vysshaia Partiinaia Shkola pri TsK KPSS, 1958); L. Slepov, *Mestnye partiinye organy* (Moscow: Vysshaia Partiinaia Shkola pri TsK KPSS, 1954); and A. F. Gorkin, *Partiia i sovety* (Moscow: Vysshaia Partiinaia Shkola pri TsK KPSS, 1955).

varies according to the size of the primary organization itself (in organizations with less than fifteen members, no *bureau* is created; only a secretary is elected to serve as the organization's executive officer). To head the *bureau,* every primary organization also elects a secretary, who must be a man with a certain minimum of seniority as Party member. He must also be confirmed by higher Party headquarters, in some cases even by the Central Committee. But we can assume that as a rule the selection of the candidate by higher headquarters precedes his election by the members of the primary organization. The election is rarely more than a formal ratification of a *fait accompli.* In fact, as we have seen, Party secretaries (and, indeed, other *bureau* personnel) are freely transferred from one assignment to another by the Central Committee or other higher agencies.

Territorial Party organizations, from town or district up to province and Union Republic, are organized in analogous fashion.[6] There the supposedly sovereign body is not the full meeting of all the members, but a conference, to meet at least once a year, of elected delegates from all the lower organizations. Between this conference and the executive branch, the *bureau,* which includes three or more secretaries, an intermediary body exists. This is the Committee or, in the case of the Union Republics, the Central Committee. Party committees are set up to function as deliberative and decision-making bodies smaller in size than the annual conferences—hence, less unwieldy and able to meet more frequently. As we shall see, there have been long periods in the history of the Party during which these territorial committees lost virtually all their functions, did not meet, or, if they did meet, merely ratified the actions of the *bureau* or its secretaries. There are some indica-

[6] As of January 1, 1961, the Party contained the following numbers of territorial organizations:

Central Committees of Union Republics,

Oblast committees and *krai* (territory) committees	157
City and town committees	602
Raion committees within large cities	343
Rural *raion* committees	3202

Figures from *Partiinaia Zhizn,* No. 1 (1962).

tions that in recent years the territorial Party committees have regained some of their functions, at least as arenas for discussion and perhaps controversy.

The organization of the Party is somewhat more complex at the national level, though it remains analogous to that of the lower organizations. Here again supreme authority resides, according to the Party statutes, in the Congress of delegates from all the lower organizations. Today this Party Congress is supposed to meet at least once every four years; since the death of Stalin it has met more frequently. In the early years of the Soviet regime its meetings took place once every year. After 1925 there was a two-year interval; then one of three years; another of four; another of five years; finally came a period of thirteen years during which no Congress met.

Until 1925, Congresses were always the scene of lively open debates over fundamental policy issues, as well as over personnel changes. Yet even in these early years of Soviet rule the Congress could not really be an effective source of authoritative decision-making. A body of several thousand voting delegates, meeting for a week or so, is much too unwieldy an organization to exercise its authority in any meaningful fashion. In the early years of the regime, meetings of the Congress were preceded by weeks or months of intense debate within the Party, a process of issue-raising and discussion that prepared the ground for meaningful debate. But this habit, too, was curbed by the rule against factionalism, as well as by the Party leaders' phobia against any show of disunity within the Party.

In addition, the independence of the Congress was curbed by the fact that its delegates, ostensibly elected by the Party member-ship, came more and more to be handpicked by the Party's highest administrative leadership. Thus, with the passage of time, the sovereign authority of the Congress exhausted itself in listening to announcements, reports, and policy speeches by the leaders, in approving or ratifying their actions since the preceding Congress, and in electing prepared slates of candidates to the various high Party offices. Since 1927 all decisions and resolutions passed by Party Congresses have been passed unanimously.

The complete domination of the Congress by the Party's executive agencies began even before the Revolution of 1917 and was vigorously promoted by Lenin, to say nothing of his successors. This process of making the Congress into a subservient ratifying agency must be narrated in some detail.

Long before the Revolution, the actual governing body of the Party had been a standing committee, the Central Committee, chosen from among the delegates to the Congress. Its function was to serve as a deliberating and policy-making center between meetings of the Party Congress. According to the present statutes of the Party this is still its function, and it is to meet at least once every six months. In the years immediately following the Revolution the Central Committee in fact met far more frequently and actually did function as the Party's main decision-making body. But several developments soon made it more and more difficult for the Central Committee to fulfill this role, one being the continual growth in its size, as shown in the following table.

Year	Members*	Candidates	Total
1912	7	5	12
1917 (April)	9	5	14
1917 (August)	21	10	31
1918	15	7	22
1919	19	8	27
1920	20	12	32
1921	25	15	40
1922	27	19	46
1923	40	17	57
1924	50	35	85
1925	63	43	106
1927	71	50	121
1930	69	63	132
1934	71	68	139
1952	125	111	236
1956	133	122	255
1961	175	155	330

* For the names of the members and candidates elected in 1962, see *Spravochnik Partiinogo Rabotnika,* Issue 4 (1963), pp. 159–163.

To some extent, this increase in Central Committee membership may reflect no more than the equally rapid increase in the Party's over-all membership, summarized in the following table:

Year	Members	Candidates
1917 (fall)	240,000	
1918	300,000	
1919	314,000	
1920	612,000	
1921	733,000	
1922	532,000*	117,000
1923	386,000*	99,000
1924	736,000†	128,000
1925	643,000	445,000
1927	887,000	349,000
1930	1,261,000	712,000
1934	1,874,000	935,000
1939	1,589,000	889,000
1952	6,013,000	869,000
1956	6,796,000	420,000
1959	7,622,000	617,000
1961	8,873,000	843,000

* Sharp decrease in membership due to a purge designed to eliminate bandwagon jumpers, careerists, and others not deemed worthy of membership.

† Sharp increase in membership due to mass recruitment shortly after Lenin's death.

SOURCE: V. M. Zasorin and N. F. Vikulin, *O novom ustave partii* (Moscow: Izd. "Znanie," 1961), p. 47. (Figures rounded off.)

During the civil war, Lenin also seems to have tried to obtain a Central Committee which in its composition matched, somehow, the heterogeneity of the Party membership; this attempt to create a balance of groups within the Committee may have contributed to its growth. We shall see presently that the creation of smaller sub-committees led to a decrease in the Central Committee's power. This loss of authority proceeded simultaneously with its growth in size, and it would be difficult to say which of the two phenomena was cause and which effect; obviously, they reinforced each other.

Even while the Central Committee was relatively small, it was often difficult to get a quorum together during the turbulent years of the civil war. Most members were important functionaries in the Party's rapidly swelling apparatus, some of them permanently stationed away from Moscow, others away from the capital on frequent trips. They often had more pressing matters to worry about. Finally, the Central Committee lost some of its power because the growing heterogeneity of the Party made it an arena of conflict. Various factions within the Party, as we have seen, were represented in it during periods when Lenin felt that he could not afford to be too intolerant toward them.

Both increase in size and growing heterogeneity of the Party were closely linked with its galloping bureaucratization; this factor, too, contributed to the waning of the Central Committee's power. The growth of Party bureaucracy is often explained by Lenin's overriding desire to keep the Party under control or by his strong predilection for bureaucratic organization and procedure. His partiality for Prussian methods notwithstanding, even in Lenin's mind there were countervailing tendencies, dreams about a socialist society without bureaucratic controls or any other methods of domination and administration. To such dreams, as we have seen, Lenin and his Party were firmly committed at the time they came to power. We are interested here in two elements of this vision. One of them was the belief, firmly held in 1917–18, that the coming political order would bring true self-government to the people of Russia, and that therefore the state would wither away once the soviets had seized power. There would then be no further need for institutions of domination and repression, no requirement of armies, police forces, courts, jails, governments, or bureaucracies and boards of experts. All public business would be reduced to simple controlling and accounting manipulations that could be handled by every citizen, even the simplest (every kitchen maid, as Lenin said). For this reason, the need for bureaucrats would be eliminated, because the simple assignments left could be rotated frequently among all the citizens.

It became clear very soon after the seizure of power that this kind of self-government was not about to develop. To manage a chaotic, starving, and disintegrating empire during a period of civil war was a formidable task that required a government machinery staffed with capable and experienced administrators, not kitchen maids or any other semiliterate representatives of the masses. But the people who had performed such services for the pre-revolutionary political order were hostile to the Bolshevik regime; their numbers were small to begin with, and large numbers of potential government servants had left the country. Those who remained were pressed into service, but they were suspected of disloyalty to the new government. In order to govern the country despite these severe handicaps, Lenin and his colleagues found it necessary to use the Communist Party as a control mechanism existing side by side with the government, infiltrating and penetrating its structure, guiding and supervising its activities. This condition alone led to the proliferation of Party activities, made the Party similar to the government in many essential respects, and, in particular, contributed to the rapid bureaucratization of its structure and functioning.

But there was an aggravating factor. Although Lenin and his colleagues had to retreat from their dreams of immediate self-government for all Russians, they still maintained unrealistic conceptions about the Party itself. The masses might not be able to assume full control over all public affairs, but the Party could—indeed, in the opinion of its leaders, every single party member was able and ready for governing tasks. Rationality and universal talents, in fact, were attributed to all Party members. The leaders seem to have considered all communists wise and capable administrators fit for any assignment they might be given, public administration specialists whose leadership would assure that under all circumstances correct decisions would be made. If only there were a sufficient number of such Party members who could be placed in charge or control of all public institutions, the entire government would consist of wise legislators (in Rousseau's sense of the word), and the welfare of the nation would be in good hands. This image of the Party membership, however, proved to be equally utopian and had to be abandoned. It turned out that a distinction between "good" and "bad" members had to be made, the former to be distinguished from the latter purely on the basis of their performance and behavior record, indicating that unworthy persons were being recruited. Moreover, even those who had meritoriously served the Party under conditions of revolution did not always turn out to perform well as supervisors or leaders of government agencies. It became apparent that the talents and personality traits which make people courageous and resourceful professional revolutionary agitators and organizers may render them unfit for administrative duties in an established government.

Incompetence on the part of loyal communists was therefore added to the difficulties facing the Party now that it was confronted very suddenly with a bewildering multiplicity of administrative tasks. At this point Lenin's manifest preference for bureaucratic methods of decision-making reasserted itself. Wherever inefficiency, confusion, or other governmental difficulties arose, his favorite solution was to replace spontaneity and autonomy with bureaucratic controls, to centralize channels of authority, to transform decision-making processes into bureaucratic routines. In thus transforming the Party into a well-controlled political machine, he used two devices. One was to weaken the party's representative institutions by creating smaller and less unwieldy committees to function as inner cabinets; the other was to circumvent open debate altogether by placing authority for making important decisions into the hands of more pliable administrative organs.

In line with the first of these measures, the most important step was taken in 1919 at the Eighth Party Congress. At that Congress two permanent subcommittees, or Bureaus, of the Central Committee were created which were given the task of functioning as the Party's highest policy-making bodies. They were called the Organizational Bureau (Orgburo) and the Political Bureau (Politburo). The former, by far the less important of the two, was to deal with problems of party structure and personnel. The Politburo was to deal with all important political decisions; it became the Party's inner cabinet and was recognized as such from its beginning. Membership in the Politburo invariably carried with it the highest possible prestige and authority. Throughout its existence, it remained a cabinet-size body which could meet frequently and discuss the most diverse matters with relative lack of formality. The first Politburo had five members and three alternates; although over the years it slowly grew in size, it never attained more than double its original membership, whereas the membership of the Central Committee multiplied by more than twenty. Very quickly, therefore, the Politburo assumed the supreme policy-making functions that had resided in the Central Committee, and the latter's influence declined accordingly, as we have seen.

It has been asserted already that the decline in the influence of representative bodies within the Party was hastened by the growth of bureaucratic controlling agencies. One of these, the Central Control Commission, was, like the two Bureaus, a subcommittee of the Central Committee. The Central Control Commission was created in 1921 for the purpose of curing and preventing inefficiency, red tape, and mismanagement within the Party, and of reviewing the performance of all Party members. It functioned as an inspectorate and auditing board and also, at times, as the principal administrator of party purges—a purge being a review of all members' activities for the purpose of determining whether or not they should be retained in the Party. It existed until 1962, still as a commission under the Party's Central Committee, fulfilling some of the same functions, but probably retaining little political significance. Its new name, Central Audit Commission, may have summarized its principal function. In November 1962, the plenary meeting of the Central Committee changed the status of this commission in very interesting and significant fashion by merging it with an analogous agency of the Council of Ministers, the Commission for State Control. The newly created body is called the Committee for Party and State Control and is subordinated to both the Council of Ministers and the Party's Central Committee. It is an outstanding symbol of the new tendency to obscure the boundaries between the Communist Party and the government. Its duty, apparently, is primarily to report on evasion of rules by managers and other persons endowed with administrative authority. For this purpose, it seems to rely, at least in part, on information from informants at the grass roots.[7] At the same time, for the purpose of organizing this kind of bureaucratic intelligence, the new Committee has field organizations at lower administrative levels.[8]

A far more important addition to the Party was the Secretariat. It was created in 1919, at the same time as the two Bureaus, to fulfil the household functions that must be carried out in any large organization: keeping records, handling the flow of correspondence, preparing agenda, keeping calendars of activities, and maintaining communications with the field. Before the creation of the Secretariat, most of these duties had been carried out by one man, Iakov Sverdlov, who apparently carried most of the necessary information in his head—a one-man secretary or office manager. His untimely death in 1919 made the creation of a formal secretarial office necessary. Ostensibly, the new agency was to serve only such ancillary functions as have been listed above; in this it might be considered comparable to the Adjutant General's office in a large military organization. Morever, in carrying out these service activities, the Secretariat was to be responsible and accountable to its parent organization, the Central Committee. It very quickly, however, developed into the administrative nerve center of the Party and more and more assumed control over all Party activities and policies.

The principal steps in this direction were as follows: first, Lenin used the Secretariat for the purpose of re-establishing control over the local and territorial units of the Party. In the main, this objective was accomplished before his death in 1924. Once the autonomy of the local units was curbed, a long-range trend toward usurpation of policy-making by the Secretariat began to manifest itself. In other words, the differences between deliberation, decision-making, and administration, never firmly established in the Party, were obliterated more and more, control over all these functions being vested to an increasing degree in the appointive office of the Secretaries rather than in the representative organs of the Party.

[7] See *Pravda* (June 26, 1963).
[8] See the decree of the November 1962 Plenum which set up the new committee. *Spravochnik Partiinogo Rabotnika,* Issue 4 (1963), p. 199.

The chief method by which the Secretariat gained this ascendancy was its control over personnel. The individual members of the Party came to regard the Secretariat machine as the most formidable superior whose cues must be followed by all who wished to stay and advance in the Party. Office holders felt this dependence even more strongly; this condition applied not only to local and territorial secretaries, but, in time, to all Party officials, including those ostensibly elected as delegates to conferences and congresses or even those elected to such higher deliberative bodies as the Central Committee. In effect, therefore, even these supreme policy-making agencies of the Party, which ostensibly were the parent organizations of the Secretariat, came to be staffed, at least indirectly, by people handpicked by the Secretariat itself. More precisely, the Party's representative as well as administrative institutions came to be packed with supporters of the man who headed the Secretariat. This, as of April 4, 1922, was J. V. Stalin.

Stalin's father was a Georgian village cobbler turned factory worker. Young Josef was sent to a seminary to prepare for the priesthood, but was converted to Marxism and expelled from divinity school. Years of vigorous activity in the revolutionary social democratic movement of his native land led to the usual experience in tsarist jails and in Siberia, but also to some prominence within the revolutionary movement. Lenin came to value him for his enterprise, his organizational talents, his loyalty, and because they thought alike about the national minority problem. He co-opted him into the Bolshevik Central Committee in 1912. Having spent the early years of World War I as a political exile in the arctic wilds of Siberia, Stalin returned to Russia in the spring of 1917 to participate in the Revolution as a member of the Bolshevik top command. He played no conspicuous role in the October Revolution and, in general, was far less known, both inside and outside the Party, than some of its flashier orators, brilliant writers, or public leaders. Yet he remained a member of the Central Committee and, after the seizure of power, entered the Soviet cabinet, though only in the relatively minor post as Commissar for Nationalities. During the civil war his most conspicuous role was that of political commissar during several important campaigns of the Red Army. Far more important for his career, however, was his inclusion in virtually every major controlling and policy-making body of the Party's high command. From the very beginning of its existence, he was a member of the Politburo, and, equally important, he was the only Politburo member who also belonged to the Orgburo from the day of its creation. In addition to the People's Commissariat for Nationalities, he was given the important Commissariat of the Workers' and Peasants' Inspection, a governmental inspectorate and bureaucratic controlling agency set up in 1921 for the purpose of streamlining the government administration and curbing inefficiency. This assignment was a token of Lenin's high regard for Stalin's talent as an administrator and trouble-shooter. Moreover, from the time of its creation, Stalin was the main power behind the Secretariat, and it was only fitting that in 1922 he was made Secretary General of the Party.

At the very moment Stalin assumed formal command over the Secretariat's machine, which already had demonstrated its formidable power over local and provincial party organs, Lenin fell ill and began to leave the Party without his guidance. He rallied once more and resumed control for a few months, but had a paralyzing stroke in 1923 and died in January 1924. His death was a severe blow to the Party, which had depended so much on his leadership and was so much a projection of his personality, and it led to years of severe disorganization and conflict. The nature of this conflict can be described in various ways. It can be seen as a clash of issues, a debate over policy alternatives in many different areas. It can also be depicted as a power struggle between different sets of leaders and followers, or between different types of Bolsheviks. Or, it can be viewed as an attempt on the part of the Party to restructure itself now that the universally recognized leader had departed from the scene. All these aspects of the interregnum that followed Lenin's death (and, in fact, began during his first serious illness) are closely intertwined; the full story is far too complex to be told here. Our interest should focus on two matters; one is the restructuring of the party's decision-making processes, and the other is the nature of the top leadership that emerged in the course of this transformation.

The structural changes in the Party after Lenin's death can be regarded as the completion of developments that had begun in the years before—the strengthening of the Politburo and the Secretariat at the expense of local and territorial organizations and the Congress and Central Committee. The bureaucratically inclined administrators of the Secretarial apparatus, whose power Stalin symbolized, inexorably swept out the romantic revolutionary intellectuals who had flocked to Lenin around 1917 and had formed the more conspicuous members of his entourage. In the process of removing this old guard from leadership, they also swept out the last remnants of freedom of discussion and the members' rights to participate in decision-making. The Congress was transformed into a rubber stamp as early as 1927; at that time some opponents of the Secretary General were still permitted to address the delegates, but their speeches were drowned out by the widespread hooting and whistling of the Congress members, now acting as Stalin's loyal claque. During the next few years, all important decisions were made in the Politburo, but the Central Committee still exercised some veto power. Even after the last opposition members had been removed from the Politburo in 1930, some of Stalin's former opponents retained their seats in the Central Committee. In fact, between 1932 and 1934, years of crisis and unrest within the Party and the country, Stalin was at times outvoted in the Central Committee and had to yield. Yet he was already so firmly entrenched as titular head of the Party that he could rally, and he then proceeded to make any further insubordination impossible. Between 1934 and 1938 the Party was so thoroughly shaken up that we may well say Stalin destroyed it. No one was safe against his suspicion and vindictiveness, neither members of the Central Committee, People's Commissars, First Secretaries of provinces and Union Republics, nor even members of the Politburo. The vast majority of those who had been prominent in the Party before or during the Revolution were eliminated; most of Lenin's former associates and collaborators were killed and their positions given to a new generation of Party administrators, many of whom had joined the Party only after the Revolution. This revolution within the Party was accomplished by agencies from outside: the secret police and Stalin's personal secretariat. Through these institutions, Stalin succeeded in ascending to absolute dictatorship of the Soviet Union, ruling like an oriental despot with unchecked arbitrariness and capriciousness. And the spirit of arbitrariness and capriciousness, of bloody vindictiveness and ferocious cunning, was imparted to the entire Party, as those who wished to survive had to practice the dictator's methods of government. Meanwhile, all public utterances about Stalin spoke as if he were a superhuman genius with almost divine attributes.

Stalin destroyed the party of Lenin, but his own party grew apace. It may not have been sovereign within the entire political system, but in the Stalinist trinity of Party, police, and government apparatus, it probably ranked highest still. The Politburo remained the center of policy-making and high-level deliberation, insofar as we know, even though many important decisions were obviously made by Stalin without consulting this Party cabinet. The Central Committee, no longer a deliberative body, now was reduced to a ratifying agency, although ostensibly it remained the focus of all authority in the Party; all important decisions of the Party were (and still are) published in its name; and the vast party bureaucracy, the "apparatus," nominally remained in its service. To it all agencies report and are responsible; by it they all are created, at least according to the party's by-laws. In this sense, the Central Committee, rather than the Congress, became the formal locus of sovereignty within the Party. But in fact the sprawling bureaucracy of the "apparatus" long ago became an appendage of the Secretariat, which is in fact the nerve center of the Party's entire permanent bureaucracy. With its many departments and sizable staff, the Party Secretariat has become a complicated structure as large as the entire government of a small state. Its organization has changed frequently and is today in flux, but at all times it has had departments or other agencies corresponding to the many functions performed by the Party and the entire political system. It has been an inner government within the national government apparatus.

The various agencies deriving their authority from the Central Committee include a number of specialized institutions, such as schools and academies, archives, libraries, and research organizations, including the Institute of Marxism–Leninism and the Academy of Sciences. Furthermore, the Central Committee is the parent organization for a judiciary body, the Committee for Party Control, which functions as a disciplinary court and a court of appeal for Party members facing expulsion or other sanctions. Finally, there is the party bureaucracy proper which takes the form of bureaus and departments (*otdely*) of the Central Committee. In fact, this central Party administration is an extension of the Secretariat.

Some of the departments of the Secretariat deal primarily with intraparty activities—for example, the Ideological Department (formerly the departments for Agitation and Propaganda), concerned with the formulation and dissemination of Party doctrine, and the departments for Party Organs, which deal with personnel policy. But the Ideological Department is concerned also with instructional work in non-Party agencies, and the department of Party Organs also supervises the work of such organizations as the Komsomol and the trade unions. There are departments dealing with education, science, and cultural matters; a number of departments concerned with foreign policy and relations with foreign Communist parties; and an armed forces department, called the Main Political Administration. This Department helps obscure the boundaries between party and government because it is jointly administered by the Secretariat and the Ministry of Defense. A Special Department may still be in existence; it has a somewhat similar relationship to the police branch of the government, the Committee for State Security.

The remaining departments are concerned with policy formation and supervision of activities in the national economy. Three bureaus were created in recent years, one for agriculture, one for heavy industry and construction, and a third for light industries; they coordinate the work of various more specialized departments in these three areas. A much more drastic experiment in restructuring was begun in March 1962, when a plenary meeting of the Central Committee decreed the complete reorganization of the Party into two separate branches, one for agricultural affairs, the other for industrial matters. Henceforth there were to be two branches of the Party, an urban and a rural one, each with its separate pyramid of primary, local, and territorial organizations. This thorough reform was canceled in November 1964.

Since 1956, the functional organization of the Secretariat has been complicated by the existence of two special Central Committee bureaus, one for the Russian republic (RSFSR), and another for Central Asia. These two bureaus supervise bureaucratic machinery similar to that of the over-all Secretariat, so that some of the Central Committee bureaus and departments exist in duplicate or triplicate—one each for the RSFSR, for Central Asia, and for the USSR as a whole.

In summary, the Secretariat was created in 1919, originally, to do the work that one man had previously performed. A small team of experienced Party officials built it up, and it became a large bureaucratic machine in which all the threads of Party work come together—the administrative heart of a 10-million-member organization and a 200-million nation. Stalin's role in this organization was that of a bureaucratic chief who became the top decision-maker, the boss of all personnel, the arbiter of all disputes and disagreements. He secured and maintained this commanding position by acquiring formal rank in all the important administrative machines. A member of the Central Committee since 1912, he belonged to both the Politburo and the Orgburo and chaired them both. As General Secretary he headed the Party bureaucracy. He sat in the national government as a member of the cabinet and during World War II made himself chairman of that body as well, and commander-in-chief of the armed forces with the highest military rank. To accomplish all this and perform his work, he seems to have possessed boundless ambition, ruthless determination, exceedingly high organizational talents, remarkable ability to set his subordinates against each other, and, last but not least, an unbelievable gift for mastering details of information.

Holding these posts, carrying out this work of commanding an entire country, Stalin performed a job that undoubtedly was essential for the continued functioning of the system as it developed under his hands, and yet was almost impossible for any one man to perform. Stalin was essential because in any administrative machinery there has to be one final authority. In any political system there has to be a sovereign to whom final appeals can be made, who acts as court of last resort and arbiter of all disputes. In a political system as authoritarian as the USSR, this apparently has to be a single man, just as the *purely administrative* part of government in Western countries is always headed by a single man carrying full responsibility—a Prime Minister or a President. Since in Western countries ultimate sovereignty still lies with the voters, these government chiefs are themselves under control. But in the USSR sovereignty belongs to the Communist Party—itself a bureaucratic agency. Its chief can tolerate no competition or checks. One might argue that a committee or board or a small oligarchy might carry out the functions Stalin performed. But there, too, disputes and disagreements would inevitably arise. Someone must be chairman, because someone must make final decisions. Moreover, since decisions taken at the top level of the Communist Party often were life-and-death decisions for the very top leaders involved, the chairman had to be an authoritarian figure, an irremovable boss, a master of the machine. In this sense, Stalin was an essential institution, the keystone in the Soviet political structure.

And yet, like a President of the United States (or even more so),[9] the Number One man in the Soviet Union faces a task that is inevitably beyond the powers of one man. In order to be an effective leader who manages his country well without endangering

[9] A President of the United States can solve his problems somewhat by being only nominally in charge of many of the agencies he formally heads or controls. But Stalin could ill afford to give any of his subordinates so much autonomy.

his own rule he depends on the knowledge of detail that clearly is beyond one individual and on a communications system that makes him independent of his subordinates. Stalin's solution lay in two devices: One was to prevent too much accretion of power to anyone of his subordinates by the arrangement which one might call the bureaucratic division of powers. All bureaucratic organization must distribute functions and jurisdictions among various subordinate agencies according to their competence. Although this may protect the top management, it is primarily a rational division of labor. But in the USSR the bureaucratic division of powers went further. Competences and jurisdictions were divided in such a fashion that various agencies interfered with each other and supervised each other, existed parallel to each other and duplicated each other's work. This may have created a certain amount of inefficiency, but it allowed Stalin to set his subordinates against each other. Inefficiency thus was a price paid for control and protection. The other device Stalin used to maintain one-man control over the entire Party and nation was to build up a personal secretariat apart from the formal structures (party, government, police, armed forces) which he headed, although its personnel must have been recruited from among these agencies. Almost nothing is known about this secretariat except for the name of its chief, Poskrëbyshev. This does not, however, diminish the importance it had for Stalin.

The entire machinery of government, in the Party and beyond it, was built, in effect, by one man and around one man, and was tailor-made for his needs. Consequently, if he were ever to fall or eventually to die, it would be threatened, even though one might argue that something very similar would some day be built in its place. So long as the Soviet political system is fundamentally bureaucratic (hence, without a constitutional order which effectively regulates the process of acquiring and wielding political authority), two things seem inevitable: first, the system requires a Number One man of virtually dictatorial authority; because he is essential, he must be regarded as an institution. Second, we can assume that his departure from the political scene (whatever its nature) inevitably will precipitate a succession crisis, unless such a crisis precedes his fall, in which case his fall marks the accession of another Number One man.[10]

[10] I make these statements with considerable diffidence, for the obvious reason that, since the removal of N. S. Khrushchev from his position of leadership, the Soviet Union has ostensibly been under the rule of a genuine duumvirate. This in itself is not without precedent, Khrushchev himself having once managed the system with a partner, N. A. Bulganin. Most Western political scientists tend to assume, however, that the Brezhnev–Kosygin duumvirate cannot maintain itself for long and will have to give way to open one-man rule. Any *strong* commitment for or against this assumption would be unwarranted.

Chapter VII
The Party Since Stalin

When the Nineteenth Congress, the first such gathering since 1939, met in Moscow in October 1952, the political atmosphere in the USSR was filled with foreboding. The obvious fact that the dictator was aging was driven home by mounting evidence that his paranoiac suspicions of even his closest collaborators were about to lead to a new large-scale purge of the Party leadership. This impending shakeup could be viewed also as an attempt by Stalin to decide the knotty problem of his succession. As a responsible political leader and architect of the Soviet system, Stalin must have been worried lest an interregnum like that following Lenin's death once again disorganize and demoralize the ranks of the Party.

The Party rules say nothing about a General Secretary; indeed, they do not provide for a Party leader at all. Instead, they are worded as if all authority within the party ultimately flowed from the membership through its delegates in the Congress. In reality, as we have seen, all authority was concentrated in the hands of the General Secretary. Under him, a complex division of powers pitted a handful of his highest lieutenants against each other. There was, first of all, the chief of his personal secretariat. Second, there was the Politburo, its nine members nationally regarded as the most important political leaders. Even within their ranks was a hierarchy, since the four or six senior members of the Politburo seemed the strongest: each of them, in addition to his Party post, also controlled important parts of the Soviet administrative machine, such as the police, the armed forces, or heavy industry. These were the Politburo Ministers.

Once Stalin died, these senior Party leaders could be expected to begin at once struggling with each other for succession to his place. It would be a struggle both for and against power; for it could not be foreseen which would be more important to each of these potential contenders—to strive for his own ascendancy or to prevent all others from succeeding Stalin and, possibly, to work out some new arrangement leading to collaboration and coexistence of all the former lieutenants. Undoubtedly, any struggle or bargaining would be based on the power and influence each of these leaders possessed by virtue of his control over a vital sector of Soviet public life. At the same time, any conflict, or indeed any working agreement, might involve debate and maneuvering in some of the decision-making bodies of the party, such as the Politburo, the Central Committee, or even a Congress. In any event, some conflict and a good deal of politicking were inevitable because neither the formal statutes nor the informal political culture of the Party provided for an orderly, regularized succession.

At the Nineteenth Congress, Stalin took two important steps designed to solve the succession problem before it became acute. The first of these steps was to single out one of his lieutenants for conspicuous and extraordinary honors, thus implicitly but clearly designating him as his senior deputy and hence his successor. This man was G. M. Malenkov, a man of wide experience in Stalin's secretariat, in industrial management, as well as Party and police work. The second step was to weaken the position of all his other lieutenants by two measures. First, he deprived the Politburo Ministers of their ministries by promoting them to the rank of Deputy Chairmen of the Council of Ministers. Secondly, he abolished the two Bureaus of the Central Committee (the Politburo and the Orgburo), replacing them with a larger, hence weaker body, which was called the Presidium of the Central Committee. The Politburo elected in 1939 had had 9 members and 2 alternates; in the Presidium the power of the members was diluted because its membership was 25 members and 11 alternates. In the weeks after the Congress, the dark clouds of an impending major purge gathered more and more thickly. We know now that even the highest leaders under Stalin began to fear for their lives. However, five months after the Congress, Stalin was dead.

At once a period of lively politicking began. Perhaps the first step taken by the highest Soviet leaders was to undo the structural reforms made at the Nineteenth Congress. The former Politburo ministers resumed command over the administrative empires Stalin had taken away from them. Moreover, the Presidium was sharply reduced in size; with ten members and four alternates, it was again similar to the Politburo that had existed until 1952.

Events since then have been followed with avid attention by outside observers. But even though we have been able to register the results of the power struggle which ensued after Stalin's passing, its actual workings have, for the most part, been hidden from public view. For instance, it was easy to see that the chief of the Soviet police system, Lavrenti Beriia, together with his top aides, was eliminated after an unsuccessful attempt to seize control; and we even know or can reconstruct some elements of the process that resulted in his and his collaborators' downfall late in 1953. But we do not know nearly enough to subject this important event to a thorough political analysis of the kind that would show us how *in general* such issues are decided, and what political, psychological, international, and other factors account for both Beriia's attempt and his failure. We simply have not got sufficient specific information about the events and maneuverings leading to his fall. What seems to have happened is that the police chief ordered his security troops to occupy strategic places in Moscow and possibly other parts of the USSR. Apparently, at the very moment when he was ready to seize control and remove his rivals, these rivals seized him, and he was shot either at once or after a speedy trial by a military kangaroo court. The more interesting questions that arise from this outline of events cannot be answered. One would like to know, for instance, by what process of communications the leaders concerned learned (or failed to learn) about the thickening plot. It would be equally rewarding to know to what extent, and at whose initiative, Beriia's rivals got together for the purpose of planning preventive action. We would wish to know the role of the troops and the troop commanders involved, both police and regular units. Obviously, they must have been involved in a situation in which loyalties conflicted. How interesting it would be to find out what factors determined the stand they took!

Similarly, baffling questions that remain unanswered are raised by the subsequent rise of Khrushchev, a process that must be summarized here. As we have seen, Stalin died after having designated G. M. Malenkov as his successor, at least by implication. Indeed, once he was dead, Malenkov assumed offices previously held by Stalin: he continued to work in the Party Secretariat, clearly as the senior Secretary, and also was made Chairman of the Council of Ministers. Within a few weeks, however, he gave up his secretarial position, remaining as head of the government. His place in the Secretariat was taken over by N. S. Khrushchev, a man far less well known outside the country. The question is who or what prompted Malenkov to resign from his high Party position. Did he do it on his own initiative, in the belief that it would be advantageous to him to concentrate his efforts on the job of Prime Minister? Was he forced out by his peers within the Party, who wished to prevent excessive concentration of power in the hands of a single person? The constant emphasis of Soviet ideology during this period on the principle of collegiate management makes the assumption plausible that such apprehensions were rife among the Party leaders. But, if his peers forced him out, it would be interesting to know precisely how such a political maneuver was accomplished and what forms it took.

A drawn-out tug of war then ensued between Malenkov and Khrushchev, the details of which are equally obscure. It ended with the fall of Malenkov and his demotion to a position of obscurity and minor responsibility. His demise brought with it additional dissension and political antagonism within the Party— a prolonged period of jockeying for positions and finally a dramatic clash between two factions, that of Khrushchev and that of Molotov and Kaganovich, to name only the principal figures. The clash took on some novel forms. Within the Presidium, the Khrushchev faction was in the minority, and in a decisive meeting he and his supporters were defeated. Having foreseen such an outcome, however, Khrushchev called together a meeting of the Central Committee, where a majority sided with him and defeated the Presidium. Khrushchev seems to have been aided substantially by the then Minister of Defense, Marshal Zhukov, who helped speed far-away members of the Central Committee to Moscow in military airplanes. For trying unsuccessfully to defeat and unseat the Khrushchev faction, the Presidium majority was subsequently denounced as an anti-Party group, its leaders ejected from their high posts and given administrative assignments of little importance.[1] The man they had tried to defeat used his victory to assume leadership over the Party, though his power and the manner in which he used it undoubtedly were very different from Stalin's way.

Nikita Sergeevich Khrushchev was a prominent representative of the generation of Party leaders who came out of the ranks of workers and peasants, joined the Party during the civil war, and rose to positions of great authority at the time of the Great Purge in the second half of the 1930s. At that time, these leaders stepped into the offices vacated by people who are today being rehabilitated as innocent victims of Stalinist terror. In the light of this observation it is interesting to note that Khrushchev's first prominent assignment was to purge the Ukrainian Party of "enemies of the people." He was in charge of the Ukraine when the purge reached its most orgiastic phase, and at that time he was given credit for the thoroughness of its operations.

A generalized portrait of this generation of leaders would stress their lower-class origin and their relative lack of formal education. This low educational level must not by any means be interpreted as indicating a lack of intelligence, but it can perhaps be assumed to imply little or no commitment to intellectual values, including those of intellectual honesty and independence. At the same time, the successful leaders of this generation displayed a good deal of pragmatism, as well as ruthlessness. They showed no compunction against jailing, torturing, and killing anyone whom Stalin or

[1] The present membership of the Presidium is listed in *Spravochnik Partiinogo Rabotnika,* Issue 4 (1963), pp. 164 and 200.

Ezhëv designated as an enemy of the people. In contrast, the men whom they helped remove very often showed compunction in dealing with former comrades-in-arms. This might be rephrased by saying that the first generation of Stalinists, who were the last to be purged in 1937–38, were loyal primarily to the Party and only incidentally to Stalin, whom they had followed for many years because he seemed to them to be pursuing the correct course. Precisely because they felt at one with the Party, they could at times show tendencies toward cultivating the cult of their own personalities, since, after all, the Party had exalted them by giving them their very great responsibilities. In comparing the Khrushchev generation (i.e., those younger men who survived the Great Purge) to the pre-Khrushchev generation of Stalinists who were eliminated, one has the feeling that the Khrushchevs were loyal less to the Party than to its leader, and that this absolute loyalty, in their case, led to a careful cult of self-effacement.[2] It should be understood that these are not the only character traits that explain the rise of Khrushchev and his peers, i.e., the generation of top leaders who survived Stalin. They are only the traits that may have distinguished them from those who did not survive the last year of the Great Purge. What both of these groups had in common was, of course, the syndrome of attitudes and skills that we have attributed to successful members of the Party *aktiv* in general.

One note of caution must be added: In the preceding paragraph, N. S. Khrushchev is portrayed as a man of self-effacing loyalty to Stalin. One implication of this portrayal might be that he lacked principles as well as courage, that he was a careerist and opportunist who succeeded because he was more successful and more ruthless than his rivals in following the dictator's cues. This may, however, be an erroneous impression. Even under Stalin some rose to high position because they boldly took the initiative and got things done. Those who fell were either timid souls who did not have the courage to act on their own or else were daring entrepreneurs whose actions resulted in failure. It should be

[2] For a biography of Khrushchev which makes these points see Lazar Pistrak, *The Great Tactician* (New York: Praeger, 1961).

remembered, in this context, that in the last few years of Stalin's life Khrushchev displayed considerable daring in promoting his abortive scheme for agricultural reforms.

If the rise of Khrushchev and his peers can be explained as a function of the ascendancy of Stalin as an absolute dictator, his victory over Malenkov, Molotov, and Kaganovich cannot yet be explained satisfactorily, simply because we do not yet have the wisdom of hindsight. Many hypotheses have been advanced, all of them on the basis of flimsy evidence. Khrushchev's ascendancy has been explained as a victory of the professional politicians over the managerial elite, whose spokesman Malenkov was assumed to be. But the assumption that Malenkov spoke for this group is difficult to prove; moreover it must be confronted with the fact that Malenkov rose within the Party through his work in the Great Purge in Stalin's Secretariat. He was thus as much a professional politician as Khrushchev. Nor does this hypothesis take into account the subsequent fall of Molotov and Kaganovich, who clearly were professional politicians rather than government managers. Their demise has been attributed to a conflict in which the provincial Party secretaries won over the central leadership of the Party; in this explanation, the Secretariat as well as the Central Committee are seen as strongholds of the provincial secretariat, and Khrushchev as their exponent, whereas the 1957 Presidium is viewed as the last bastion of the old Stalinist prominents. Each hypothesis raises more questions than it provides answers; and again it is probably too early to deal with these questions.

One thing seems clear: Khrushchev's victory obviously spelled defeat for at least two factions within the Party. The ouster of Malenkov removed a man who had become the symbol of a policy of relaxation, in economic policy and perhaps in other areas as well; the fall of Molotov and Kaganovich removed men of Stalin's own Old-Bolshevik generation who maintained the need for strict centralization, doctrinal inflexibility, and possibly also Stalinist police methods of government. Khrushchev's rise is therefore the victory of a skillful professional politician who carefully steered between the extremes of dogmatism and opportunism; in a different political system, a man of his type might wish to call himself a "progressive conservative." Scholars in future generations may perhaps come to the conclusion that his emergence was little more than the result of political skill combined with a political *style* that seemed, at least for a while, to be in tune with the requirements of the moment. His subsequent retirement suggests, however, that there were limits to his skill and to the appropriateness of his style of operation and other leadership qualities. With Brezhnev and Kosygin, a slightly younger set of leaders has assumed command, men whom all observers identified as Khrushchev's most loyal followers, if only because their careers were so obviously and for such a long time dependent on his. Whether this latest change of command will bring with it substantial changes in the style and method of government in the USSR, or whether it is itself the result of such changes, remains to be seen. Many questions are still unsolved. For example, is the institution of one-man dictatorship yielding to a pattern of collective management, or must the eventual emergence of a single dictator still be considered an essential feature of the Soviet political system? In line with this question, theories concerning the immutability of so-called totalitarian systems will sooner or later have to be re-examined. Beyond this there is a host of questions that may never be solved concerning the processes by which Khrushchev's retirement was effected.

Let us return to the changes in the style of government. It should be pointed out that differences of styles are more than just aesthetic differences. New modes of operation directly affect the contents of the policies; *how* things are done determines in part *what* will and will not be done. And some features of the style of Soviet politics since Stalin's death must be noted—with due caution, to be sure, since political life is subject to change, and on occasions change may be retrograde. Perhaps the central symbol of recent changes in style as well as policies has been "destalinization." This word denotes the obviously reluctant and half-hearted attempt of the Party to re-evaluate the role and person of the late dictator.

There have been several milestones in the progress of destalinization. One was the immediate reaction to Stalin's death, which took
the form of a public resolve by all the surviving leaders to rule
the country and the Party in the "Leninist" spirit of collegiality.
A feeling of relief must have swept the high command of the
Party when the leader passed away, and it may well be that a
genuine revulsion against the excesses of his method of government found its expression in this stress on collegiality and the
criticism of the "cult of personality." At the same time, both
criticism of Stalin and the caution with which it was expressed
betray the hesitancy these leaders must have felt at expressing any
position very strongly, lest it do them political harm in a very
fluid situation. The Party and the outside world were therefore
caught by surprise when the Twentieth Congress, in 1956, was
exposed to a passionate denunciation of Stalin. This famous
"Secret Speech" by Khrushchev was the second milestone in the
history of destalinization. It brought with it a concerted effort
to undo some of Stalin's works, an effort which was symbolized
by the rehabilitation of many of his victims and the rewriting of
the Party's history. Among observers in the West there seemed
to be a general consensus that power relationships within the
Party's top command were now similar to those prevailing in 1934,
when Stalin was no more than first among equals, and when the
Central Committee still functioned as a forum for meaningful
discussion. The semblance of collegial rule was followed, however,
by Khrushchev's victory over his rivals, which clearly made him
more than merely the first among equals. And yet, his ascendancy
led to a much more drastic destalinization speech, this one given
in public rather than behind closed doors, at the Twenty-second
Congress, in 1961. History will once again have to be rewritten.
Stalin's rule, and with it all present-day relationships within the
Party, will once again have to be reevaluated in conformance with
Khrushchev's most recent revelations.

The entire process of destalinization which, with ups and downs,
has been going on since March of 1953, must be seen as both
cause and effect of persistent pressures for greater freedom of

discussion within the Communist Party.[3] There are many indications of this tendency. One of them is the simple fact that Khrushchev's rivals were demoted and denounced but not killed or jailed or even ejected from the ranks of Party membership. They remained Party comrades for the time being, even though this appellation might be conveniently omitted in their successors' speeches. Not only did they remain in the Party, with, to be sure, positions of minor responsibility,[4] but from the proceedings at the Twenty-second Congress it became apparent that at least one of them, V. M. Molotov, still went on fighting for support of his ideas, making use of his right as a Party member to appeal to the Central Committee. Open debate has begun in the USSR on many issues of public policy. These issues range from aesthetic doctrines through history and the social sciences to economic policy and military strategy, covering matters of vital importance to the nation as well as trivia. One may conclude that within the Party, as well, issues that ten years ago were considered settled and taboo are today being debated. There is no freedom of speech in the Party or in the public, but there seems to be much greater freedom of discussion than before; and the higher in the Party, the greater this freedom is likely to be. Sooner or later the actual freedom of discussion will strive to be recognized formally as freedom of speech. That these strivings are already being voiced within the Party was indicated by N. S. Khrushchev, who at the Twenty-second Congress felt it necessary to reject the demands made by unidentified comrades that the Party rule against factionalism be abolished. The fact that such a demand needs to be rejected in a public address shows how strongly it must have been voiced.

In order to explain this striving for greater freedom, many of us tend to think at once of the power struggle. Khrushchev as well as his successors, so we speculate, have permitted some freedom

[3] Needless to say, a full understanding of the destalinization campaigns and related ideological developments is possible only in light of contemporary political problems within the USSR, the entire communist bloc, and the world as a whole.

[4] When his turn came to be ousted from command, Khrushchev himself became a beneficiary of these more modern methods of leadership circulation.

of discussion in order to hold the Party together. Perhaps they have done so to court the loyalty and support of the "liberals" in the Party; more likely, they have granted concessions under pressure; quite probably they even have been trying desperately to hold the line of doctrine and discipline in the face of mounting pressure for greater freedom. At the same time, one might assume that the Party and its leadership can afford to grant some of this freedom of debate because of its success in establishing and stabilizing its rule and implanting its ideology in the minds of the members. Moreover, to withdraw the scant concessions made so far might create problems of morale within the Party with which the leaders do not wish to cope.

In speculating about their motives—and we can do no more than speculate—we must not forget the changes in the broader environment within which these leaders must operate, an environment of increasing heterogeneity and complexity that more and more defies unified control by a single man. Hence the Party must concede greater autonomy and flexibility to its own subordinates, so they can maintain some control and direction. At the same time, Soviet society, having crossed the threshold of industrialization and great-power status, is today at a crossroads with signs pointing in several different directions. Within the Party there must therefore be sharp disagreements concerning the need and desirability of reforms, as against conservative adherence to tried and proven methods and policies. Undoubtedly, there are factions in the Party today—or, if not factions, then divisions of opinion and mood and cliques formed around the spokesmen for these different political lines. In turn, these divisions no more than reflect and express the growing heterogeneity of the entire Soviet elite and the growing complexity of Soviet society, with its inevitable clashes of opinion, its different professional groupings, its conflict of generations, its divergent class interests.

As a result, there has been within the Party considerable pressure for greater autonomy, for increased participation by the members, and for greater security from arbitrary treatment. In turn, the leaders have felt more urgently than before the need to streamline the organization, to loosen the creaky joints of a political machine growing ever larger and more complex, and to raise the morale of the people who work in the machine. Referring to the Stalin era as certain "mistakes" in Party management, the Party boasts that "The Party . . . steadfastly initiates measures which in the future are to exclude altogether the possibility that such mistakes be repeated."[5] The leadership naturally desires to maintain control over the Party even while making such adjustments—indeed, precisely through making them. These pressures and desires are symbolized by the new rules, or by-laws, which the Party adopted at its Twenty-second Congress in the fall of 1961. In introducing these new rules, Frol Kozlov called them the *basic law* of the Party, thus correctly implying that they were, in effect, the Party's constitution.[6] Amendments and revisions of the Party Constitution have been made very frequently since the RS-DRP adopted its first set of rules in 1898. But the changes made in 1961 are more important than most of the revisions that have been written in several decades, even though, as Kozlov himself pointed out, "the fundamental Leninist organizational principles of the structure and functioning of the party . . . remain unchanged."[7] The changes might be summarized as follows:

First, the new rules provide greater security to the individual Party member. They confirm the secrecy of the ballot in all Party elections, even though during the discussions preceding the Congress there had been some argument against the secret ballot. Expulsion procedures have been made a good deal more stringent than they were before, and a member's right to appeal disciplinary action taken against him is spelled out with greater care. The suggestion made by some members during the preliminary debates that the rules provide for occasional mass purges of the membership was expressly repudiated. Many older Party members may remember from bitter experience that the necessity for mass purges was denied as early as 1939, but that purges occurred nonetheless.

[5] From a resolution of the Twenty-second Congress, *Spravochnik Partiinogo Rabotnika,* Issue 4, (1963), p. 23.
[6] *Pravda* (October 29, 1961).
[7] *Ibid.*

Still, it may be comforting to have one more assurance that they are a thing of the past.

More important than the safeguards for individual members are the changes which aim at ensuring freer debate of issues by the entire membership. A number of new provisions work in this direction. Among them is the statement that all members are free to communicate with any Party agency and have the right to press for a reply. By thus legalizing communications outside regular bureaucratic channels, the Party violates its own deeply engrained bureaucratic instincts and traditions, thus indicating how strongly the leaders feel the need for untrammeled communication with the rank-and-file membership. The rules furthermore guarantee every member's right to criticize any Party member freely, regardless of his rank or post in the Party. Like the right to communicate outside of channels, this provision encourages the rank-and-file members to speak up against little Stalins in charge of local and provincial organizations. Like all laws, it is therefore two-edged. It can be applied to curb abuses and arbitrariness, but it can also be used to promote abuse and arbitrariness of the center, at the expense of the lower units' autonomy. Incidentally, the little Stalins are warned in the new rules that the suppression of any criticism from below is a crime against the Party.

The right to debate freely is elaborated further. For one thing, the new rules give all members the right to advance their opinion on any issue whatever until that issue has been settled by a vote of the membership. Here we simply have a reaffirmation of an old principle of "democratic centralism"; and the stress in this provision is as much on the discipline and obedience every member must have once the Party has made a decision as it is on the freedom to debate. In fact, all the inconsistency of "democratic centralism" is revealed in the implicit assumption that a political issue can ever be closed—that there can ever be a problem that must no longer be debated because a vote has been taken and the Party has been committed to action. The entire process by which discussion simply died in the Party is attributable to this idea that a matter remains settled unless the highest agencies of the Party, perhaps the General Secretary himself, declare it once again to be debatable. Hence if the Party rules went no further than to reaffirm the right to discuss an issue freely until it was settled, they would not break new ground. But the new by-laws do go further. For the first time, they lay down rules according to which the membership itself can reopen a settled issue. These rules are quite stringent. Nothing but a mighty groundswell of opinion can force a debate on the leadership. But a step has nevertheless been taken by, at least, recognition of the possibility that a discussion might be started from below. (For the technicalities, see Article 27 of the Party rules.)

Finally, the new by-laws indicate the leaders' desire to loosen the bureaucratic rigidities of the Party and provide for greater participation of the membership at large. Dictatorship and bureaucracy easily cause apathy among those outside the ruling machine, as any American working in a big bureaucratic organization is likely to know. This apathy is a sign of poor morale. It is also a waste of good talent; and, because it perpetuates the power of the professional decision-makers, it may lead to all the undesirable and irrational manifestations of Parkinson's Laws. It is in this light that we must understand some of the new provisions. One of these calls for increased participation in Party work by rank-and-file members. It asks that the Party's professional bureaucracy increasingly be divested of its functions, and that these functions be taken over by committees of rank-and-file members, not only on the level of the primary organization, but also in the local and territorial organizations. To those who read this provision several analogies may come to mind. They may be reminded of the *zemstvo* committees that were created in tsarist Russia in the wake of the emancipation reforms; again, the academic reader might be reminded of faculty committees or student government bodies formed in basically authoritarian institutions of learning for the purpose of both mitigating and sugarcoating bureaucratic rule.

While committees are to take over much of the work of the Party, the *aktiv* is to be kept in motion. We have seen that the turnover in secretarial assignments has always been rather fast. The new rules make a reasonably rapid turnover of personnel mandatory for all Party organs which are filled on the basis of elections. At every regular election, at least a quarter of the Central Committee and Presidium members are to be replaced; and the proportion of committee and bureau members to be eliminated rises as we go down to lower levels of the Party. At the lowest levels, at least half of the personnel in town or district committees as well as of primary organization bureaus must be replaced by new people. Furthermore, the number of terms any person may serve on all ruling Party organs at the national level is limited to three; secretaries of primary organizations are limited to two terms of office. Exceptions may be made in the cases of "particularly outstanding Party leaders," if at least three fourths of the vote by secret ballot is in their favor.

Party rules have often been disregarded in the past. More frequently, they have been used to serve the interests of those leaders who managed to pack the decision-making bodies with their supporters. Furthermore, being broad, general, and flexible, the rules leave many details unstated. These details of organization and procedures are determined by instructions issued by the Central Committee. According to the situation of the moment, the leadership therefore can interpret the new Party rules narrowly or liberally. At the same time, the new rules do make it somewhat more difficult for any one leader to pack the leading Party organizations with his supporters. The rules may in fact be a desperate attempt to hold the line against the groundswell of unrest and dissatisfaction. But they must at the same time be recognized as the Party's first serious departure from the Stalinist tradition.

Part Three

The Managers

Chapter VIII
Principles of Government

Article 42 of the new Party rules contains the following paragraph: "Party organizations must not act in place of government, trade-union, cooperative, or other public organizations of the working people; they must not allow either the merging of the functions of party and other bodies or undue parallelism in work." With this statement, the new rules reiterate that Party agencies must neither usurp nor duplicate the functions of government, a demand that has been made insistently and persistently since the Bolsheviks took over the reins of government in Russia.[1]

Article 42 is part of Chapter V of the new rules, which deals with the territorial organizations of the Party below the national level. Some observers[2] have therefore wondered whether this attempt to maintain the boundaries between the Party and the government (as well as other agencies) is intended not to apply at the highest level. To be sure, we have observed already to what extent the Central Committee and its Presidium interweave with the Council of Ministers and other high government organs. But the

[1] Another authoritative document states the same ideas as follows: "How does the Party play its leading roles in the conditions of the dictatorship of the proletariat? It acts through the government and mass public organizations, guiding their efforts towards one single goal. But, in guiding all the state and public organizations, it does not supplant them. Party leadership may be compared with the art of the conductor, who strives for harmony in the orchestra but, of course, does not try to play for every musician. The Party ensures the implementation of its policy, acting through its members working in the state apparatus and public organizations." *Fundamentals of Marxism–Leninism*, p. 526.

[2] For instance, Leonard Schapiro, "The Party's New Rules," in *Problems of Communism*, XI, 1 (January–February, 1962), 31–32.

degree of interweaving at the top is no greater than at any other level of administration; and, however intricate the articulation between Party and government, the two structures can and must be seen as distinct hierarchies with different functions. For the purpose of analyzing the system and establishing some abstract model of it, the difficulty it has had in maintaining clear boundaries between the various structures does not necessarily matter.

THE SCOPE OF GOVERNMENT

In our attempt to differentiate between the Party and the government, we have asserted that there were analogies between the Soviet political system and the American corporation. If this led us to see the Party as the owners and stockholders—and the Party Presidium as the Board of Directors—the government must be viewed as the equivalent of management. Government is the service of the hired administrators whose job it is to carry out the policies broadly outlined by the sovereign owners. Government therefore is responsible to the Party. It has been created by the Party, and the Party reserves and exercises the right to make changes in the government structure whenever it so desires. In fact, the organization and procedures of government in the USSR have been characterized by the frequency and incisiveness of change imposed on government by the Party. The sovereign has experimented freely with new devices of administration; it jealously seeks to guard against the entrenchment of political institutions as irremovable vested interests. In this it has not always been successful. As anyone familiar with governmental, corporate, academic, or other bureaucracies in the West must be aware, any institution, once created, is difficult to abolish because its removal creates hardships and problems in conversion, in anticipation of which pressures for continuing the ongoing organization inevitably arise. All complex organizations have some tendency for self-perpetuation.

Despite this built-in conservatism, the structure of government changes even in Western societies. Change, however, is infinitely slower in the West, not only because existing structures fight for their continued existence; they also fight against the creation of new organizations; in addition, there is usually a constitution which provides a rough structural blueprint and thus protects the government against excessive tinkering by whoever is in power. In the Soviet Union, the Constitution does not provide this protection; it is regarded far more as a symbol or summary of the existing structure of government than as an immutable blueprint; it is descriptive rather than prescriptive, and consequently has been changed as often and as easily as the government organization it describes. Soviet spokesmen do not hesitate to acknowledge the descriptive nature of the Constitution. A recent article states, "The Constitution fixes what has been achieved and gained, and in consequence develops with socialist construction."[3] Nor is the structure of the government protected by the pressure of vested interests or by public opinion. Even if they do operate in the USSR, their strength is insufficient against the Party's determination that changes must be wrought. The structure of government in the Soviet Union is, therefore, far more flexible and changeable than in constitutional political systems. This is a relative, not an absolute, difference. Even though the flexibility of institutions deserves to be stressed, one must keep in mind that all structures have a tendency to entrench themselves, that all change therefore engenders resistance because careers, power, ideologies and commitments of various kinds are at stake every time the administrative machinery is restructured. And if the changes are drastic, as they were in February 1957, the resistance may be dramatic, as it turned out to be in June of the same year, when the majority in the Party Presidium unsuccessfully sought to oust the man who was wreaking major reforms. Similarly, Khrushchev's eventual fall from power may have been precipitated, among other things, by the abandon with which he continued to restructure both the Party and the government.

Constitutions protect the government from the people, as we

---

[3] V. Kotok, "Constitutional Law," in P. S. Romashkin, ed., *Fundamentals of Soviet Law* (Moscow, 1962), p. 48.

have just seen. They are also designed to protect the people from the government. The principal device for accomplishing this is the separation of powers and the resulting equilibrium of checks and balances which is to prevent governmental arbitrariness and excessively drastic action. Here again, in practice we may find that some degree of power division can be found also in the Soviet government; but in theory the principle is repudiated.[4] Soviet ideology is statist. It asserts that government in its own system is beneficial; and the beneficial force should be strengthened rather than curbed. Hence the idea of artificially dividing powers among rigidly separated jurisdictions is alien to Soviet political culture. Therefore, law-making, administration, as well as adjudication all emanate from the one central government agency, the Council of Ministers.

At the same time, simply because the government is structured, power is in fact divided. Rule-making power, administrative authority, the power to supervise and control, and various other functions are distributed among a vast multiplicity of agencies, each having jurisdiction over a broad or narrow sector of public life in the USSR. For arranging matters in this fashion, which might be called bureaucratic division of powers, there are several obvious motives. One is the sheer complexity of government in modern industrial society, which compels even the most centralist ruling group to structure the government into a multiplicity of jurisdictions. Seen in this light, the bureaucratic division of powers is essential for the sake of promoting governmental efficiency. At the same time, it is safe to say that it is more than a mere stream-lining device. It can also be promoted for the purpose of protecting the ruling oligarchy or the dictator from the government by setting various agencies and jurisdictions against each other. In previous chapters we noted that under Stalin the entire Soviet political system was a system of checks and balances designed to protect

---

[4] "A characteristic feature of the system of Soviet state organs is the unity and interconnection of all its component parts. The Soviet state organs do not oppose each other, are not isolated and self-contained organizations; on the contrary, they are in constant interaction." A. Denisov and M. Kirichenko, *Soviet State Law* (Moscow, 1960), p. 195.

the dictator against any potential rival. Some of the thorough re-structuring that has been accomplished since Stalin's death may be explained by the hypothesis that criteria of efficiency became stronger while the dictator's urge to have potential rivals check and paralyze each other disappeared—at least, temporarily. This hypothesis obviously presupposes that the bureaucratic division of powers may take different forms, these forms depending on the specific purposes that motivate the division.

The task of the government, we have said, is to manage the USSR in line with the broad policy directives emanating from the Communist Party. If we disregard the relationship between government and Party, we might say, more generally, that the function of the government is to regulate public life, to formulate public policy by making binding rules concerning the behavior of individuals and groups, to manage agencies set up to carry out public policies, to enforce the observance of all rules by the citizenry, and to adjudicate conflicts that may arise in their interpretation. Such a statement is sufficiently abstract to apply to governments in all political systems. Certainly it would apply to the government of the United States. Soviet government and American government, then, have at least in common that they both function as rational political authorities in modern industrial societies, and that vague and superficial structural similarities are related to this function. The observation undoubtedly is trite; yet even the self-evident deserves, at times, to be stated, if only to present a complete picture. Structural similarities are increased somewhat when comparisons are made, not with the government of the United States, but with those of continental Europe. They, again very superficially, have been the more immediate models for the organization of Russian and Soviet governments. For instance, in administrative details such as the structure and functioning of the ministries of Justice and the Interior, the Soviet Council of Ministers seems at times to be created according to continental models, specifically, the French.

But the task of this book is to show in what the government of the USSR differs from those of other countries. In discussing the relationship between government and Party, we have touched on some important differences. Among others that will emerge from this presentation, the most outstanding, perhaps, is the fact that the *scope* of government activity in the USSR is immensely wider than in other political systems. Government is the authoritative regulation of public life. But in the USSR virtually all life is public, and all human activities are subject to public policy. Even this statement, of course, applies, in some fashion, to our own political system. The most liberal government today can be expected to regulate the economic life of the country and to interfere directly or indirectly with the most personal problems of the citizens —their education, their family life, their pattern of consumption. The difference between the Soviet Union and other systems lies not so much in the mere scope of government activity as in the manner in which the public authorities regulate the lives of the citizens, and also in the intensity of control. In all modern systems, public policy regulates virtually all human endeavors. But in the West, the authoritative rules of government tend to be less specific. They leave a greater amount of decisions to the citizens, individually or collectively. In this sense, the individual retains a greater degree of both freedom and privacy.

To convey an idea of the scope of government activities in the USSR, the following activities might be listed. They do not by any means exhaust the full range of action taken by the Soviet government, but do give us a general idea of the variety of pursuits undertaken:

1. The government maintains public order. Its civil laws and family law regulate the rights and obligations of citizens toward each other. Its criminal law specifies the manner in which public authority should deal with offenders against the public order. It maintains courts and law enforcement agencies for the purpose of adjudicating conflicts or offenses and executing legal decisions.

2. The government conducts relations with foreign states, maintains a military establishment, and by other means prepares the defense of the country.

3. The government maintains the educational system. The first

two functions enumerated above should not have surprised any reader. The third might not be surprising, but it is to some extent a distinguishing feature of government in the USSR. In contrast to the United States, where some educational institutions are private, all educational facilities, from kindergartens to the highest postgraduate academies, are created and operated by the government. Their curricula are worked out by public authorities; their personnel are public officials. And the entire educational machinery is geared to the needs of society, as defined by the government, for a citizenry trained in various skills and indoctrinated with official views.

4. All scientific work in the USSR is organized, planned, sponsored, and supported by the government, whereas in our society, this kind of activity is distributed among various public authorities, private institutions of learning, and business corporations.

5. Virtually all health care, insurance, and social security activities in the Soviet Union are carried out by agencies of the government. Hence physicians and all other medical personnel are public officials too, as are attorneys, social workers, and summer camp counselors.

6. Entertainment, art, and leisure-time pursuits are organized either by the government directly or, in some instances, indirectly under its control. Club houses, for instance, are maintained by many trade unions and by the Party's youth affiliate; chess clubs or amateur groups in the various arts may have virtually independent status. But, until very recently, sports clubs were under the jurisdiction of the government, and today theaters, opera houses, the movie industry, radio, television, and a major proportion of all publishing facilities are still government-controlled. Even the activity of organized religions, although ostensibly separated from the government, is subject to control by a government agency.

7. Last, but not least, the economy of the Soviet Union has been almost completely nationalized. Virtually all enterprises are public enterprises, owned and operated by the government, including all industry and communications and most of the distributing system, with the exception of some retailing of agricultural

produce. Some crafts and much of agriculture are carried out by enterprises which take the form of producers' cooperatives. Even here, the operation is geared so tightly to the public sector of the economy that in all but form these cooperatives are public enterprises. In most of their activities they conform to the production plans formulated by the government.

If it seems to the reader that the government of the Soviet Union is in total control of all human activities, he should be told that the Party's plans for the future indicate that the public sector is to be expanded still further. The platform ratified by the Twenty-second Party Congress, for instance, envisions the gradual disappearance of producers' cooperatives in agriculture—they are to be replaced by state-owned farms; it further foresees a significant narrowing of the functions of the family, because neighborhood schools gradually are expected to be replaced by boarding schools; and a number of other planks in the platform fit into the same pattern.

Thus the scope of government activities in the USSR seems truly all-encompassing. We might expect the size of the government service to have attained tremendous proportions (by size we mean the number of government employees in proportion to the total adult population). Figures regarding this are not available in sufficient quantity.[5] Even if they were, they might turn out to be meaningless, for in a society where virtually all organized activity is managed by the government, the state merges with society, and almost everyone becomes a civil servant. The government turns into the one and only employer, and the entire society becomes something like a company town writ large, or, to return to our previous analogy, a business corporation writ large. The notion of "government," however, should perhaps be restricted to include only the supervisory, managerial, or administrative personnel—the overhead of staff. Again we do not possess adequate statistical data to make a reasonable estimate of the size of governmental overhead in the Soviet Union. If we did have such data,

[5] For the number of people occupying certain specified administrative command positions, see *Narodnoe Khoziaistvo SSSR v 1962 g.* (Moscow, 1962), pp. 33–35.

they might surprise us by indicating that government in the USSR is, if anything, smaller than the analogous overhead in the United States. This vague guess is based on the following considerations: First, the size of the administrative overhead does not necessarily increase in proportion to the directness of interference and control. On the contrary, the indirect regulations of the economy and other areas which government exercises in the United States may in some cases be so cumbersome that it requires as sizable an overhead as does direct management of the Soviet type. Moreover, since federalism and localism are far more deeply engrained in the American political system than in the USSR, as we shall see, a far greater number of governments exist side by side, at times competing with each other. But even if the sum total of government servants—national, state, and local—in the United States is found to be less than the number of their Soviet colleagues, the comparison becomes meaningful only if the size of government in the USSR is compared with the total United States overhead—business as well as governmental—for all the activities which in the Soviet Union are performed by public authorities. Once this comparison is made, the administration of the USSR may in fact appear less formidable and less cumbersome, and possibly more efficient, than its United States counterpart.[6]

THE BUREAUCRATIC NATURE OF GOVERNMENT

Having voiced, however timidly, my suspicion that government in the Soviet Union might be less cumbersome and perhaps even more

[6] Other factors that reduce the total administrative overhead of the Soviet system are the underdeveloped state of service industries, the absence of social or economic pressures for conspicuous waste and planned obsolescence, as well as readiness to solve many problems by far more summary procedures than would be tolerable in the United States. For elaborations, see Lynn Turgeon, *The Contrasting Economies* (Boston: Allyn & Bacon, 1963), pp. 257–258; also see David Granick, "Soviet and American Management; Comparisons," in Joint Economic Committee, U.S. Congress, *Comparisons of the U.S. and Soviet Economies,* Part I (Washington, D.C.: Government Printing Office, 1960), p. 146; and Norman Kaplan, "Research Administration and the Administrator: USSR and United States," *Administrative Science Quarterly,* VI, 1 (June, 1961), 51–72.

efficient in some respects than its American counterpart, I may be accused of irony if I now go on to say that Soviet government is bureaucratic. "Bureaucracy," in everyday usage, is a term of opprobrium implying inefficiency, waste, pettiness, heartlessness, and organizational hypertrophy, if not, indeed, rule by bland mediocrities or narrow authoritarians. This is the image the word evokes among Americans, and it has the same negative connotation in the Soviet Union. Bureaucracy, in the language of the USSR, is a perversion of good government.[7]

In the present book, the term "bureaucracy" is used with considerable ambivalence. When contemporary social scientists employ it, they tend to define it as the rational, purposive, and planned management of some human affairs through large and complex organization. Bureaucracy thus becomes virtually synonymous with management, provided the unit administered is sufficiently large and its objectives sufficiently diversified; bureaucracy, indeed, is rational management on a comparatively large scale. By defining it thus we implicitly give it a positive value and regard it as a progressive phenomenon, for the conscious, planned organization and management of human affairs appears as the imposition of order over chaos, the triumph of reason over blind fate. In this light bureaucracy, its structure and operations, turn into man's tools for the mastery of his environment, inventions comparable to the improvements made in material production.

Implicit in this evaluation of bureaucracy is the assumption that the adequacy and usefulness of managerial organizations, the degree of their "rationality" (to use a much-abused term) can be verified or measured. Students of bureaucracy have, in fact, elabo-

---

[7] Official Soviet ideology claims that Soviet socialism has eliminated the last residues of bureaucracy, which Lenin called the "worst internal enemy of a society building socialism." Bureaucracy, claims the authoritative textbook, is *par excellence* a bourgeois feature. "Under capitalist conditions, bureaucracy is a system of government in which power is in the hands of an official administration divorced from the people, in effect uncontrolled by them and serving the interests of the exploiter classes. It is obvious that bureaucracy is not an inherent feature of the working-class state, for this state is established by the people, serves its interests, and is under its control." *Fundamentals of Marxism–Leninism,* p. 529.

rated criteria of structure and functioning against which actual administrative organizations may be measured. Taken together, these several principles constitute models of what might be called the ideal bureaucracy, an organization that accomplishes its tasks efficiently, smoothly, predictably, and justly.

But no one familiar with the history of political ideas and ideals will be surprised to learn that the "ideal" bureaucracy constructed out of such criteria of evaluation is unattainable, at least in its imagined perfection. The perfect bureaucracy is utopian, for several reasons. First, careful examination of the various models presented by the social scientists will reveal that they are made up of contradictory criteria. For instance, the hierarchic command principle is in perpetual conflict with the need for decentralization and deference to experts. To work well, an actual bureaucracy must find an eternally uneasy balance between centralizing and decentralizing urges. More generally, a bureaucracy functions well only if each of its "rational" features is present only in moderation. Carried out with excessive zeal, such necessary principles of rational management as discretion and secrecy, communications through channels, or regard for rules and regulations turn into paralyzing poisons.

Furthermore, bureaucracy will always run into difficulty with and have to make adjustments to the sad fact that it must deal with human beings who, once they live or operate within an administrative machinery, will for many reasons be tempted to subvert it or to use it for their own ends. Although the perfect bureaucracy of which many an administrator seems to dream is one from which human beings have been eliminated (they must either be replaced by machines or turned into machines), except, perhaps, as objects of administrative decisions and as products of bureaucratic processes and manipulations—such brave new worlds *en miniature* have so far remained dreams. In real life, bureaucracies with every step they take encounter the resilience and resistance of obstreperous individuals as well as primary groups and other nonbureaucratic social organizations. Again, the *perfect* bureaucracy would have to wipe out such groups or incorporate them totally within the administrative organization. Whether or not one regards this idea as obnoxious, it seems to be an impossible task.

More than that: it seems clear that the perfect bureaucracy, or an absolute degree of bureaucratization, is also a ludicrous idea. If it could be devised, it would defeat its own purposes, for over-organization becomes chaos, and total regulation or control over human affairs would kill all initiative and prevent all change. The idea of subjecting life or any of its aspects to regularized procedures, to orderly, well-thought-out routines, has static, conservative connotations. In the modern world, where technology, social organization, and other global affairs are undergoing explosive change, the possibility of imposing rules and routines on life must appear entirely ludicrous. And yet, it is precisely what must be attempted if man is to gain control over some of the forces the species has unleashed. The postulate derived from this dilemma is to devise structures and processes of rational management that can effectively cope with changes in society and technology. But this, again, seems an impossible demand.

Karl Marx, in his younger years as a radical democrat (rather than a Marxist), speculated about the ideal democratic order. Following Rousseau, he saw it as a political system in which the gap of alienation between the government and the people, between the state and society, had been bridged forever. The withering away of the state that Marx foresaw as one of the final consequences of the victory of the proletariat is nothing else than the complete merger of political into social life, because then the people truly would rule. In one of his earliest writings, Marx attacked this problem of bridging the gap between state and society by postulating a truly democratic constitution, a perfect constitution that would change in step and in tune with changing circumstances. This, of course, is a denial of the very principle of constitutionalism, which implies a fixed order of procedural rules for the game of politics. Similarly, the idea of a perfect bureaucracy that maintains itself while nicely coping with a revolutionary world is, it seems, a denial of the very principle of bureaucratic management.[8]

Like the perfect constitution which dialectically negates and thereby renews itself, the perfect bureaucracy has never been created anywhere. Instead, the observer must distinguish between different degrees of bureaucratization. Each of the two extremes has its own built-in irrationality. In administrative systems of a very low degree of bureaucratization, rational order would be perverted by the intrusion of many prebureaucratic features. At the other extreme of the continuum, bureaucratic order would be frustrated by its own virtues—by overorganization, overplanning, overregulation. Many, if not all, existing bureaucracies combine features from both extremes.

In summary, bureaucracy is rational management—the imposition of planning and purposive control over human affairs. Undeniably it is an absolutely essential device of government and administration in the world of modern technology and complexity. Yet this device is forever imperfect because it has difficulties, inefficiencies, and irrational features built into its very structure and workings. The study of bureaucracy therefore includes the study of the interesting syndrome of ills which constitute the pathology of planned and rational management.

Soviet government, being bureaucratic, shares all these symptoms of "bureaupathology," to use a term coined by Victor Thompson. The typical behavior of government officials that seems to irritate many of their superiors, subordinates, and citizen-clients seems to be universal in the contemporary world. Nonetheless, such behavior often appears to be even more frequent and more

[8] I thoroughly agree with the views of Ralf Dahrendorf concerning the inevitability of change in the modern world and the essential function of conflict in facilitating and adjusting to it. According to this view, the perfect *bureaucratic* order—an arrangement without disruptions and malfunctioning, an absolute orderliness, regularity, or indeed a perfect Weberian rationality—appears as an evil utopia; and any social system approaching the Weberian model is pathological. But the pathology is, in a sense, self-limiting, because all attempts to construct and perpetuate a perfectly functioning bureaucratic social system are condemned to failure. See Ralf Dahrendorf, *Gesellschaft und Freiheit* (München: R. Piper, 1963), Chapter 5.

ineradicable in the USSR than in Western business corporations and government agencies, for a number of reasons. For one thing, bureaucratic behavior in the Soviet Union is not mitigated by the real checks on bureaucracies in societies where public authority seeks to curb corporate authority, where elected representatives are pitted against the executive branch, and where judicial redress against bureaucratic arbitrariness is somewhat more easily obtained. But another reason for the seeming predominance of bureaucratic behavior is that all-pervasive scope of public authority in the Soviet system which we have already mentioned. It is this vast scope of government activity which makes the whole country into one vast organization and completely eradicates the difference between public and private government. All administration in the USSR is public administration. Hence life for all Soviet citizens is a great deal more like life in a company town or on an army post, where everyone is subjected to a single line of hierarchic authority.[9]

Hierarchy. One of the ground rules underlying all bureaucratic organization is the monocratic principle according to which all administrative bodies are structured as hierarchies. Bureaucracies are command systems in which all participants obey, are responsible to, and report on all activities to a single line of command, a centralized, pyramid-shaped hierarchy (the line) which receives all information and issues all directives. In the Soviet Union, this rule takes the form of the principle of *edinonachalie* (literally, "monocracy"), according to which in any one governmental agency one man is in command and bears all responsibility for the success or failure of the agency. The Soviet government shares this commitment to the monocratic principle of organization with those parts of governments in the West which are usually called the executive branch or the administration. In both cases, this commitment is directly related to the dependent status of the administration, a feature to which we shall have to return. The executive is dependent in that it supposedly exists for the purpose of carrying

---

[9] In emphasizing the pathology of bureaucracy I do not, of course, wish to pretend that democracy and consititutional government do not have pathologies of their own.

out the laws and the commands of the people's representatives—be they elected legislative assemblies or the voting constituency (in the West) or the ruling party (in the USSR). In all cases, the main policy lines are supposedly provided by superordinate structures, even though in actual life the relationship may be far less simple. Still the executive or administrative branch is felt to be carrying out a national policy, whoever may be formulating it. The supposed unity and coherence of such a national policy finds symbolic expression in the office of the chief executive, whose title may be President, Prime Minister, or Chairman of the Council of Ministers. All *executive* authority flows from him. All administrative agencies are under his command and direction. Every subordinate agency is headed by a single chief who, within his narrower jurisdiction, represents the chief executive, his authority filtering down to him through the channels of the bureaucratic hierarchy.

Precisely because of its dependent status virtually the entire government machinery of the USSR is organized like the executive and administrative branch in Western political systems. Those functions of rule-making and policy-making which in the West are, at least formally, the prerogative of the legislative branch, are not, in the final analysis, carried out by the government in the USSR, but by the Party, which, again formally, is outside the structure of governmental institutions.[10]

Lest there be confusion on this point, we must state very clearly that its dependence on the Communist Party does not necessarily weaken the Soviet government. On the contrary, it is very strong and powerful. But this statement, too, must be clarified and qualified. Most probably, the government's dependent status is both a source of strength and a source of weakness. It renders the bureaucrat more powerful in dealing with the citizenry and liberates him, in significant measure, from the popular control to which bureaucracies in some Western countries are subjected. The Soviet bureauc-

[10] It should be pointed out in this connection that the vast Party apparatus itself is organized, and functions, in accordance with principles of bureaucratic management. The entire political system thus appears as a unified, though complex, bureaucratic structure, and in outlining the characteristic traits of the government apparatus we are in fact making statements applicable to the Party and its many affiliate organizations as well.

racy is not a *responsible* bureaucracy in the sense in which this term is customarily used by Western political scientists; the Soviet bureaucracy is not firmly controlled by "the public," be that taken to mean the electorate and its representatives in legislative assemblies or the congeries of interest groups impinging on Western bureaucracies, or even the special clientele of industries or trade associations that may control a bureaucratic agency originally created to control those very interests. But even though the Soviet bureaucracy is not responsible to any such groups, it is to some extent responsive to pressure. Certain standards of service to the public are on occasion enforced in response to public protest. There are a number of channels, both formal and informal, through which the citizen can voice his complaint when he is confronted with bureaucratic arbitrariness or failure to perform public services. Yet the volume and effectiveness of public pressure is much less than in many Western countries for several reasons. One is the statist political culture which assumes that the citizens are servants of the state rather than vice versa; another is the ultimate sovereignty of the Party, which operates the political system according to a hierarchy of values in which many objectives have much higher priorities than that of service to the public; finally, there are structural or procedural differences, among them the virtual absence of judicial redress against bureaucratic wrongs. Only in rare instances does Soviet law allow the citizen to sue bureaucratic agencies before a court of law; instead, formal avenues of complaint usually proceed along administrative lines such as those customarily used in the armed forces of most countries. The Soviet citizen, like a rank-and-file soldier, may wish to complain about arbitrary treatment, and formal procedures for this purpose are established. But it is up to the higher authorities whether or not they wish to heed a given complaint.

In any event, the bureaucracy is far less subject to "popular control" than some of its Western counterparts. At the same time, it is more dependent, hence weaker on the whole, because its position is that of the Party's servant. As the hired hands of the sovereign party, Soviet administrators receive policies and guidelines from the political command above them. Yet, as we have seen, this observation must be qualified even further. For one thing, it should be remembered that at the very top of the bureaucratic hierarchy the Party command merges to some extent with the government command. In the measure to which this overlapping occurs, the Soviet bureaucracy has some of the characteristics of a *ruling* bureaucracy—a self-appointed and self-perpetuating government service responsible to none. Second, the principle of *edinonachalie* as well as the recent moves toward decentralization may be seen as mitigations of the bureaucracy's dependence on the Party. This might be restated by saying that dependence on the Party applies, as it were, in the final analysis; it is the background, the setting, within which the bureaucracy operates with some degree of independence. Finally, the growing complexity of Soviet society and the increasing dependence of the Party on expert staff work may operate to strengthen a trend toward greater independence of the bureaucrats, not only because their expertise is essential to the party, but also because, in time, a service tradition may develop within the government administration similar to that of the European civil service, with the effect of making governmental officialdom a more independent and generally acknowledged status group. In the perennial struggle between political generalists and administrative specialists, both have their advantages, though each is dependent on the other. One might speculate that the secular trend favors the specialists; for, if the hypothesis of the managerial revolution is at all meaningful as applied to Western business corporations, it might also have some meaning as regards the Soviet political system. Conversely, it could be argued that precisely the greater authority and independence of the professional specialists in material and human engineering so diversifies and heterogenizes the Soviet system that professional decision-makers, specialists in aggregating and integrating conflicting opinions and interests—in short, professional politicians—are needed more urgently than ever before.

The above speculations have been noted only to show that an unambiguous answer to questions about the flow of authority between the public, the Party, and the government bureaucracy cannot be given. Merely to classify the Soviet administration as an obvious example of a *one-party* bureaucracy, as some scholars have done, is not sufficient. To be sure, the views of the Party will prevail in the final analysis; but the complexities of the relationship hiding behind such a convenient label must be spelled out.

We began this discussion by observing the commitment of the Soviet government to the monocratic or hierarchical principle of *edinonachalie*. Although firmly entrenched today (with the reservations noted) it was not at first accepted by the system. In the beginning of Soviet rule the command principle was felt to be in conflict with socialist rhetoric, with its stress on equality and communal self-government. But, since about 1930, hierarchical organization has been imposed and become an unshakable dogma, even though Soviet society seems to have its share of people who have not yet learned to accept the rank order by which bureaucracy lives. Still, in the USSR, such rebellious or antiauthoritarian spirits must be extremely cautious in expressing their views, even if they can back them up with quotations from Marx and Engels.

A much more serious challenge to the monocratic principle comes from the nature of modern bureaucracy itself: it has become so large and complex, its tasks so manifold and technical, that the single line of command has a strong tendency simply to break down. It does this because of two closely related developments. First, because of the modern bureaucracy's sheer size and complexity, the top command must delegate and decentralize more and more of its activities, and therefore is in mounting danger of losing control. Second, more and more of the actual decisions will have to be made by specialists whose work the "line commanders" or administrative chiefs may not even understand, even though they sign the orders, dramatize their role as decision-makers, and are held responsible for the results. In consequence, Soviet government is characterized by that same "imbalance between ability and authority" and suffers from all that "tension generated by the conflict between specialization and hierarchy" which seem to trouble all giant organizations in other parts of the world.[11] In the USSR, this tension expresses itself, among other ways, in the conflict between the principles of *edinonachalie* and *kolegial'nost*. According to the former, the chief of any agency is responsible. He takes credit for efficient performance and is blamed for failures. Like a military officer, he is *in command*. But, in line with the principle of "collegial responsibility," he is expected always to consult his colleagues (subordinates) in whatever bureau, committee, or council he happens to chair. In other words, he is obliged to consult his staff and subjects himself to sanctions by disregarding their advice.

This conflict between the command principle and the collegiate principle symbolizes a perennial tension inherent in all bureaucratic organizations everywhere. It takes the form of a never-ending struggle between line agencies and staff agencies. But it can be seen also as a conflict between two contradictory criteria of structural rationality: The hierarchic principle is not easily reconciled with the principle of structural differentiation.

Structural Differentiation. According to all students of bureaucracy, rational management must incorporate a functional division of labor. Where regularized, orderly routines are to take the place of arbitrariness or *ad hoc* decision-making, administrative functions must be distributed among numerous agencies having limited jurisdiction over strictly specified areas, in which they are or become competent. Implicitly, if not explicitly, most writers in the field of administration and management measure the maturity or rationality of various bureaucracies, or, perhaps, the degree of bureaucratization, by the degree to which functions are differentiated and jurisdictions or competencies divided. Rationality thus comes close to implying complexity. Stated in this oversimplified form, the notion of rationality obviously takes insufficient cognizance of the fact that all schemes of bureaucratic organization have their typical inadequacies and difficulties. Complexity itself comes into conflict with equally rational centralizing urges; public adminis-

[11] The quotations are from Victor A. Thompson, *Modern Organization* (New York: Alfred A. Knopf, 1961), pp. 6 and 78.

tration specialists have long recognized a perennial conflict between functional bureaus and generalist administrators, between staff and line; and their discussions show that there can hardly be agreement on any one best scheme of organization. Moreover, any implication that there might be an ideal way of differentiating bureaucratic functions is vitiated by awareness that the tasks of administration change rapidly; hence the bureaucracy must be reorganized repeatedly so as to remain in tune with changing tasks and to cope with emerging problems. All that can be said in this context is that the Soviet leadership has shown itself conscious of these organizational problems and that it is perpetually struggling toward greater rationality in administration. Much of this book deals, after all, with structural changes the Party has made in the political system so as to adjust to newly emergent problems.

Structural rationality, of course, is only one of several essential elements of managerial efficiency, as we have seen. Yet bureaucratic hierarchs often overestimate its value or, rather, are so preoccupied with structural problems that they forget about other matters—a typical symptom of bureaupathology. They do this easily because the managerial ideology is imbued with the idea expounded here that the task of bureaucracy is to subject blind and chaotic life to the rule of reason through organization. From this, bureaucrats are prone to conclude that all organization has inherent rationality and is therefore preferable to nonorganization or, as Soviet ideology would term it, to spontaneity. In short, bureaucrats, including those managing the USSR, are prone to become organization-happy. Their guiding principle of thought and action seems to be, "When in trouble, reorganize." No one can read the proceedings of Communist Party Congresses, Central Committee Plenums, and similar meetings without becoming aware of how strongly this principle is engrained in communist thought. Almost every Resolution the party ever publishes is written according to the following pattern: achievements made in the most recent past are noted with pleasure; shortcomings are then viewed with alarm; remedial action is then proposed. High on the list of priorities for remedial action inevitably is an improvement in organizational work, or a reorganization.

Needless to say, there are numerous problems which cannot be solved by a mere re-structuring of administrative agencies.[12]

Rules and Regulations. One of the most characteristic elements of bureaucratic rationality is the effort of administrative and managerial agencies to behave predictably as well as justly by subjecting their own activities to rules and regulations, by applying general rules dispassionately and disinterestedly, avoiding differential or arbitrary treatment of individuals. In its attempt to impose rational management on all human activities, bureaucracy must strive to convert its own activities into well-planned and controlled routines.

If the Soviet system were to be evaluated on the basis of this single standard, one would have to say that it has achieved a relatively high level of bureaucratization. Its officials are expected to operate according to strict rules which may take the form of laws, decrees, or regulations. Observance of these general rules is controlled by the Party, the numerous bureaucratic or governmental controlling agencies, the police, the public prosecutor, the courts, as well as the public which, as we have seen, may bring violations of rules to the attention of such supervisory agencies. Nepotism, favoritism, bribery, prejudice, and other violations of the principle of disinterestedness are considered criminal offenses. Moreover, Soviet government, in the almost half century of its existence, has developed standard organizational patterns and operating procedures which have converted many instances of decision-making into well-established routines. In short, the USSR would score reasonably high on this standard of rationality by which students of administration evaluate different bureaucracies.

This standard itself, however, may be subject to some challenge. To be sure, in theory, strict observation of rules and regulations may indeed appear to be "rational"; in fact it is obviously preferable to utter arbitrariness and to unequal treatment of citizens. At the

[12] That Parkinson's Law concerning the inevitable proliferation of bureaucratic agencies applies in the USSR is doubtful, both because of the chronic scarcity of trained or experienced personnel and because of the Party's vigilance. It may in fact be unrealistic with respect to Western political systems as well.

same time, many students of organizational behavior are aware that excessive preoccupation with the observance of *petty* or *trivial* regulations is a pathological feature of administration, hence non-rational and dysfunctional to the purposes of the agency in which it is practiced. The observance of rules and regulations is therefore a standard that must be applied flexibly. When applied unthinkingly and rigidly, it turns into a tyranny and arbitrariness of its own, into a special form of administrative irresponsibility.

Even a cursory study of the Soviet press or of Soviet novels and short stories dealing with administrators will reveal that this kind of "excessive rationality" has always been prevalent throughout the government. Rigid adherence to trivial and petty rules is so pervasive in all bureaucratic organizations that every reader must be familiar with it. The most obvious explanation for it, perhaps, is to say that it provides security for administrators who are insecure (for whatever reasons); and that at the same time, as every friend of Josef Schweik knows very well, it can be a subtle method of sabotaging the workings of the organization with impunity. In this case, even the deviant gains reasonable security.

But, just as the hierarchic or monocratic principle of command must be tempered by the principle of structural diversity, so adherence to rules and routines must be made tolerable by a countervailing principle. Accordingly, we can find in all bureaucracies, including the Soviet political system, a certain fluidity of rules and regulations, if only because of the ease with which the highest authorities can change laws, rules, and procedural standards—and have in fact changed them. Again, such flexibility must appear an essential element of rational management, but here, too, rationality consists only in moderation. If changeability and elasticity are carried beyond a certain undefinable point, the rapid and frequent changes in the rules under which the bureaucracy operates convert flexibility into arbitrariness and capriciousness. Again, this is a problem facing all large organizations, but it may be more pressing in the USSR, for a number of reasons.

Rationality is tempered and subverted also by that pattern of evading the rules in a multitude of ways which is called "corrup-

tion." That corruption prevails in the Soviet government administration could be taken for granted even if we did not have recurrent
confirmation of the fact from criticism voiced in the Soviet
press.[13] Soviet officials, after all, are human; and any bureaucracy
can be expected to contain a small proportion of people who are
subject to illegal influences—bribes, blackmail, national prejudice,
or loyalty to kinfolk and friends. The precise proportion of officials
who may be corrupt is impossible to ascertain; the proportion may
have varied greatly from one period to another. Also, Western
observers may be prevented by their own preconceptions about the
Soviet regime from making an adequate estimate. We cannot
even make informed guesses about the way in which the peculiarities
of the Soviet system affect the corruption ratio. For instance, does
the severity of the sanctions imposed on officials found guilty act
as an effective deterrent? Indeed, does the harshness of these
sanctions reflect the views of the Party concerning corrupt practices,
or are they a hypocritical smokescreen designed to conceal the
Party's attitude of toleration toward such phenomena?

Instead of attempting an assessment of the prevalence of corruption in the Soviet administration, we can do no more than offer
tentative explanations for its existence. One such explanation would
be that modernization is a more recent phenomenon in the USSR
than in Western bureaucracies. The influence of the peasant way
of life is still strong, and this tradition includes firm loyalties to
primary groups, sharp national prejudices, and in general a far
weaker commitment to the bureaucratic rule of regulation. Second,
living standards in the Soviet Union have been well below those of
Western countries. Scarcity reigns, even with regard to some of the
bare essentials of material comfort. The pay scale of the average
Soviet bureaucrat seems to be quite modest, and the lure of illicit
wealth may therefore be considerable. In the last decade, to be
sure, the general standard of living has risen very rapidly; but so

[13] Khrushchev himself devoted much time at the November 1962 meeting
of the Central Committee to a bitter complaint about theft, bribery, waste,
high living, and other corrupt practices in high places, and an order of the
Supreme Soviet Presidium, dated February 20, 1962, made bribery a capital
offense. The text of this is in *Spravochnik Partiinogo Rabotnika,* Issue 4
(1963), p. 533.

apparently has the appetite of the average Soviet citizen. Indeed, Soviet society appears to be in the throes of a groundswell of rising expectations—the spirit of materialism characterizing the consumption-conscious people of North America may finally have made itself at home in communist Russia. Furthermore, as we shall see in some detail below, the Soviet bureaucracy is a highly competitive organization in which shrewd, ruthless, and amoral manipulators or operators seem to have the best chance of rising to higher positions. Lack of principles thus appears to be rewarded, and any system in which this is true runs the risk of encouraging corruption. This rise of the manipulators is not an inherent structural feature, but a matter of Party policy: the Soviet political system, as operated by the Party, tends to reward success, and it often does so regardless of how that success was won. The successful production manager, the skillful organizer, the smooth manipulator of men, and other administrators who get their work done seem to feel themselves at liberty to disregard rules, to cut corners, to act in arbitrary fashion; and much of the time they seem to be getting away with it. Deviations from the rules are punished severely only when they are not mitigated by success.[14] We shall subject this phenomenon to additional examination below.

Corruption is a harsh word, and there are many scholars who seek to avoid using such terms. A more neutral way of describing deviations from general rules would be to speak about the intrusion of informal organization and practices into the formal bureaucratic structure and procedures. There have beeen periods in which Western scholars tended to regard Soviet society as essentially unstructured. They saw it as an undifferentiated mass of people held together artificially by a hard crust of dictatorial government imposed by the Party. Such views may still have their adherents. But Western social scientists have by now discovered a social structure beneath communist rule, and have, consequently, become aware of the prevalence of informal organization patterns interwoven with the political system. When these patterns of informal organization

[14] Occasionally, this principle that success excuses all sorts of rule violations is questioned in the Soviet press. See, for instance, *Izvestiia* (December 2, 1960), pp. 3–4.

H. A. IRONSIDE
MEMORIAL LIBRARY

were first discovered, they came as a distinct surprise to many Western students. But by now we are familiar with the recurrent forms they take. Some of these have already been mentioned in this book. In Part Two, for instance, we became acquainted with the phenomenon of "family relations" (*semeistvennost*), which was defined as a protective alliance between the Party and the agencies it supervises and controls. Obviously, *semeistvennost* need not include the Party, but can also be a protective alliance between various governmental agencies, in violation of established chains of authority and responsibility. Another way in which informal organization asserts itself is in the chronic tendency of Soviet administrators to evade managerial responsibility by passing the buck to ever higher agencies. The practice is so endemic that the Party has always considered the enforcement of managerial responsibility one of its most crucial tasks, as we saw in the opening paragraph of Part Three. The reason for the prevalence of buck-passing must be seen in the risks bureaucrats at every level of the Soviet administration are forced to take; in the final analysis, buck-passing is a reflection of the considerable amount of discretion given to administrators—again in the name of *edinonachalie*—as well as of the insecurity they feel.

The administrator's fear of taking risks implies a fear also of making innovations. As in all giant organizations, untested practices are shunned because they may lead to failure; and failure wrecks careers. Routines, in contrast, are safe; the success indicators by which superior authorities appraise the administrator's performance are established in terms of routines. We so much identify conservatism and the fear of innovation with bureaucratic managers that we can readily accept the definition of the "bureaucratic personality" as ". . . people who have a definition of themselves and the world that excludes novelty or change."[15] Soviet spokesmen, however, prefer to regard both bureaucracy and the fear of innovation as deplorable. Their textbook complains about "those who like an easy life [and] are often tempted to use over and over again the methods which were suitable yesterday or the day before yesterday, but

[15] Maurice R. Stein and Arthur J. Vidich, "Identity and History," in Maurice R. Stein, Arthur J. Vidich, and David Manning White, *Identity and Anxiety* (Glencoe, Ill.: Free Press, 1960), p. 19.

which today clearly need to be replaced. . . ."[16] The persistence of such complaints attests the persistence of bureaucratic conservatism in Soviet government. In the political system of the Stalin period, these typical features were reinforced by the severity of the sanctions imposed on those who failed, as well as by the rigidity of Party dogmas. This rigidity could be overcome only in response to emergencies, so that policy-making came to consist of solving emergencies as they came up. A careful study of bureaucracies everywhere might, perhaps, reveal that unforeseen emergencies are at the basis of many or most decisions taken by top administrators. Perhaps their function can be defined primarily in these terms, for, in the absence of emergencies, routines do keep the organization going even without its chief. But, if this is correct, then the commonly accepted notion that bureaucracy rationalizes the affairs of man by subjecting life to established routines becomes more and more unrealistic. On the contrary, rational problem-solving can be achieved only by transcending routine, by taking initiative, by experimentation, innovation, and the breaking of rules. We shall return to this theme presently.[17]

[16] *Fundamentals of Marxism–Leninism,* p. 687. For complaints that economic managers discourage innovation because it disrupts or upsets well-established routines and threatens to decrease profits or output, see *Pravda* (July 2, 1960), p. 1; and *Izvestiia* (July 3, 1960), pp. 1 and 3.

[17] Most students of large organizations would probably agree that innovation and initiative are discouraged, the larger and more complex the organization becomes—since modern bureaucracy favors the routinization of decision-making. Perhaps this is not rationality at all, but a very specific form of rampant irrationality, a species of immobilism marked by growing inability to make meaningful decisions, hence a growing ineptness at solving social problems. It would be extremely interesting to compare the Soviet political system with that of the United States in this respect. Doing this, we might find that the two systems are characterized by different types of immobilism: in the USSR, bureaucratic routinization paralyzes the administrators of the executive agencies, even while the masters of the entire vast machine remain relatively free to experiment, innovate, and make drastic changes in the entire political structure. In the United States the picture seems reversed: Although administrative agencies seem often to be relatively independent of the government, hence free to make policy decisions, immobilism reigns at the top of the political system because the social forces are so evenly balanced or the veto groups are so strongly entrenched that meaningful innovations can only rarely be made. Then again, it might be argued that, in the United States, not even the individual agencies are free to innovate. To be sure, they may be relatively free from central political

Structured Communications.   For a number of reasons all bureaucracies seek to control the flow of various kinds of information by
establishing formal channels of communication.[18] Such channels
are essential in order to provide all subordinates with precisely that
information and those orders they need to perform their functions.
They enable the recipient of such knowledge or commands to distinguish essential and authoritative communications from incidental,
unreliable, or spurious ones. At the same time, formal communications channels are important control devices because they help
determine the subordinates' access to information, to their superiors,
and to their peers. At the same time, they also seek to regulate the
relations of the bureaucratic organization with the world outside.

If the principle of structured communications were carried to
its logical (and perhaps absurd) conclusions, the perfect bureaucracy would be one in which all information essential to the top
hierarchs flows upward in the form of standardized routine reports,
while nothing flows downward or laterally except on a strict
"need-to-know" basis, and all communications with the outside
world are filtered through public relations channels. Even though
this ideal state is rarely attained, all bureaucracies, including the
Soviet government, seek as much as possible to keep their operations and information secret not only from the outside world, but
also from their own personnel. For the hierarchs, secrecy is essential because all power shuns the light of publicity. For subordinates,
secrecy is an important weapon because in many ways knowlege
withheld is a source of both power and prestige.[19]

---

control, and hence seemingly independent; but this independence allows
them only to function as conservative forces, in obedience to the same veto
groups that keep the central government immobilistic.

[18] Here we speak only about the communication of information. For a
discussion of the communication of sentiment within the Soviet system, see
Chapter XIV on socialization.

[19] I should be inclined to explain the conspicuous secrecy-mongering of
the Soviet government as exaggerated bureaucratism. The reasons for the
exaggerated degree of secrecy probably can be found in the traditional political culture inherited from tsarism, in the conspiratorial origins of the
Communist Party, and in the hostility with which the USSR and the outside
world have faced each other. For a treatment stressing only these fortifying
factors, see Walter F. Hahn, *Internal Motives for Soviet Secrecy* (Washington, D.C.: Institute for Defense Analyses, 1963).

Again, it is obvious that the perfect plan of communications channels is not likely to function smoothly. Figuratively speaking, it consists of blocks, barriers, filters, sieves—that is, of devices that seek to keep information from flowing—as well as pipelines, pumps, sprinkler systems, and other machinery for disseminating information. The two kinds of devices contradict each other; and a well-functioning communications system must balance them finely so as to get the right kind of information, orders, and reports to the right people at the right time, despite the many barriers and despite the many temptations to pass on too much, too little, too early, too late, or to the wrong persons.

Since the perfectly balanced communications system cannot be devised, all bureaucracies, including the Soviet administration, are plagued by typical pathological symptoms, jointly known as out-of-channel communications. Every administrator engages in illicit communication for the good of the system, to get things done, to expedite the flow of information the clogged channels fail to carry. In addition, countless individuals tune in on the ever-present rumor and gossip mill, which exists for the sake of individuals—rumor-mongering being a device to get attention or respect, and rumor-listening being a source of information essential for survival and success within the organization. Finally, all bureaucratic organizations occasionally find that some individuals deliberately leak confidential information to selected publics, in order to gain advantages in intra-agency competition and conflict. These and other informal communications habits[20] are so inevitable that bureaucracies often seek to incorporate them in the process of rational management by monitoring out-of-channel communications or even participating in them (for instance, by deliberately planting rumors or leaking information). One of the important functions of the Communist Party in the Soviet Union is to perform this monitoring service; the Control Commission, the security police, and the press also play their parts in this activity.

[20] A persistent phenomenon of this kind is the political joke, which the regime regards as illicit and offensive, because jokes are filled with the spirit of negativism, destructive criticism, and hostility. Insecure rulers cannot afford a sense of humor, and bureaucratic rulers are inevitably insecure, as Victor Thompson, among others, has convincingly demonstrated.

Expertise. Rationality in bureaucracy furthermore means a striving for expertise. Tasks and the authority to perform them should, in a rational administration, be delegated to persons who are qualified by ability, training, and experience. Specialized functions should be assigned to the experts—a modest version of Plato's wish that the Philosophers be Kings. In the final analysis, this stress on expertise can be reduced to the demand that the recruitment of administrators be based on schooling and examinations open to all, and that their further assignment and promotion be determined by their performance. Both of these desiderata are easily stated, but almost impossible to realize with complete "rationality."

First of all, the principle of basing personnel assignment and promotion on past performance, as well as the more general need for controlling performance that bureaucracy as rational management of human affairs implies, make it necessary for administrative chiefs to inform themselves perpetually about the performance of all their subordinates. To do this rationally—that is, impersonally, objectively, or, if you please, scientifically—bureaucracies must elaborate standards of performance for all the types of work done by subordinates, against which their work can be measured. To find such objective standards is one of the most troublesome problems of bureaucratic management of all types, and the Soviet political system has been no more successful than other large organizations in solving this problem. The task involved here is to reduce complex human behavior to comparable, hence measurable, data; to evaluate, on a comparative and competitive basis, such elusive things as leadership, merit, promise, and success; and to determine, in a vast administrative machinery, individual responsibility for successes and failures. The difficulties involved will be obvious to anyone who has ever had to grade students' essays, helped determine promotions, or participated in the process of picking from among several candidates the one who is to be given an administrative responsibility. In real life, such choices and evaluations will often be determined in part by human factors that have little or nothing to do with past or potential performance. But bureaucratic management must seek to eliminate such "irrelevant" criteria. To choose personnel rationally, it must define performance, success, and failure in measurable terms. All bureaucracies do this, even though those elements of behavior which can be quantified and compared objectively are often incidental, if not altogether irrelevant, to over-all quality of performance and long-range probability of success in attaining the organization's objectives. Still, lacking more reliable criteria, military commanders at times seem to assess the battle-readiness of a troop unit by the straightness of its ranks during parade; public prosecutors are evaluated on the basis of the number of convictions they have obtained; college teachers by the number of articles they have published (I once knew a dean who wanted to be strictly fair and therefore not only counted the number of publications, but refined his evaluation of competing professors by adding up the pages of their publications); welfare agencies by the number of cases they have "processed"; agencies of all kinds by their success in cutting costs. Undesirable, and indeed unplanned, behavior results from these definitions of performance standards, because inevitably the subordinate individuals and agencies will strive to fulfill those demands that are the visible and measurable criteria of success, neglecting standards that lend themselves less readily to quantification, even though they may be the more vital goals. Performance becomes mechanical. All efforts are skewed by the exclusive attention paid to trivia. Means turn into ends.[21]

Soviet publications and pronouncements give never-ending evidence that this kind of bureaucratic hypertrophy is built into the entire Soviet system. A typical example might be taken from education. Teachers' success is measured by the number of students passing their courses, just as some universities in our society measure their greatness by the number of students they graduate each year. The fewer failing marks, and the fewer students who have to repeat the course, the more successful the teacher is rated. As a consequence, teachers tend to give passing grades where they

[21] One of the saddest examples of such mechanization of a life process is the massive perversion of higher education in the United States through the urge to find measurable criteria of academic progress. The result has been the "objective" test, measuring many abilities and skills, some of them trivial, but unable to measure wisdom, maturity, or judgment. Yet passing such tests has become the overriding goal of higher education.

are not warranted; or, if the examination is to be given by others, they will cram their students instead of teaching them. When Soviet educationalists speak of "formalism" they mean just this—mechanical, rote methods of memorization that require neither explanation nor understanding. More generally, "formalism" is the perennial and undefeatable urge of bureaucrats everywhere in the Soviet system to comply with the visible and measurable success criteria without regard to the more meaningful goals. In the Soviet school system, the inevitable consequence of formalistic teaching is that secondary school graduates have no real knowledge, no interests, no ability to think independently, and indeed no honesty, because copying and plagiarizing are practiced universally.[22]

Irrationality also creeps into the original recruitment of higher government officials. Previous discussions of elite recruitment within the Party have shown already that it is not possible to distinguish sharply between the rational qualifications for office (such as skill, training, and experience) and the nonrational qualifications, such as loyalty and personality. No bureaucratic organization can afford to recruit personnel, however well qualified, who do not measure up to these nonprofessional standards; indeed, it has already been made clear that personality traits as well as political attitudes help determine the very performance of the administrator. Here, too, therefore, the distinction between rational and nonrational qualifications for office simply breaks down or becomes meaningless.

Part One of this book presented a sketchy survey of the recruitment problems faced by the Soviet government in the first decades of its existence, a period when those few who were qualified could not be considered loyal, while the loyal communists had no professional qualifications; and all this time, with the growing complexity of the administrative apparatus, the need for government officials multiplied with tremendous rapidity. The Soviet government bureaucracy for many years was unable to cope with this problem to its own satisfaction and had to manage as best it could with makeshift solutions. The only possible course for the Party to follow in

[22] For massive evidence of this, mostly taken from the Soviet educational journal, *Uchitel'skaia Gazeta,* see Frederic Lilge, "The Soviet School Today," *Survey,* 48 (July, 1963), 93–95.

these years was to recruit anyone who had any qualifications what-soever. People with professional training were pressed or lured into government service even though they could not be trusted to have any loyalty to the communist regime. Called "bourgeois spe-cialists," they were always suspect and were closely supervised by superiors, colleagues, and subordinates who were members of the Party; they were severely hamstrung by regulations designed to keep them in check; if and when difficulties arose, they were the first to be blamed, and severe sanctions were often meted out to them as warning examples, including carefully staged public trials resulting in death or long prison sentences. Side by side with the bourgeois specialists, the Soviet government service recruited great numbers of people whose only qualification was that they were deserving communists who had demonstrated their worth by their work as members of a conspiratorial revolutionary party. If these Old Bolsheviks were members of the revolutionary intelligentsia, they at least had some higher education. But this alone did not necessarily render them qualified government administrators, even though some of these experienced revolutionaries proved to be extremely capable and at times brilliant officials. But there were never enough bourgeois specialists or experienced Party members. Hence a large proportion of bureaucrats in the new Soviet government service had to come from the semiliterate mass of those who supported the revolution, workers and peasants with hardly any formal education who had little more than eagerness or willingness to qualify them for service in the bureaucracy. Special schools and speed courses were created for the purpose of giving the masses, especially the industrial working class, the rudiments of a higher education; and many a high official serving the Soviet government today received his formal training in these "workers' faculties" or similar institutions. The purges of the 1930s and the devastations of the war helped to postpone the time when a new generation of Soviet citizens could at last be raised, the new Soviet intelligentsia whose ranks might for the first time yield sufficient numbers of persons in whom profes-sional and political qualifications might be combined. There is no doubt that this goal has by now been reached.

Today, Soviet bureaucratic agencies recruit their personnel in a manner similar to that used by government and corporate bureaucracies in the West. They can rely on the system of schools and universities to provide specialists in all possible fields; and the public school system is therefore the chief—in fact, virtually the only—reservoir from which new civil servants are recruited. Since all schools and universities are operated by the government, the school system can be carefully geared to the demands made by the various government agencies, so that the number of graduates as well as their curricula correspond to the specifications of the bureaucracy. This system never works perfectly, since the requirements of the administration may change more rapidly than the time it takes to give proper professional training; hence by the time a year's crop of specialists is graduated, its services may no longer be required, whereas specialists of a different kind, who are needed urgently, have not been produced by the school system. Still, to the extent that planning is meaningful in the production of experts, the system works quite well. In addition to relying on the general network of schools, some agencies, such as the armed forces and the Ministry of Foreign Affairs, have schools directly under their own jurisdiction. These may vary greatly in level. They include military cadet schools providing primary and secondary education to prospective army and navy officers, high-level academies, and a great variety of in-service training programs.

Little is known in the West about the actual work of the Civil Service Commission, which has usually been a cabinet-level agency of the government. No generalizations can be made about promotion practices, job security, and the rate of mobility from one agency to another, though in a thorough study of the Soviet administration all these questions would have to be studied. Nor can we make meaningful statements about the status of the government servant within the community as a whole. Such statements would make little sense because virtually everyone not a worker, a peasant, or a professional party official must be considered an employee of the government bureaucracy. The bureaucracy coincides with virtually the entire white-collar population. Perhaps the only relevant observations that should be made here are some impressions concerning relations within the ranks of the administrators: These relations seem to be governed by two principles which are obviously in conflict with each other. On the one hand, the status pyramid of Soviet officialdom seems, if anything, even steeper than the exceedingly steep pyramid along which elite strata in the West are arranged; if this statement is incorrect, then at least the *appearance* of sharp stratification is greater, because official rhetoric gives more open recognition to the need for status and rank differences. Rank-consciousness, deference to superiors, sharp gradations in pay scales—these and other symptoms of stratification are acknowledged and justified more openly in the USSR. Moreover, since the government bureaucracy coincides with the society as a whole, there is a greater convergence of the social with the official status scale than in Western societies. On the other hand, the growing importance of professional specialists as decision-makers and their recruitment into the hierarchy of administrative chiefs, which we have mentioned before, continually tends to complicate the simplicity of the pyramidal structure, as the generalists of the command hierarchy would like to preserve it. Hence the status system itself is in a constant state of tension and flux.

COMPETITION AND CONFLICT

Within the Soviet governmental system, keen competition goes on between individuals and between groups. This statement may surprise those who believe that competition is eliminated under socialism, or that bureaucratization tends to eliminate it. Indeed, when Western social scientists began to study the structure and behavior of bureaucratic management and to formulate criteria of rational administration, competition and conflict were not incorporated into their theoretical models. More recently, however, more and more students of managerial organizations have recognized that competition and conflict inevitably occur in such systems and fulfill important and even necessary functions in making them work. The chief hierarchs within a bureaucracy, too, may deplore competition and conflict within their organization, but, if they are at all sophisticated, will recognize their inevitablity and put them to use. So it is in the USSR, where the architects of the administrative system have made competition an integral part which they seek to foster in a variety of ways.

There is, first of all, a great amount of competition among individuals. It is directly related to the existence of a status hierarchy, or, more generally, of a steeply graded system of rewards, within a society that is relatively mobile. Despite the mobility, room close to the top is very limited. Moreover, sanctions for those whose performance is criticized have in the past been extremely severe. Although this may discourage substantial numbers of Soviet citizens from competing for high rank and great authority, enough people still do participate in the general scramble for promotion that competition appears very keen; and since not even the most highly placed officials are ever really secure, the impression is that it gets keener the higher we look toward the top of the pyramid.[23]

Competition between individuals easily turns into competition between groups. Since the incentive system to which all administrators are subject rewards success and punishes failure, personal competition includes an intense struggle for the factors ensuring success. Therefore, in fighting for his own advancement, every bureaucrat must also fight very strongly for his agency so as to make it strong, efficient, and resourceful. Since there is a perpetual scarcity of the factors (material, personnel, jurisdiction, latitude of decision-making, assignments that can be attained, inside information, etc.) that make an agency competitive, the personal interests of administrators tend to convert bureaucratic agencies into interest groups and lobbies. One of the surprising effects of this situation is the importance of *bargaining* as an essential and ever-present feature of the administrative process in the USSR (which therefore is a thoroughly political process as well). The stakes of the bargaining process we

---

[23] In his recent book on bureaucracy, *Modern Organization,* Victor Thompson observes the perpetual insecurity of hierarchs, owing to the great contrast between authority and ability; from this he derives their tendency to insist rigidly on the prerogatives of rank and to make the status pyramid ever steeper.

have just mentioned. The partners who become involved in it include subordinates and superordinates, controlling agencies, competitors, suppliers, customers, trade unions, and the representatives of local government. Because of its importance, bargaining has led to the emergence of a profession which is not officially acknowledged as existing; its members are not on any agency's table of organization. This is the profession of the full-time bargainer, who is called "pusher" (*tolkach*) in Soviet parlance. On the payroll of his organization, he may be listed as a bookkeeper or a doorman or in any other way; but his function is to act as contact man, to keep his eyes and ears open, to cultivate good public relations in those places where they count most. In short, the *tolkach* is a combination lobbyist and salesman. His very existence demonstrates the excessive clumsiness and immobility of giant bureaucratic government.[24]

Seen in this light, competition among the various organizations composing the government administration appears like a perversion or an abuse which serves personal aims and frustrates the goals of the system as a whole. But in fact it is promoted and organized by the regime itself, in line with a broader effort to ensure all citizens' cooperation, educate them for teamwork, and promote their creativity. By encouraging different agencies to compete with each other in a great variety of ways, the party obviously wishes to appeal to group loyalties and put them into the service of the entire community. Moreover, a material basis is given to such group loyalties by the practice of letting all the members of a successful agency share to some extent in the financial and psychological rewards that

[24] "An important development in corporate dealings with the 'institutional' customer is the rising role of the intermediary. These are not individuals and businesses in the chain of distribution but in the chain of contact and influence. Some intermediaries simply become employees of corporations. . . . Other people act as free-lance agents bringing together buyer and seller for a fee—the 5 per-centers or influence peddlers. One cannot say categorically that their activities are mischievous, but neither can one take a purely benign view of such tenuous relations between producer and consumer." (Wilbert E. Moore, *The Conduct of the Corporation* [New York: Random House, 1962], p. 268.) Professor Moore in this statement might be describing the *tolkach;* and his ambivalent appraisal of that role echoes the mixed feelings this phenomenon engenders among Soviet leaders.

go to the successful. Recognition as well as censure are given to teams and organizations as much as to individuals; one of the most characteristic features of the Soviet educational system is the emphasis it lays on teamwork, the care with which it organizes work, play, and other activities so that they are carried out within and for a group—the "collective," as all teams and organizations are called. Group competition thus is an essential part of that "socialist emulation" which Lenin built into the workings of Soviet society to serve as the necessary incentive until a truly collectivist breed of men with a higher communist ethic could be reared.

Yet this planned competitiveness coexists with unplanned and unwanted group conflict; and it may well be that the spontaneous struggles are both more frequent and a more intrinsic part of the social system than competition promoted by the Party. Behind all the plans and all the coordination which seem to face the observer, perennial conflicts of interests may be dividing not only the social fabric, but indeed the fabric of the governmental organization itself. The Soviet administration, in other words, may be racked by the struggle of interest groups. And this competition not only undermines the bureaucratic order which the hierarchs seek to maintain, but also may lead to more serious malfunctions—planlessness, bottlenecks, "family relations," localism,[25] and corruption.

The prevalence of such "irrational" behavior demonstrates the strong urge toward interest-group formation within the Soviet administrative machinery. And yet we must speak about such groups in a rather hypothetical tone, for two reasons. One is the great danger of being misunderstood concerning the implications of group conflicts within the Soviet system. Interest groups are a phenomenon familiar to students of constitutional-democratic societies, and many such students would automatically conclude that their presence implies a democratic system. But this is a hasty conclusion. Their existence in the USSR does not mean that they interact in the same fashion and through the same political structure as in Western countries. Even the prevalence of competition and bargain-

[25] Localism *(mestnichestvo)* is the perennial tendency of Soviet officials to act in such a fashion that their local interests are satisfied, even at the expense of broader national interests.

ing does not necessarily indicate the existence of democratic processes as they are understood in the West. In short, attributing
interest groups and interest conflicts to the Soviet system does not
imply that the USSR is in any essential respects similar to the
United States. If we destroy false notions about the Soviet Union
as an allegedly monolithic command structure completely controlled
by the Party bosses and marked by central planning from above and
blind obedience from below, we do not then have to assume naively
that the only alternative to such an unreal political order is the
democratic model. The existence of interest groups, of competition
and bargaining, means that within the Soviet administration there is
politics. But this is bureaucratic politics which deviates considerably from Western notions of democracy. Bargaining and
politics in the USSR go on within the framework of a set of goals
which a recognized central authority has determined, whereas in
the United States and similar political systems there is no central
authority. Government in the United States provides no goals;
it is no more than an arbiter or broker in conflicts of interest. In
short, the Soviet political system contains an institution (the Party)
which claims to know the public interest. In the United States none
dares make this claim—or none gets away with it unchallenged.

The other reason why we should speak with hesitation about
interest groups in the USSR is that they are extremely difficult to
identify. The temptation to speak about allegedly identifiable groups
on the basis of grossly insufficient evidence has been too great for
many people writing in this field. Groups are difficult to identify
because their formation is the result of a great number of determi-
nant factors. For one thing, even without knowing very much about
Soviet politics, we are entitled to assume that monolithic unity has
never been more than an unattainable goal and that, instead of
reaching it, Soviet bureaucracy has been faced by the same conflicts
that all large administrative structures face—between specialists and
generalists, staff and line, field agencies and central headquarters.
Nothing more need be said about the structural consequences
of the personal competition among top-ranking administrators
and the resulting struggle for control of the success factors. But

we might place this competition in another perspective by linking it to the political control system created by Stalin. In a previous chapter this system was described as a bureaucratic division of powers. Stalin, we saw, attempted to secure himself against potential rivals by creating an administrative machine characterized by a multiplication of overlapping authorities which controlled each other, competed with each other, and often duplicated each other's work. Hence jurisdictional fights over control of different administrative areas were endemic in the Soviet administration; the questions of who was to carry out any one particular policy or who was to control the limited resources was always controversial. It must be understood, finally, that such jurisdictional conflicts are inevitably linked with policy disagreements, because control over scarce resources spells the ability to commit them for specific purposes. And here, by a devious route, we have returned to the trite observation that group formation is inevitable in a complex society where limited resources must serve an infinite variety of socially accepted tasks.

All policy disputes, as well as simple jurisdictional squabbles, must ultimately reach the Communist Party and be carried out within it. Hence bureaucratic interest-group politics is likely to be linked to policy conflicts within the highest boards of the Party command. Both are therefore also inextricably intertwined with the fierce personal power struggle among the political and bureaucratic leaders.

The resulting image of the group structure of Soviet politics is exceedingly complex and vitiates any attempt to divide the Soviet political system into a simple set of easily defined groups. It may make some limited sense to talk about the military elite, the industrial managers, the atomic scientists, the legal profession, or a host of other professional groups as identifiable interests; again, it may be true that there are identifiable groups based on ties of loyalty to individual leaders—a Khrushchev faction, a Molotov faction, perhaps even a Gomulka lobby; and this semifeudal kind of bureaucratic vassalage may reach deep down to the very grass roots of the system. Such loyalties and cohesions may indeed exist, but without doubt they are complicated and made tenuous by a multiplicity of divergent loyalties and interests. Just as, in the West, the very real solidarity felt by all officers of the armed services may be undermined by the fierceness of interservice rivalries, or the *esprit de corps* of all army generals by the conflicts between the spokesmen of artillery, armor, special forces, and the like, so also we can expect all Soviet bureaucrats to be guided by many divergent interests—professional, ideological, personal, temperamental, local, and others. In short, we should beware of any Kremlinologist's simple scheme of dividing the Soviet administration into easily identifiable interest groups. We know they must exist, but we cannot know their structure and composition.[26]

One final problem adds to the difficulties we have in analyzing the group structure of Soviet politics: the reluctance with which the spokesmen of the Soviet system themselves discuss it. In this respect, they are conforming to the ideological dogma of the unshakable, monolithic unity of their system.[27] This very dogma is a typically bureaucratic attitude shared by hierarchs in many other giant administrative structures. All bureaucrats find it difficult to recognize the pluralism reigning in their administrative empire, because the actual heterogeneity and the polycentric autonomy of the various substructures fly in the face of the monocratic principle to which they are so thoroughly committed. Pluralism thus is regarded as a perversion of sound bureaucratic practice. Competition, conflict, and bargaining processes are considered illegitimate and must therefore be carried on surreptitiously. This unwillingness or inability to recognize the importance of "informal organization"

[26] Consequently, statements made by Western observers who interpret changes in policy or organization as the result of interest-group conflicts must remain speculative, even though they often sound very plausible. For one of the numerous examples, see Harry Schwartz's guess (*New York Times* [December 15, 1963], p. E3) that Khrushchev's decision to embark on a crash program to develop chemical industries was a victory of the consumers' and chemical industries' chiefs over the lobby of armament and steel executives, space program administrators, and the like.

[27] The only concession Soviet writers have, so far, made to the reality of growing heterogeneity in their society is to predict the increasing influence of "societal" organizations in decision-making. For a typical statement, see N. G. Aleksandrov, *Pravo i zakonnost v period zavernutogo stroitel'stva kommunizma* (Moscow, 1961), p. 56.

makes it extremely difficult for the outsider to study the actual workings of any bureaucratic machine. It also creates a perpetual strain
in the organization itself, because it leads the hierarchs to reassert
their formal authority ever more strongly. The gap between the
principles of formal structure and actual functioning tends to grow
wider and wider.[28]

CREATIVITY, OR THE UNITY OF CHAOS AND ORDER

The preceding dicussion was designed to show that features of
irrational behavior, including "corruption," cannot be sufficiently
explained on the basis of personal motives, but are a function of the
competition that goes on within the Soviet bureaucratic system. It
is for the sake of his organization as much as for his own promotion that the administrator hoards material, conceals resources, and
plays the black market, that he bargains, lobbies, engages in empire-
building, falsifies reports, and breaks countless rules that have been
imposed on him. But it is not only his own organization that
stands to benefit from such disregard of rules and regulations. In
many ways, the entire political system may gain from such activities.
For, in general, rules are broken primarily for one purpose: to get
things done, to accomplish those tasks which the regime has imposed
on its various agencies. Or perhaps it would be more apt to say
that violations that are condoned tend to be violations that help the
administrators meet their objectives. Seen in this light, deviations
from bureaucratic norms are a way of making cumbersome administrative systems work through unorthodox, and at times imaginative,
methods. The rule-breaker among bureaucrats often is the innovator, the entrepreneur, the productive and creative individual. Creativity thus can take the form of deviance, even corruption.

Innovation, in all established systems, tends to be disruptive and
therefore engenders defensive, conservative forces. Most often it
is also risky. Innovation through rule-breaking in the USSR shares
both these characteristics. It involves the innovator and his whole

---

[28] For a theoretical discussion of this process, see Victor Thompson,
Modern Organization (New York: Alfred A. Knopf, 1961), p. 123.

"shop" in serious risk, because rule-breaking, as we have stated, is condoned only if it brings results. In the case of failure, it invites serious sanctions; and even if it leads to successful performance, there is always the possibility that the superordinate hierarchs may take credit for the successes won. Moreover, the system, to its own disadvantage, must remain suspicious of unorthodox innovation, because, *precisely if it is successful,* it threatens to upset the routinized channels, procedures, and structures to which the masters of the entire machine are so deeply committed.

This fruitful tension between bureaucratic principles and their violation can be observed in another of its manifestations when we examine the general structure of the government administration and the individual hierarch's position within it. One phenomenon often noted by students of Soviet government is the multiplicity of controlling agencies to which any one Soviet bureaucratic office is subjected. Any administrator, on any level and in any specialty, is performing his duties under the eyes of the Communist Party, the political police, the regular law enforcement agencies and the rule of laws in general; he is subjected to financial control by banks and auditors; whatever his work, it will be guided by a production plan setting performance targets of various kinds; his enterprise or office may be inspected by officials of the Control Commission or, indeed, by representatives of the press.

This necessity of having to account for administrative action to a multiplicity of publics is similar to that faced by the official in government or corporate bureaucracies in the West, although the reasons for the situation are different. In the West, we can attribute it to the prevailing pluralistic authority structure of the entire society. Various authorities independent of each other impinge on the administrator's work, and if he is to be successful, he must know how to aggregate the conflicting interests that impose themselves on him. In the Soviet Union, we may, perhaps, speak of an incipient pluralism which, in the long run, might transform Soviet society in the Western image. But this tendency is still counteracted by the sovereignty of the Communist Party. It has been customary, in the West, to explain the multiplicity of controlling agencies as an expression of Stalin's (or the Party's) distrust of all officials, of the urge to heap controls upon controls so as to prevent even the slightest tendencies toward bureaucratic autonomy. Most observers would be quick to add that the proliferation of control agencies has created the jurisdictional fights, the overlapping lines of authority, and the administrative chaos we have already sought to describe. The multiplicity of parallel authorities has generally been regarded as an intrusion of gross irrationality into Soviet public administration. At the same time, most Western students seem to have assumed that this irrationality was a price the Party willingly paid for the tight control the system allegedly provides. This interpretation undoubtedly contains a grain of truth. But it suffers from the same defect as all other theories of Soviet government which overstress power considerations, which think of Soviet politics exclusively in terms of control and jungle warfare. The fact is that the Party aims not only to stay in control, but also to promote certain policies; and it may well be that the proliferation of controlling agencies is a highly rational device, from the Party's point of view, because it not only protects the rulers from bureaucratic autonomy, but also promotes policies that in the eyes of the ruling elite have highest priority.

We shall try to argue in favor of this hypothesis after noting one additional feature of public administration in the USSR which seems to have a highly irrational character: students of Soviet government are in general agreement that Soviet officials, on the whole, tend to be inordinately harassed. The rat race of competition is fierce. The hours spent on duty are extremely long. The demands which the regime makes on officials' time, energy, and ingenuity seem to be chronically excessive. This fact is not altered by the argument that in making such demands on its servants the Soviet administration may not be very different from corresponding bureaucracies in the West. Again, the chronic overburdening of officials can be regarded as one of the contributing factors of the evasive tactics we discussed under the heading of "corruption" and "informal organization."[29]

[29] For a vivid description of a manager's worries and illegal activities, see Vladimir Voinovich, "Khochu byt chestnym," *Novyi mir,* 2 (1963).

The irrational tempo of work typical of Soviet administration, where periods of feverish activity alternate with periods of slack and exhaustion, is another consequence of the same situation.

We have suggested before that these informal and "irrational" practices fulfill the function of enabling officials to meet their performance goals. This proposition should now be re-stated to say that it enables them to meet their *most urgent* or most important performance goals. The Soviet political system, impinging on the individual administrator through a multiplicity of supervisory hierarchies, imposes a corresponding multiplicity of goals, objectives, or standards of behavior on him. Not all of these can possibly be met; in fact, some of these values or standards may at times be in conflict with each other. Adherence to the bureaucrat's objectives and role expectations must therefore be *selective*. Now, as we have observed, the regime tends to punish violations of standards only if they are not mitigated by success; the enforcement of standards is similarly selective. In this sense, the entire administrative system may be thought of as corrupt, because the selective enforcement of general rules is clearly a form of corruption.

But the entire system may also be regarded as a highly rational device for accomplishing the Party's goals without incurring any political risks. That the Party has a multiplicity of objectives we have tried to make clear in Part One of this book. They are formulated and passed down as assignments or behavior standards through a multiplicity of agencies. But some of them are pegged so high, and many of them so contradict others, that any one of them can be attained only by violating some others. In this situation, the responsibility for action rests with the individual bureaucrat. Contrary to the popular image of an official in a planned and centralized political machine, he is not a mere automaton simply carrying out orders. Instead, he is a man endowed with *edinonachalie,* which gives him a surprising amount of leeway for individual initiative, inventiveness, and entrepreneurship—surprising at least for those who believe that the Soviet system does not provide possibilities for leadership and creativity at a level below that of the Party's high command.

Endowed with a good deal of discretion in deciding which of the goals imposed on him by the multiplicity of authorities he must fulfill, and which he can dare to neglect, this Soviet executive should not necessarily arouse our envy. His relative freedom of action spells heavy responsibility. Moreover, since a conflict of goals often forces him to violate some of the commands he has been given, he cannot act without enmeshing himself in violations.

In attempting to minimize the risks he thus faces every time he acts, the successful administrator's most valuable skill may consist in sensing to which of his objectives the Party assigns the highest priority and which standards it is least risky to neglect or violate. In this, too, he is similar to his Western colleague; and just as his Western counterpart may be guided by the actions of professional politicians in balancing conflicting interests, so the Soviet official is aided in recognizing the Party's current hierarchy of values by the professional politicians in his own primary organization. Moreover, while the Party provides political guidelines for steering through a maze of conflicting instructions, the laws and the courts function as legal authorities to cut through conflicting interests. The administrator's greatest danger, apart from general failure, lies in sudden shifts of (political or legal) opinion within the Party, sudden decisions to crack down on some violations that have heretofore been tolerated. At such times, the responsible bureaucrat will feel the full sanctions of selective enforcement.

For the Party, this corrosion of administrative routine by shifting political considerations seems to have the advantage of combining sovereignty in general rule- and policy-making with flexibility in applying the rules. Speaking through the multiplicity of controlling and guiding agencies, the Party can contradict or reverse itself without ever seeming to do so. It can effect subtle shifts in policy emphasis without ever changing any formal decisions it has taken. It can, furthermore, unload much blame for failures and rule violations on the hapless bureaucrat carrying all the risks of *edinonachalie*. Meanwhile, the tasks that have highest priority do get done, because all participants in the system are well aware of the Party's hierarchy of values. In this sense, the entire machinery works quite well precisely because of its seeming inefficiencies—it functions well because it functions differently from the way the planners intended.[30]

It may well be that what has been described above is a system of public management best suited for an emergency administration, i.e., for government of a political system in which crisis is chronic. If this analysis is correct, we might expect the system to become more and more dysfunctional as the USSR becomes a mature and relatively settled industrial society. Still, it may well be that crisis and emergencies are endemic in mature industrial societies because of the rapidity of technological change and the consequent instability of the entire social order. If that is correct, then the synthesis of chaos and order, of bureaucratic rules and their systematic violation, might be a model toward which contemporary government is moving in all highly industrialized societies. Certainly the problems of Soviet government—both the formal Soviet structure and the entire political system—and the patterns of organization and functioning that have been sketched in these pages appear strikingly similar to prevailing patterns of management in all modern administrations, governmental as well as corporate. Indeed, Wilbert E. Moore's model of the business corporation as an administrative system could well have served as an outline for the present chapter.[31]

Having said this, one ought to proceed to asking further questions; but at this point little more can be done than to ask them. If it is true that there are similarities between the Soviet system and

[30] Similar thoughts about the beneficial effect of seemingly inefficient management procedures have been expressed in Joseph S. Berliner, *Factory Management in the USSR* (Cambridge: Harvard University Press, 1957), where informal organization is seen as the life blood of Soviet economic life; also, occasionally, in Alec Nove, *The Soviet Economy* (New York: Praeger, 1961), for instance in his remarks about the rationality of the irregular tempo of work ("storming"); and in Andrew Gunder Frank, "The Organization of Economic Activity in the Soviet Union," *Weltwirtschaftliches Archiv*, LXXVIII, 1 (1957), 104–156.

[31] The principle features of this model are (1) the division of labor, (2) hierarchy, (3) indirect communication channels, (4) codified rules, (5) informal organization, (6) competition, (7) conflict, and (8) "socialism." Wilbert E. Moore, *The Conduct of the Corporation* (New York: Random House, 1962).

bureaucratic structures in the Western world, should one not point out that there are significant differences between various bureaucracies? Indeed, students of administration would point out that there are various types or patterns of management. R. Likert has made an interesting attempt[32] to define four types of bureaucratic systems, according to a considerable number of different criteria. He labels these systems (1) exploitative authoritarian, (2) benevolent authoritarian, (3) consultative, and (4) participative. Without discussing the adequacy of his definitions or the usefulness of his scales (some of them seem to depend too much on highly subjective judgment), I suggest that the Soviet government under Stalin came closest to his first type, and that since Stalin's death it has been moving closer to the second and third patterns. Government under Khrushchev and his successors may be closest to what Likert calls consultative authoritarianism, but includes also some features of the participative pattern. The reader may find support for this assertion in the subsequent chapters of this book.

[32] R. Likert, *New Patterns of Management* (New York: McGraw-Hill, 1961).

Chapter IX
The Council of Ministers

When a Soviet citizen speaks about "the government," chances are that he means the Council of Ministers[1] and the sprawling system of agencies directly subordinate to it. Within the entire system of governmental institutions which comprise the managerial part of the political structure of the USSR, the Council of Ministers is the leading organization in only one of the two most important branches. It corresponds to what in American politics would be called "the administration," the other main branch of government, if we may call it this, being the legislature. In form, the Council of Ministers and its dependent institutions are created by and dependent on this representative branch of government—the soviets—which in theory constitutes the heart of socialist democracy in the USSR. But in fact the Soviet citizen's language usage is correct, because the Council of Ministers is indeed the organ that carries the bulk of those burdens which we have called managerial or governmental.

The Council of Ministers consists of a Chairman, some First Deputy Chairmen and Deputy Chairmen, about a dozen Ministers, a somewhat larger number of Heads of various other cabinet-level agencies, and, *ex officio,* the fifteen Chairmen of the Councils of Ministers of the constituent republics of the USSR. It is appointed by a decree of the Presidium of the Supreme Soviet; the Council of Ministers is therefore a creation of the Soviet parliament. Some, but by no means all, of its members are deputies in the Supreme

---

[1] Before March 15, 1946, Ministries were called People's Commissariats, and the "government" we are now discussing bore the name of Council of People's Commissars. See p. 118.

Soviet; there is no recognition of the principle of a division of powers which might prevent outsiders from addressing the Supreme Soviet, if these outsiders are cabinet officers. The formal dependence on the representative assembly is largely fictitious. In practice, the Council of Ministers is responsible to none—or certainly to no constitutional authority. Its actual responsibility is to the Party, and that means in practice to the Central Committee and its Presidium. The place of the Council of Ministers in the central administration might be clarified if we compared the Presidium of the Central Committee to the Cabinet in the British system of government; in this analogy, we would then have to see the Council of Ministers as the gathering of the highest permanent civil service personnel, the permanent Under-Secretaries. And, in fact, the Council of Ministers is composed very largely of career specialists who have risen in the civil service. Politically they are often no more significant than the highest career civil servants in Western political systems. Few members of the Council of Ministers hold high rank in the Party, as we have noted.

Obviously, also, this body of fifty to sixty members is much too large to function as a deliberative body. There have been repeated moves to create an inner cabinet. The last of these was the Presidium of the Council of Ministers, created in 1953.

RESPONSIBILITIES OF THE COUNCIL OF MINISTERS

The Council of Ministers, then, is the peak of the administration. It has final authority in the organization of all ministries and other cabinet-level agencies and is therefore responsible for the structure of the executive branch, if we may call it that. But it also is the principal source of legislation in the Soviet Union. First of all, the Council of Ministers is charged with the task of drawing up the national economic plans—from those covering five, seven, ten, or fifteen years to the shorter-range annual and semi-annual ones. These plans assume the form of law once they are passed by the Supreme Soviet, but may in fact be binding on the citizens before this formal act. In all fields of endeavor, indeed,

the Council of Ministers is in the habit of preparing laws which
are often published as "drafts" and in that state go into effect at
once, possibly long before the Supreme Soviet has had a chance
to "pass" or ratify them. Much legislation, or what must be regarded
as such, does not take the form of laws or draft laws at all, but is
published by the Council of Ministers as decrees (*postanovleniia*)
or orders (*rasporiazheniia*). Such executive acts can be issued on
the authority of laws which leave details to the discretion of the
executive. The Supreme Soviet or its Presidium has the right to
veto them but has never done so. Some of these decrees and
orders are classified and are not made public; they are legally
binding, nonetheless.

The importance of the Council itself lies primarily in its law-
making function. The administration or execution of these laws
is the task of the individual ministries and other cabinet-level
agencies (State Commissions) whose heads belong to the Council
of Ministers. It is also the task of the fifteen Socialist Soviet Republics constituting the Soviet Union. The fact that their "prime
ministers" belong to the All-Union Council of Ministers *ex officio*
symbolizes the subordination of the constituent republics to the
federal union and entitles us to consider them, at least in part,
as executive agents of the central government. We shall return
to this last point in a more detailed discussion of Soviet federalism.

For the sake of convenience, the ministries and boards of the
central government might be divided into two categories—those
dealing primarily with economic matters and all others. For most
of the noneconomic ministries and state commissions, institutions
analogous in jurisdiction and functions can be found in Western
(and especially Continental European) cabinets. They include
the ministries of Foreign Affairs and Defense, the tasks of which
need no elaboration. They would include also the Ministry of the
Interior, which, like its Continental counterparts, organizes the
police and fire protection force and registers the population and
its changes in birth, marriage, death, and residence. In the British
government, the analogous cabinet agency is called the Home

Office. The Ministry of Finance also has its counterparts in non-Soviet political systems. It functions as the nation's treasury department and tax collector, and shares budget-making functions with such additional cabinet-level agencies as the State Bank, The State Economic Council (Gosekonsovet), and the State Planning Commission (Gosplan). An important agency attached to the Council of Ministers is the Commission of Soviet Control, which functions as a general inspectorate. Lenin created it in 1920, under the name of People's Commissariat of Workers' and Peasants' Inspection (abbreviation: Rabkrin), for the purpose of promoting administrative efficiency and curbing red tape and other bureaucratic abuses. It has since changed its name several times but retained its functions. Its head has usually been an experienced Party leader of the highest rank. In November 1962 it merged with an analogous institution of the Communist Party Central Committee.[2] Finally, we might include among the most important noneconomic ministries the Central Statistical Administration, the task of which need not be explained further, and the Ministry of Higher Education, which is directly in charge of all institutions of learning above the level of secondary schools. At various times in the history of the USSR, other activities have been elevated to cabinet rank or demoted to the status of a department within an existing ministry. An example might be the Civil Service Commission, which at times has existed within the Ministry of Finance, while at other times it has been directly subordinate to the Council of Ministers. One additional noneconomic agency deserving of mention is the Committee for State Security (KGB)—the political police of the regime. It too has undergone frequent changes in organization and name, as we shall see in Chapter XIII, devoted entirely to the role of the political police in the Soviet system.

Among the ministries and boards dealing with economic problems, some are general planning and service organizations: the State Planning Committee, the State Economic Council, the State Bank, the State Scientific and Economic Council, the State Commission for Foreign Economic Relations. Other ministries and

[2] See p. 168 above.

commissions exert control over specific branches of the economy, such as the merchant marine, railroad communications, mining and resource conservation, power station construction, shipbuilding, atomic energy. Their very names remind us of regulatory agencies in the federal government of the United States, such as the commissions dealing with aviation, telecommunications, interstate commerce, securities exchange, and so forth. But the similarity of names may be deceptive. At least some of the agencies of the Council of Ministers operate rather than regulate. The Ministry of Merchant Marine operates the commercial fleet; the Ministry of Railroad Communications runs the railroads; the Ministry of Postal Service and Telecommunications manages post offices and telephone exchanges. These ministries, at least, are more similar therefore to such agencies as the Tennessee Valley Authority, which operates its power stations, or the Atomic Energy Commission, which is in the business of producing fissionable material. They are thus analogous to public corporations.

Until some years ago, all economic ministries had direct managerial functions for entire sectors of the economy. The number of these ministries was far larger than it is today; for each branch of industry or production, there was a ministry. It was as if there were, say, a Secretary for Chemical Industry in the United States President's cabinet who had complete control over DuPont, Dow Chemical, Union Carbide, and all other chemical industries, large or small, in the entire United States. Until May 1957, the list of ministries dealing with branches of the economy read like an economist's chart of the country's principal lines of production. These ministries included the following:

Aviation industry	Power stations
Merchant marine	Agriculture
Defense industry	State farms
Railroads	Grain products
Radio engineering industry	Automobile industry
Shipbuilding	Machine building
Transport construction	General machine building
Chemical industry	Heavy machine building

Medium machine building[3]

Instrument-making and automation devices

Machine tool and appliance industry

Constructional and road machine building

Oil industry enterprise construction

Power station construction

Tractor and agricultural machine building

Transport machine building

Electrical engineering industry

Paper and wood products industry

Urban and rural construction

Light industry

Lumber industry

Oil industry

Meat and dairy products industry

Food products industry

Construction materials industry

Fish industry

Construction

Metallurgical and chemical industry enterprises construction

Coal industry enterprises construction

Coal industry

Nonferrous metallurgy

Ferrous metallurgy

The list was always subject to frequent changes. Like giant corporations, most of these ministries, in turn, were divided into divisions (*glavki*) dealing with various branches of the industry. Under the command of each *glavk* were enterprises or combinations of enterprises, some of the largest ones being designated as *trusts* or *kombinaty*. Directly or indirectly, therefore, all enterprises were subordinated, in a straight line of command, to the minister in charge of a particular branch of production.

PROBLEMS OF ORGANIZATION OF THE COUNCIL

The proliferation of ministries within the cabinet, which resulted from this tendency to have a cabinet-level agency for every major branch of the economy, became most pronounced in the late 1930s. Undoubtedly, it divided the management of the country's vast economic empire into more manageable administrative units[4] and may also have put production experts from the various production branches more directly in charge. At the same time, such a multiplication of cabinet posts created problems of coordination

[3] This name probably conceals an agency managing the production of nuclear weapons.

[4] See Merle Fainsod, *How Russia is Ruled,* 1st ed. (Cambridge: Harvard University Press, 1959), p. 332.

that must at times have become overwhelming. Each bureaucratic agency sooner or later became an interest group of its own—a pressure group engaging in bureaucratic imperialism, considering other ministries as its rivals and in many ways working against the joint interest of all, the public interest, as defined by the Party. Hence the need for coordination grew apace with the proliferation of ministries. One method of achieving it was to create, within the unwieldy Council of Ministers, an inner cabinet or supercabinet. The first such body was the State Committee of Defense, created after the beginning of the German invasion of Russia. It consisted of those ministers, then still called People's Commissars, who were also highest-ranking party members, in short, the Politburo ministers. This Defense Committee was dissolved after the end of the war, but a similar inner cabinet was created in 1953, after Stalin's death. It was called the Presidium of the Council of Ministers, and it consisted of the Chairman and the Deputy Chairmen. We do not have sufficient information to conclude whether it ever functions as regularly as did the wartime Defense Committee. Another device for mitigating the proliferation of ministries was a reversal of the trend: the reduction of ministries by a process of consolidation. This was attempted repeatedly, at times with timidity and at other times with boldness, but always led again to the multiplication of cabinet-level agencies.

In May of 1957, however, a more thoroughgoing reorganization of the cabinet, which was more than just a reduction in the number of ministries, was undertaken. In effect it amounted to their almost complete abolition in anything except name—and in many cases even the designations were changed. In today's Council of Ministers there are only about 15 ministries and about 20 boards or commissions.[5] These new economic ministries and commissions are supposed to function primarily as planning and coordinating boards and as inspectorates. They are to regulate rather than operate the branch of the economy over which they have jurisdiction.[6] They have therefore diminished significantly in both size

[5] In 1964, six of the commissions were once again redesignated as ministries, and one additional ministry was created.

[6] For a definition of their functions, see *Spravochnik Partiinogo Rabotnika,* Issue 3 (1961), p. 264.

and power. A wholesale transfer of many of their personnel into new managerial organizations (to be discussed later) accompanied this redefinition of their task. No attempt will be made here to understress the differences between a private or corporate economy and one that is nationalized and centrally planned, yet it seems clear that in their function the economic ministries and boards in the Soviet Council of Ministers have come closer to the regulatory agencies of the United States Government. We can assume that the tasks of the ministries, under the present scheme of organization, include at least the following: (1) The ministry's function is that of coordinating the activities of enterprises in a given branch of the economy. Coordinating probably includes such matters as setting standards and specifications of production, providing efficiency experts and troubleshooters, giving directives on price policy, collaborating with other agencies in determining standards of safety and other problems of labor relations. In short, the ministry performs many of the functions which in the West are carried out by the trade associations and cartels or by the governmental regulatory agency. The difference between the Soviet ministry and these Western institutions lies not in what is done, but in how it is done—not in what decisions are taken but in how they are arrived at. The cartel makes decisions on the basis of agreement among the members; the regulatory commission makes rules on the basis of public policy and industry pressure (lobbying). In the Soviet ministry, industry-wide agreement and articulation of interest from below are undoubtedly taken into consideration; but much greater weight is likely to be given to public policy as formulated by the Council of Ministers and the Party's Central Committee. The Ministry therefore is a more authoritative institution than the trade association or even the regulatory commission which, in the American political system, proverbially is prone to be dominated by the very interests it is set up to control. Moreover, the amount of regulation and the intensity of control which the Soviet ministry can impose on its industry is very much greater than that exercised by a regulatory commission in the United States. (2) At the same time, the ministry undoubtedly does act as a lobbyist or spokesman for the entire industry within the Council of

Ministers. Of course, the interests it defends differ from those that are important to corporate business in the United States, and the bargaining process in which the ministry is involved as the spokesman for the entire industry must take very much different forms. But still there is some very general similarity in the relationship between the industry, the regulatory agency, and the central government. We have said that the interests defended by the Ministry differ from those of the Western business community, which is interested in obtaining orders, crowding out competitors, obtaining permission to charge higher prices, and other ways of increasing its profits and its power. In the Soviet economy, the aims of the ministry's lobbying activity include such things as greater allocation of scarce material and human resources; lower production quotas; jurisdiction over areas of activity that are also of interest to other industries; and managerial autonomy in a host of problem situations. (3) Futhermore, the ministries have jurisdiction over research and development activities that are related to their particular industry. (4) Finally, they can be expected to coordinate the recruitment, training, assignment, transfer, promotion, and demotion of personnel. In this connection, we can expect them to be directly concerned with curricula in institutions of higher education. This concern, too, is shared by at least some business and professional associations in Western systems, although it may be exercised in very different fashion.

Except for some of the intricacies of Soviet federalism, which will be discussed later, little is startling about the organization of a typical ministry in the USSR. Each ministry is headed by a Minister; it is divided into departments or branches headed by Deputy Ministers or Assistant Ministers. A number of these highest civil servants form a small advisory group called the collegium. When the Soviet government was first created, it was these collegia rather than the ministers themselves which were in charge of the ministries (then called People's Commissariats); theoretically, at least, the People's Commissar was no more than first among equals in the collegium, which he chaired *ex officio*. The effectiveness of this collegiate management of the executive departments seems to have varied from one commissariat to another and from one period to another. At the time of the first five-year plan this collegiate system was replaced by the command principle (*edinonachalie*) which placed the commissar fully in charge of his commissariat. This principle is still in force today, although its abuse has been denounced as an outgrowth of the "cult of personality." A minister today is obliged to consult his subordinates in the collegium, though he is not bound to follow their advice; at the same time, the collegium has the right to appeal against his decision to the Council of Ministers. In addition to the collegium, a ministry may organize a large advisory council or *ad hoc* committees made up of senior civil servants of the staff, together with leading officials from the field. The tendency in the last years seems to have been to encourage more and more such participation by the agencies in the field; and as we have seen already, a sizable portion of the entire ministerial machinery has already been dismantled. In the measure in which the ministry turns from an entrepreneurial command to a regulating and coordinating agency, we might expect also an erosion of the principle of *edinonachalie,* at least as applied to the minister, and hence some strengthening of the influence of the collegium. If this occurs, the ministries may come to resemble American regulatory commissions even in some of their formal structure. Whether this possible trend away from the command principle may also find expression in the noneconomic ministries is a question that cannot yet be answered.

Like any national bureaucracy, a ministry will have a complex staff organization as well as field agencies. The organization of the staff, the number and kinds of departments and subdivisions, will naturally depend on the various activities the ministry is expected to undertake. Nothing further needs to be said about this at the moment. But we shall have to discuss at some length the lines of authority to the field, because they are somewhat complicated, owing to the structure of federalism in the USSR.

LINES OF AUTHORITY IN THE REPUBLICS

The Union of Soviet Socialist Republics is a federation of fifteen constituent republics, the rights of which will be discussed below.

Here it should be noted only very generally that the republics (their full designation is Union Republics) have a certain limited degree of autonomy, which expresses itself in government activity. Each Union Republic, in fact, has a government organized very much like the national government, with a Council of Ministers designated, at least formally, by an elected republican parliament called the Supreme Soviet. Within some of these republics there are so-called autonomous areas inhabited by strong concentrations of minority nationalities; such an autonomous area may be designated as a republic, a territory (*krai*), or a province (*oblast*). All the Union Republics are divided into provinces; within the provinces there are districts and cities; within the district (*raion*) there are towns and villages. On each level, the government is organized in an analogous manner, although, of course, the organization becomes less complex down the scale from the national to the local level; still, the structural similarities are striking. On all levels, there is an elected body called Soviet and an administration, appointed by the Soviet, which in the republic is still called Council of Ministers and on lower levels bears the name Executive Committee (*ispolkom*).[7] At each level, the government (Council of Ministers or Executive Committee) is divided into a number of executive departments or, at the level of the republic, Republic Ministries. And in every case, such an executive department has in effect a dual responsibility. On the one hand, it is responsible to the *ispolkom* or Council of Ministers of which it is a part; and, at least formally, it therefore is accountable to the soviet which has appointed its chief administrator. On the other hand, each agency within a local or territorial government is also subordinate to the corresponding department or ministry exercising corresponding functions on a higher level. This general pattern is complicated by two equally general phenomena. First of all, there are executive departments on various levels below that of the federal union which do not have a counterpart in the next higher government. For instance, there may be functions of a purely local nature for which

[7] From the Central Committee Plenum of November 1962 to the November 1964 Plenum, an *oblast* had two separate soviets, one for cities and industry, another for agriculture.

the district or provincial Executive Committee does not have an administrative organization. In such cases, the local administrator is responsible only to his own Executive Committee or to its Chairman. At the same time, there are central ministries or territorial departments which have no counterpart in lower Executive Committees. Such agencies then work through field organizations that are directly subordinate to the center and have no responsibility to the local government of the area in which they operate. This last pattern of concentration of some of the administrative work in the hands of agencies working directly out of Moscow was very strong before the reforms of 1957, but has been curbed considerably since then, as we shall see.

Some examples might illustrate the way in which local and central governments divide responsibilities between them. In economic production, craft cooperatives and other minor enterprises might be administered and supervised by the Executive Committee of a district or even a town; but an important factory in the same town would be within the jurisdiction of a central entrepreneurial agency—a *glavk* before the reforms of 1957, a territorial economic council today. Its relations to a comparatively small community might therefore be as tenuous as that between a major corporation and its small-town home in the United States. Politically, the town might be more dependent on the large plant than vice versa; or else they might coexist as more or less independent sovereignties.[8] Again, local police forces (called militia in the USSR) will be under the command of a police chief who belongs to the local Executive Committee and is responsible to it. At the same time, he will perform his duties along guidelines established by, and under the supervision of, the republican Ministry of Law and Order and the provincial authorities corresponding to it. In that sense, he must be considered a field agency of the ministry. But at the same time, police troops, frontier guards, or other field agencies of the same ministry may be stationed in the town who are not subject to supervision by the local Executive Committee but report

[8] See Norton Long, "The Corporation, Its Satellites, and the Local Community," in Edward S. Mason, ed., *The Corporation in Modern Society* (Cambridge: Harvard University Press, 1960).

directly to a higher headquarters, perhaps even the ministry itself. Finally, while certain auditing functions may be performed by local or provincial Executive Committees (again under the rules and regulations promulgated by the all-Union Ministry of Finance or the Commission of Party and State Control), both the Finance Ministry and the Control Commission will have their field organizations reporting directly to Moscow and performing functions not under the jurisdiction of the local government.

A pattern emerges here which is familiar to Americans and, indeed, to the citizens of all large modern states: Various administrative tasks are allocated to different types of agencies on an *ad hoc* basis. Some are performed locally; other, more ambitious, tasks are performed directly by the federal government; and some by intermediary agencies. But all the activities of territorial and local governments are subject to the laws, rules, and supervision of the All-Union Council of Ministers. This is a pattern rather similar to that prevailing in France, where the *département* and the town or village have a certain degree of autonomy concerning local matters; but at the same time both the Prefect and the Mayor are obliged to carry out the orders of the central government, so that local government functions as the field organization of the national administration.

In its details, this administrative scheme has changed frequently and is still today subject to much experimentation in the Soviet Union. Within the last decade, the Party appears to have worried more than usual about the structure of national economic management. The problems here are complex. Planning economists have questioned the theoretical framework of the economy, including investment calculations and price mechanisms. The determination of investment priorities has always been a thorny issue. Bold changes in the incentive system have been proposed. In this chapter, we are concerned only with changes in the administrative framework of economic planning and management.

As early as 1953 the Malenkov government made an attempt to reduce the number of central ministries, but abandoned it after a few months. During the following two years or so it tried, again not very successfully, to decentralize economic management by placing production enterprises under the jurisdiction of authorities at a lower level than those under whose charge they had been before. Both experiments were repeated on a much larger and bolder scale in 1957, after Khrushchev had become the chief of the government. We have noted already that he abolished large numbers of ministries and transformed most of the remaining economic ministries of the federal cabinet from production management agencies into coordinating and regulating boards. Having thus stripped the ministries of their entrepreneurial functions, he created regional planning and management boards called Economic Councils (*sovnarkhozy*). Roughly one hundred of these councils divided the entire country between themselves into what seemed to be more manageable economic regions. Within these regions they were to take charge of the entire economy, so that production and exchange within each region might be coordinated. The *sovnarkhozy* thus are managerial organizations directly responsible to the Council of Ministers for the functioning of the economy in a given territory. They were staffed with career civil servants transferred from the erstwhile ministries[9]; but their highest decision-making boards or cabinets appear to be made up primarily of top-ranking industrial executives and the highest Party and government officials of the region. Where the territory of an Economic Council coincides with a province, the pattern seems to be that the provincial Party secretary (*obkomsek*) serves as its chairman.

A somewhat similar reorganization of planning and management took place in the field of agriculture. Here, too, the existing ministries of agriculture seem to have been stripped of some of their entrepreneurial functions and remain responsible primarily for science and education. Planning and production, as well as accounting, were placed under the jurisdiction of territorial agencies covering one or several districts (*raiony*). Their main task, according to the comments of the Soviet press (e.g., *Pravda,* March 24,

---

[9] Other personnel from the ministries was transferred to the State Planning Board (Gosplan), now apparently reorganized for short-range planning. The task of making long-range economic plans were given to a newly organized State Economic Council (*Gosekonsovet*).

1962), is to promote efficiency in the management of farms by manipulating incentives, appointment of suitable personnel, inspection, and agronomic advice. Thus all local farm management will be incorporated in these new administrative units; and the field offices of various ministries previously supervising and coordinating some farm activities have been abolished.

Analogous moves toward decentralization were taken also in noneconomic fields of activity. For instance, the federal Ministry of Justice was abolished in 1956 and Ministries of Justice were set up in the fifteen constituent republics, while the federal Council of Ministers, for purposes of coordination, created a Juridical Commission in the place of the old ministry. Similarly, the federal Ministry of Health now shares more responsibilities with the Ministries of Health of the Union Republics; apparently the republican Ministries of Health deal with concrete health problems, whereas the federal Ministry defines standards of medical care, coordinates, regulates, and guides medical work, passes on drugs, and supervises and inspects medical institutions.

For the national economy, the 1957 reforms created one additional agency: economic councils for larger economic regions, charged with planning, coordinating, and supervisory functions. There were thirteen of these regions in 1957, and in February of 1962, after about nine months of preparatory discussions, they were rearranged into seventeen. The Russian Socialist Federative Soviet Republic (RSFSR) is divided into ten such regions, the Ukrainian republic into three. The remaining four regions comprise the following areas: one region coincides more or less with the Kazakh republic; another comprises the three Baltic republics; yet another the three Transcaucasian republics; and another includes the four Central Asian republics. Like the *sovnarkhoz,* such a regional council is administered by career civil servants, presumably from the old economic ministries; the highest-ranking of these specialists have appointments as Deputy Chairmen. The Chairmanship itself is held by top-ranking regional government or Party leaders. To express this in the terminology of Western politics: the administrators are career civil servants, experts in their special fields, whereas the final decisions are made by political appointees. We can no more than surmise the functions of these regional boards. Apparently they are supposed to coordinate and supervise the work of the *sovnarkhozy* (see *Pravda,* February 23, 1962).

The decentralization measures of 1957 apparently did not work satisfactorily. By 1960 a process of "recentralization" began which mitigated some of the reforms. Some planning and management functions reverted to national authorities in Moscow. Some of the economic regions have recently been merged into larger units, and in the fall of 1962 the number of *sovnarkhozy* was reduced by more than half (from 103 to 40 or 42). The chief complaint about the 1957 reforms seems to have been that the new provincial management councils placed the interests of their territories above that of the nation—as if this could not have been predicted! Yet the spirit of reform and experimentation still is rife in Soviet economic management and in the government administration as a whole, and much of what was created in 1957 has remained.

CENTRALIZATION VS. DECENTRALIZATION:
THE PURPOSES OF RECENT REFORMS

Western observers, in trying to explain these rather drastic reorganizations, have succumbed to the temptation to regard them as moves by N. S. Khrushchev and his successors, first to diminish the power of the central economic-managerial elite and increase that of the regional Party chieftains, and later to correct the excesses resulting from this restructuring. This may indeed be one of the effects of the first reform and may also be one of the motives. In connection with arguments that focus on power struggles within the Soviet elite, one might speculate in addition that the creation of the 100-odd Economic Councils also weakened, to some extent, the Union Republics. But we deprive ourselves of insight into the workings of the Soviet political system if we focus too exclusively on assumed power struggles between interest groups and their leaders. The reforms of 1957 and subsequent years can also be explained very plausibly in terms of efficiency calculations. It makes sense, in a sprawling industrial empire like the Soviet Union, to decentralize economic planning and management once a certain threshold of industrialization has been passed. It makes sense, economically, to permit or even encourage regional coordination and cooperation once the industrial basis for a modern economy has been created and the most pressing shortages of material and manpower have been overcome. Moreover, sending the staff personnel from the ministries into the field not only relieved some of the unbearable bureaucratic glut from Moscow; the reforms also remedied a feature of economic inefficiency that had grown more and more disturbing. This was the tendency for all production ministries to secure themselves against shortages by a policy of vertical integration. "Vertical integration" is the name we give to the effort of large business corporations to make themselves independent of their suppliers by acquiring other firms providing critical materials. An example of vertical integration thus would be the motor car corporation that seeks to own its own iron ore and coal mines, the ships in which to transport these materials, steel mills, rubber plantations and rubber factories, and the like. This procedure is precisely what the economic ministries attempted in the USSR, at times on a most ambitious scale.[10] In order to become independent of other ministries, and hence free from the fear of unforeseen and disastrous shortages, each of the ministries attempted to produce some of its necessary materials, structures, and equipment by itself, even though other ministries had been given exclusive jurisdiction over such production lines. From a narrow point of view, this was essential and beneficial. But from the point of view of over-all economic efficiency in a planned economy straining every fiber to raise the total output, the phenomenon of the farm equipment ministry or the ministry of fisheries operating its own brick kilns or building homes for its personnel or even manufacturing its own motors and machines—

[10] See the Decree of the Central Committee Plenum of February 14, 1957, in *Spravochnik Partiinogo Rabotnika*, Issue 1 (1957), pp. 112–119. See also A. Denisov and M. Kirichenko, *Soviet State Law*, p. 266.

all this was extremely wasteful and had to be curbed. This is at least one of the aims of the reorganization. At the same time, the tendencies to hoard scarce materials and to pursue narrow sectional interests at the expense of nation-wide coordination of effort have, to some extent, simply been transferred from the functional divisions on the All-Union level (the ministries) to the territorial planning boards or the provincial managerial committees. This, at least, is the conclusion that can be drawn from the repeated complaints about localism in the Soviet press.

In referring to these reforms as a series of steps in the direction of decentralization, caution is indicated, especially since some of these steps were later retraced. What is being decentralized in Soviet government in these years is not final authority, but only decision-making (or *administrative*) power. In fact, it may well be that by delegating administrative authorities of various kinds to territorial organizations, the final policy-making authority of the Party and its leaders has been strengthened. Students of public administration would assert that administrative power can be delegated only to the extent that policy-making authority is centralized. At the same time, the concentration of authority at the center may indeed make administrative decentralization mandatory if the whole system is not to go down in chaos, and the administrative machinery Stalin left to his successors undoubtedly was in need of sweeping reforms. On the one hand, he had concentrated in his hands far more decision-making functions than any single chief executive could possibly handle; on the other hand, his method of delegating power had been dictated by fear and suspicion, by security calculations rather than by considerations of efficiency. The result was a swollen control machinery on top of an inefficient bureaucracy consisting of competing and overlapping hierarchies. The entire structure made for a tremendous amount of wasted motion and wasted human energy. Stalin's death might have been seen as the moment in which this apparatus should have been overhauled and streamlined. But the vacancy at the peak of the pyramid of command had to be filled before the administrative machinery could be reshaped. In this sense, those students are proved correct who maintain that centralization (of authority) must precede decentralization (of administration). Khrushchev had to establish his authority before he could tinker with the structure.

Moreover, it might be argued that the terms "centralization" and "decentralization" are not very meaningful to describe the reforms since 1957. Soviet government has always burdened subordinate organizations with tremendous responsibilities and at times with more discretion in decision-making than they desired; yet it has always been jealous to retain final authority for the top of the hierarchy. This situation has not changed at all. What is subject to experimentation is the precise method of decentralization and centralization, the specific functions allotted to various parts of the total organism; and every devolution of some authority away from the center is likely to lead to the center's assuming new and different functions so as not to upset the balance. Hence when managerial authority is passed down to Union Republics and *sovnarkhozy,* the federal government assumes regulatory and supervisory tasks it had not carried out before; and managerial decentralization therefore can be accompanied by new standardization measures and the imposition of nation-wide uniformities in production, reporting, statistics, and other administrative methods.[11]

Khrushchev's reforms might be seen in analogy with secular trends in Western large-scale business organizations. Typically, they were created by ruthless captains of industry who single-handedly ruled the vast corporate empires they created. But as these empires became larger and more complex, autocratic command by their creators outlived its usefulness; and if the creators, like Henry Ford, continued to hold on, their reign at times endangered the very existence of the organization. Their death or their ouster was therefore followed by sweeping reorganizations, including a significant measure of administrative decentralization. To use Likert's terminology,[12] the trend of development in modern corporate

[11] See U. S Department of Commerce, Bureau of the Census, "The Soviet Statistical System: Labor Force Record Keeping and Reporting Since 1957" (Washington, D.C.: Government Printing Office, 1962), pp. 1–3.
[12] See p. 243.

business has been from the exploitative-authoritarian pattern of management toward the benevolent-authoritarian, consultative, and, finally, participative patterns. Such a trend is discernible also in the USSR. The following quotation from a textbook on public administration illustrates the phenomenon:

> . . . the structural evolution in General Motors and du Pont . . . is typical of the distribution of decision making in all expanding organizations, whether public or private. What usually happens is that a strong executive who is both creative and aggressive has made the original decisions which were responsible for the organization becoming large and prosperous, but as it becomes larger, he finds himself incapable of relinquishing either power or decision making to subordinates. He continues to play the game close to his vest, often to the great annoyance and anxiety of his subordinates. There comes a time when he must leave because of internal crisis, superannuation, or death. Group management succeeds personal management, and the decentralization of decision making results.
>
> In General Motors the aggressive organizer . . . was ultimately followed by Alfred P. Sloan, Jr., who introduced decentralized management and is sometimes regarded as the father of the idea which we are emphasizing at this point, namely, the distinction between corporate and operating levels.
>
> Sloan's idea was that the corporate level should not concern itself with operating decisions and details but with high policy on matters which affected all divisions, and maintain supervision over the operating units by means of communication and feedback, ...[13]

To this one might add only that real life is never so simple as abstract principles; and under Khrushchev as well as his successors the principle of distinguishing between corporate and operating levels was violated at least as persistently as in Western administrative structures. One reason for Nikita Khrushchev's removal from leadership quite plausibly may have been the failure of his reforms to provide the Soviet government with a smoothly functioning economic administration.

[13] J. M. Pfiffner and R. V. Presthus, *Public Administration,* 4th ed. (New York: Ronald Press, 1960), pp. 257–258.

Chapter X
The Soviets

Tomorrow is the day of the yearly election of the Well-Doer. . . . Certainly this in no way resembles the disorderly, unorganized election days of the ancients, on which (it seems so funny!) they did not even know in advance the results of the election. To build a state on some non-discountable contingencies, to build blindly—what could be more nonsensical? Yet centuries had to pass before this was understood!
                                                        ZAMIATIN. *We*

In theory, the Council of Ministers is responsible to the Supreme Soviet, just as all lower executive organs are responsible to their respective soviets. Before a discussion of the details of this relationship, it might be advisable to present a brief survey of the history of the institution of the soviet.

BEGINNING OF THE SOVIETS

In October 1917, the Bolsheviks seized power in the name of the Soviets of Workers', Peasants', and Soldiers' Deputies. When, some weeks later, the Constituent Assembly met—the first nationwide representative body the Russian people had elected on the basis of the universal, free, equal, and secret franchise—this gathering was dissolved, again in the name of the government of soviets, on the grounds that the soviets were more faithful representatives of the nation. Soviets (councils) originally were revolutionary action committees formed by elements from among the lower classes (workers, peasants, and rank-and-file military personnel), with a great deal of spontaneity, both in 1905 and in 1917. Very similar grass-roots organizations made their appearance in France in 1789, and in Hungary in 1956. Their flexible organization, or, rather, the anarchic principle built into them, as well as their close ties to the masses of the people, make them ideal organizations of local and regional government in periods of revolution and disorder, when the previous system has dissolved in chaos. Soviets are flexible because they are unstructured, and their personnel is in a perpetual process of turnover—or at least this was true of the soviets at the time of the 1917 revolution. Because of this high rate of turnover, they were as faithfully representative of mass moods and opinions as any organization could be. At the same time, because of their close ties with the poorest layers of the population, these revolutionary action committees tend to show a strongly repressive egalitarian spirit, negative in that it tends to exhaust itself in the mere destruction of the existing social and political structure. In that sense, the representativeness of the revolutionary soviets is limited, too, because what is represented is primarily the spirit of revolt against the previous system rather than meaningful positive aims. It becomes apparent also that the much-praised flexibility of the soviets, their faithfulness in representing or reflecting changes in the mood of the masses, becomes a liability as soon as positive governmental tasks confront the new revolutionary regime. At that point, sensitivity to changed opinions can turn into fickleness which may make it impossible to develop, and stick to, any long-range policies. Hence it may well be that soviets or similar organizations are functional to any political system only in periods of revolutionary crisis. They are symptoms of a system's complete dissolution.[1]

The Bolsheviks' initial attitude toward the soviets was one of suspicion, based on an awareness of precisely this character. As the expression of "spontaneous" mass moods, the soviets were regarded as unreliable by Lenin; and their possible usefulness to the Party was at first underestimated by the Bolsheviks. This feeling of caution was reinforced by the fact that in the first months of 1917 the soviets were dominated by people of the non-Bolshevik Left—Mensheviks and Social Revolutionaries or their followers. To the measure in which these non-Bolshevik forces were replaced

[1] See Oskar Anweiler, *Die Rätebewegung in Russland, 1905–1921* (Leiden: E. J. Brill, 1958).

by greater and greater numbers of Bolsheviks, Lenin and his Party became willing and eager to make use of them for the purpose of maintaining Party control over the masses and channeling their revolutionary energy into directions conforming to Party strategy. The soviets, in other words, became an ideal instrument for completely overthrowing the existing political order and establishing a communist regime.

This positive attitude toward them was fed appreciably by the belief that they could be useful even beyond the purely negative revolutionary tasks. Soviets could serve the Party not only for purposes of destroying the old system, but also as mass organizations for governing the new one. After all, the coming society was not to be ruled by the Party, but by the masses of the people—a dictatorship of the working classes—and this was to take the form of government by soviets. The Party's commitment to these organizations was therefore fortified by a super-democratic rhetoric, in which soviets were hailed as a new and better form of democracy, something like the town-meeting idea applied to the entire nation. Justification for this was found in Marx's comments on the Paris Commune of 1871; in fact, the soviets were described as reincarnations of that commune. When Lenin said, a few years after the revolution, that communism could be defined as soviet democracy plus industrialization ("Communism is soviet government plus the electrification of the country"), he was still expressing this notion.[2]

The initial structure of the system of soviets reflected this commitment to the principles of direct democracy, albeit with some limitations. The most serious limitation, perhaps, was in directness of representation at higher levels of government. During the first two decades of Soviet rule, the voting population elected only the

[2] Echoes of this can be found in Hannah Arendt's article on the Hungarian revolution of 1956 in which she describes soviets in very similar terms. The soviets as an alternative to constitutional democracy seem to appeal to her because they would have spelled the destruction of the communist dictatorship. Otherwise, it is hard to fit her praise of the soviets into her usually deeply conservative views. Hannah Arendt, "Totalitarian Imperialism," *Journal of Politics* (February, 1958). See also her book, *The Human Condition* (Chicago: University of Chicago Press, 1958), pp. 216–217.

deputies in the lowest local soviets. Higher, territorial, soviets were composed of delegates from the lower-level assemblies, so that a ladder or pyramid of soviets existed, each of which drew its deputies from all the chambers directly below it. The top of the pyramid was therefore composed of people who represented the electorate only through several intermediary steps of delegation. It was formed by a national legislature, the Congress of Soviets; and even this body, which theoretically was the sovereign law-making institution, further delegated its authority. Since it was too large and met too infrequently to function as the nation's parliament, it formed a permanent subcommittee to fulfill these very functions. This subcommittee was the Central Executive Committee (TsIK), or, after 1924, the All-Union Central Executive Committee (VTsIK), which came closest to being the equivalent of a national legislature. In its turn, the TsIK delegated its executive powers to the cabinet, which until World War II was called the Council of People's Commissars (*Sovnarkom*). In analogous fashion, lower-level soviets formed Executive Committees (singular form: *Ispolkom*), and these in turn appointed Bureaus composed of the full-time professional administrative chiefs.

Special features of this representative system included provisions for the rotation and recall of deputies. In theory, this was to make the soviets absolutely sensitive to shifts in public opinion. In practice, it became a device for enabling the Party to remove deputies it considered undesirable. The franchise, incidentally, was not equal between 1917 and 1936 (see Chapter II). This inequality was to emphasize or strengthen the proletarian nature of the Soviet regime. Another bow made initially to the idea of the workers' democracy, and to the traditions of the Paris Commune, was the establishment of the collegial principle in administration with which we are already acquainted. Administrative chiefs were to be no more than first among equals within the collegium of their commissariat or lower organization.

A curious attempt to balance the upward and downward flow of authority was manifested in the provision that individual lower soviets were fully responsible to higher soviets, even though the latter, after all, had been created by all the lower bodies under their own jurisdiction. The idea that a government created by the people (or its representatives) should be able to enforce its decisions is, of course, familiar to all students of democratic theory, even when it takes on the radical aspects of direct democracy, as in the writings of Rousseau. But in the revolutionary period the spirit of anarchy was so strong, centrifugal tendencies so pronounced, that this principle of the subordination of lower soviets was at first controversial.

Another outstanding feature reflecting the spirit of Rousseau, and one which has become an integral part of Soviet political culture, was the absence of any division of powers. Soviets, on all levels, were to be the fountainheads of legislation and administration, as well as adjudication. In the hands of this one and only directly representative body all political functions were to be concentrated.

The entire structure of soviets, in the initial years of the regime, strongly expressed the spirit of direct democracy, of rule by the masses. Consequently, Soviet government was plagued by all the tensions and strains that are inherent in such populist theory and practice. The soviets were sensitive to mass moods and to shifts in opinion; at the same time they were easily swayed by small cores of political manipulators. Strong anarchic and centralistic tendencies coexisted within the system. In their policies, soviets tended to be solicitous of the masses; and yet they were instruments of the tyranny of the majority. They were placed in a constitutional order, and at the same time saw themselves as sovereign, and therefore free to disregard all traditional rules of the political game. For all these reasons, soviets as originally created in the throes of revolution were not very effective tools for governing a country, and this fact, together with the efforts of the Party to maintain its own *de facto* sovereignty, explains the very rapid demise of the soviets as organs of self-government. Inherently weak, the soviets were deprived of their initial autonomy by the rules of "democratic centralism," which allowed the small caucus of the Communist Party within any soviet organization to establish its leadership. The same rules of democratic centralism, as well as mere arguments of efficiency and expediency, were used to establish the preponderance of executive over legislative agencies, of central over territorial and local chambers. In short, the Party succeeded in a very short time in taming the soviets into service organizations for carrying out the Party's policies.

We shall omit a discussion of the details of this process; indeed, we shall not deal at all with the development of the soviets during the first two decades of the regime. Instead, we shall sketch the structure and function of these institutions as they emerged from the 1936 Constitution, the basic provisions of which still apply today. Let us begin by examining the manner in which soviet deputies are elected.

ELECTION OF SOVIET DEPUTIES

Soviets exist at all levels of the Soviet political system—the federal Union, the fifteen Union Republics, and the Autonomous Republics; at the level of the region or territory (*krai*), the province (*oblast*), the district (*raion*), and in each town and village. Each soviet is elected directly by its constituents—the national and Republican soviets for four years, the lower ones for two-year terms. The four-year sessions of the Republican soviets do not coincide with those of the All-Union chambers; nor are local elections held at the same time as those for the Republican and federal soviets. The political life of all citizens is therefore marked by frequency of election campaigns. In any normal four-year period, there are likely to be four such events, one for the All-Union Supreme Soviet, one for the Supreme Soviet of the Republic, and two for provincial and local assemblies.

The franchise, which until 1936 was discriminatory and, to some extent, indirect, is now direct, universal, and equal for all citizens over eighteen years of age, with the customary exceptions of the insane and convicted criminals deprived of their citizens' rights by a court of law. All citizens of voting age are eligible for election to local and provincial soviets; for membership in the Supreme

Soviet of Union Republics, the minimum age is twenty-one; for the federal Supreme Soviet it is twenty-three. Deputies are chosen in single-member constituencies. No electoral district elects more than one deputy to any one chamber. The technicalities of conducting elections are in the hands of an election commission appointed by the local authorities—subject, undoubtedly, to the rules of Party nomenclature.

Candidates for election are placed on the ballot as the result of a nomination procedure which, at least in outward appearance, has some similarities to a very informal primary election. Candidates for soviet seats are nominated by various formal organizations or by seemingly spontaneous peer-group associations. The list of groups that may propose an individual for inclusion on the ballot includes the Communist Party and its youth affiliate, Komsomol; trade unions, cooperatives, and cultural societies; and also *ad hoc* assemblies of workers, farmers, employees, and military service personnel. In short, the field seems wide open for the spontaneous expression of public opinion. Once nominations have been made, each constituency will have a conference of representatives from the various organizations that have participated in the nominations game; these conferences result in the selection of one candidate for each constituency. His name alone will appear on the ballot. These conferences can become real debates in which even the public may participate. However, with surprising regularity debate becomes superfluous because, by strange coincidence, the nominations usually are in agreement beforehand. All the various representatives of the public seem to have picked the same individual as the community's favorite son. The reason for this, of course, is that the rules of Party nomenclature are applied in the very nomination process.

Once the candidates for soviet seats have been selected, a nationwide election campaign follows, in which the voters are urged to show their support of the regime and their feeling of identification with the nation by coming to the polls without exception and casting their ballot for the candidates of the "bloc of communists and non-Party people." These campaigns may last as long as two months. Like all such efforts everywhere, they are designed to rise to a higher and higher pitch of intensity and urgency. The climax of the campaign is reached when the Central Committee of the Communist Party issues its platform for the coming legislative period.

The ballot handed to each voter contains the name of the one candidate who has been selected and the organization that has nominated him. The voter elects his candidate by dropping the unmarked ballot into the ballot box. He votes against the candidate by crossing out his name; for this purpose he may wish to step into the voting booth which supposedly ensures the secrecy of the vote. Naturally, the assumption is that only those who wish to defeat the candidate will trouble to step into the booth. It therefore takes courage to vote negatively; and yet, occasionally, a candidate does not obtain the necessary absolute majority (candidates are elected if they obtain an absolute majority of those entitled to vote in the constituency). In those cases of grass-roots resistance, the election is declared invalid and must be held again, after another round of nomination procedures.

It takes courage not only to vote against "the people's" candidate; it takes equal courage not to vote at all—even going to the polls late in the day has been frowned upon by the authorities. Election day is a public holiday, a celebration of solidarity, on which the voters are expected to compete with their neighbors and with other communities in a contest of citizenship and loyalty. The constituency which earliest of all manages to achieve a 100 percent turnout will receive praise and congratulations. How much pride the average citizen takes in such competitive achievement is difficult for us to guess; but for the bureaucrats and party chiefs in charge of the community this may be an important success, indicating to their superiors their leadership capabilities. Even when this interest of the leaders in making a good showing is taken into consideration, the percentage of voters who actually participate in elections is still surprisingly high.[3] Moreover, the number of nega-

[3] Proportion of eligible voters who actually participated in elections for the Supreme Soviet of the USSR: 1937, 96.8 percent; 1946, 99.7 percent; 1950, 99.98 percent; 1954, 99.98 percent; 1958, 99.97 percent; 1962, 99.95 percent. Figures are from N. G. Aleksandrov and A. I. Lepeshkin, *Osnovy Sovetskogo Gosudarstva i Prava* (Moscow, 1962), p. 175.

tive votes has usually been kept to a very small percentage. How accurately the regime reports the election results is anyone's guess. That there may be some juggling of these figures is suggested by the curious fact that the official figures given by the Soviet government for "no" votes in the 1962 election are well below those given by Moscow radio on the morrow of the election day.

NUMBER OF NEGATIVE VOTES

	Soviet of the Union	Soviet of Nationalities
Preliminary figures broadcast by Moscow radio	797,000	1,200,000
Official figures	746,563	464,115

COMPARABLE OFFICIAL FIGURES FOR PREVIOUS ELECTIONS

1958	580,641	363,736
1954	247,897	187,357

SOURCE: *New York Times*, March 18, 1962.

Given the obviously contrived character of the universal turnout and the near-unanimity of most elections, we must inevitably ask ourselves why the regime takes the trouble to set this elaborate machinery into motion once every twelve months or so. Since opposition has been rendered ineffective for decades, why is this annual display of solidarity with the regime put on with such dubious spontaneity? A number of answers can be given; taken together, they might explain it to the reader's satisfaction.

First, the annual election may satisfy the psychological need of the political elite to obtain repeated plebiscitary reassurances that they have the sympathy of the masses. At the same time, the overwhelming majorities may serve to convince many citizens that such sympathy is widespread. A solid mass of affirmative votes confronts the individual doubter or dissenter; and even though he may suspect the voting statistics to be fraudulent, his deviant attitude may nonetheless be shaken by them. In both cases, despite rational awareness that the monolithic unity shown by the vote is contrived, the count of "yes" votes may have the desired psychological impact. Seen in this light, Soviet elections are magic rituals which may be quite effective.[4]

Furthermore, elections might be attempts to gauge popular support for the regime or, conversely, to pinpoint areas of non-support and discontent. Yet, it seems that they cannot be a very reliable or sensitive measure of this. They do, however, provide a seemingly reliable yardstick for something related to this: Election results (both participation and "yes" votes) are a gauge for measuring the effectiveness of the local political machine. The local or territorial Party chief who cannot deliver as many votes as his colleagues may not be in trouble quite so deeply as an American party chairman who fails in delivering votes, because votes are not so vital a commodity to the Communist Party as they are to an office-seeker in the United States. But he is in trouble nonetheless. Lagging participation or an increase in negative votes proves to his superiors that he has been remiss in his educational efforts or that he has alienated his constituency by excessively unpopular policies. Elections thus are examinations in which the educators rather than the pupils receive passing or failing marks. At the same time, elections are themselves educational devices: campaigns attempt to acquaint the people with issues, in however ritual a fashion. They are thus occasions for the regime to explain itself and sell itself to its subjects, to legitimize its rule.

Closely related to this purpose, elections, and even more the nomination process and the ensuing campaign, are designed to give the masses (or at least great numbers of activists among the

[4] Read, for instance, the following incantation (italics added):

"The leadership of the Communist Party over the soviets (so teaches Leninism) expresses itself above all in the fact that through the soviets the party tries to place into key governmental posts its own candidates, its best workers. *In this the party succeeds because it enjoys unlimited confidence among the Soviet People.*

"This circumstance can be seen with particular clarity in the example of elections of deputies into the organs of state power, where the party comes forth not by itself but in an [electoral] bloc with those outside its ranks. *The results of the elections for the organs of Soviet state power demonstrate that almost all voters unanimously vote for the candidates of the bloc of communists and non-party-members.* The bloc of communists and non-party-members is the clearest evidence of the moral unity of the Soviet people, firmly allied with each other in the struggle for socialism." A. I. Lepeshkin, *Mestnye organy vlasti sovetskogo gosudarstva* (Moscow, 1957), p. 28.

masses) a sense of participation in politics. The population as a whole is encouraged to participate in nomination meetings; its representatives get the chance to sit on election commissions and to take an active part in agitational work. Finally, the holiday atmosphere of election days gives the regime an opportunity to display in gay and solemn ritual its symbols of authority and faith. Election day is a red-letter day in the Soviet calendar. It gives the citizens' political life a distinct rhythm. Bureaucratic chiefs use it as a target date for meeting important production quotas. It is thus a day of dedication and rededication, the occasion for solemn confessions of faith and loyalty. The importance of such Holy Days for any political system should not be underestimated.

FORM AND FUNCTION OF PRESENT SOVIETS

Having examined the electoral process in the USSR, we now turn to the soviets themselves. Theoretically, all soviets are the supreme organs of self-government on their respective level, with the proviso that this self-government is subject to the overriding authority of higher soviets. Within this limitation, soviets are supposedly the source of all legislation; they are the fountainhead of all administrative and judicial authority, the ultimate source of all government appointments; and they have the power to review and veto all administrative acts.[5] Yet soviets meet at relatively infrequent intervals and for only brief periods. They are therefore largely inoperative as organs of day-to-day government.[6] For these

[5] This does not mean that legislation and other acts for which the soviets are ultimately responsible must be *initiated* by the Soviet. On the federal level, for instance, laws and other matters voted upon by the Supreme Soviet most often originate in the Central Committee of the Party and/or the federal Council of Ministers, less frequently in the Presidium of the Supreme Soviet. The Supreme Court of the USSR also has the right to initiate legislation, but does not seem to have made use of it.

[6] A recent Soviet textbook proudly claims that all national legislation is made by the Supreme Soviet and then tells the reader that between 1936 and 1960, this national legislature passed "more than 130 legislative acts." (A. Denisov and M. Kirichenko, *Soviet State Law* [Moscow, 1960], p. 215.) If it is remembered that some of this astonishingly scanty legislation is trivial, it becomes clear that the Supreme Soviet is, in fact, not the place where important decisions are made.

purposes they delegate their various powers to smaller committees and to executive agencies.

At the level of the federal Union and the Union Republics, the representative assemblies are called Supreme Soviets. Of these, the national Supreme Soviet alone consists of two chambers, the Soviet of the Union and the Soviet of Nationalities. All Union-Republican Supreme Soviets are unicameral.

To elect the Soviet of the Union, the entire nation is divided into electoral districts in such a manner that any one deputy represents roughly 300,000 citizens. The Soviet of Nationalities is made up of representatives from the country's nationality groups as follows: 25 deputies from each Union Republic; 11 from each Autonomous Republic; 5 from each Autonomous Province (*oblast*); and 1 from each National Region (*krai*). In addition, each chamber contains eight deputies elected by the members of the armed forces. The term of service for the entire Supreme Soviet, as was noted in the preceding chapter, is four years. By-elections are held to fill vacancies if they occur within the four-year legislative period.

The Supreme Soviet as presently constituted was elected on March 18, 1962. This election sent 791 deputies to the Soviet of the Union, and 652 to the Soviet of Nationalities.[7] In their social composition, these two chambers represent a fair cross-section of the population, as shown by the following table. It must be understood, however, that in each of the occupational categories, Supreme Soviet deputies are likely to be taken from the very highest ranks. For instance, most of the 59 members of the armed services who sit in the present Supreme Soviet can be expected to be Marshals, Generals, and Admirals. Genuine workers and farmers among the deputies most likely are people who have distinguished themselves by outstanding work or other highly meritorious service.

A Supreme Soviet usually meets twice a year for a period of a few days, rarely exceeding one week. Each house meets separately

[7] These are record figures, owing to the growth of the Soviet population. Figures for the two previous Supreme Soviets are as follows:

Soviet of the Union:	Election of 1954—708 deputies	
	Election of 1958—738 deputies	
Soviet of Nationalities:	Election of 1954—639 deputies	
	Election of 1958—640 deputies	

COMPOSITION OF SUPREME SOVIET AS ELECTED IN 1962

Party career officials	244
Government administration	220
Military	59
Factory directors	28
Collective farm chairmen and state farm directors	118
Scientists	60
Artists and writers	47
Engineers	14
Teachers and physicians	47
Agronomists	26
Industrial workers	310
Agricultural labor and collective farm peasants	220
Labor union officials	12
Functionaries of the Komsomol	7
Judges and public prosecutors	2
Newspaper editors	2
Cosmonauts	2
Society for Cultural Relations with Foreign Countries	1

and proceeds to organize itself by electing its chairman and a number of deputy chairmen. Each house also appoints a credentials committee to verify the credentials of all the deputies, and a small number of standing committees—a committee on proposed legislation, one on the budget, one on the economic plan, and one for foreign affairs.[8] Subsequently, joint meetings of the entire Supreme Soviet alternate with separate meetings of the two chambers. The joint meetings are held for the purpose of listening to the government's reports and for making appointments or confirming appointments made by the Presidium of the Supreme Soviet. At such joint sessions, moreover, members of the government may answer interpellations submitted by individual deputies. In short, when it meets as a unified body, the Supreme Soviet reviews with inevitable approval the acts of the government during the preceding

[8] S. G. Novikov, *Postoiannye Komissii Verkhovnogo Soveta SSSR* (Moscow: Gosiurzdat, 1958).

months and confirms the slate of cabinet appointees for the subsequent period. In their separate meetings, the two chambers discuss proposed legislation and the government budget. Minor amendments frequently are proposed and incorporated in either laws or the budget. Debate is perfunctory and seems to arouse little interest among either the deputies or the population. Amendments of the budget proposed from the floor of either house appear to be motivated, as a rule, by the interests of the deputy's local constituency.

At the end of the few days' session, a newly elected Supreme Soviet will have achieved the following: It will have created its own internal organization, including the appointment of a Presidium, about which more will be said below. The Supreme Soviet will have approved the reports of the outgoing ministers and confirmed the appointment of a new Council of Ministers. If it is time for a new national budget, it will have passed the budget, with minor amendments, confirmed all laws promulgated during the past months by the Presidium of the Supreme Soviet, and passed new laws and constitutional amendments proposed by the government. The number of old laws confirmed and new legislation passed usually is surprisingly small. Many decisions which in other political systems would take the form of laws are laid down as executive decrees or orders and require no confirmation by the Supreme Soviet.

The Presidium of the Supreme Soviet, at least formally, is an important institution with wide powers. It is to function as a permanent committee of the entire Supreme Soviet, empowered to act in its name, subject only to later confirmation. Much important legislation is promulgated in its name, as we have seen.[9] Honors and awards, too, are presented in the name of the Presidium; and its signature appears under all appointments of ministers and assignments of foreign service personnel to diplomatic missions abroad. Finally, it acts as the collective head of state of the USSR, the Chairman functioning as the individual head of state for certain ceremonial functions, such as that of receiving foreign ambassadors. The Chairman has often been an honorably retired politician of

[9] It takes the form of orders (*ukazy*) or decrees (*postanovleniia*).

high rank, someone we would call an Elder Statesman. But a
recent Chairman, Leonid Il'ich Brezhnev, was in his fifties and still
an active political leader of highest rank when he was appointed
in 1960; he has since attained the highest position in the Communist Party. The man who succeeded him as titular head of state
was Anastas Ivanovich Mikoyan, a veteran politician also of the
highest rank. The Chairman of the Presidium is assisted by fifteen
Vice-Chairmen, who inevitably turn out to be the Chairmen of the
Supreme Soviets of the fifteen constituent republics of the Soviet
Union. In addition, there are sixteen members and one Secretary.

The Supreme Soviets of these fifteen republics function in
analogous fashion. All are unicameral and all have between 400
and 500 deputies elected, like their All-Union colleagues, for four
years. Republican Supreme Soviet elections were held in 1947,
1951, 1955, 1959, 1963, and 1965. Like the Soviet of the Union,
the deputies are elected in single-member districts of roughly
equal size within each republic. Since the number of deputies in
each of these Supreme Soviets does not differ greatly, but the
population of the several Union Republics does, the size of electoral
districts varies greatly from one republic to another. For instance,
whereas about 150,000 voters elect one deputy in the RSFSR, in
the Armenian Socialist Soviet Republic one deputy represents no
more than about 5000 voters.

Soviets on lower territorial levels are correspondingly smaller,
although, surprisingly, those of the largest cities contain several
hundreds of deputies. Like the assemblies higher above, they delegate their authority to executive and judicial organizations. At
regular intervals, they hold brief perfunctory sessions without any
real debate. They mechanically approve whatever their chairman
may have placed on the agenda, listen to solemn declarations of
policy, and then disperse.

Local soviets have developed one institution that may fulfill
more than these parade functions; a group of standing committees
has been established. These have vaguely defined advisory, supervisory, and inspection capacity in such matters as local industry,
local consumer services, road-building, communications, health,

education, entertainment, trade, and the budget.[10] As committees of the local soviet, they consist of deputies, but also draw in other citizens, especially representatives of various civic organizations. They may submit reports to the parent soviet and may offer resolutions, but have no power of enforcement. Hence they can undoubtedly be disregarded by administrators most of the time and may be no more effective than are weak Parent-Teacher Associations against strongly entrenched boards of education. Nonetheless, these standing committees of local soviets are of interest because activists from the community who are not members of the soviets are encouraged and co-opted to work with them. They therefore serve as agencies for socialization and indoctrination and for obtaining grass-roots volunteer work on communal projects. The work of the local soviet may be somewhat meaningful for many citizens because of these committees, just as participation in the PTA or a Mayor's race relations committee may shake at least some citizens in our society out of their apathy toward local government. Yet this does not conceal the basic powerlessness of the local soviets, or indeed of soviet chambers on any level. They may indeed serve as subsidiary agencies for communicating with the masses and giving them a sense of participation, but they do not govern or even participate in the process of decision-making, except in a ceremonial or symbolic fashion. The press in the USSR has frequently acknowledged this by deploring the lack of effective communication between the soviets and their executive agencies. According to these complaints, soviet assemblies are not informed about current administrative problems, policies, and acts. Executive agencies virtually disregard them. They pay no attention to criticisms and complaints offered by the soviets, not even bothering to suppress such criticism. Hence, even the watchdog functions of soviets are severely curtailed in practice.

The question as to why the institution of soviets has continued to be maintained thus arises inevitably; and it is not certain whether a really convincing answer can be given. We cannot assume that

[10] See A. Denisov and M. Kirichenko, *Soviet State Law* (Moscow, 1960), p. 277.

the soviets simply survived beyond their time of functioning and that the Party simply never took the trouble to abolish them because other dysfunctional or obsolete structures have been removed without difficulty or ceremony by the sovereign party. Obviously the Party still views the soviets as a useful machinery. Nor is it plausible to believe that this usefulness lies primarily in the democratic façade the soviets present to the outside world or to the Soviet citizens. The leaders of the Party are not really so concerned about public opinion at home or abroad that they would maintain this elaborate political shell merely for the sake of presenting a favorable image. We might argue, indeed, that the soviets equally serve the function of dramatizing the political disenfranchisement of the population: by meeting only for the ceremonial approval of decisions already taken, by reducing their activities to unanimous resolutions and well-timed applause, the soviets effectively symbolize the servile role of the citizens they represent, and are in that sense truly representative institutions.

Soviet writers themselves stress the role of the soviets as agencies of socialization by regarding them as the most important tools of "drawing the masses into government work," of providing some form of mass participation in public life; and because soviets, somehow or other, take in all the citizens, Soviet spokesmen tend to rate them more important in this regard than such mass organizations as trade unions, the Komsomol, and the numerous other citizens' organizations. They predict that in the coming years and decades the soviets' ability to make the masses participate will increase; that their membership will be enlarged and will rotate more regularly; that soviet meetings will become more frequent; that the number and responsibility of the standing committees will be enlarged; and that the authority of soviets will be strengthened.[11] If and when such changes take place, the Soviet press will hail them as tokens of the democratization of the Soviet system. A somewhat cynical outsider might, instead, observe that the bureaucratic hierarchs in charge of the system have learned to manipulate those

[11] See, for instance, N. G. Aleksandrov, *Pravo i zakonnost v period razvernutogo stroitel'stva kommunizma* (Moscow, 1961), pp. 51–53.

they so contemptuously call "the masses" somewhat more smoothly and skilfully—that the methods of sophisticated personnel management are spreading to the USSR.

In addition, soviets are useful as important sources of psychological rewards and as safety valves for popular discontent. Membership in a soviet is a conspicuous honor for those citizens on whom it is conferred, and the honor is accompanied by some material benefits. The representative assemblies of the USSR are gatherings of Notables without power or influence, but Notables nonetheless; and to belong to them is likely to be a very important status symbol for the individual. Furthermore, meetings of soviets can be regarded as briefing sessions in which the Party, or, more precisely, the government, accounts for its current problems and policies. Finally, soviets do function as safety valves for popular discontent, because each deputy provides a channel of access to the administration for all citizens seeking redress. In a thoroughly bureaucratized political system, where complaint rather than litigation is the customary manner of protesting against alleged violations of citizens' rights, such channels of access can be very important. Apparently, the typical member of a soviet, especially the Supreme Soviet of the federal government, receives a considerable number of complaints or appeals for help from constituents, which the deputy most likely will pass on to the appropriate executive agency. Undoubtedly, this does lead to the redress of some injustices or irregularities; and Soviet political scientists point to the role of the soviet deputy with pride: "The close every-day contact between the deputies and the electorate is one of the most characteristic features of Soviet socialist democracy."[12]

Again, however, the outsider has some reason to be a little skeptical about these claims. There is, as mentioned already, little evidence that the government administration pays much attention to such complaints. Why should it? After all, the deputy has no power to follow through. The effectiveness of this safety valve, moreover, is curbed by additional factors. First of all, certain hardships and

---

[12] A Denisov and M. Kirichenko, *Soviet State Law* (Moscow, 1960), p. 365.

inequities are basic features of the system, and no complaining will remove them. Indeed, the wise deputy will refrain from passing on to the authorities those complaints that attack essential elements of the soviet way of life. Second, many deputies, especially those of the highest soviets, have no roots in the constituency they represent, do not reside there, and have little interest in its citizens, especially since they are in no wise dependent on them for re-election. There is a sufficiently rapid turnover of deputies to emancipate them from their constituencies even more. Thus, even as safety valves the soviets serve only in a very limited fashion.

Chapter XI
Federalism and Local Government

Because government on the local level affords more opportunities for engaging the rank and file of the citizenry, or at least the activists among them, in more or less regular volunteer work, a first glance at the Soviet political scene could give the impression that democracy—or, better, participation—is more meaningful on lower levels of the system than on the higher ones, where participation seems both more perfunctory and more sporadic. It this were true, it would be a strange reversal of the situation prevailing in the United States, where popular apathy in local politics seems to co-exist with a livelier interest in national issues.[1] But it is probably not true at all.

THE SUBORDINATE STATUS OF LOCAL GOVERNMENT

In reality, grass-roots participation in politics seems to be no more meaningful on the local than on the national level in the USSR. It does not appear to have any greater effect on decision-making by the bureaucratic chiefs and does not take the citizen closer to the centers of authority. Nor is it likely to give the individual much more of a consciousness of sovereignty, and thus to satisfy his democratic or socialistic yearning for self-government. Participation in local government seems to be little more than a perfunctory democratic exercise.

This is the case for several reasons. One of them, already mentioned, is that the local executive, although nominally respon-

[1] Whether this is a realistic image of the intensity of participation on the several levels of American politics is a question with which we cannot deal here.

sible to its soviet, actually pays little or no attention to it and functions independently. Soviets and their citizens' committees thus work in a void; their resolutions are cries into the wind. Executive officials can disregard them with such impunity because even their formal dependence on the soviet is a farce: the appointment of an Executive Committee by a soviet is purely a matter of form and at times remains entirely unobserved. Very often, Ispolkom chairmen are appointed and transferred without even having been delegates in the soviet that appoints them, or even without having been residents in the area they are about to administer. This is true also for other members of the local Executive Committee. The entire local administrative staff consists of bureaucrats, belonging to various nation-wide hierarchies, whose assignments are made by their superior personnel officers in consultation with that Party headquarters which has the *nomenklatura* over the specific office. A typical Ispolkom consists of the Chairman, who is the local government head; a Vice Chairman; a Secretary; and several other members. These are likely to include the First Secretary of the local Party Committee and possibly also some of the following: the First Secretary of the local Komsomol organization; the commander of the local military garrison; the commander of the local police forces; managers of the most important local industrial enterprises; heads of the most important departments of the local Ispolkom. In large communities, the Ispolkom, even after the most recent reorganization, may be so large that it develops an inner cabinet, called the Bureau. Whatever the size and inner structure of this local executive, it is clear that this bureaucratic body simply represents the local chiefs of various national administrations, military and civil. The individuals composing this committee are likely to have their roots in the various hierarchies they serve, rather than in the local community to which they have for a short time been assigned. They will regard themselves as officials having a difficult job to do, in which the mere citizen should not interfere.[2]

[2] The formal structure of local government is outlined in A. Lashin, *Mestnye Organy Gosudarstvennoi Vlasti v SSSR* (Moscow: Gospolitizdat, 1955); and A. I. Lepeshkin, *Mestnye Organy Vlasti Sovetskogo Gosudarstva* (Moscow: Gosiurizdat, 1957).

Another fact that renders the citizens' participation in local government more or less meaningless is the lack of sovereignty even of the local executive. Local autonomy used to be so strong in the very early years of the revolution that the country was in a virtual state of anarchy. However, these centrifugal tendencies were curbed during and after the civil war, with the result that local autonomy was destroyed. Government in villages, towns, provinces, and even in the constituent republics of the Union has been transformed into an administrative agency of a strongly centralized bureaucratic state. Technically, this was accomplished by the introduction of the principle of dual subordination for all executive bodies below the all-union level. Every soviet is, formally, responsible both to its constituents and to the next higher soviet. Similarly, every local or territorial executive is, formally, responsible both to the soviet that has, in theory, appointed it, and to the executive agencies of higher soviets, thus ultimately to the All-Union Council of Ministers. Local Ispolkomy are in effect the local arm of the All-Union government; and it is understood that orders from any higher administrative office override the commands given by a lower one. This makes it apparent that the so-called dual subordination of local and territorial administrations is largely fictitious. In reality, their responsibility goes upward in a direct hierarchic line, by-passing the local soviet for all practical purposes.

Matters are a little more complicated for the persons serving as department chiefs within a local Ispolkom, or as ministers in a Republic's Council of Ministers. Each one of these is fully responsible both to his own Ispolkom or Council-of-Ministers Chairman and to the superordinate agencies of his own administrative branch. Once again the ancillary role of local government becomes apparent when we realize that many a member of a Chairman's staff owes his very appointment not to his ostensible superior (the Chairman) but to the specialized administrative service within which he had made his career. This increases the likelihood that heterogeneity and tension will prevail in local and territorial executive branches, which must tend to weaken them further, however omnipotent they may appear to the local constituents.

FEDERALISM

A discussion of Soviet federalism should be inserted at this point because the relationship of the fifteen Union Republics to the federal Union can be seen as an application of the principle of dual subordination. The solutions are intended to accommodate the special problems of a multinational society in which large areas are inhabited predominantly by ethnic minorities. They have been shaped, moreover, by ideological commitments and conflicting political considerations. There had been considerable conflict within the Communist Party, since long before the October Revolution, concerning the principles to be adopted in the treatment of national minorities and the implementation of these principles. Autonomist and centralist inclinations clashed many times. In the course of the past decades, the regime has experimented with a considerable variety of forms and policies. Some of these matters will be discussed in Part Four of this book. The present chapter will deal only with the formal structure and administrative arrangements that characterize the resulting Soviet federalism.

According to the Constitution of the USSR, the following prerequisites must be fulfilled before a Union Republic can be created: (1) The area to be given this supposedly sovereign status must be situated at the frontiers of the Soviet Union, presumably so that the right of secession formally granted to Union Republics can be exercised. Since in practice, the exercise of this right would be considered a hostile act,[3] this cannot be the real reason for the provision. Perhaps there *is* no real reason, and all the complicated legislation concerning the status of Union Republics is a farce. If it is not, then perhaps the real reason for locating Union

[3] "The basic principle in the programs of the Communist Parties on the national question is that each nation has the right to self-determination, including secession and the formation of an independent state. The granting of such a right does not at all mean that each nation is invited, or, still less, compelled to secede, to break state ties with the nation with which it formerly belonged in a single state. Such an interpretation of the right to self-determination would merely play into the hands of international capital, which is interested in dividing the nations of the socialist countries and then crushing them one by one." *Fundamentals of Marxism–Leninism,* p. 604.

Republics only on the borders of the USSR is to be found in the fact that the national minorities in whose names these republics are created usually spill over into neighboring countries. Azerbaidzhanis are concentrated both in the Azerbaidzhan Socialist Soviet Republic and across its borders in Iran. The same is true of Turkmens, Uzbeks, Kirghiz, and Tadzhiks, Armenians, and Moldavians, as it was true of Karelians and Finns. The creation of "sovereign" states for these nations thus automatically leads to the existence of *irredentás* outside the Soviet Union, which could be used as the pretext for expansive moves. (2) In order to attain the status of a Union Republic, a territory must have a population of at least one round million. (3) The nationality in whose name the Union Republic is to be created must constitute the majority of its population. It is not clear from the wording of the Constitution whether this requirement is valid only at the time the constituent Republic is created or whether it remains valid. If the latter, then the Constitution is probably being violated; certainly in one of the Union Republics, that of the Kazakhs, the "native" population has probably become a minority; and in the Karelo-Finnish SSR, Russians probably were in the majority from the very beginning. The day may not be far away when Latvians, Estonians, and Lithuanians, too, will be minorities within their respective Republics, if they have not become this already.

There are today fifteen Union Republics. Each has its own Supreme Soviet and Council of Ministers. In the formal relations between constituents, Supreme Soviets, Councils of Ministers, and Ministries, federal and Union-Republican agencies, the principle of dual subordination applies throughout. Each Council of Ministers is responsible both to its local Supreme Soviet and to the All-Union Council of Ministers, just as each Supreme Soviet is, in theory, responsible both to its electors and to the All-Union Supreme Soviet and the laws it passes. In the organization of Ministries, the principle of dual subordination has led to a somewhat complicated division of jurisdictions between various types of executive agencies. There are, first of all, federal agencies, called All-Union Ministries, which have their field agencies in various parts of the USSR, but have no counterpart within the cabinets of the constituent republics. Conversely, there are local agencies, known as Republican Ministries, which do not have a counterpart on the federal level; and, finally, Union-Republican Ministries as well as other administrative agencies exist on both levels, in which case the Republic's Minister is responsible both to his own Council of Ministers and to the corresponding Ministry in the All-Union cabinet.

The care with which formal arrangements of this sort seem to provide for a distribution of jurisdictions and responsibilities between the federal government and the several Union Republics, while at the same time taking into account the inevitable over-lapping of these responsibilities, is deceptive. Although the formal structure seems to give the Republics autonomy in managing their primary education, their public health and welfare programs, their minor industries, and many other matters, in practice national autonomy means little more than the right to use the native lan-guage as the official language in schools, courts, and other public agencies. It does not mean the right to pursue any policies that are in conflict with national policies. In all areas of administration, the Republics are subordinate to the federal government; and the fed-eral Constitution, in granting certain rights to the Republics, makes clear that all residual rights lie with the federal Union. The Repub-lics have no recourse against acts of the federal government com-mitted on their territory, nor any control over the field agencies which report directly to Moscow. Conversely, any decree or order passed by the Council of Ministers of a Union Republic can be vetoed by the Presidium of the All-Union Supreme Soviet. Even the budgets of the Union Republics must be approved by the fed-eral Council of Ministers; and until 1956, the federal government went so far as to hand the fifteen republics item budgets rather than the lump budgets they now receive.

Central control is exercised by Moscow in a more subtle form through its personnel policy affecting the Republics. As we shall see in Chapter XX, non-natives have usually occupied key positions in the governments of some of the Union Republics. We shall try to connect this practice with long-range efforts toward the acculturation of the non-Russian nationalities and the political socialization of their elites; for it is these efforts which undoubtedly have motivated the ostensibly federalistic policies of the USSR in constructing its government.

In addition to the fifteen Union Republics which constitute the Union of Socialist Soviet Republics, there are other autonomous territories: nineteen Autonomous Socialist Soviet Republics (ASSR), nine Autonomous Provinces (oblast), and ten National Regions (*krai*). The national *krais* seem to be comparatively large territories inhabited primarily by peoples on a comparatively low level of civilization. Thus they seem to be somewhat analogous to the Indian Territories of the old American West.[4] The Autonomous Republics and Provinces are more akin to the Union Republics, but lack one or more of the prerequisites for Union-Republic status. Moreover, they have no formal rights different from any other administrative areas, except the right to use their own language as the official language. The federal government has created and abolished them or changed their boundaries at will. During or shortly after World War II, five such territorial units were dissolved because their people had shown themselves disloyal to the USSR or were deemed security risks. These were the Volga-German ASSR, the Chechen-Ingush ASSR, the Crimean ASSR, the Kalmyk ASSR, and the Karachai National Krai. These governments were abolished and the populations deported to hardship areas. Three of them were re-created in 1957 and their peoples repatriated: the Karachai Krai and the Kalmyk and Chechen-Ingush Autonomous Republics. Even the Volga-Germans have by now been "rehabilitated."

This very brief discussion of the federalistic structure of the USSR might be summed up by saying that formal national autonomy in its various shapes has been a convenient device for achieving a number of ends. Most of them are related to the problems of

[4] To the extent that the Soviet regime wishes to promote the rapid acculturation of the "natives" in these territories to modern ways of life, the *krai* may be significantly different from an Indian territory, not to mention an Indian reservation.

imposing a new way of life onto a large society which is considerably more heterogeneous than the melting pot of the New World. Against the difficult problems created by this cultural heterogeneity of the Soviet population, other benefits derived from formal federalism have been of minor importance. These would include the gain of two additional United Nations seats for the USSR and, perhaps a favorable impression created in various circles at home and abroad by the seemingly liberal nationality policy of the Soviet government. As we shall see in Part Six of this book, the problems arising out of the cultural heterogeneity of the entire nation have not by any means been solved. At the same time, it may well be that the rulers of the USSR face them with even greater confidence, feeling that a solution will come forth in the long run. Whether or not this is their attitude, respect for the formalities of Soviet federalism does not seem to motivate them very strongly. In this connection, it is interesting to note that the Khrushchevian administrative reforms of 1957 and 1962 took relatively little cognizance of the federalist structure; and in some of the discussions concerning the creation of economic regions, there even seemed to be an implicit desire to by-pass the Union Republics and lesser autonomous areas and thus to weaken federalism by creating a different network of territorial organizations.

THE FUNCTIONS OF LOCAL GOVERNMENT

We are thus brought back to a point made earlier in this chapter, namely, the subordinate and ancillary position of territorial and local government organizations. Each higher unit of government functions first of all for the purpose of supervising the work of lower soviets and executive committees. Each higher Executive Committee feels itself directly responsible for the performance of all the Executive Committees under its jurisdiction. But what, then, are the functions of the lowest government units, the soviets of towns and villages? What remains for them to do on their low level in the administrative structure?

The functions of local government are as varied as that of the

Soviet government in general. Some of them are shared by local governments in all modern societies. Among these are traffic control and the maintenance of the local police, as well as the maintenance of public records concerning births and deaths, marriage, divorce, residence, and sojourn. In the USSR, such registers include also military recruitment records; in fact, local soviets, somewhat analogous to American draft boards, also carry out the actual recruitment of all those liable to do their military service. Furthermore, like towns and cities throughout Europe, local soviets maintain local services and utilities, from power plants and bus lines through primary schools to theaters, cinemas, parks, and other entertainment or recreational facilities. But public facilities in the USSR also include medical services, clinics, hospitals, ambulances, and the like; they include restaurants, cafes, and cafeterias; indeed, they include the retail distribution system of commodities and services for the consumer, from farmers' markets through repair shops to specialty and department stores. In fact, local governments are very much preoccupied with the management or supervision of economic enterprises, many of which are under local jurisdiction.[5]

Economic activities organized and supervised by local soviets (even though under the auspices of regional and national plans) include not only the distribution system, but also craft cooperatives, certain aspects of farming, and small industry. Finally, local soviets are in charge not only of road building and maintenance, but also of building construction, for residences as well as public buildings. Because a great number of these activities for which local soviets are responsible require the use of funds, personnel, equipment, and material that must be allotted or obtained from other agencies of the government, local soviets also have the important function

[5] The reforms of 1962 which divided both the Party and the government into separate branches for industry and agriculture must have led to a thorough redistribution of economic jurisdictions. How this affected local governments is difficult to assess. The proposal at the time was to take local industries away from city and even provincial soviets and place them instead under the regional *sovnarkhoz*. Nor is it clear how the reversal of this structural reform in 1964 has affected the role of local government in economic management.

of bargaining with higher authorities for goods or services to which, according to plans, the locality is entitled. At the same time, local soviets will have to bargain equally hard for a definition of administrative objectives which are capable of being attained, given the resources of the community. Since the higher authorities must be besieged with such lobbying from all the localities under their jurisdiction, this may not always be very effective. But, as in the case of American advertising, this simply means that everyone must redouble his efforts so as not to be left behind his competitors—in this case, the neighboring communities.

In the fulfillment of their various tasks, however, local soviets are severely handicapped not only by the scarcity of resources (especially if they are to be used for providing benefits to the consumer) but even more, perhaps, by the centralization of the entire economy. Especially in larger towns and cities the most important economic activities are likely to be outside local jurisdiction. If, until 1957, large enterprises were directly subordinate to a production division (*glavk*) of a ministry, they have, since 1957, been under the jurisdiction of a *sovnarkhoz*. In either case, the local soviet had no jurisdiction over the enterprise and little control over its activities. In this sense, local soviets are in somewhat the same boat as local governments in the United States in their relations with large corporate enterprises within their boundaries. In both societies, there is a tendency toward domination over local government by the large industrial units, or at least of independent coexistence of local government with private-business government. In the USSR, this trend has gone so far that many towns have virtually become company towns. This is so because large enterprises—strong and influential, whereas town governments are weak and carry little weight—have tended to usurp many of the civil functions theoretically belonging to local soviets. Factories or other large establishments have undertaken a very large amount of housing construction. They have built roads and bridges, laid sewers, provided local transport and a host of other services, always responding to their own special needs and interests. As a result, city soviets have relatively little to do that is of great importance.

Their prestige and status within Soviet officialdom, already quite low, has suffered from this fact. Furthermore, city soviets usually are powerless in any conflict between industrial interests. Such conflicts are carried out over the heads of the city fathers, who might as well not be in existence. Finally, it has often been impossible to engage in rational city planning. Instead, cities have grown helter-skelter, in accordance with the short-range needs of industrial magnates and in disregard of any broader interests. A conference on city planning and construction (the first of its kind to be held in Russia) which met in the summer of 1960 brought out the fact that many Soviet cities are without a development plan; that actual construction, as well as the choice of construction and development sites, is done in uncoordinated fashion by different authorities, and many vital aspects of city development remain totally neglected.[6]

To sum up: Despite federalist forms and a brief history of local autonomy, territorial and local government authorities, though nominally responsible to local soviets, are primarily agencies of a highly centralized bureaucracy. Moreover, since local matters are decided by many agencies which may be responsible to local government authorities not at all, and which in fact may not even trouble to establish effective liaison with them, local government often is as helpless and ineffective in regulating matters of local concern as local governments are in the United States. Since the structures of government in the two countries are so dissimilar, these striking similarities may, perhaps, be accounted for by a certain inevitable centralizing effect of large-scale industry.

[6] "Yesterday in the Kremlin," *Pravda* (June 8, 1960), p. 1. See also "Industry and the City," *Izvestiia* (May 4, 1960), p. 4; "Several Questions of Soviet Urban Development," *Pravda* (June 1, 1960), pp. 2–3; and Timothy Sosnovy, "The Soviet City," in Joint Economic Committee, U. S. Congress, *Dimensions of Soviet Economic Power* (Washington, D.C.: Government Printing Press, 1962), p. 327.

Part Four

Government in Action: Control over the Behavior of Citizens

Introduction

The preceding chapters were devoted to a general survey of the structure of government in the USSR. The picture which emerged was that of a bureaucratic organization with a bias for hierarchy, command, and centralization, plagued like other modern large-scale organizations with sharp conflicts between various principles of organization and management and between different policy goals. This very general image of the political system must now be made more specific by discussing some of the most important functions served by this political machinery. This will have to include a survey of the concrete problems faced, of the institutions created to cope with them, of the manner in which these institutions work, and of the policies that guide them. Our survey will have to include the process of economic planning and the institutions involved in it; the resolution of conflicts by the judicial system; the control of deviants by non-judicial methods and agencies; the process of elite recruitment; the policies toward national minorities; and many other topics. This partial list of government activities has been given only to remind the reader that the scope of government is wider in the USSR than in traditional liberal governments; at least, it is acknowledged to be as wide as society itself.[1] The political

[1] It should be clearly understood that even in liberal political systems such agencies as the press, the economic institutions, youth organizations, peer groups, religious bodies, and all other associations are also part of the political system. It is therefore only seemingly true that the range of institutions to be examined is greater in the USSR than in the West. In all societies, the range of groups and activities to be surveyed by the political scientist is far wider than that of the "government" properly speaking.

system of the Soviet Union merges with society not only in fact, but also by law. Groups and activities which are civic in other political systems are governmental or Party-affiliated in the USSR. Actually, even then the scope of political domination is wider yet than that of the government; for government, as we have seen, is only one of the agencies of the Party, and the Party also works directly through grass-roots organizations that are not, strictly speaking, governmental. These include not only its own ideological indoctrination machine and its youth affiliate, but also trade unions, seemingly voluntary associations such as civil defense groups, and neighborhood or peer groups of various kinds.

For the sake of clarity, all the problems and policies with which Parts Four and Five deal will be discussed under two broad headings: control over the behavior of citizens; and economic and social problems. Obviously, these are distinctions of convenience which may inject their own distortions into the presentation. In describing a complex subject where everything is related to everything else, this is unavoidable.

*   *   *

The USSR often is called totalitarian. We shall discuss the meaning of this term, and its applicability to the Soviet system, toward the end of the book. Here we shall attempt only to describe. Yet in describing we may wish to use adjectives that distinguish Soviet politics from other political systems. In discussing the regime's efforts to control its citizens' behavior, it is very tempting to use the word "totalitarian" because of the seemingly total control which the Party imposes on the actions of individuals and the people as a whole. The reasons for this attempt have been discussed in Part One. The aim might be described as the bureaucratization of all social life. From our discussions of the nature of the Soviet administration, we may very well conclude that this attempt is likely to be self-defeating: with the growth in size and complexity of the government organization, hierarchic control becomes less and less feasible. Social life goes on within a chaos of overlapping and competing bureaucratic structures. Still, for the individual citizen, this may very well mean an almost total regimentation of his life.

Several controlling institutions have already come to our attention. Many of these were economic ones, such as the Finance Ministry and its local subordinates, which collect taxes, audit the financial records of all enterprises and agencies, and exert budgetary control over all parts of government; also the government banks, which control all monetary transactions between various official agencies, and the Commission on Soviet Control, which duplicates some of these supervisory and auditing functions. For the average citizen, controls over his economic behavior take various forms. The tax structure affects the distribution of material rewards. Government control over administered prices for all consumption goods regulates consumption; and the movement of commodities is further determined by government management of the entire retail distribution system and of the many social services provided to citizens. We shall take a closer look at these services when discussing the welfare-state features and other material rewards offered by the Soviet system.

General political supervision over all activities is, as we have seen, provided by the Communist Party. In his many endeavors, the citizen encounters it in the form of the primary organization at his place of work, the Party caucus in all other organizations to which he might belong, and the indoctrination machinery with its many agencies. To this ever-present guidance system we might add a general feature of the bureaucratic state, the penchant for licencing and recording various activities which in some other political systems might be pursued entirely without the participation of governmental agencies. The citizen's professional career is more carefully regulated than in many other societies, and its milestones are recorded in a permanent service record, the Labor Booklet, which thus becomes an essential identification document for each individual. His movements from one town to another are regulated with the help of an internal passport, without which travel becomes impossible. Residence is controlled by the fact that housing in larger towns is obtainable only through allocation of living quarters by some official agency or that material for individual dwelling construction can be obtained legally only from the government. Even some leisure-time activities are organized, supervised, and obtainable only with the help of official permits. Everyone in the West who has ever served in the armed forces, or any American who carries "Blue Cross" insurance is familiar with some of these seemingly inevitable formalities of the bureaucratized life.

In the following pages, devices to control the citizens' behavior will be discussed a little more specifically under four headings: law, terror, socialization, and rewards.

Chapter XII
Law

One occasionally encounters expressions of surprise that the Soviet political system includes laws and courts. This surprise is usually based on a simplistic conception of Soviet communism as arbitrary absolutism and lawless terror, together with an equally naive identification of law with free enterprise and constitutional democracy. The assumption that Soviet government is lawless government is fed also by various scholarly works denying the existence of law in the USSR because the laws that do prevail in the Soviet system do not conform to the definitions of law these scholars have accepted on the basis of their own training in Roman or Anglo-Saxon law. In turn, these learned rejections of Soviet claims that theirs is a law-minded system find some support in the Bolsheviks' skeptical attitude toward law at the time they seized power in Russia.

In the earliest years of the regime, the Bolsheviks believed that law and courts were features of the hated past. They would disappear presently, especially if the regime helped all other remnants of capitalism to disappear; and, once removed, law would not return. Laws were regarded as expressions and supporting props of capitalist property relationships, which would simply wither away once capitalism had been destroyed. The courts, according to Bolshevik views, were bastions of tsarist reaction or of bourgeois exploitation. Criminality, they argued, was the symptom of a sick society; hence, once they had cut out the cancer of capitalism, criminal behavior, too, would disappear, and laws or courts dealing with crime could be abolished. Meanwhile, the Party or its enforce-ment agencies would mete out "revolutionary justice" to all its enemies, based on the law of the revolution, which was, of course, a denial of all previous law. We might reduce all this to two basic assumptions: first, that the existing legal system propped up tsarism and capitalism, was therefore counter-revolutionary, and must be smashed; second, that the revolution would usher in pure communism, a society in which all people would spontaneously and without the constraint of formal law behave toward each other in brotherly fashion. Consequently, when the Bolsheviks, shortly after coming to power, abolished all courts and closed the law schools, they thought these institutions would never return.

The New Economic Policy of 1921, as we have seen, was a return to freedom of enterprise in various fields. The consequent recognition of property rights and business relationships made it necessary to reintroduce laws regulating these rights and relation-ships; and the regime hastily enacted entire codes of law, copied from Western European models—bourgeois law to fit the bour-geois features of the transitional regime. The haste and studied carelessness with which they adopted these codes symbolized the contempt they still felt for these laws and the hope they still nurtured of soon being able to dispense altogether with a legal system. These expectations burst forth with renewed vigor at the time the NEP was abolished and the first five-year plan evoked another spell of revolutionary euphoria. Once again everything bourgeois, every feature of class exploitation and class differences, was to be destroyed once and for all time. Law, too, was now to disappear forever like the kulak and the NEPman. Yet a few years later, the regime once again reversed itself on this, as on so many other matters. Its spokesmen asserted the need for law in what was now to be called a socialist society. The Party insisted that capital-ist law would give way, not to a lawless state, but to socialist law. Disgrace and death were the fate of all the Bolshevik legal philoso-phers who had predicted and advocated the withering away of law. It is easy to see, in retrospect, why they had to be "liquidated:" their theories assumed that law exists only where exploitation, domination, and other inequities associated with class societies still reign. But the Soviet regime now wished to proclaim itself a just society without exploitation or class struggle; and yet its rulers had also convinced themselves that law was essential to the functioning also of this kind of society.

"Soviet law," writes a Soviet authority, "is a system of rules established by the state to promote the consolidation of the social order which helps society advance toward communism.

"Socialist law and legality consolidate and safeguard the social and state system and its economic foundation . . . and ensure the development and strengthening of socialist relations in society."[1]

As a very general description of the function of law in the USSR, this statement can be accepted. But it is really too general to be satisfactory. Even a cursory view will reveal that law in the Soviet Union fulfills a number of related functions. It provides rules and institutions for settling disputes between individual citizens. In connection with this, law must, of course, define the individual's rights and obligations. To a limited extent, law also settles private citizens' claims against public authorities, again on the basis of defined rights and duties. More broadly, Soviet law establishes rules and institutions for the resolution of any kind of conflict, including disputes between different authoritative rules and commands. Disputes between various public authorities, especially between different economic enterprises, provide a major share of the business of Soviet legal institutions. In the main, administrative law codifies the rules covering the relations of government agencies to each other and to their employees. But there are specific codes of labor law defining the rights and obligations of employees and employers; and a separate system of commercial courts, called State Arbitration Boards (Gosarbitrazh) resolves conflicts and disputes between Soviet economic enterprises on the basis of business law, whereas rules concerning money, credit, budgets, and related matters are set down in codes of finance law. Furthermore, in its criminal branch, Soviet law establishes norms of behavior toward individuals and toward society and its institu-

---

[1] P. Romashkin, *Fundamentals of Soviet Law* (Moscow, 1962), p. 20.

tions, and provides rules and procedures for punishing those who violate these norms. Finally, as constitutional law, it defines a broad framework of rules and institutions that supposedly govern the entire political system. The basic function of all law in the USSR might, perhaps, be said to provide working rules for the smooth functioning of the entire social system and to protect this social system and its political order from anyone hostile to it. Law in the Soviet Union constitutes a protective superstructure over a system of human relations that still falls short of the communist ideal and therefore must protect itself against its own people. Moreover, it is an important socialization device—a method of teaching the Party's norms of behavior to all citizens and, with the help of sanctions, of making such behavior a conditioned response. Law has a certain majesty which argues in its favor against any attempts to challenge the norms which underlie it. And the drama of the courtroom trial easily lends itself for use as an educational device to impress object lessons on all participants and onlookers.

After a prolonged period of hostility to the very idea of law, the Soviet political system has thus emerged firmly committed to the use of law and courts. The discourse of its social scientists or publicists, in fact, is highly legalistic. Soviet treatises on its governmental system remind us of the learned legal writings of the German school before World War I, in which professorial bureaucrats and bureaucratic professors defined the constitutional order of the Empire or the Prussian kingdom in terms of neatly divided jurisdictions, and managed to reduce even the doctrines of liberal constitutional democracy to bureaucratic tables of organization. In both cases, the rule of law is proudly boasted, and the law and order prevailing are contrasted with the disorder and resulting injustice rampant in the Western democracies. In both cases, the Western observer should not be blind to the degree of order and predictability, to the *Rechtssicherheit* established by the Prussian and the Soviet states. In both cases, law attained important functions within the political system because the rulers realized that *Rechtssicherheit* is a bureaucratic necessity.

Whether or not the political order so firmly committed to the rule of law deserves to be called a "state according to law" is, perhaps, a matter of definition. In the West, this usually is meant to express the principle that basic human rights, as defined in some constitutional document, override the will of the party in power, or that the regime is bound by well-established sanctions to observe certain basic rules of behavior toward the citizens. Because of this, the concept of the "state according to law" is squarely opposed to the idea of the *raison d'état*. Yet in the Soviet system, this "reason of state" clearly overrides all legal considerations. The rule of law may indeed protect individual citizens from arbitrariness, but it does so only incidentally. The limits of legalism are reached when obedience to the laws is inopportune for the ruling party. To be sure, the laws are kept flexible so they can be bent. But many times the Party has simply disregarded the laws or, as if on afterthought, changed them so that they conform with its lawless practices. The sheer magnitude and complexity of the administrative task facing the regime also encourage this procedure, and so does the regime's bureaucratic nature, i.e., the rule-of-command principle. Complexity, size, rapid changes in problems and tasks, the ease with which new rules can be enacted—all these factors lead to an overwhelming volume of legislation in the Soviet Union. A body of laws, decrees, and regulations has been developed which is so vast it can no longer be surveyed.[2] It is also full of contradictions and inconsistencies, and undoubtedly also full of loopholes. Many a Western lawyer might find this jungle of legislation vaguely familiar; yet a legal system so unwieldy and labyrinthine mocks the idea of the state according to law.

Still, the very existence of law and of a legalistic rhetoric with which the regime seeks to legitimize itself has the tendency to propel the political system toward the state according to law. Where law has once been established, if only for the purpose of serving bureaucratic reasons it seeks to assert itself against the remnants of arbitrariness and the *raison d'état;* and it must strive also for con-

[2] In recent years, Soviet jurists have clamored for the elimination of obsolete laws that have never been repealed; and progress has been made by the Union Republics in writing codes of labor law, family law, land law, criminal law, civil law, criminal procedure, and civil procedure.

sistency, clarity, and publicity, even though this striving, too, can be explained as a bureaucratic necessity. In short, the legal profession, called into life for the purpose of guarding "socialist legality," must develop professional standards of its own which compel its spokesmen to resist *breaches* of legal norms and to clean up the chaos of conflicting or obscure legislation. In fact, the legal profession in the USSR does seem to represent legality in a running political controversy going on within the Soviet system, a controversy Harold J. Berman has called the struggle for law. What is this struggle for law? Perhaps it is several things, among them the attempt to rely more and more on law as the regulator of interpersonal and interinstitutional relations in the Soviet Union, eliminating administrative arbitrariness.[3] The struggle for law then would be a struggle for the further bureaucratization and routinization of management in the Soviet system. Beyond this, it might be viewed as an attempt to de-politicize the juridical process, an effort to transform legal procedures from a tool of the Party into ground rules that bind even the sovereign elite. By this very definition, we have, of course, indicated the difficulties of this struggle: as we well know, a sovereign by his very nature does not care to submit to any binding restrictions.

CIVIL AND CRIMINAL LAW

After these general remarks, we shall now take a closer look at various elements of Soviet Law. Since we have summarized the Constitution in a previous chapter, little need be added about constitutional law; it does, in a fashion, provide the basic norms on which the entire legal system is based. Since some of the provisions of the Constitution are observed in the *breach* or are formal window-dressing concealing real political relationships, the entire legal system does, of course, rest on a somewhat shaky and, if you wish,

[3] In an interview with the American correspondent Henry Shapiro in November 1957, Khrushchev still complained that Soviet educational institutions were turning out too many lawyers. But since then the Party's chief ideological journal has called for an increased reliance on law and lawyers to ensure the smoother functioning of the Soviet system. See *Izvestiia* (November 19, 1957), and *Kommunist* 16 (1963), 36.

phantom-like basis; and, like the Constitution, it is easily circum-
vented. Constitutional law nonetheless is of some importance to
Soviet bureaucratic managers because it does provide guidelines
for defining the complicated relations between the countless administrative agencies of the governmental system. The legalistic treatises
of law professors that are published in Soviet journals are no mere
academic exercises but are rather essential guides for administrators
and constitute the framework within which such branches as administrative and business law are elaborated.

Business law, which provides the rules for the organization of
economic enterprises and the relations between such enterprises, is
a highly interesting branch of Soviet law. An entire network of special commercial courts carries out this body of rules; and a corps of
lawyers attached to the staffs of major enterprises give the necessary
legal advice to the managers. The ground rules on which this commercial law operates might be summarized as follows: Economic
enterprises deal with each other through contracts. Many of these
contracts are concluded, not at the discretion of management, but
on the basis of plans; and the State Arbitration Boards (Gosarbitrazh) among other things enforce the writing of contracts which,
according to plans, ought to have been made. Once made, whether
on the basis of the plan or not, contracts must be served. In case of
default by one or several parties, litigation may ensue, and Gosarbitrazh courts may award damages to the injured enterprise. Some
of this may sound, and indeed is, similar to the basic rules of business law in the West. However, in deciding on litigation between
enterprises, Gosarbitrazh is less concerned with safeguarding the
contractual rights of the injured parties than with furthering the
interests of the Soviet economy as a whole. The public interest, as
defined by the Party, overrides the interests of any one administrative unit.

Little need be said about private law in the USSR.[4] It defines the
personal rights of individuals, including property rights; deals with
torts and damages; and regulates family life, including such matters
as divorce, alimony, and inheritance. A sizable portion of individual

[4] In line with Continental usage, the Soviet term is civil law.

litigation in Soviet courts seems to be devoted to divorce and alimony settlement.[5] Many other conflicts between individuals, which in our society would turn into litigation, are apparently channeled into administrative procedures or settled by peer-group pressure.

As for criminal law, a number of features are noteworthy. First of all, we must be aware that the "hierarchy of crimes" in the Soviet Union is different from ours. This term refers to the degree of heinousness attributed to different offenses, as measured by the severity of the punishment the law specifies for them or by the severity of the punishment actually meted out.[6] Not only is this hierarchy of crimes different, but it has also shown itself subject to frequent changes, in line with the Party's current preoccupations. At any time certain deviations from its standards assumed alarming proportions, the Party could declare them capital offenses, either by a formal change of the criminal law or by a publicity campaign impressing on all judges the need to be particularly relentless in the struggle against these specific crimes. Despite such fluctuations, which in some form may occur in all modern societies, the hierarchy of crimes has shown certain regularities. Political crimes have been considered so dangerous that the regular court machinery did not even deal with them; instead, combatting them until recently belonged to the jurisdiction of the political police. If espionage or other dealings with a foreign power were involved, the alleged culprit faced a military tribunal, even if he himself were a civilian.

[5] A clubwoman in Bay City, Michigan, asked me a few years ago, "How come the Russians have divorces, when they don't have any property?" Readers are invited to think of the most suitable reply.

[6] That different societies have different hierarchies of offenses should be a familiar fact to everyone in America, where criminal laws differ from region to region and from one subsociety to another. For instance, most Americans, if asked to range the three following acts in order of their offensiveness, would list them as follows: (1) wanton infliction of bodily harm, (2) fraud, and (3) drinking a glass of beer. Yet I know some institutions of higher learning where a student caught drinking beer would face expulsion; one caught cheating on an examination would receive a failing grade in the course; and one cruelly endangering the life of a fellow-student during a fraternity hazing would be placed on disciplinary probation for a number of weeks. Obviously, the hierarchy of crimes at those schools is in conflict with that accepted within the legal system.

Next in severity have always been offenses against the economic order, including public property, work discipline, currency regulations, or the prohibition against illicit trading, private enterprise, or the use of hired labor. Such offenses are regarded as particularly severe, even though the actual damage done may be petty in the eyes of the Western observer. Conversely, offenses against private rights are punished far more mildly, even though the object involved may be very much greater. There have been some complaints by Soviet citizens, recently, that the government does not give sufficient protection to private property. In the last few years, the government has been especially eager to clamp down on people who live by illicit trade instead of socially useful labor (as defined by the regime). A law passed in May of 1961 referred to such people as "parasites and drones" and specified exile and compulsory labor as their punishment.[7] At the same time, death was decreed to be the proper punishment for a number of crimes hitherto punishable only by prison sentences; among them were serious offenses against public property and currency regulations; crimes of violence committed by convicts in correctional institutions, and certain cases of rape, threats against the life of regular or voluntary policemen, and accepting bribes.[8] The Soviet press has given considerable publicity to the numerous cases in which death penalties have been imposed for such derelictions.

Criminal procedure follows the model of continental Europe in many of its details. A pretrial investigation, during which the authorities keep the prospective defendant in custody, precedes any criminal trial. Western Germany, among other countries, still follows the same procedure. The purpose of this investigation is to determine whether the evidence at hand warrants prosecution; it thus fulfills somewhat the same function as a grand jury investigation. Until recently, defense attorneys were not permitted to inspect

[7] *Izvestiia* (May 5, 1961). See also Khrushchev's renewed attack on parasites and drones, *Izvestiia* (April 26, 1963).

[8] For full reference to the pertinent laws or decrees, see Reinhart Maurach, "Todesstrafe in der Sowjetunion," *Osteuropa*, XIII, 11–12 (November–December, 1963), 745–753.

the records of these pretrial investigations, but now appear to have received this right. Bail and writs of *habeas corpus* are Anglo-Saxon devices which are absent from criminal procedure in the USSR (or in most other European systems). Until recently, criminal courts proceeded on the basis of the presumption of guilt; the burden of proving his innocence was on the defendant. Even though this procedure, too, is now at least controversial in the Soviet Union, the emphasis still is on protecting society rather than on giving the defendant the benefit of all possible doubt.

The government's task of protecting itself against those it considers criminals is made easier by various features of Soviet criminal law. One of these is the fact that the law codes define some crimes, including such capital crimes as treason and sabotage, rather loosely. In its all-inclusiveness, the penal code article defining treason reminds one of that famous old Article of War which said that any behavior harmful to the Army, or any behavior not becoming an officer and a gentleman, could be punished as the court-martial might direct. Partly because of this looseness in the definition of offenses, courts have habitually defined crimes by analogy from actions specifically identified as criminal in the codes. In addition, the Soviet government has not hesitated to enact *ex post facto* criminal legislation to punish people for actions that were not specifically defined as crimes at the time they were committed. Finally, in trying alleged offenders, Soviet courts are in the habit of stressing not only the misdeed itself, but also motivation, intent, and the defendant's past record, activities, and often even his social origin. More than in other societies, the entire person usually is on trial, and sometimes even the entire category of persons he represents.[9]

[9] In December 1958, the federal government published fundamental guidelines for the criminal legislation to be enacted and codified by the several Union Republics. These fundamentals included provisions forbidding punishment except on the basis of a regular court trial; punishment by analogy; and punishment for any crimes not enumerated and defined in the Criminal Code. Contrary to the expectations of some leading Soviet lawyers, it did not specify that an accused should be assumed innocent unless proven guilty. Even now, the practice of Soviet courts still is to assume his guilt and to find him guilty if his guilt was *probable*. See A. Bovin, "Istina v pravosudii," *Izvestiia* (February 9, 1962).

COURTS

The court system of the USSR is centralized and standardized, despite the federalistic framework of the government. So, in fact, is the entire legal system, because the constitutions and law codes of the several Union Republics are virtually carbon copies of each other. In all the republics, courts of first instance, called People's Courts, exist in every *raion*. Provincial courts, fifteen Union-Republican Supreme Courts, and the Supreme Court of the USSR, act as courts of the first instance in certain specified cases, and as courts of appeal and review for cases tried in lower courts. The military establishment has its own ladder of courts; this system merges with the civilian judiciary in the federal Supreme Court, which has a military department. Judges in all courts above the level of the People's Courts are appointed by their soviets for five-year terms. They can be removed and are subject to disciplinary action. They also tend to be under considerable public pressure, via the news media, especially the press. The alleged independence of judges in many political systems is no more than fiction; in the Soviet Union it is hardly even that.

People's Courts consist of judges and lay representatives of the community. One judge and two assessors conduct any trial. The judges are elected for five-year terms; the assessors are drawn from a panel of citizens elected by the same process. Any assessor remains on call for two years, but serves no longer than ten days during the year. Even though they may not have much formal legal training, apart from short courses taken at the Ministry of Justice or even correspondence courses, judges nonetheless have professional status as against the assessors, if only because of their professional experience. In the courtroom and during deliberations the judge presides, but the assessors are his or her equals; and the majority decides on all questions. There is no division of functions between judges and assessors as there is between an American judge and the jury.

Soviet court procedure is informal. The trial is no contest between litigants or between accuser and defendant, with the judge acting as a seemingly detached umpire. Nor are the rules of evidence as stringent as they are in an American court. Instead, the Soviet judge actively seeks to determine all the relevant facts. He and his assessors ask questions and interrupt testimony at their discretion. Compared to litigation in the United States, justice in the Soviet Union is far more informal, quick, and cheap. It may also be a good deal more summary; that is the price paid for speed and informality. At the same time it seems to convey a certain humane atmosphere. A large percentage of people's judges are women, who conduct trials in a somewhat maternal fashion, briskly and sternly, but with compassion and warmth. Despite all its formal similarities to the Prussian tradition of justice, the character of the Soviet court is thus markedly different from that of a German *Amtsgericht,* where the judge is likely to address his listeners in the tone of a company commander.[10]

A team of attorneys, organized in a lawyers' association, is attached to every court to provide legal counsel for anyone who desires it at fees established by regulation. Attorneys in any trial are expected not only to assist their clients, but also to help the court determine justice, even if in doing so they act against the seeming interest of their own client. They are expected not to suppress any evidence if it is damaging to their client, nor to be too persuasive in defending an accused of whom the government obviously wishes to make a warning example. Attorneys have been disbarred or otherwise punished for placing their clients' interests above that of the community, as defined by the Party. Again, the Soviet system makes the trial, not into a contest, but into a collective effort to do justice; it is in this effort that the attorneys are to participate. In this sense, they represent the community, or the regime, no less than

[10] In attempting to explain this difference, one might argue that the Soviet People's Court is in fact closer to the people: the typical People's Judge differs from his German colleague by (a) less formal legal training, (b) less obvious origins in the upper classes, and (c) less social distance from the lower classes by virtue of salary and status difference. In contrast, in a German court, the upper class has authority to sit in judgment over another part of society, about which it knows and cares very little. See Ralf Dahrendorf, *Gesellschaft und Freiheit* (München: R. Piper, 1963), Chapter 8, especially p. 195.

does the public prosecutor or the judge. Here, too, the attempt to determine the "general will" militates against anything like the separation of powers or the recognition of conflicts as legitimate.

THE PROCURACY

Like the entire legal system of the USSR, the office of the public prosecutor has been modeled, at least in its outward forms, on analogous continental institutions. Called the Procuracy (*Prokuratura*), it is one of the most centralized agencies of the Soviet government, the Procurator (*Prokuror*) of any Union Republic being appointed directly by the Procurator General of the federal Union. Its powers and functions are far wider than those of public attorneys in the United States.[11] A Soviet procurator not only acts as prosecutor in criminal trials. He also supervises the criminal investigation forces; he has the powers of arrest and detention; and he functions as inspector of prisons. In recent years, the procuracy has also been in charge of reviewing the work of the political police.

In addition to these functions, which are related to the investigation, prosecution, and punishment of crimes, the procuracy functions as the guardian of legality throughout the governmental system. Procurators review all legal acts and may challenge them. They may protest decisions of civil or criminal courts and force retrials. They may compel economic enterprises to redraw contracts made with each other; and they may ask that any administrative decision they deem to be illegal be reconsidered. To back up this broad authority, procurators also have what amounts to a subpoena right, in that they may demand from all governmental agencies any information, documents, or other materials they wish to inspect. These are formidable powers indeed. They make the procuracy a highly sensitive and politically important tool in the hands of the regime, and the Party has always taken particular care in staffing it.

This brings us back once more to the "struggle for law" discussed previously in this chapter. Undoubtedly, such a struggle is always

[11] A useful Soviet survey of the functions of the procuracy, containing a lengthy bibliography, is V. G. Lebedinskii and Iu. A. Kelenov, *Prokurorskii nadzor v SSSR* (Moscow: Gosiurizdat, 1957).

latent within the Soviet political system. One might, perhaps, expect the procurators, as guardians of socialist legality, to be in the forefront of this struggle; in fact, there is some evidence that procurators have at times attempted to combat the arbitrariness of the political police and the high-handed disregard for legality displayed by local Party leaders. Yet, hand-picked as they are, they will obviously not carry this struggle further than the Party wants it to be carried. The procurator's struggle for law will therefore be kept within the confines of the bureaucratic system in which the top of the hierarchy decides how much legality is or is not useful to the regime. Whether we can expect law schools, professors, or Ministers of Justice to be more independent in the fight for the supremacy and consistency of the legal order remains to be seen.[12]

[12] Recent trends in the "Struggle for Law" are discussed in Harold J. Berman, "The Dilemma of Soviet Law Reform," *Harvard Law Review*, 76, 5 (March, 1963), 929–951. See also Harold J. Berman, *Justice in the USSR* (Cambridge: Harvard University Press, 1963), Chapter 2.

Chapter XIII
Terror

". . . the more power an actor has, the less power he needs to exercise. . . . A relatively powerless actor must employ 'powerful' instruments."
Felix E. Oppenheim, DIMENSIONS OF FREEDOM

Flexible and well attuned to the interests of the regime, criminal law in the Soviet Union provides sanctions against anything the Party considers undesirable behavior. Yet it has never been the only means for curbing dissenters and deviants and enforcing compliance with desirable behavior. On the contrary, from its very beginnings the Soviet political system has been characterized by its readiness to apply extralegal sanctions against anyone those in control deemed undesirable, and to use terror and arbitrary force to cow the people into submission and collaboration. From its earliest days, in other words, the Party has sought to achieve legitimacy by fear. The methods it has used for this have changed; so have the agencies conducting terror and their place within the political system; and so, finally, have the categories of citizens chiefly affected by terror.

DEVELOPMENT OF THE USE OF TERROR

During the civil war, the Soviet regime boastfully called itself a proletarian dictatorship, defining dictatorship as "government not based on law." In other words, the Party itself proclaimed violence and coercion to be the main methods of government. Bolsheviks were in general agreement that the first task of their new regime was to coerce certain classes of the population or even to destroy them. In fact, this was a strange outgrowth of their revolutionary euphoria: some Bolsheviks seem to have been convinced that all that remained to be done to bring about communism was to jail or kill off all capitalists. On the other hand, the terror unleashed by the Bolsheviks can be seen simply as a function of the civil war. The revolution had divided the country into politically hostile camps, all of them desperate, all of them ready to kill indiscriminately for the purpose of legitimizing themselves by terror and eliminating all possible foes. Civil wars tend to be the bloodiest and dirtiest of all wars, because the antagonists view their enemies not as honorable foes, but as despicable traitors. In civil wars, quarter is rarely given. Prisoners are shot because to keep them alive is politically risky. During the Russian civil war, both sides proceeded even more drastically than that: counterrevolutionary troops, having conquered a city, would often round up large numbers of workers and kill them, assuming, undoubtedly, that by doing so they were killing the Bolshevik revolution. As we have seen, some of the managers of the Red Terror made similar assumptions about the beneficial results of killing all capitalists. Their attitude might be summarized as "shoot first; ask questions later," or, as Lenin is supposed to have said, "It is better to kill a thousand innocent people than to let one genuine counterrevolutionary run free." This seems like a hysterical reaction to an admittedly desperate situation, at least from the comfort of hindsight.

The unceremonious, easygoing fashion in which Bolsheviks during the civil war did away with human lives is demonstrated by the way in which a minor official, almost casually, killed the tsar and his family when White forces approached their place of confinement in the Ural Mountains. He acted in order to prevent his prisoners from being liberated, because this would have been an important psychological victory for the enemies of the revolution. As important as these prisoners would have been to the Whites, so unimportant were they to the Reds: the Council of People's Commissars received a report of the tsar's summary execution and casually passed on to the next item on the agenda.

Although the Red Terror was directed primarily against members and supporters of the old ruling classes, it turned its attention toward anyone who challenged the Bolshevik regime, such as the leaders of the Left-Socialist Revolutionary Party, who, after supporting the October Revolution, rebelled against it in the summer of 1918; other non-Bolshevik socialists (Mensheviks, Anarchists, Socialist Revolutionaries, and others) who were gradually forced to go underground during the civil war; rebellious peasants who resisted food requisitioning or who turned vast areas of Central Russia into an autonomous peasant republic for more than a year.

The institution especially created for the purpose of carrying out the Red Terror was the All-Russian Extraordinary Commission for the Fight Against Counterrevolution, Speculation, and Delinquency in Office, colloquially called the Chrezvychaika, but better known under the abbreviation Cheka. Even today, a Soviet security police agent is likely to call himself, proudly, a Chekist. Created six weeks after the October Revolution, the Cheka was nominally responsible to the Sovnarkom, but in practice it answered to none. Lenin appears to have had boundless confidence in its head, F. E. Dzerzhinski, a veteran of the revolutionary Marxist movement in Poland, whose personality was a rare mixture of decency and incorruptibility, asceticism and aesthetic refinement, aristocratic upbringing and devotion to the cause of the working class, visionary idealism, the practicality of a capable manager, and the cold-blooded ruthlessness of a hangman. The Party as a whole seems to have viewed the Cheka and its open terror with some ambivalence—either as a necessary evil or, with burning pride, as the avenging sword of the revolution.

Whatever doubts the Party members may have harbored were likely to be intensified by the fact that the Cheka attracted a rather mixed lot of members. The organization contained many idealists of a certain ruthless purity—a type personified by Dzerzhinski—but it also included sadists and hatemongers and, furthermore, careerists or opportunists, including people with a reactionary or counterrevolutionary political past who joined the Cheka because it obviously was the safest agency or because its members enjoyed certain prerogatives, not to speak of a peculiar license. There is some evidence that the membership of the Soviet political police has retained this character throughout its history. At the higher level of its organization were often persons who combine the professional skills and the authoritarian personality traits of the policeman with fanatical devotion and loyalty to the Soviet way of life and its leadership. At the lower levels, however, one frequently encounters various kinds of deviants, among them persons whose authoritarian bent borders on the pathological, as well as people who have been pressed into police service after they were caught committing some kind of offense. Political police work everywhere seems to attract or recruit weak, insecure, sometimes actually sick personalities.

The secret police, however, has never been the only agency charged with wielding terror, i.e., violence applied or threatened. Apart from the Red Army, which during the civil war was perhaps the chief instrument for attaining legitimacy by force of arms, the Party membership itself often ruled by direct force, either individually or, as in the case of the Kronstadt uprising, organized as a combat force. In other words, Party members often behaved in sovereign fashion, taking the law into their own hands. In addition, the Party during the civil war systematically and successfully wielded terror against various elements of the population by organizing and unleashing the resentment of the poor against the rich in such organizations as the workers' Red Guards and the rural Committees of the Poor. It turned the country over, as it were, to those who had been the most underprivileged under previous regimes; and, although the Party managed, on the whole, to control or direct their spontaneous resentment, this guided class war looked like the arbitrary and terroristic rule of the mob to those who previously had been privileged and comfortable—a terrifying experience for people accustomed to deference. Finally, the Party during the civil war made ample use of the threat of starvation to force people into obedience. These were times of starvation for the entire country, of course; but by controlling the distribution of food supplies, the Party held the life of all citizens in its hands. Possession of ration cards was a matter of life and death, and so was the possession of a job which entitled its holder to a ration card. In short, not only the civil war situation, but also the economic ruin of the country meant that terror in many forms was an ever-present element of the political order.

Once the civil war was won and legitimacy of the most basic sort had been achieved, the regime itself felt that deliberate and open terror had outlived its usefulness. It may well be that this judgment was premature. To be sure, the revolutionary war had ended in victory, and the Party was definitely in power. But the Kronstadt rebellion, the continuing peasant war in Russia's central provinces, the cleavages in the Party, and the continued trouble in national minority areas, among other facts, showed the shakiness of the regime's hold over the country. Notwithstanding, the Cheka was abolished in February of 1922, and the deliberate class warfare organized by the Party during War Communism was replaced by more benign methods—persuasion, permissiveness, and material incentives. Some of the Party leaders seem to have had a surfeit of heroic, desperate, and bloody methods. The Red Terror had been so costly, so intolerable a moral burden to its own organizers, that some of them may have turned from it with a feeling of relief. Others may have had no such scruples, but nonetheless convinced themselves that the continuation of the terror would be political suicide for the regime. In any event, the Party deliberately turned away from mass terror; of this change the abolition of the Cheka was a symbol.

Yet, although mass terror was foresworn, terror continued, though on a smaller scale. The regime continued to deal with real and suspected saboteurs and counterrevolutionary agents in summary, extralegal fashion. It no longer executed people as casually as before; in fact, during the 1920s executions appear to have been relatively few. But it jailed or exiled people into places hardly fit for human habitation. The concentration camps which the Cheka had set up in the fall of 1918 for "enemies of the people" continued in existence even after the Extraordinary Commission had been abolished. The reduced terror of the NEP period was directed against all those who would not make their peace with the Bolshevik regime and continued their attempts to dislodge it—in short, against political, religious, and national activists ranging from bishops and conservative adventurers to Menshevik and Social Revolutionary organizers who thought they could still agitate among workers or peasants. After 1926, extralegal procedures were applied also against communist oppositionists who had been expelled by the Party; up to that time, Party members, even former members, had enjoyed immunity from the terror.

After the abolition of the Cheka, the chief agency for the surveillance and punishment of politically undesirable persons was a division within the People's Commissariat of the Interior called the State Political Administration (GPU). Formally subordinate to the Commissariat, the GPU was somewhat more limited in its authorities than the Cheka had been. In its security work it was to be guided by certain procedural rules, whereas no rules whatsoever had limited its predecessor organization. After the formation of the federal Union of Socialist Soviet Republics, the GPU was detached from the Commissariat of the Interior and made an independent staff agency of the Sovnarkom. It was now renamed the Unified State Political Administration (OGPU). The OGPU became a formidable political force, with its own armed forces of over half a million men, an elite enjoying considerable prestige and material privileges. Its influence increased rapidly and its terror flared up in full furor during the first years of the drive for industrialization, especially during the open class warfare against free enterprise in agriculture. In many ways, this period of the first five-year plan was a repetition of methods used during War Communism. Once again revolutionary fanaticism gripped many supporters of the regime and made them ready to kill anyone standing in the way of the Party. Once again organized class warfare and deliberate starvation combined with other violent methods in coercing the population; once again Party and Komsomol members supplemented the political police in the application of terror methods; and once again the revolutionary years finally gave way to a period in which the Party renounced terroristic methods and abolished the agency of terror. For two or three years after the full fury of collectivization had spent itself, a number of Party leaders who wished to steer a milder course prevailed in the highest councils of the Party. In July 1934, the Soviet government dissolved the OGPU and transferred its functions to the Commissariat of the Interior (NKVD)—later, the Ministery of the Interior (MVD)— that agency again to be subject to a few restrictive procedural rules. Yet, only a few months after, terror again became the dominant method of government in the USSR: the Great Purge, which started in December of 1934 with the assassination of Sergei M. Kirov and which lasted for four years, firmly established the political police as an all-powerful branch of government, virtually independent of the Party or the formal Soviet administration and subject only to the will of Stalin. It created an atmosphere of fear and universal suspicion that may have lessened since Stalin's death, but certainly has not disappeared. It made terror so all-pervasive that one was fully justified in summing up the entire Soviet political system by calling it a police state.

TERROR UNDER STALIN

The Commissariat for the Interior was far more than merely the chief terror organization. To administer these specific functions was the task of one of its subdivisions, the Main Administration for State Security (GUGB). In 1941, this agency was taken from the jurisdiction of the NKVD and transformed into a separate cabinet-level administration, the People's Commissariat for State Security (NKGB), or, since 1946, Ministry of State Security (MGB). Under the direct guidance of Stalin's personal secretariat, this security force penetrated all branches of the political system, including the Communist Party itself. Its operations called for a complex organization. As an agency for gathering political intelligence and for investigating suspects, the political police comprised a network of field units which, very much like the Party, paralleled the organizational structure of the entire society and reached into every single administrative unit of Party and government. Just as every public organization has its Party primary organization which reports about the organization through its own Party hierarchy, so the MGB has its "Special

Department" (Osobyi Otdel; abbreviated OO), which is the grass-roots detachment of the security police. For special tasks of enforcement, the MVD and MGB used to have their own military forces deployed throughout the country. In special political-police jails, interrogators would seek to obtain confessions of guilt and denunciations of associates from arrested suspects. For determining the punishment alleged political offenders were to receive, the MGB had its own special boards which made their decisions in the absence of the accused or his counsel, and without the right of appeal. Administrative sanction thus imposed could take many forms, ranging from severe pay cuts ("exile at the person's place of work"), through exile to or from specified places, to forced labor in concentration camps or confinement in one of the dreaded "isolator" camps. The police had the authority to pass out sentences of up to five years' duration in this summary fashion; and they could renew these sentences any number of times.

Management of the corrective labor camps, which at times contained millions of prisoners, made the security police into one of the largest economic empires within the entire Soviet system, and virtually a state within the state. Under Stalin, the population of these camps may be said to have constituted a social class of its own, large and important enough to be regarded as a major element of Soviet society, with a discernible structure of its own. Vast construction projects—factories, dams, canals, railroads—as well as a host of other operations, such as mining, lumbering, and many branches of manufacture, employed great numbers of prisoners, either exclusively, or side by side with free labor. Where only convict labor was used, the MVD–MGB at times seems to have been completely in charge of the entire work project; in other cases, the police functioned as a labor exchange, farming out its inexhaustible pool of convicts to various enterprises at a considerable profit to its accounts. In short, loyalty and security risks in the USSR were put to work by the police at hard labor in places so inhospitable that less coercive methods of recruitment would hardly have succeeded in providing a sufficient labor force. If one disregards the cost of this program of using forced labor—the waste of lives, the considerable overhead, not to mention the unspeakable inefficiency described so strikingly in Alexander Solzhenitsyn's *A Day in the Life of Ivan Denisovich*[1]—he might therefore conclude that the Soviet economy derived a good deal of benefit from its police state. Whether these benefits outweigh the serious economic and political disadvantages is a matter of controversy. One interesting fact entering such a discussion is the economic and political benefit which the security police itself derived from managing such a vast economic empire, including material benefits and tremendous bargaining power. Once established, the system of labor camps undoubtedly helped perpetuate the MVD–MGB and its operations. One might even suspect (although this cannot possibly be proved) that some of the mass arrests of suspects which occurred again and again were undertaken because the police were given a quota of arrests to fulfill. One might speculate that such a quota was based, in whole or in part, on the need for additional labor in the camps where death, disease, and weakness continually thinned the ranks of the workers. Nor is it, perhaps, farfetched to assume that the bureaucratic incentive system, where performance is measured by raw quantities, provided a built-in stimulus for making large numbers of arrests. And, finally, the political climate in the days of Stalin's rule was one of universal suspicion and fear. The police chief in the United States who expects every traffic patrolman on his force to fill his daily minimum of citations to prove that he is doing his job properly silently assumes that there is no dearth of lawbreakers. Similarly, the Party or police chief in the USSR who

---

[1] Anyone familiar with the reality of Soviet corrective labor camps and the recklessness with which they wasted health, lives, and talents will be offended by the hypocrisy of the Soviet ideologists who write as follows: "Capitalism makes use of technical progress and improved organization of production to intensify exploitation and to increase absolute and relative surplus-value. The employer introduces machinery not because it saves labor, but only if it costs him less than the wages of the workers it displaces. The motto of capitalism is 'to extract as much as possible from the worker.' The slogan of socialism is 'to extract as much as possible from machinery.'

"Of course, under socialism, too, a definite standard of labor intensity, dictated by the rhythm of the production process, must be maintained. But socialism excludes an intensification of labor which drains the worker of his strength and destroys his health." *Fundamentals of Marxism–Leninism*, p. 583.

may have expected his subordinates to carry out certain minimal numbers of arrests or obtain a quota of confessions to prove their political vigilance must have assumed that there were vast numbers of spies, wreckers, and other enemies of the regime.[2]

The function of this impressive machinery within the total political system might be summarized as follows: First, the security police serves as an indispensable gatherer of political intelligence, a polling agency for gauging public opinions and sentiments. In societies which treat the expression of unapproved opinions as subversive and criminal, communications from the constituents to the rulers can flow only through the channels of police investigators; without the police, the elite would be left virtually without any feedback. From the point of view of assessing the mood of the citizens, the fact that those whose mood deviates from the Party's norm face "corrective" sanctions is almost incidental. In short, simply because the security police wields a terrifying punitive apparatus, we should not be blind to its importance as a communication link.

The most important element in the communications network thus established undoubtedly is the informer, that seemingly plain and ordinary citizen who, unsuspected by his peers, informs the security police about their behavior and stated opinions. This is a difficult subject to discuss because, obviously, no reliable information about informers is available, neither concerning their number at any particular time during the history of the USSR, nor their manner of recruitment, remuneration, organization, nor the ratio of professionals to amateurs, of full-time to part-time agents. It would be interesting, but for the time being quite impossible, to gain insight into the motives of people who report their peers to the police, though one thing is clear: all citizens are under constant pressure from the regime to watch their colleagues, neighbors, friends—indeed, their relatives—and to be vigilant against possible enemies. This continual call for vigilance is, in effect, an attempt to make every citizen a volunteer agent of the security police. As

[2] For further remarks about the paranoid assumptions on which the work of the political police is based, see p. 332.

in so many other fields, the Soviet system seeks to involve a maximum number of people at the grass-roots level in active participation.[3] We cannot know how successful it has been in this attempt at various times; still, the very possibility that anyone might have an urge to be especially "vigilant" must act as a significant curb on unorthodox words and behavior.

One other very important series of related questions about the work of the security police is impossible for outsiders to answer: How effective is it as an agency for gathering and communicating the moods and opinions of the citizens? How accurate are its methods of collecting intelligence? How realistic is the image of grass-roots sentiments it sends to the top of the hierarchy? On these questions the few bits of evidence available are contradictory. On the one hand, the one provincial archive of the Party that has fallen into Western hands contains straightforward, unvarnished situation reports indicating either a remarkable degree of detachment or an ability to suppress ideological preconceptions. On the other hand, the Great Purge and similar episodes make the security police appear virtually as helpless victims of mass hysteria which they themselves helped create in the first place. Finally, the very existence of a terror apparatus, or even the people's belief that it exists, inhibits deviant behavior and the expression of any political opinions whatever, so that communication between citizens and rulers tends to break down or be distorted even before it reaches the communications machinery of the police.

In order to obtain a general idea of who the victims are who feel the sanctions once the intelligence has been gathered, we should become familiar with the notion of preventative punishment, or *prophylactic justice*. For this precisely is the aim of administrative sanctions. The security police in the USSR seeks to ferret out and punish not those persons who have committed crimes against the public order, since the courts can handle them. The security police aims to catch and punish those who are *likely* to commit offenses in the future, who are considered *inclined* toward treacherous,

---

[3] Khrushchev expressed this as clearly as possible: "Figuratively speaking, every citizen has the duty to consider himself a policeman (*militsioner*)." *Izvestiia* (April 26, 1963).

subversive, or disloyal acts. Prophylactic justice is based on the same principles as American attempts to eliminate loyalty and security risks from public employment. In both cases, the security police operates on the basis of certain behavioral norms, and seeks to locate, isolate, and eliminate those individuals who deviate from these norms. The character traits of the "desirable" or "acceptable" or "safe" citizen may include not only his actual behavior and manifest opinions, present and past, but also his associates and relatives, his national, ethnic, or religious origin, and perhaps other features with which he is involuntarily endowed. In both cases, the individual is judged not only by what he has said and done, but also by the categories according to which he can be classified. Seen in this light, prophylactic justice marks the ultimate erosion of all notions of individualism and of due process. The citizen is treated not on the basis of his actions or even his thoughts, but on the basis of the potential thoughts and acts attributed to the people whose background or characteristics he happens to share.[4] This method of eliminating and punishing potential deviants is typical not so much of the "individual terror" directed against selected citizens who have in fact manifested deviant attitudes, but rather of the "mass terror" in which punitive action is taken against entire categories of people or the population is alerted to be especially vigilant about them. Mass terror was applied to the "bourgeois specialists" in Soviet services in the late 1920s and early 1930s; against the peasantry at the time of collectivization; against the Party's Old Guard during the Great Purge; against soldiers and civilians who had fallen into enemy hands after World War II; against virtually all the national

[4] That the idea of prophylactic justice is still very attractive to the Soviet regime was made clear by a speech Khrushchev made in April 1962 before a Komsomol congress. Suppose, he said, a man comes to the police and says, "So-and-so wants to kill me." All the police can then tell him is, "Take it easy, man. As long as he has not done you any harm, there is nothing we can do to him. But don't worry. If and when he kills you, you can be sure we will catch him, and he will be punished." But, said Khrushchev, in the case of antisocial elements, parasites, and loiterers, the Soviet regime is going to render them harmless prophylactically by forcing them to do socially useful work—presumably under supervision, if not behind barbed wire.

minorities at various times. Inevitably, its result was massive deportation of the people belonging to the categories to be eliminated.[5]

A great variety of explanations has been offered to account for the widespread and repeated use of individual and mass terror throughout (and beyond) the period of Stalin's rule. Some of the most plausible of these explanations might be combined into the following theory: The Soviet regime's readiness to apply terror was a function of the desperate urge they felt to storm the heavens of industrialization. The Party must have been fully aware of the strong resistance it had to overcome in this effort, resistance motivated by hostility either to communism or to the industrial way of life. This awareness determined the Party leaders to whip the nation into collaborating; and they were all the more readily prepared to use such negative incentives because other incentives were lacking. Material rewards were scarce for decades; the ideology was wearing thin and revolutionary enthusiasm had spent itself quickly; indeed, large elements of the Leninist ideological heritage were dysfunctional to the industrialization drive and could be replaced only by terror. Terror, then, could be defined as the shoving aside and crushing of all those who could not or would not adjust to the superhuman demands the Party made on Soviet society, as a shock treatment for those who clung to even a shred of the fabric of the old society, and as a hysterical reaction of those entrepreneurs of industrialization who despaired when they became aware of the lack of sympathy for their effort in the hearts of peasants, religious believers, nomads, intellectuals, and even workers and Old Guard Party members. And the method of applying punishment prophylactically on the basis of negative loyalty indications is nothing else than the bureaucratization of class warfare, the transformation of political struggles into regulated routines and computerlike operations.

Seen in this context, Stalin's personal traits, his paranoia and

[5] Instances in which prophylactic justice of this kind was applied in the West to large numbers of people include the so-called denazification of Germany after World War II on the basis of automatic arrest categories, the forced "relocation" of people of Japanese ancestry from the West Coast in 1942, and certain aspects of antisubversive legislation in the United States.

vindictiveness, are only incidental. These traits themselves were nurtured by the problems of industrialization, and so was the crisis brewing in the Party in 1934, which led to the Great Purge. Similarly, the scapegoatism practiced by the Party, as well as the society-wide paranoia, can be seen in this light. Blaming political enemies for all the hardships industrialization engendered was, of course, a deliberate and cynical device; and the citizens' excessive "vigilance," their readiness to assume guilt by association or to convict on the basis of "self-criticism," were artificial creations of the Party and the security police. But both the scapegoatism and the universal hysteria could be fanned and used only in a society involved in a superhuman effort, which led to terrible inefficiencies and hardships. Add to this a chronically ticklish international situation and an equally chronic and troubling nationality problem, magnified by the wartime acquisitions of new territories, and the use of terror as a major method of government begins to make sense, if we can empathize with the desperate and determined people who ruled Soviet society, seeking to accomplish the impossible in record time. This explanation, perhaps somewhat commonplace, seems less contrived and more "economical" than a reference to the unique requirements of totalitarian systems for recurrent orgies of blood-letting, especially if this idea, in turn, is supported by the assertion that such systems have no other method of ensuring social mobility and a turnover of elites.[6]

Perhaps one more observation deserves to be added about the function of the security police: Throughout its history, it has been used as an important instrument in the foreign policy of the USSR, as an agency of military intelligence and counterintelligence, espionage, and covert political work of many different kinds similar to that carried out by our own Central Intelligence Agency. The apparatus of the security police in this function has overlapped and meshed in intricate fashion with those of the military establishment, the diplomatic service, and the international network of communist parties. Since this book concentrates on the domestic

[6] For the best expression of the idea criticized here, see Zbigniew K. Brzezinski, *The Permanent Purge* (Cambridge: Harvard University Press, 1956).

policies of the Soviet regime, we shall not dwell on these ramifications of the police apparatus.

Instead, we must round out this sketch of methods of extralegal compulsion, as practiced under Stalin (and, in large measure, also under his successors), by adding a number of features which can be distinguished from terror or from the work of the security police, even though they might, at the same time, be regarded as an extension of terror methods and police-state devices to the entire social fabric and to daily life. However we classify these practices, they are not easy to describe precisely because they are all-pervasive, almost part of the atmosphere or the style of life. We might, perhaps, summarize this style of life by saying that the Soviet regime has tried, with considerable success, to mobilize informal but very palpable peer-group pressure for the purpose of controlling the actions and words, and, hopefully, even the thoughts, of individual citizens. The Party has sought to make the citizens amenable to such pressure by assiduously preaching the primacy and the sovereignty of the collectivity over any of its individual members. In addition, it has always maintained that it had the exclusive right to define public attitudes and social norms of behavior, and has always used the massive means at its disposal to spread these norms until a majority of citizens, or at least a majority of citizen-activists, had internalized them. Once this degree of socialization had been achieved, peer-group pressure, mobilized by the Party or its activist spokesmen, could be applied to deviant or unreconstructed individuals. One factor that has helped the Party considerably in perfecting this system of pressures for conformity is the cramped housing situation prevailing in the cities of the USSR which has made it difficult for the individual to attain even a minimum of privacy. Instead, he lives as if in a goldfish bowl, his life an open book to his neighbors. Partly because of the housing shortage, the very notion of individual privacy has become very dim or disappeared altogether from the minds of many Soviet citizens, and the collective concern of all peers for every member of the group has become part of the natural order of things. The collectivist rhetoric has apparently reinforced this attitude. Many Soviet citizens appear to take it for granted that their peer group leaders have a right to inquire into all their activities, and that in fact the individual should, on his own initiative, make regular and full reports to his peer group about his life and activities. This routine reporting is complemented by more formal exercises in "self-criticism," during which the individual is urged to examine his political and moral conscience in the presence of his peers and openly recognize his failings. All of this might be compared to the religious ritual of the confession, were it not so much more a public performance. Moreover, whereas the confession may be said to function primarily to unburden the sinner's conscience and enable him to go on living despite his sinful inclinations, peer-group pressures and self-criticism meetings aim far more directly at adjusting the individual's behavior. Both devices seek to make conformity to group norms self-enforcing by backing it up with vague but strong community pressure. That such pressure is as much a perversion and corrosion of regular judicial processes as naked terror must be self-evident.

TERROR SINCE STALIN

In the decade since Stalin's death, his successors have publicly decried the excesses of mass terror and have backed their words with actions of various kinds. They have rehabilitated some of the victims of terror, benefiting by this corrective action not only the surviving kin of the Old Bolsheviks purged in the 1930s, but also thousands of citizens exiled, after mass raids, because they belonged to a nationality group or some other group singled out for annihilation or decimation. Fairly early after Stalin's death, his successors decapitated and significantly weakened the entire police apparatus, in line with the liquidation of its former chief, L. P. Beria. Conforming to the pattern of decentralization practiced in many other areas of administration, the federal Ministry of the Interior (MVD) was abolished in 1960 and its functions transferred to analogous ministries in the fifteen constituent republics. (Two years later, on September 3, 1962, the name of the MVD in the RSFSR was changed to Ministry of Public Law and Order.) At the federal Council of Ministers, a Committee on State Security (KGB) remains in charge of combatting political crimes. Meanwhile, there has been an obvious decrease in the number of inmates in corrective labor camps and an apparent willingness to experiment with more benign methods of correction emphasizing rehabilitation rather than punishment.[7] Finally, the security police has been deprived of some of the authorities it wielded before, most important among them that of inflicting punishment through administrative boards without even a modicum of due legal process. In short, the talons of the terror apparatus have been clipped somewhat. Without doubt, the basic elements of the machine remain in existence and may still be in use, albeit on a reduced basis. The Party's pronouncements continue to stress the need for "socialist legality" and warn against police arbitrariness; but they also go on preaching unflagging vigilance against any persons who might disturb the Soviet way of life.

The picture, already obscure because of the lack of sufficient evidence, is ambiguous because of the contradictory aims of the regime. It seems plausible to assume that the economic disadvantages of using prison labor on the previous gigantic scale have impressed themselves on the Party leaders. In a rapidly maturing industrial economy, manpower is too precious to be wasted in such reckless fashion. Moreover, the men in the Kremlin may also have convinced themselves that mass terror endangers and damages the political system more than it benefits the ruling elite, perhaps because the guardians of loyalty and security have arrogated too much unchecked power in their hands, or because legitimacy achieved through dread rests on too insecure a basis. Perhaps the Party has come to the conclusion, anyway, that it has in fact

[7] For a discussion of the broad range of changes in this regard, see Paul Barton, "An End to Concentration Camps?" in *Problems of Communism*, No. 2 (1962), 38–46. For a report on a new kind of labor camp, the Corrective Labor Colony Settlement—a penal institution without walls or guards —see article by D. Pankov, *Izvestiia* (October 5, 1963 and November 11, 1963).

gained legitimacy in sufficient measure so that it can now rely on more open legal procedures for controlling deviant citizens. Because more and more citizens have obviously accepted the values of the regime as their own, the Party can rely more and more on the population itself to keep its deviant members under control. In other words, peer-group pressure can be mobilized not only in periods of intense class warfare, but also in periods of growing stabilization; in the former circumstance, a struggling regime encourages militant minorities that sympathize with the revolution to take the law into their own hands; in the latter, the party enforces its well-established rule by fostering majority tyranny. In both cases, the forms may be very similar. Indeed, we can assume that any individual Soviet official must regard the terror apparatus and the political police in general as a threat, and that even the number-one man in the system may look at it that way. Political police forces in any system are a potential threat not because of the troops and weapons they have at their disposal, but because they have the power of knowledge. Their files, containing all the most embarrassing information about even the highest citizens, are political dynamite which can explode under the very individual or group theoretically controlling the police and dependent on their work. In short, the political police is useful, but also dangerous. Its entire operation tends to have a disruptive effect. Police officials have a professional interest both in being suspicious and in fostering suspicion. The political police plays the role of watchdog and accuser, hence also of a disrupter and troublemaker. In looking at any society that makes use of political police forces one gets the impression that these forces spend much of their time (and of the national resources) in chasing phantom enemies of their own imagination or even creation. After all, even if there are no subversive conspiracies, the police must justify its continued existence; it does this by conjuring up imaginary threats, and fulfills its bureaucratic achievement quotas by unearthing sufficient numbers of suspicious characters.[8] If the Communist Party of the Soviet Union has, since Stalin's death, limited the powers of the police,

[8] See p. 323.

it may well be because the leaders became aware of these dangers. In all political systems, Soviet or Western style, vigilance against the political police is a vital necessity.

What was said above concerning the renewed and intensified use of peer-group pressure refers to a variety of experiments the Soviet regime has undertaken in recent years. All these experiments have in common the transfer of police and/or judicial functions from formal administrative agencies of the government to informal groups at the grass-roots or community level. Soviet spokesmen write about these transfers of governmental functions as steps toward the withering away of the state, hence as tokens of the incipient transition of Soviet society from socialism to communism, "signifying the further development of Soviet democracy and the strengthening of the role of the community in the communist education of the toilers."[9] Two such novel institutions deserve to be discussed—the Comrades' Courts formed by residential neighborhood assemblies or by the employees gathered at a place of work, and the squads (*druzhiny*) of Young Communist activists which function as auxiliary police and as universal censors of behavior. Comrades' Courts, discussed since 1959, set up formally in 1961, and still somewhat on an experimental basis,[10] sit in judgment over individuals from their own neighborhood or workshop. They are entitled to mete out various minor punishments or recommend more drastic action by higher authorities. But, in effect, they seem to decide primarily whether or not the individual being "tried" fits in or should be cast out of his peer group. In making this decision, Comrades' Courts direct their attention to various kinds of antisocial behavior, including quarrelsomeness, malicious gossip, drunkenness, slovenliness, wife-beating, promiscuity, vandalism, petty theft, and unsatisfactory work discipline. Their main function is defined as that of helping to educate their

[9] Decree of the Presidium of the All-Union Central Council of Trade Unions extending the jurisdiction of the Workers' Comrades' Courts. *Spravochnik Partiinogo Rabotnika*, Issue 4 (1963), p. 554.

[10] Witness the decree of the Presidium of the Supreme Soviet of the Russian Republic (RSFSR), October 23, 1963, adding numerous and thorough amendments to the statute on Comrades' Courts. *Izvestiia* (October 25, 1963).

fellow-citizens to a positive attitude toward work, socialist property, the socialist way of life, collectivism, mutual help, and respect for the rights of others;[11] they assume jurisdiction for the individual's behavior not only at his place of work, but also in public places and even in the home. In contrast, the vigilante squads of the Komsomol are organized to function as auxiliary police. They are to keep order at mass gatherings and in public places and appear to be on the lookout for any citizens offending against the community's (or the Party's) standards of taste in behavior, dress, entertainment, or choice of associates. They are supposed to use persuasion, warnings, or adverse publicity against offenders against such standards or may turn them over to more formal legal authorities in case of serious or repeated violations. As soon as they were created, it became evident that they would frequently overstep the limits of their authority, taking the law into their own hands. Some of these volunteer policemen seem to be narrow-minded, prying minds; some have been roughnecks who used physical violence against those whose behavior they found objectionable. In the Soviet press, there has been a good deal of discussion of these practices.[12] But popular resentment has also led to violent resistance; and this has caused the government to pass severe laws against such resistance: the police and its auxiliaries apparently have to be protected against the Soviet people.[13] In both cases, the Party obviously has created institutions of coercion and intimidation which apply sanctions in cases where no formal law has been violated, and where therefore the public prosecutor and the courts have no cause to step in, despite the vagueness and all-inclusiveness of Soviet criminal laws. Moreover, in all these cases, the Party uses the spontaneous resentment of the most narrow-minded, the most indoctrinated, and the most authoritarian citizens, including juveniles with questionable motives, to intimidate all

[11] "Polozhenie o tovarishcheskikh sudakh," in *Spravochnik Partiinogo Rabotnika,* Issue 4 (1963), p. 555.

[12] See, for instance, the complaints in *Komsomolskaia Pravda* (October 6, 1960), p. 2; (December 13, 1960), p. 2; and (September 22, 1960), p. 4.

[13] Ukaz Prezidiuma Verkhovnogo Soveta SSSR, in *Spravochnik Partiinogo Rabotnika,* Issue 4 (February 15, 1962), p. 532. See also Postanovlennie Prezidiuma Verkhovnogo Soveta SSSR (April 4, 1962).

those who dare exercise or manifest some shreds of individuality and nonconformity. In these new institutions, terror has become a popular institution.[14]

Soviet commentators hail this development as part of the withering away of the state and the blossoming forth of true democracy. A distinguished law professor asserts that "the Soviet state will rely less and less on compulsion and more and more on *education* and *organization*",[15] and indeed one might consider comrades' courts and Komsomol *druzhiny* as educational institutions of a peculiar kind. As a matter of fact, all coercion has educational effects, just as all organization is a form of compulsion. Another recent Soviet writer is a bit more forthright in discussing the creeping terror of these organizations: "In communist society," he writes, "governmental-legal coercion will completely disappear, and with it the institutions which carry it out. However, coercion will continue to exist in the coming society. Only it will be practiced directly by the society, by societal organizations, by the public. . . . Political power will transform itself into societal power."[16]

[14] For details, see also Jeremy R. Azrael, "Is Coercion Withering Away?" in *Problems of Communism*, XI, 6 (November–December, 1962), pp. 9–17.

[15] P. Romashkin, "Soviet State and Law at the Contemporary Stage," in *Fundamentals of Soviet Law* (Moscow, 1962), pp. 19–20.

[16] A. K. Belykh, "O dialektike otmiraniia gosudarstva," in *Sovetskoe gosudarstvo i pravo*, No. 1 (1963).

Chapter XIV
Socialization and Legitimation

Of course, the way of life, and labor and social relations, play a decisive part in developing people's social consciousness and high moral qualities. But it would be incorrect to make everything depend on objective factors alone [that is, on the given social system]. Communist education of the working people is an incessant concern of the Party, the state, mass organizations, and collectives. An important part is played here by the press, radio, cinema, television, literature, theater, and graphic arts. Skilful use of all these media can greatly accelerate the law-governed process of the development of communist consciousness and morality, and therefore the transition to communism.

FUNDAMENTALS OF MARXISM–LENINISM

To repeat: the widespread and habitual use of terror is an admission of insecurity, weakness, and lack of legitimacy, just as the habitual use of bully tactics in personal relations betrays weakness or an inner sense of weakness. Moreover, terror is an unreliable as well as costly method of obtaining compliance with the will of the regime. Vigilance easily snowballs into mass hysteria. The cost in human lives is always heavy and, in the long run, prohibitive. Terror alienates the citizens as much as it cows them; and by doing both it stifles initiative, innovation, and progress. Finally, it is insufficiently discriminating and eliminates many loyal and useful individuals who did not in fact threaten the political system. Some of these drawbacks apply not only to mass terror as practiced by the police, but also to the pressure for conformity exerted by neighborhood kangaroo courts and Komsomol vigilante squads.

A much more reliable and dependable method of achieving compliance is to condition the citizens so as to make them accept the values and goals of the elite, to make them internalize the Party's will so that it becomes their own. Such a process of conditioning is usually called "socialization"; and if it is conditioning specifically to the political system, it may be referred to as "political socialization." Socialization is a process that must go on in all human societies and political systems, because no society or political order has yet been devised in which the members can function and succeed, and yet not disrupt the social or political structure, by merely following the instincts and drives with which they may have been born. All social behavior is learned behavior; and socialization is the process in which men learn to function as members of their own societies.

Socialization is so closely linked with legitimation that the two processes should be named in the same breath. Socialization functions to make the individual into a useful and successful member of his society by teaching him the prevailing behavior pattern and role expectations. Legitimation is that process which makes him accept the system as it is; it causes him to develop positive, approving attitudes toward the system and its institutions, toward those who exert leadership in it as well as toward the process by which they have been selected for their prominent positions. Because men seem to have a propensity for challenging relationships of inequality, this, too, is probably a process no political system can dispense with.

The universality of the socialization and legitimation processes may at times be overlooked because the processes may be so spontaneous, nondeliberate, or informal, that they escape the notice even of the outside observer. The insider, that is, the member of a given society, is likely to be entirely unaware of these processes. In his eyes, what is in fact a schooling for life in a specific social system becomes a schooling for life in general, since he is not aware of alternative ways of life. Socialization processes, moreover, attract little attention of those who observe comparatively static or traditional societies, since the very process of growing up in a traditional or stable setting seems to accomplish the tasks of socialization and legitimation. Similar processes may also be obscure in very heterogeneous or rapidly changing societies because they may abound in subcultures and subsocieties, each having its own standards of behavior and specific methods of conditioning its members. Because of this variety, the outsider may overlook the socialization devices that pervade the entire society; and, again, these may be so spontaneous and informal that they escape attention.

PROCESSES OF SOCIALIZATION AND LEGITIMATION

In the Soviet political system, some of these observations apply as well. Simply by growing up as a Soviet citizen, any human being is bound to absorb and internalize the most general rules of behavior determining individual successes and failure in that system. Simply by being born of Soviet parents and reared in Soviet schools, a child is bound to adopt the political culture of his environment. By receiving his training and employment from the Soviet state, the citizen is likely to adjust himself to the ways and manners prevailing in that organization. Moreover, by growing up under the ever-present tutelage of the Communist Party, he may come to take its political leadership entirely for granted. To use the technical expression: in his eyes, the Party and its leaders, simply by having been in charge for as long as he can remember, may be endowed with legitimacy, and so may the countless citizens to whom the system has granted some particular authority. In a similarly informal and unnoticeable fashion, the American reader of this book may have learned to respect as legitimate the authority of the President, of his teacher, or of the policeman; and he may also have learned to take for granted the wealth of some and the poverty of others. In other words, he may have accepted the legitimacy of private property and property differences.

Still, the Soviet regime has not been able or willing to rely on the spontaneous processes of socialization and legitimation which work on those who simply grow up in the system. We have had ample proof of this in the preceding chapter. The principal reason for this unwillingness to let spontaneous socialization do its work, of course, is that it has been a revolutionary regime which sought to overthrow the inherited, traditional political culture and promote a completely new one. The spontaneous processes working on the growing child therefore were not just insufficient; they were in fact considered hostile—part of a past the regime wished to overcome. Hence the spontaneous socialization forces working in the parental home, in the village, the church, the peer group, and other features of the social environment, had to be counteracted by a process of counter-socialization or resocialization, and the revolutionary origins of the regime logically demanded a vigorous effort at legitimizing the new ruling party.[1] The need for such education and reeducation programs was felt all the more urgently after the regime engaged in its crash program for industrialization, which by its very nature required a major psychological readjustment of all citizens, if they did not wish to be shoved aside or crushed by the giant machine their society was becoming.

The Communist Party has always acknowledged the need for a continual process of socialization, beginning with Lenin's realization that the Soviet regime was held together by a mixture of coercion and conviction; and it has always aspired to a situation in which coercion could be dispensed with because communist convictions had spread among the widest masses of the population. "It must be our endeavor," said Khrushchev to a congress of communist youth leaders, "to make every young person regard the interests of the nation as his own most vital interests and thus to make them turn into ideologically committed fighters."[2] And the basic ideological textbook of the Party states this as follows: "The society that is building communism sets before itself a lofty ideal—gradually to do away with all compulsion and administrative regulation of relations between people, replacing them by measures of social influence and education. Only such a society is able to

[1] Particularly the family, which in more stable societies is the first and perhaps most important agent of socialization, was of doubtful and often negative value to the regime, because it was bound, in the main, to transmit prerevolutionary life patterns. This is one of the reasons why the regime, in the first fifteen years of its existence, sought to destroy the family. To be sure, in line with the cultural counterrevolution, the Party rediscovered the usefulness of the family as a socialization agent, but even now the family is no more than an auxiliary device in this process.

[2] *Komsomolskaia Pravda* (April 21, 1962).

achieve the task of eradicating all violations of law and order and abolishing crime, for it creates the necessary conditions for this by ensuring the growth of material security and a rise in the level of culture and political consciousness among the working people. Voluntary, conscientious fulfillment of their duties becomes a rule for all."[3] In the long run, the aim of socialization, in fact, is to make all citizens internalize the Party's goals to such an extent that everyone is a communist. "As time goes on," says the same text, "the ideology of the party, its principles and standards of life will become the possession of all of society. Actually, every person will then become a conscious Communist."[4]

Forms of Indoctrination. Of the various methods of socialization and legitimation used by the Soviet rulers, other than the terror described earlier, the most obvious one is indoctrination. Indoctrination assumes a number of forms. First, it comes to the individual as formal citizenship education. All children in the Soviet Union receive school instruction in topics that convey the political ethos of the regime—history, social studies, and philosophy. The length and intensity of such instruction increases at every higher educational level. What the content of such instruction is, we have indicated in Part I. Taught by teachers and professors who have "majored" in these subjects at teachers' colleges or specialized higher institutions of learning, these courses are compulsory for all students. That these subjects are often taught in perfunctory and boring fashion is due partly to the catechismal rigidity of the Soviet official dogma, and partly to the nature of compulsory mass instruction in any subject. Obviously, the regime could not succeed in the task of indoctrination if it left it to classroom instructors of this sort. Therefore, the Party supplements the effort of these teachers and professors by an elaborate publicity machinery which it operates directly. This is the *agitprop* operation of the party, usually referred to as "ideological work," which has been mentioned in Part II. It attempts, among other things, to spread the official social doctrine among the general citizenry by means of

[3] *Fundamentals of Marxism–Leninism*, p. 672.
[4] *Ibid.*, p. 690.

books, pamphlets, periodicals, and other visual material such as posters and exhibits; through lectures, seminars, discussions, and informal orientation talks.[5] Some of these (and other) indoctrination messages reach the broadest mass audiences regardless of whether the individuals wish to receive them or not. Others are available to those citizens who are interested or who feel the need to demonstrate an interest in them.

While the Party's Agitprop machine addresses itself to the entire population, the younger generation's classroom indoctrination is supplemented by the work of the Party's youth auxiliaries. To be sure, no more than between one third and one half of the young men and women above the age of fourteen have usually been members of the Komsomol (Full name: All-Union Leninist Communist Union of Youth, or VLKSM); and in some periods, such as the years immediately before and after World War II, the percentages have been far lower.[6] But the vast majority of younger children (ages ten to fifteen) are members of the Young Pioneers. This communist scout movement functions primarily as a socialization and indoctrination agency, wherein the youngsters learn discipline, obedience, cooperativeness, patriotism, and other boy scout virtues that will supposedly help integrate them into adult society.

[5] Some of these techniques, and the need for improving them, are discussed in *Ideologicheskaia rabota partiinykh organizatsii* (Moscow: Gospolitizdat, 1956).

[6] Komsomol membership is open to boys and girls between the ages of fourteen and twenty-seven, but many of its leaders are older (at the Thirteenth Komsomol Congress, in 1958, 52 percent of the delegates were above the age limit, then twenty-six). From an initial enrolment of about 22,000 in 1918, the membership has grown as follows:

1919	96,000	1933	4,500,000
1920	400,000	1936	3,600,000
1922	247,000	1941	11,000,000
1924	400,000	1945	15,000,000
1925	1,000,000	1949	9,283,289
1927	2,000,000	1954	18,825,327
	1962	19,400,000	

Figures are from Ralph T. Fisher, Jr., *Pattern for Soviet Youth* (New York: Columbia University Press, 1959) and *Komsomolskaia Pravda* (April 18, 1962).

It might be useful to distinguish not only between different methods of indoctrination, but also between different kinds of material presented to the receivers of indoctrination. The broad background information of history, social studies, and philosophy, which in their totality constitute the dogma of Soviet communism, represent only the more formal part of indoctrination. This is always supplemented by the ceaseless dissemination of the current Party line on domestic problems and world affairs. Such up-to-date information and comments on recent events are unleashed onto the citizenry in a never-ending, broad and fast stream of messages from which there seems to be no escape. True, not everyone can be expected to read the daily newspaper or the wall newspaper tacked onto the bulletin board; many people may never set foot in the reading rooms their village, town, or employer provides; election campaigns may leave them unmoved, and they may doze during agitation meetings. But the posters, billboards, and electric-light signs remain visible to all passers-by, and only the deaf can fail to hear the messages that come forth from the local radio station through loudspeakers fixed permanently in public places—markets, squares, parks, canteens. Government publicity is as inescapable in the USSR as commercial advertising is in the United States; and, except for being noncompetitive, it takes very similar forms. Likewise, much of the verbiage poured forth is apparently taken in by the hapless citizens as uncritically, unthinkingly, and noncommittally as we ingest political oratory, church sermons, and commercial advertising.

The institution that makes this running indoctrination possible is the absolute monopoly which the Party, indirectly or directly, wields over all media of communications, including all publishing ventures, from mimeographed wall newspapers to books, all radio and television facilities, and the two news-gathering agencies. By wielding this monopoly over the printed or publicly spoken word, the Party, aided by the government and various other subsidiary organizations, can control the contents, form, subject matter, and manner of presentation or interpretation of all public communications. It can thus indoctrinate the citizens not only positively (by structuring all messages in accordance with the Party line) but also negatively (by keeping any alternative views from being voiced; by eliminating facts, interpretations, or even moods not in line with the party's views). In short, the entire communications business, in the largest sense of the word, is in the hands of the political machinery. This monopoly is not disrupted by the very considerable degree of decentralization prevailing in the publication of the printed word. The Party's Central Committee publishes a daily newspaper, *Pravda* (Truth), as do many of its subordinate territorial organizations. The national government and many republican, provincial, and city governments publish dailies of their own. The variety of specialized newspapers and periodicals in the USSR is as great as the complex division of labor in a modern industrial society demands. Every skill and profession, every interest, every separate reading public and every organized group in Soviet government, economics, and daily life, has some serial publication responding to its needs for specialized information and news. Inevitably, this variety of publications and publishers spells a certain amount of difference in opinions and interpretations. The strategic conceptions expressed in *Krasnaya Zvezda* (Red Star), the newspaper of the Central Committee's Military Department, have at times differed from those printed in the journal of the General Staff, *Voennaia Mysl* (Military Thought). Various literary journals, at the present time, are managed by spokesmen of different literary schools. The Komsomol paper, *Komsomolskaia Pravda,* is likely to clash with professional educators, and their journals, on a variety of educational problems. Issues concerning economic management will be viewed differently by economists and production engineers, and their respective journals.

In Part I of this book it was pointed out that in every practical field of endeavor, the line and staff personnel who must solve countless managerial and engineering problems discuss them candidly and in commonsense terms, often with little regard to ideological taboos. Nonetheless, controversy and heterogeneity are kept down by a number of devices. First, much of the news appearing in provincial and local papers is in fact printed in Moscow, which distributes its plates by air, or dictates its articles by wireless in a manner similar to the way wire services and newspaper chains operate in the United States. Moreover, all publications, with due acknowledgment of their variety and conflicting views, are official publications in that they are produced by recognized public organizations. Soviet law strictly forbids the private ownership of printing and publishing facilities, including even duplicating machines. To close the chain of controls over the printed word, all publications are subject to several stages of censorship. In the case of books, the censorship agency is the Main Administration for Literary Affairs and Publishing (Glavlit) in the Ministry for Education.[7]

Despite real differences of opinion which are expressed continually, the total output of printed and spoken words in the USSR thus tends to appear strikingly uniform in tone and contents, at least to the outsider. Whether the various control methods enumerated above create this homogeneity or whether they merely reinforce it might be an interesting question, but can probably not be answered. Lest we answer, with undue haste, that the uniformities of Soviet thought and communications are the result of direct control and coercion, we should reflect on some of the uniformities of political opinion in the Western world, which develop with seeming spontaneity, yet can at times be striking. There are instances in which editorial opinion as expressed in newspapers and on television in the West has spontaneously shifted as widely and as rapidly as the Soviet press does in the wake of a change in the Party line.[8]

[7] See Merle Fainsod, "Censorship in the USSR," *Problems of Communism,* No. 2 (1956).

[8] Examples can be adduced most easily from interpretations of international affairs; for instance, the shifts of American press opinion concerning Fidel Castro or Syngman Rhee, and the remarkable change in attitudes toward Germany and Japan.

"Through the years I have noted that *Time* is run on what might be called the Theory of Instantaneously Reversible Infallibility. That is, what is propounded with great skill and energy and conviction on one Friday as an eternal Truth is neither denied nor explained the following Friday when a diametrically opposed eternal Truth is propounded, with equal vigor and conviction." Statement by Irwin Shaw, in *"Time:* The Weekly Fiction Magazine," in *fact,* I, 1 (January–February 1964), 19.

To sum up: The Soviet citizen hears a great deal about current events, whether he is interested or not. The higher his status, the more he is expected to keep himself informed; and in a variety of ways his peers and his superiors manage to check on his zeal in keeping up with the news. All he learns is selected and interpreted for him, and presented in a form and style which the Party considers appropriate.

The Arts as Media of Socialization.   But this does not exhaust the list of socialization methods. Rather, they include a number of other important devices. One of these is the Party's control over all artistic endeavor and over all entertainment media. Style and content of all artistic creations and entertainment are prescribed to those who practice the relevant professions. Their work is planned and supervised, and their careers are controlled, by the government or the Party in the bureaucratic fashion pervading all Soviet public life. The methods employed for this purpose include central control over the essential tools—theaters, musical instruments, artistic materials, printing presses. Party and government, through their countless branch agencies, are the only patrons and distributors of art and entertainment. Hence they can control their style and content; and the relevant professions are organized in unions or guilds which act as vehicles for these controls. For instance, the Union of Soviet Writers, closely supervised by the cultural department of the Central Committee, commissions works, sets themes, determines permissible forms, voices criticism, and may veto the publication of a manuscript. Membership in good standing in the Union is the first prerequisite for having one's work published. Similar controls shape the works of painters, sculptors, composers, actors, movie producers, and even circus performers.

The rationale behind this monopolistic control over art and entertainment is the argument that all these activities are acts of communication. All communications, however, must convey messages acceptable to the regime if they are to be permitted. The people (as represented by the Party and the government) will not allow anyone to express hostile or deviant views and cannot be expected to permit foes or deviants to use materials owned by the people for such purposes. The people have the right to prevent their own property from being used for purposes that are frivolous, useless, or wasteful; hence the right—nay, the duty—of those authorities who speak for the people to determine the form and contents of all artistic and entertainment production.

The principal guidelines the Party has imposed on Soviet art in this connection might be summarized as follows: First, all art must be presented in forms that are easily understood by everyone. Art must be uncomplicated. If it is visual, it should also be naturalistic; if it is music, it should be harmonious and folksy. Aesthetic sophistication therefore is frowned upon. There must be no experiments with bold or bizarre forms, no flights into excessive abstraction, obscure symbolism, erudite allusions, or other departures from the familiar and the conventional. Such ventures are condemned as "formalism," which thus comes to mean any preoccupation with aesthetic problems, any conception of art as an end in itself or for itself, or of art as a means of individual self-expression. Art should serve not the artist, nor a select public or connoisseurs, but has a social purpose and derives its sole justification from this purpose. This determines its forms.[9]

Second, the contents of all art and entertainment must conform to the aims of the regime. Stated most generally, art is supposed to please and to educate. It must glorify the regime and its achievements, and condemn its enemies. It should engender confidence in the Soviet system by dwelling on its advantages and promises. Although it may, and indeed ought to, portray dissenters and shortcomings or insert dissonances, the inevitable victory of the forces of progress (i.e., the Communist Party) must never remain in doubt. In Soviet art and entertainment, the good guys always

---

[9] "Socialism . . . frees culture from the oppression of the money-bags, affording the artist the opportunity to create not in order to pander to the depraved tastes of a small handful of wealthy fat-bellies, but for the masses. Does this infringe the freedom of the artist? Not in the least." *Fundamentals of Marxism–Leninism*, p. 612.

win. The ending always is happy. The concluding note inevitably is one of triumph and optimism.[10]

In short, Soviet art, in style and content, has been strikingly similar to the "heroic art" of the Third Reich, and even more to the products of what many observers today call Western mass culture. Soviet painting reminds us of *Saturday Evening Post* covers; Soviet compositions, of American "light classical" musicals. Soviet architecture, until a few years ago, seemed modeled on the Woolworth building, the Flatiron building, or other monstrous relics from lower Broadway. It would be very intriguing to speculate on the reasons for these similarities between a seemingly spontaneous artistic production and one that is so obviously directed, or between commercialized art and politicized art; but such musings would go far beyond the framework of this book.

Called "Socialist Realism," this canon for artistic production, which combines a popular-naturalistic manner with an optimistic mood, has had the sanction of the Party for the last three decades. To dwell on the currents and factions within the artists' community and their relations with the regime and with each other, however pertinent to the study of Soviet politics, would get us involved in excessive detail. But pertinent it surely is; for as soon as artistic style becomes a matter of public policy, divergent conceptions of or attitudes toward art turn into political issues. But then, since virtually all professions in the USSR are in the public employ,

---

[10] "Those who are creative in the field of culture carry a heavy responsibility. Literature and art not only reflect the life of the people, but also mould the human mind. The idea of the indivisible bond of literature and art with the interests and the struggle of social classes and, in socialist society, with the life of the entire people, was theoretically substantiated by Lenin who put forward the principle of the partisanship of literature. Bourgeois propagandists viciously attack this principle, seeking to prove that serving the interests of a definite class and conscious pursuance of a definite political line are incompatible with freedom or artistic creation. But this is a futile attempt." *Ibid.*, pp. 611–612.

It must, of course, be conceded that most, including some of the greatest, works of art have been produced in conformity with the tastes and demands of the consumers of art, and in material dependence on them. In fact, many immortal masterpieces have been produced under dictatorship (secular or religious).

almost all disputes among professional specialists tend to become political issues.[11]

The obligation of artists to convey in their work a mood of confidence and optimism, a sense of the inevitable happy ending, can be regarded as part of a much more general effort to generate a perpetual mood of optimism and confidence in the population. Seen in this light, the entire indoctrination work of the Soviet regime might be described as an attempt to make its subjects think only positive thoughts, to keep smiling, and to repress all discontent. Sour faces and grumbling voices are a vote of nonconfidence in communism and therefore a manifestation of disloyalty; at the least, they are considered disturbing and disruptive. Happiness is obligatory. Thus even the individual's mood, his affect, are political matters, and subject to regulation.

Summing all this up in a somewhat more comprehensive fashion, we might define the goal of all indoctrination as follows: The Soviet regime endeavors to teach its citizens to react to any situation in a highly stereotyped manner. There is a correct word and correct facial expression for every occasion; and any citizen who wants to succeed in the system is well advised to use them. This attitude can be illustrated by the cartoon on page 349 and a Soviet joke: Two men run themselves breathless to catch a bus. If they miss, they will be late for work and subject to sanctions. They manage to catch it, and one man even finds a seat. As he lowers himself onto the seat, he emits a groan of retrospective exasperation. Whereupon his friend says, "Come now, Ivanovich; how often have I warned you not to talk politics in public?"

Much of this may by now come naturally. On many issues, conformity no longer has to be enforced, but only reinforced. At least the opinion leaders are so well in tune with official thinking that they swing with the political wind without having to be reindoctrinated every time it shifts.

At the same time, in this process of the stereotyping of affect

[11] A thorough discussion, with inconclusive results, of Party policies concerning art and literature took place at the June 1963 Plenum of the Communist Party. For the major speeches, see *Pravda* (June 20, 21, 22, 1963).

we see terror and indoctrination merging in subtle fashion. In any one instance it is impossible to say whether the individual's response is the result of police terror, peer-group pressure, or the steady stream of educational and exhortative messages rushing in upon his consciousness. All the forms of terror and all the forms of indoctrination intimately support and back up the others; each makes the other more acceptable as a "normal" phenomenon. All are responses to the party's need for reinforced legitimacy.

"SPONTANEOUS" SOCIALIZATION

At the beginning of this chapter we noted that simply growing up in his society socializes the individual for life within it and that this process operates in all societies, including the USSR. Indoctrination and the manipulation of affect, we saw, are used because the regime is unwilling to rely on these spontaneous socialization processes. At the same time, spontaneous socialization, too, goes on in the Soviet system. Yet even its processes seem, to the outside observer, to be somehow contrived and manipulated. This impression is conveyed because the public life in which the citizens participate is given a certain didactic, paternal, or parental character: open political activities and events are deliberately dramatized, as it were, by those who stage them, so that they become educational experiences. We have observed this, in passing, when discussing the various steps of the electoral process, which functions not only to recruit soviet deputies, but, far more important, as a device for citizenship education. Similarly, court trials not only serve to adjudicate disputes, but also to teach socialist legality to all participants and observers. Trade unions are not nearly so important to the regime as agencies for collective bargaining and the safeguarding of workers' rights as they are as socialization devices which teach labor discipline and other constructive attitudes. Service in the armed forces is a socialization device of outstanding importance, especially for citizens from among national minorities and the less educated (virtually all young men with higher education are exempt from military service; only the "masses" are drafted). Military service not only instills the values and behavior patterns of the Soviet way of life into the recruits; the armed forces act also as an important recruiting pool for the Party and the Komsomol. Similar observations can be made about a host of other activities involving citizens, activists, or Party members, from Young Pioneer scrap collection drives or civil defense activities to ceremonies, parades, and mass demonstrations.

In fact, it must have become quite clear by now that, in the eyes of the Party, all activities of Soviet life, because they are carried out within a *kollektiv,* organized by and dependent on the Party, function as socialization processes, if only because the Party can use them for the purpose of mobilizing peer-group pressure on deviant citizens. This is what is implied in Khrushchev's recent remark to youth leaders, that "the most important strength in the fight against evils is *publicity*"; for the collective life is public life. This, too, is expressed in the official textbook on ideology, which says, "The chief part in communist education will more and more pass directly to the collectives. The social practice of the socialist countries has already shown that the most effective means of struggle against egotistic individualism, which is the main opponent of communist morality, lies in counterposing active collectivism to it. . . . The socialist collective exerts a tremendous influence capable in case of need of re-educating and turning into useful members of society even the most apparently incorrigible persons."[12]

A good deal of organizational life involving younger citizens seems to function *primarily* as a socialization process.[13] This is true not only of the school and classroom experience, but also of the extracurricular activities carried out under the auspices of the Komsomol and its children's auxiliaries. In examining both the school and the communist youth organization, we discover a certain latent conflict of purpose within and between them.

As in other societies, the school of the USSR not only gives professional training, which enables the students to obtain for themselves meaningful places within the occupational structure. It also is supposed to provide training in "life adjustment"—in short, socialization; and it does so by structuring the students' experiences in and out of the classroom so as to make the school a didactic replica of the total society. The authoritarian relationship between teachers and pupils contributes toward this kind of life adjustment in the USSR; and so does the mixture of authoritarianism, uniformity, collectivism, and managed competitiveness which pervades the classroom situation. Students in Soviet schools are given to understand from the very beginning that they are, in a sense, wards of the state and incur a lifelong obligation in return for the training they receive free of charge. Life in their classes teaches them that they are, individually and collectively, responsible not only for their own performance, but also for that of the entire *kollektiv* and every one of its members. The curriculum itself undoubtedly conveys to the students a sense of the regime's priorities. Dormitory life, in institutes of higher learning, easily

[12] *Fundamentals of Marxism–Leninism,* p. 684.

[13] This, too, is a trite observation, for in *all* societies, the life and activities of the young are a continual process of socialization.

lends itself for purposes of socialization; and since the Soviet regime now aims to replace more and more of its present primary and secondary schools with boarding schools, where the pupils live during the entire academic year, the opportunity for structuring the entire life experience of the younger generation grows to unprecedented proportions. One of the most effective socialization devices of all is students' self-government, that playful initiation into the practices of bureaucratic politics and democratic centralism which gives budding organization men their first chance to show leadership potential, at the same time compelling all to conform to officially approved standards of behavior through seemingly spontaneous and democratic self-enforcement. In short, as schools in the West not only contribute to the growth of knowledge and skills, but function also as training grounds for adult life in general ("training for democracy"), so the Soviet school socializes the young citizen, indoctrinates him with the accepted values, and trains him for the competitive rat race of organizationmanship. It may seem to the outside observer that the tremendous stress Soviet schools place on learning skills and professional knowledge leaves less time for the socialization functions. But, in fact, one function does not preclude the other.[14]

Still, the schools can safely lay stress on professional training and academic learning, because socialization for life in the bureaucratized society is also carried out outside the school. For people of school age, the Little Octobrists, Young Pioneers, and the Komsomol provide this schooling for life. During the school year, the students who belong to these organizations spend much of their free time in them; and the students' self-government activities, as well as the various community service projects they are encouraged to undertake, are guided by these Party youth affiliates, just as adult political life is guided and infiltrated by the Party.

[14] Indeed, the school socializes not only the children, but also the parents. Parents not conforming to officially approved ways in rearing their children may be counseled by school personnel. This may begin as early as nursery school, that is, within the first year of the child's life (see p. 372). See Mark G. Field, "Soviet Medical Institutions," in *Survey*, No. 48 (July 1963), 86–87.

During vacations, a large proportion of school children spend several weeks in Komsomol and Pioneer camps. Much of their leisure time is thus managed by an organization which has made the political socialization of youth its primary goal.

For upward-mobile aspirants to elite positions, moreover, the Komsomol provides the initial schooling and proving ground. By attaining responsible positions within the Komsomol, young men and women show the Party their leadership potential. By being active and prominent in youth activities guided and supervised by the Komsomol, they prove their worth as mass organizers or agitators. Leadership in student self-government or various youth associations is an opportunity to acquire and test the many skills needed by the successful organization man, the trusted bureaucratic hierarch. By providing and supervising opportunities for developing, manifesting, and testing such leadership potential, the Komsomol thus performs a socialization function analogous to that played by the many extracurricular activities, especially the fraternity life, on many American college campuses. In both cases, two education or socialization processes go on side by side, meshing and interfering with each other. One provides the academic learning; the other gives schooling in leadership. Those successful in one attain academic excellence; those who advance in the other become Big Men On Campus, while maintaining their gentlemanly "C" average. Both processes prepare the student for upward mobility. But while the school trains professional specialists, the Komsomol trains professional politicians and organization men. As in America, there is a good deal of antagonism and contempt between those who commit themselves fully to either of these two different educational processes. Moreover, educators in the USSR seem to think no more highly of the Komsomol than their American colleagues regard Greek fraternities. In both cases, the educators tend to lament the fact that so much of the students' time is wasted on activities which appear frivolous or useless or outright incompatible with academic pursuits. Meanwhile, the Komsomol leaders sound exactly like fraternity elders when they retort that their extracurricular schooling is an essential complement to the mere "book learning" imparted in the classroom, that they are helping educate the "whole man" and the future leaders of society.[15]

SUMMARY: ROUTES TO LEGITIMATION

In the present chapter, we have surveyed a variety of socialization processes in the Soviet political system. Our point of departure was the inadequacy of terror as a device to obtain legitimacy and compliance. Terror, as we said, is complemented by indoctrination; and both have tended to be supplanted by subtler—and, if you wish, more insidious—methods of peer-group pressure, through which conformity to behavior and belief patterns is more and more self-enforced by the community. More and more of the values and orientations of the Soviet political elite have been internalized, if not by the population, then by the articulate opinion-makers. The Party's views are turning into a self-enforcing General Will. Both terror and frantic indoctrination recede in importance, remaining in existence only as reinforcement devices. They are used with greater caution because they have revealed themselves to be unreliable and dangerous. We have seen this to be the case with regard to terror. It is true also of indoctrination. When carried to the point of frenzy, indoctrination leads to excessive doctrinal rigidity; and this hinders the ruling elite in orienting itself to, and solving, the problems of an increasingly complex industrial society. When doctrinal rigidity becomes too dysfunctional, indoctrination itself must be braked.

Today, terror, in the fullest sense of the word, may be little more than a memory; yet even this memory is bound to affect the behavior of many citizens. Still, criminal law and the bureaucratic authoritarianism of all social relations in the USSR probably suffice to keep potential deviants in line. Indoctrination is still practiced, but less feverishly than before, because the regime has gained legitimacy. It can rely on peer groups to enforce the General Will.

[15] An interesting debate on academic versus extracurricular education, which was fought in the pages of *Komsomolskaia Pravda* in 1961, is reprinted in *The Soviet Review*, III, 4 (April 1962), 3–15.

Indoctrination remains in two forms: one is the very specialized one of current news and current slogans, which inform the citizens of the Party's day-to-day interpretation of events. The other is a set of vague and empty formulas, a catechismal litany chanted ritually and unthinkingly—a rhetoric flowing from everyone's lips in the predictable phrases of Sunday sermons and Independence Day speeches, affecting Soviet listeners no more than those exercises do their Western counterparts. This gradual turn from terror-plus-propaganda to peer-group pressure, this lessening intensity of terror and propaganda to the point where they are used merely as reminders, is a step in the direction from permanent civil war (of the Kremlin versus the people) to a somewhat more benign (or, at least, somewhat less frantic) process of politics, in which the means of persuasion have become both more insidious and more effective.[16]

To this, a note of caution must be added. Again and again, this book assumes that the Soviet regime has attained a considerable amount of legitimacy. In other words, we take for granted that the Soviet people have come to accept the Party as their sovereign and/or their representative. Supposing this assumption to be correct, can we say that indoctrination has achieved its purpose, and that the rank-and-file of the citizenry have in fact accepted the goals of the elite? It would probably be rash to draw this conclusion.

Like the large bureaucratic structure in the West, with which the Soviet political system has so much in common, the USSR undoubtedly contains citizens who in their adjustment to the system conform to divergent basic types. Positive or active acceptance of elite values corresponds to what Presthus calls the "upward-mobile type."[17] Those whom he calls the "indifferent" may in fact be composed of two groups that could be separated—those whose attitude is one of passive acceptance and those who passively reject

16 I have expressed some of these ideas before, in discussion with Z. K. Brzezinski, who has argued that indoctrination has replaced terror as the most essential function of the Soviet system. See our exchange of views in "The Nature of the Soviet System," *Slavic Review,* XX, 3 (October 1961).

17 Robert V. Presthus, *The Organizational Society* (New York: Alfred A. Knopf, 1962).

elite values—though the line might be very difficult to draw. Active or overt rejection of elite values leads to a person's elimination from the system, so it can be disregarded. Finally, all bureaucratic systems seem to contain their share of creative individualists of the type Presthus calls the "ambivalent." This last category will be the least numerous, whereas the vast majority of the people probably belong to one or the other kind of the indifferent. It seems plausible to assume that the only ones who are truly indoctrinated are the upward-mobile characters, whereas those whose acceptance (or rejection) of elite values remains passive are merely cowed, beaten, apathetic, and resigned—products of terror rather than indoctrination. If this is so, then perhaps Soviet indoctrination does not have any noticeable effect on the minds of the masses of the citizenry; perhaps it is no more effective than American advertising. Once we raise this question, we are easily led to suppose that the entire indoctrination machinery is primarily a device by which the political elite reassures itself, a self-legitimation apparatus rather than a doctrinal message for the masses. In fact, one might come to the assumption that the whole socialization process functions primarily for the elite, that is, for the upper 5 percent of the population, while the vast majority of people are left languishing in their indifference and obscurity, so long as they are rendered harmless by control and infiltration. These questions cannot be answered with the information and means at our disposal. But they are worth raising, if only to show the limits of our knowledge.[18]

[18] I have explored this question further in an article, "The Functions of Ideology in the Soviet Political System," to be published in the October 1965 or January 1966 issue of *Soviet Studies.*

Chapter XV
Rewards

Some time after the end of the civil war, Lenin remarked that the Soviet state was held together by a combination of coercion and persuasion. In examining the twin processes of terror and socialization, we have done no more than elaborate on this statement, which, of course, applies to all states, not only the USSR. Yet one other process helps to compel citizens to collaborate with, and function within, the political system and thus keeps it together. This is the structure of rewards which go to those who do collaborate and excel in their services to the regime. Rewards might be regarded as part of the socialization process, or they might be seen as something separate; that does not matter. Suffice it to say that in determining "who gets what, when, and how," the regime has a very effective method of compelling its citizens to comply with its expectations.[1]

---

[1] Close examination will undoubtedly reveal that in all societies there is a functional relationship between the distribution of benefits and the political structure. But in the Soviet Union this relationship, like so many other features, is more subject to deliberate control and manipulation than in some societies of the recent past. To quote a Polish sociologist: "In the society which gave rise to Marx's *Das Kapital* and Spencer's *Sociology,* the emperors did not distribute bread among the urban masses, and for entry to the circus a price had to be paid which was calculated on the principle of maximal profit. The world of today is giving a new form to the questions concerning the relations between privilege systems and systems of inter-human dependencies, the relations between the privilege of disposing over means of production and the privilege of a higher share in the national income, the relations between the ability to dispose over means of production and that of disposing over means of coercion." Stanisław Ossowski, *Klassenstruktur im sozialen Bewusstsein* (Neuwied: Luchterhand, 1962), p. 228.

Rewards, then, can be defined as the mechanism for structuring the process of social differentiation, because they determine differences in material living standards, as well as status, and reinforce them by psychological distinctions (status symbols). They are therefore the direct cause of the social stratification that can be observed in the USSR. This stratification is considered desirable by Soviet ideologists. To be sure, the Soviet Union describes itself as a society without class struggle, which expects soon to eliminate class differences altogether. But because the term "class" is defined in narrow, technical terms, classlessness is compatible with inequalities; and Soviet spokesmen have indicated that they do not, within the foreseeable future, intend to do away with inequalities. On the contrary, they hope to make use of managed inequalities; and the system of rewards, as well as other things related to it, such as the process of elite recruitment, will doubtless continue to emphasize the differences between various strata of the Soviet population.

This stratification process contradicts the earliest expectations of the communist regime, which incorporated the belief that after the revolution all members of the society would collaborate spontaneously, without expectation of reward. Implicitly, this image of communist society included equality as well. In the days of the revolution, the Bolsheviks expected that their coming to power would lead to a rise in the general welfare; they took it for granted that the elimination of the exploiter classes had already raised every individual's status to that of sovereign, of a fully autonomous member in a free and sovereign collectivity. The regime very quickly realized that its expectation of spontaneous collaboration and equality was a pipedream and that incentives would have to be provided to make the citizens work and cooperate. Hence the need for a system of managed inequality and for competition in the quest for the rewards of life. "The transition to communism requires not only an abundance of material and cultural benefits, but also a new attitude to labor—its conversion into a prime vital need. Until this is so, people's labor requires a material stimulus, i.e., in the first place differential payment. Prematurely discarding this would undermine the workers' incentive to develop production and therefore hamper the building of communism."[2]

In the early decades of the Soviet regime, the deliberate promotion of inequality was regarded by its spokesmen as a temporary measure going against the grain of their socialist convictions. Since then, however, a much more positive attitude toward managed inequalities has replaced these apologetic feelings, and the process of structuring Soviet society into sharply differentiated layers has been promoted vigorously and deliberately. Salary scales in the many professional hierarchies came to be steeply graded. Individual taxes are regressive, as if to imply that those who earn high salaries ought to be allowed to enjoy them. Wherever possible, the Soviet system has tended to reward individuals on the basis of their own performance by giving them piece-rate wages rather than fixed salaries (the principal exception to this is the collective farm peasant). Outstanding success in any line of work is rewarded by a complicated and steeply graded system of bonuses which at times add up to a multiple of the base salary.[3] Various fringe benefits, including adequate housing, plush transportation, vacations, and special commissaries selling better goods for lower prices, go to those whose work the regime considers most valuable or essential. To this one might add that unofficial fringe benefits (resembling bribes, graft, and the like), are often available on a preferential basis to those in positions of authority and status, and hence to those already reaping higher material rewards. All this is reinforced by the cultivation of status differences and their emphasis through psychological rewards (status symbols) such as uniforms and badges of rank, medals, citations, and other conspicuous honors, chauffeur-driven limousines, and election to

[2] *Fundamentals of Marxism–Leninism,* p. 656.

[3] "In socialist society, the bulk of material and cultural values are distributed in accordance with the quantity and quality of labor expended by each worker in social production. Those who work more and better receive a larger and better reward for their work from socialist society.

. . . The principle of payment in accordance with the quantity and quality of work, properly applied, is a powerful means for raising labor productivity and strengthening socialist labor discipline." *Ibid.,* p. 584.

honorific posts. In the words of the official ideologists, each man's labor, in Soviet society, becomes the principal measure of the individual's social worth.[4]

The net result of this reward system is a stratified society in which power, authority, status, and material well-being are concentrated in relatively few hands.[5] Since all these emoluments are distributed in a process which the top-ranking decision-makers have set up, they can use the rewards system so as to structure individual behavior. The fierce competition raging in virtually every field of endeavor, which is exactly what the system seeks to accomplish, attests to its effectiveness.[6]

At the same time, a significant proportion of rewards available within the Soviet political system is given to all or most citizens more or less indiscriminately. Let these rewards be examined under several headings, beginning with the general living standards.

STANDARDS OF LIVING

The relevant information about living standards could be summarized by saying that the Soviet Union is in the process of becoming a welfare state. This does not mean that the government seeks to provide maximal material comforts for all citizens. It does mean that the government attempts to provide a *minimum* of such

[4] *Ibid.*, p. 602. See also the following statement: "Material incentive has been and remains an important motive force in raising labor productivity. But during the transition to communism it will be increasingly supplemented by moral stimuli until the latter begin to predominate. . . . Other measures are designed to raise still higher the glory of the working men, to educate all working people through the finest examples. Such measures include, in particular, the award of Orders, medals, and certificates of merit to the best factory workers, collective farmers and office employees, their election to central and local government bodies and leading posts in public organizations, and lastly, the attention paid every day to the people of labor by the press, radio, publications, and art." *Ibid.*, p. 682.

[5] Even though the wealth pyramid is not so steep as that of the United States.

[6] Since 1956, income inequalities have shown a tendency to go down. Wage inequalities among workers have decreased; the minimum wage has risen; regular fixed salaries are beginning to take the place of piece-rate wages; and the income gap between workers and the white collar elite has narrowed. See Murray Yanowitch, "The Soviet Income Revolution," *Slavic Review*, XXII, 4 (December, 1963), 683–697.

comforts for all. Welfare states, in this sense, are political systems which undertake to put a floor under the general living standards and, in line with this, to protect their citizens against extraordinary hardships due to disease, accident, or other misfortune.

This effort involves a wide range of operations. One of these is the management of the nation's consumer goods industries, and the attempt to produce such goods as will meet the needs of the people. Virtually everything the consumer might want to buy, with the exception of some foodstuffs and some articles he can make himself or have made by individual craftsmen, must be manufactured by the government; and even for do-it-yourself items, the consumer must ordinarily obtain his materials from the government. The task of satisfying these consumer needs has had a very low priority in the total value system of those who ruled Soviet society since the beginning of industrialization. Shortages, low quality of materials and workmanship, and tasteless standardization have therefore been chronic in consumer goods production, despite the never-ending complaints by the press and other spokesmen of the public. Until recently, the resultant elasticity of demand for consumer goods relieved the government of the need to gauge the market so as to find out what should be produced. The authorities could always be sure that all merchandise would move into the consumers' hands quickly. With the recent rise in the general standard of living, the public gives signs of becoming somewhat more discriminating, and the government has faced the need of becoming more sensitive to consumer demands and of devising methods for determining them. This task, for which no effective machinery seems as yet to have been created, will inevitably be linked with the problem of differentiation: should industry give priority to the satisfaction of upper-class demands for luxury goods, or should it answer the more basic needs of the less-privileged general population?

The government not only produces the goods demanded by the consumers, it also owns and operates the distribution system. Agencies charged with the wholesale and retail distribution of consumers' goods are managed by regional and local government organizations. An American writer, comparing this distribution machinery with that in his own country, must conclude that the Soviet system is still on a very primitive level. Quite obviously, the regime has given the development of such facilities the very lowest priority. Stores would appear understaffed and inefficient to an American spoiled by supermarkets and "service with a smile." Services to the consumer, such as repair shops, laundries, and the like, are chronically inadequate. Some of these are still in private hands (usually as craft cooperatives); others are operated by local government authorities. In both cases, they are run by people who have little (if any) bargaining power in the scramble for materials, machinery, or trained personnel. In the case of food distribution, a comparison with America shows up the underdeveloped state of all aspects of food processing, including storing, canning, freezing, and dehydration. Hence the consumer is still quite dependent on local and seasonal supplies and his diet is far less varied than that of American supermarket shoppers. The very activity of shopping remains tedious, uncertain, and time-consuming.

This situation can be explained in part by the backward methods and the low level of agricultural production that still prevail in the Soviet Union, the marginality of much of the country's farm lands, and the wars, civil wars, occupation, and wholesale destruction that have disrupted agriculture in the last fifty years. But these problems have been aggravated by the deliberate deployment of all available material and human resources for the production of capital goods, war material, and scientific development at the expense of the living standard. In the light of this policy, the Soviet Union, for most of its history, was not in fact a welfare state at all, but, if anything, an "ill-fare" state or workhouse society, in which the aim was to get the maximum effort out of everyone in return for the barest minimum of material rewards.[7] That this was the party's considered policy was made dramatically clear more

[7] It might appear as if the Soviet regime had adopted the slogan by which, according to Babeuf, the capitalists operated: Work hard and eat little, lest you be entirely out of work and eat nothing at all. Quoted by Stanisław Ossowski, *Klassenstruktur im sozialen Bewusstsein* (Neuwied: Luchterhand, 1962), p. 41.

than once. During Stalin's reign the strict austerity regimes, imposed during the first two five-year plans and after World War II, were justified in such terms; since his death, the controversy between Malenkov and Khrushchev ended with the party reasserting the priority of machine and defense production over the consumer-goods industry. One might conclude today that, in the long run, this policy of forced savings and postponed gratification has paid off. Also, the regime may have recognized that the constitutional formula, "He who does not work, neither will he eat," must be supplemented by another axiom: "He who gets nothing to eat, neither will he work." Whatever the reason, within the last ten years or so, living standards have risen perceptibly. Rationing has been abolished, although there are many commodities for which demand far outweighs supplies. Although prices for food staples and basic consumer goods have fluctuated, the general tendency has been for these prices to go down, while the general trend for wages has been in the opposite direction. A rise in the wage level simultaneous with a fall in the price level spells a marked rise in real wages, i.e., in living standards. This trend has been accompanied by some improvement in the quality and variety of consumers goods; the regime seems to be responding to voiced demands for more pleasing merchandise.[8] This form of response to increased consumer demands has been supplemented by experiments with various other methods of responding to consumer pressure: In recent years, the Soviet government has introduced installment credits for purchases of expensive commodities. The volume of advertising has increased. Market research and trade fairs have begun to gauge consumer demands. Yet all these responses appear to have difficulty keeping in step with rising expectations. The more the living standard has improved, the harder it has been to please the Soviet consumer. In his eyes, the government's response to his demands must appear sluggish and reluctant.[9] At the same time,

[8] In 1956, Soviet consumers for the first time were authorized to return defective merchandise to retail stores.

[9] See Marshall Goldman, *Soviet Marketing Distribution in a Controlled Economy* (New York: Macmillan-Free Press, 1963); Alec Nove, "Toward A Communist Welfare State?," *Problems of Communism,* IX, 1; Rachel E. Golden, "Recent Trends in Soviet Personal Income and Consumption,"

the greater the accumulation of capital wealth in the Soviet economy, the more easily and quickly can we expect a substantial rise in the general standard of living, even though the backwardness of the consumer economy, and the distance it must go in order to catch up with Western European or North American standards, still are tremendous.

Perhaps the most glaring example of problems faced by the Soviet consumer is the housing situation—urbanization in general. A chronic and serious housing shortage plagued Russian cities even before the revolution of 1917. Industrialization had begun very rapidly, and the burgeoning urban working class was crowded into hastily constructed tenements and slums. Since 1917, and especially since the beginning of the five-year plans of industrialization, housing construction has never kept pace with the growth of industry; and even for the proper care and maintenance of *existing* housing facilities insufficient time and resources were expended. The creeping loss, due to neglect, was small, however, in comparison to the disastrous destruction of dwellings during the two major wars. The resultant shortage of housing space was aggravated by the rapid urbanization of the country, which multiplied the need not only for housing, but also for the many public utilities necessary for the functioning of cities—water, gas, electricity and other fuel, sewage, garbage disposal, snow removal, telephone service, and public transportation. Perhaps we should call all these things the incidental costs of industrialization. In the USSR they have, almost without exception, been provided very inadequately.

Joint Economic Committee, U. S. Congress, *Dimensions of Soviet Economic Power*, 347–366.

Various explanations have been offered for the sluggishness of this response. The popular assumption that a planned economy cannot efficiently meet consumer needs appears to have no academic supporters, although Alexander Gerschenkron comes close when he says that the nature of totalitarian systems forbids the development of a genuine welfare-state economy (Alexander Gerschenkron, "Patterns of Economic Development," in Cyril E. Black, ed., *The Transformation of Russian Society*, Cambridge: Harvard University Press, 1960), pp. 69 ff. It seems more plausible to assume simply that the slow response is the result of deliberate choice: space ships, guns and machines still have a higher priority than butter and refrigerators.

The production authorities, from ministries down to individual enterprises, had little incentive to spend their scarce resources on such "incidentals," and the trade union leaders, who might have demanded more adequate services for their members, were smart enough to realize that the Party wanted them to concentrate, instead, on problems of productivity and labor discipline. Local government, another agency that should have provided the incidentals of urbanization, always was a budgetary stepchild, hence unable to do a satisfactory job on this problem; and any community initiative to supply some of the most essential services by a spontaneous collective effort was likely to be stifled by lack of time, funds, encouragement, or individual entrepreneurship.[10]

To be sure, private individuals or families can lease land from the local authorities at a very nominal rent and construct their own dwellings on these lots, with material purchased from the government partly on credit. There has been a great deal of such private housing construction, especially in cities devastated by World War II, and possibly also in some of the burgeoning industrial centers of Soviet Asia. But the regime has expressed apprehension about the resultant strengthening of private property instincts and practices and seems to regard this development as a threat. It may also feel that this kind of housing construction uses scarce materials in wasteful and uneconomic fashion. Whatever the reason, it has sought to restrict the practice by severely curbing the allocation of materials for such purposes.[11]

Because of this history, many cities in the USSR have a hasty, temporary look which may remind the American visitor of pictures he has seen of frontier towns or gold-rush settlements. They lack some of the services we would consider essential, such as gas, electricity, or municipal water works.[12]

The official sanitary norm of 9 square meters (about 100 square feet) of living space per person remains largely unfulfilled. In fact,

[10] Concerning the chaotic state of city planning, and the reasons for it, see Chapter XI on local government.

[11] See *Kommunist*, No. 14 (1960), p. 27.

[12] For staggering statistics about these inadequacies, see Timothy Sosnovy, "The Soviet City," Joint Economic Committee, U. S. Congress, *Dimensions of Soviet Economic Power*, p. 337.

as late as 1961 the per capita dwelling space for the Soviet population was only .05 percent more than it had been in 1926.[13] The
typical urban dwelling in the USSR still remains the house, large
or small, in which one family lives in each room, all families sharing the kitchen and toilet facilities. Since 1956 or 1957, the government has undertaken an ambitious crash program in residential
construction, concentrating its efforts on large complexes of apartment buildings; and this program has been supplemented by the
construction of private dwellings. Much of this work has suffered
from shoddy execution, but it has nonetheless relieved some of the
most serious shortages. What the government provides for its urban
citizens, at a nominal price, is not luxurious, according to middle-
class American standards; on the contrary, it is decidedly inadequate. It may be better than anything so far enjoyed by the vast
majority of Soviet citizens. And yet, progress will continue to be
slow. The program the Communist Party adopted in 1961 envisions that by about 1980 every Soviet family will finally live in
its own little apartment.

HEALTH

Medicine in the Soviet Union is socialized; complete medical care
is available to all citizens free of charge. Most people in the USSR
seem to regard this as a laudable achievement. The per capita
ratio of physicians is far higher than that in the United States.
However, many of these physicians are not nearly as well trained
as the average general practitioner in America, so the high ratio
may be deceptive. Statistical tables concerned with this often include medical practitioners (*fel'dshery*) or even midwives among
physicians; the training of such practitioners corresponds to that
received by senior medical noncommissioned officers in the armed
forces.

Soviet doctors, on the whole, are rather poorly paid. Some
augment their salaries, semilegally, by engaging in private practice.
Since this pattern seems sufficiently widespread, we can say that

[13] Timothy Sosnovy, "The Soviet Housing Situation Today," *Soviet
Studies*, XI, 1 (July, 1959), 4.

NUMBER OF PHYSICIANS IN THE USSR OTHER THAN MILITARY*
(IN THOUSANDS)

	1913	1940	1956	1959
Number of physicians	23	142	329	381
Number of physicians per 10,000 population	1	7	16	18

* This does not, apparently, include *fel'dshery* and midwives.

SOURCE: Mark G. Field, "Medical System," *McGraw-Hill Encyclopedia of Russia and the Soviet Union* (New York: McGraw-Hill, 1961), p. 343.

people who have wealth or positions of authority receive better medical care than the majority, because they can engage physicians for private service. In general, the relatively low material rewards which go to the medical profession militate aaginst recruitment to it, so that careerists and persons interested in amassing wealth are discouraged from entering it. Instead, Soviet medicine seems to attract idealists—kind-hearted, motherly, "people-oriented" persons of the type which in the United States typically turns to social work and similar helping professions. Most Western observers are impressed by the warm atmosphere of the doctor–patient relationship in the USSR, by the enthusiasm of the average physician, and by the aura of saintliness doctors have in the eyes of many citizens, who seem to feel that the physician is the rare human being in a fundamentally inhuman, machinelike social system. Some observers compare this atmosphere favorably with that prevalent in the United States, where the patient's ability to pay turns into an ever-present problem disturbing the doctor–patient relationship.

Yet the system does have an impact on the relationship between doctors and patients; and perhaps the ambiguity of this relationship is symbolic of the spirit pervading all the welfare-state features of the Soviet system. From the patient's point of view, the doctor's function is to prevent, alleviate, and cure sickness. But in fact he fulfills one additional important function: he is the only person in the social system who has authority to excuse people from work to which they have been assigned. In a society where heavy duties are imposed on all, sickness is one of the few legitimate escapes from obligations open to citizens who are tired, discouraged, lazy, or who for any other reason would like to be excused from work. This possibility encourages the citizen, at times, to simulate illness, exaggerate his troubles, or, in real desperation, deliberately induce disease or injury. In turn, the physician's task is complicated by the need to weed out the malingerers from those truly deserving his attention—a task all the more desperate because his time and materials are sorely limited. He is, after all, not only the healer of the sick, but also an officer on the staff of the government which is interested in getting socially desirable work done. The strain in the doctor–patient relationship which results from this dilemma is identical with the strain between doctors and patients in the armed forces of any country. Medical officers, after all, are in the very same situation as their Soviet colleagues: they must prevent and cure illness, but also weed out goldbricks and, in both ways, secure the combat effectiveness of their units. They must serve their patients, but also obey their commanding officers; and the commander's orders may come into conflict with the physician's professional standards.

Without wishing to minimize the impressive achievements of Soviet medicine (about which more will be said below), it would probably be no distortion of truth to say that even the humanitarian work of healing the sick is a service the Soviet regime needs precisely for the aim of maintaining its "combat effectiveness," i.e., the citizens' capacity for socially useful work. The curious fact that sanatoria, rest homes, and similar places of recovery, once administered by health authorities, now are under the jurisdiction of labor unions, indicates that the Party is interested in their use as rewards for performance, loyalty, and work discipline. Medical care, in short, is a means to promote economic growth.[14]

These reservations notwithstanding, the achievement of the Soviet government in providing generally adequate and competent,

[14] To illustrate this mentality, a Polish communist bitterly quotes a billboard slogan he saw some years ago, "Tuberculosis Delays Economic Growth." Leszek Kołakowski, *Der Mensch ohne Alternative* (München: R. Piper & Co., 1961), p. 233. Pragmatic thinking of this kind about problems which, in the eyes of some people, are strictly humanitarian and moral, is not, of course, restricted to the USSR. Who has not heard so-called liberals in the United States argue in favor of racial integration because continued segregation damages the nation's image in the world? ("Racial segregation hurts us in the UN.")

and continually improving, medical service to a nation of 220 million is very great. As Mark G. Field has written:

> The Soviet Regime has established, over the last four decades, a system of medical care and preventive medicine dispensed as a public service the scope of which goes beyond anything ever attempted in this field on a national scale. This system has both the advantage and the drawbacks of being centrally planned, controlled, and administered, and its growth is in theory geared to the general development of the society. It is financed by the state and does not depend for its sustenance on fees for services or voluntary and charitable contributions. This undoubtedly permits long-range programming and some flexibility in the sense that human and material resources can be mobilized and shifted to meet medical problems as they arise. The emphasis in the medical system has been primarily a quantitative one, but there is little doubt that the quality of services, research, and education will improve in the future as the industrialization drive levels off and more resources can be devoted to this area. At the same time, the bureaucratic and centralized nature of the medical system has the general problems of such structures: red tape, inertia, some loss of individual motivation and initiative, depersonalization of services, the avoidance of personal responsibility, heavy administrative overheads, and the "formal" fulfillment of orders and directives. Yet the total balance is undoubtedly a positive one and represents one of the most impressive achievements of the regime and the health authorities. The Soviet medical service provides a realistic and workable solution to the provision of medical services to the Soviet population.[15]

SOCIAL SECURITY

The Soviet citizens, as we have seen, does not have to worry about medical bills. Nor, given the nature of the Soviet economy, need he worry about unemployment. The system's demand for labor has been higher than the supply ever since the beginning of the industrialization program. Undoubtedly, there is some structural

[15] Mark G. Field, "Medical System," M. T. Florinsky, ed., *McGraw-Hill Encyclopedia of Russia and the Soviet Union* (New York: McGraw-Hill, 1961), p. 343. Copyright © 1961, McGraw-Hill, Inc. Reprinted by permission of the publisher.

unemployment which cannot be eliminated;[16] but the regime assumes that unused labor supplies will always be absorbed quickly. Unemployment insurance was abolished at the time of the first five-year plan, no doubt for the purpose of discouraging voluntary unemployment.

At the same time, a fairly elaborate social security system ensures the urban population against a variety of disasters due to accident, illness, old age, and death. This social security system is administered by the All-Union Central Trade Union Council (VTsSPS), through industrial unions and shop committees. Its benefits have not been extended to the collective-farm peasants. To be sure, individual collective farms may have their own social security insurance plans. But, in the main, the regime seems to assume that the peasant family will take care of any of its members who are no longer able to provide for themselves. Social security on the collective farm is therefore based on kinship traditions rather than national legislation.

For the urban dweller several important insurance schemes protect him from the blows of disability (different plans provide compensation for injuries suffered at the place of work or in line of duty and for any other disability). The benefits of socialized medicine are supplemented by sickness benefits and maternity benefits. There is survivors' insurance for indigent dependents of deceased workers; and old age pensions pay monthly benefits for those who have reached retirement age. Most of these schemes have been in existence since the years of the NEP. They have been subject to some major changes, especially at the beginning of the industrialization period, and again in 1956, when Soviet social security emerged in its present form. Most of the 1956 reforms amounted to liberalizations of the social security program.[17]

[16] In fact, the unemployment problem may be becoming more serious. See Jay B. Sorenson, "Problems and Prospects," *Problems of Communism*, XIII, 1 (January–February, 1964), 29–30.

[17] Soviet sources on the program include *Gosudarstvennoe sotsial'noe strakhovanie* (Moscow: Profizdat, 1959); A. V. Vaisfel'd and V. V. Karavaev, *Zakonodatel'stvo o gosudarstvennykh pensiiakh* (Moscow, 1959); and V. A. Aralov and A. V. Levshin, *Sotsial'noe obespechenie v SSSR* (Moscow, 1959).

The purpose of these and other benefits of social security is not only the one we have stated—that of putting a floor under the standard of living. Equally, if not more important, from the point of view of the regime, is the aim of providing these advantages as rewards for those who perform services of value to the system. Social security benefits are to act as incentives to make people work well and hard and to cause them to submit to labor discipline. A number of features of the social security system are geared to this aim. The eligibility requirements for several of these benefits are structured so as to favor workers and employees whom the regime regards as most useful. The most blatant expression of this principle is the harsh discrimination against the collective-farm peasants, who share only few of the advantages of social security. At the same time, payments even for urban workers depend on a scale which in many cases favors miners and other professions wherein work is particularly hazardous or exhausting. Labor discipline is enforced by the social security system because pension rights and various other benefits go only to those who have a specified amount of seniority in their present employment. By moving from one job to another, the Soviet worker or employee, like his American colleague, jeopardizes several important fringe benefits. Furthermore, a number of these fringe benefits are available only (or preferentially) to trade union members, to Party members, or to other kinds of activists or people who impress their superiors with their own usefulness. Thus in providing material rewards, the Soviet regime promotes social differentiation. We shall presently return to this point.

EDUCATION AND UPWARD MOBILITY

The ability to obtain an education fully corresponding to a person's abilities, achievements, and (to some extent) interests is one of the rewards the Soviet system provides for its citizens; and they seem, in general, to regard it as a very valuable benefit.

Attendance in public schools is compulsory for all children, beginning at the age of seven. The obligatory schooling provided for all children was at one time comparatively modest; four years for rural areas and seven years in towns and cities was the rule for compulsory education. In the past few years, the Soviet school system has entered a period of long-range reforms; the prevailing standard for all children is coming to be the eight-year school which they attend between the ages of seven and fifteen. This compulsory education, which roughly corresponds to American elementary and junior high schools, is supplemented by an elaborate preschool system, well developed particularly in urban areas, because many mothers are wage-earners and cannot take care of their children. Nurseries for infants and toddlers are customarily established by economic enterprises; they take care of children between the ages of ten weeks and three years. Four years of public kindergarten usually follow. The first seven years of many urban children's lives are thus spent primarily in public institutions. The long-range plans of the regime now are to transform the eight-year schools and the subsequent three-year senior high schools (they are called "middle schools" in the USSR) into boarding schools (*internaty*), so that public institutions would assume more and more of the parental functions.[18]

Students who have had their eight years of compulsory schooling are usually encouraged to take an additional three years of secondary education. At this level, the system divides itself into several different types of secondary schools, most of them combining practical work with classroom studies, often of a rather limited vocational nature; or else stressing an all-around polytechnical training. Apparently, a few secondary schools concentrate on the more abstract liberal arts and function as preparatory schools for the very gifted who are deemed fit to go directly into higher academic institutions. In general, the secondary school system concentrates on training for productive work in the Soviet economy. The Party leadership has repeatedly preached the virtues and glories of manual work. It combats the prevailing disdain for dirty hands and blue-collar professions, which seems to be particularly strong

[18] Current plans for restructuring the educational system are summarized in N. K. Goncharov, *Perestroika sovetskoi shkoly* (Moscow: Izdatel'stvo Znanie, 1959).

among the urban and white-collar population. In recent years, it has sought to bridge the gap between the laboring classes and the "intelligentsia" by admitting to higher academic institutions only those who had spent two years as farm hands or factory workers. And still, the educational system incorporates a continual process of differentiation which seeks to screen out those most talented for higher academic studies and for creative work in the arts and sciences. For the most promising or favored in this respect, the demands for a polytechnical emphasis in education and for a probational period of manual labor are waived.

Soviet educational policy for a long time has been torn between elitist and egalitarian principles. It is designed, on the whole, to give all citizens an equal chance to succeed; it seeks to provide training and assign jobs so as to make the best possible use of the individual's potential; and its spokesmen assert that *all* work should be considered as valuable and honorable as brain work—there should be no status differences simply because of differences between manual and intellectual skills. Yet all this egalitarian rhetoric cannot dispel the prevalent preference for white-collar professions or mitigate the scramble for educational advantages. Moreover, the educational system itself is geared to differentiate sharply between steeply graded levels of occupational and professional training. With all its emphasis on equal opportunities, the educational ladder reinforces status differences in Soviet society.[19] The strain between conflicting principles might be expressed somewhat differently by saying that the Soviet educational system is chronically torn between the urge to train all citizens as quickly as possible for productive work and the equally strong urge to give everyone the best education he is able to absorb. To obtain as thorough an education as talents and application permit can be seen both as an obligation and as a privilege.

The strain is mitigated to some extent by letting individual com-

---

[19] Until 1956, tuition had to be paid by students in vocational schools, secondary schools, and institutions of higher learning. This favored the children of the upper strata and strengthened certain elitist tendencies. Since then, all education has become free; and in institutions of higher learning most students receive a small stipend to allow for living expenses.

petition decide what level of education any individual is to receive. Schooling at all levels of the educational ladder tends to be demanding. Although the system provides special educational institutions for the physically or mentally handicapped, it shows little patience with slow learners among those not especially handicapped. Students are given heavy doses of mathematics, natural sciences, and foreign languages. Their memories are strained by plenty of rote learning. Those who want to make the grade have to work hard. Enrollment in institutions of higher learning is severely limited, depending on the planned need for experts in various fields of endeavor. Students for higher institutions are selected on the basis of their performance in preparatory schools, and for every one accepted there are many rejections. Political considerations undoubtedly enter into the selection process, but their importance by now has become secondary in most fields. Once accepted, a university or institute student pays no tuition, but is charged a nominal fee for his dormitory room. The vast majority of students receives a modest stipend, which is increased for those obtaining outstanding grades in their courses. Everything in this system contributes to making it very competitive.

An education is the society's gift to the young citizen. Or perhaps it is more in the nature of a loan or an investment, which obliges the recipient to repay it through socially useful professional activity. Graduates of eight-year schools who do not go on to higher educational institutions enter the so-called "labor reserve" system which functions as an employment exchange or manpower pool while at the same time providing for additional vocational training. Graduates of higher institutions are obliged to accept assignment to any jobs in which they may be needed, the educational institution serving as a placement bureau for its current crop of graduates. The choicest assignments are those in larger cities, with important agencies, or those that promise fastest promotion possibilities. Such assignments go to the better students or, at times, to those with influential connections. Graduates are obliged to remain in the first jobs to which they have been assigned for a two- or three-year period before they can by their own initiative seek to change jobs.

In summary: the educational system established by the Soviet government is centralized and standardized. It serves to answer the needs of the system for trained specialists in all fields of endeavor, and for a population with a high level of literacy, polytechnical know-how, and general education.[20] The educational apparatus is part of the reward system because, while serving the needs of the regime, it also functions as the major vehicle for upward social mobility. Excellent performance in the national school system opens opportunities for all citizens, regardless of origin, so long as the young person's talents and interests correspond to the priorities of the regime. The basic principle that guides the process of social mobility is providing full opportunities to all who have talent and who apply these talents in hard work. Having a chronic need for trained specialists in a host of different fields,[21] the Soviet regime wants everyone to climb to the highest position of responsibility, skill, and authority he is equipped to reach. This principle may be tempered by a certain amount of corruption, since personal connections play a role in helping undeserving students to obtain better jobs or be accepted in educational institutions from which they would otherwise be excluded for lack of talent. Inevitably, some wealthy youngsters have even sought to purchase examinations, hire substitutes to take exams in their stead, or otherwise cheat the educational system. Inevitably, also, political considerations affect the selection process. Finally, as we have indicated, the system tends to discriminate against the rural population and, possibly, against some national minorities.[22] Still, on the whole, it provides more open a road for talent and hard work than that of any other society.

[20] For this reason, the education process is, by and large, identical with the system for recruiting the nation's professional elites.

[21] For a thorough discussion, see Dr. Curt Zinnemann, "Das Arbeitspotential in der Sowjetunion," *Ostprobleme,* XV, 19, 595–599.

[22] For people at the bottom of the social scale in the USSR, i.e., for those in rural and culturally underdeveloped areas, the educational system is not the only, perhaps not even the most important, vehicle for upward mobility. The Machine-Tractor Stations or, today, the rural farm machinery repair shops (Repair Tractor Stations) fulfill this function for the peasant youth; and so does service in the country's armed forces. In both these

PSYCHOLOGICAL REWARDS

To complete this survey of rewards given to the Soviet citizen, it might be well to call attention to certain vague psychological benefits which may be significant for many such citizens, hard to define though they may be. One of these psychological rewards has been mentioned above: it is the widely held belief that Soviet society is wide open, with plenty of room at the top and with opportunities for advancement available to all, regardless of origin. Although, stated in such unambiguous form, the image of absolutely free social mobility is doubtless an illusion, the illusion and the egalitarian rhetoric that perpetuates it must give a considerable sense of satisfaction to many Soviet citizens. Another such illusion which spreads a feeling of well-being may be the myth that in the USSR sovereignty lies in the people, in the collectivity of common men; that the government and the ruling party are in truth the representatives of the people; and that all the nation's material wealth, her resources and her factories, her cities and the entire economy, are in fact the property of the people.[23] Even individuals who might react with skepticism to such statements can nonetheless be expected to derive a certain satisfaction from being part of a successful and growing enterprise of vast proportions. Many a member of

---

agencies, the ambitious rural youngster has a chance to become acquainted with machinery and with urban life in general. Military or naval service, moreover, temporarily removes him from his native environment and thus serves to broaden his horizon as well as wean him away from his village. Both therefore acquaint him with the world of machines and cities and draw the more ambitious away from the countryside forever. For the villager, this is an essential first step upward in the social scale. To the ambitious young Soviet citizen, his society must appear remarkably open, with room at the top for all who apply themselves.

[23] "A man reared in the spirit of socialist morality cannot look on with indifference at shortcomings, at anything that runs counter to the interests of society, even though it does not concern him directly. The feeling of being master and the sense of responsibility for the common cause inseparably associated with it constitute a major feature of the spiritual make-up of the new man. Members of socialist society have not only great rights, but great duties as well. But these are the duties of masters, of real citizens of their country, and not the obligations of downtrodden subjects." *Fundamentals of Marxism–Leninism,* p. 615.

Soviet society is proud of the achievements his regime has made.[24] Countless citizens may feel that participation in public life (which to an outside observer may appear to be no more than mock participation) enriches his life. And vast masses of ego-weak, helpless individuals may gratefully submerge their very lives in the paternal fold of the system's vast organization. Even the bureaucratization of life thus provides meaningful rewards for many a Soviet citizen.

[24] Referring to the German Democratic Republic, a West German sociologist writes: "Obviously, many people . . . note economic growth with approval even when it is hardly felt by the consumer, i.e., when it is expressed only in (uncontrollable) statistical figures. The individual here sees himself predominantly within the larger context; the values of working for the collectivity and of subordination to the common good stand in the foreground of society's system of norms." Ralf Dahrendorf, *Gesellschaft und Freiheit* (München: R. Piper & Co., 1963), p. 309.

Chapter XVI
Citizenship

"Caterpillar is People."
(Slogan printed on a calendar
distributed by a well-known
tractor and equipment company)

Let us round out this survey of the relations between the Soviet regime and its citizens by adding a few words about the general meaning of citizenship in the USSR. Most of what has to be said here is simply a summary of, or reference to, matters mentioned in previous chapters.

RIGHTS AND DUTIES

For instance, it is unnecessary to say more than a few words about the citizens' constitutional rights and duties, since these formal provisions were discussed in Part Two. As we saw, a Soviet citizen has the right to own personal property and to have it, as well as his life and liberty, protected against his fellow-citizens. He has the right to vote, to participate actively in public affairs, and to seek redress of officially wrought inequities through formal and informal complaint channels. His membership in the society entitles him to a certain minimal level of material welfare and security, including not only employment, but also education up to his ability, personal growth, and mobility up the social scale. One might say that each citizen has a share in the nation's economic and cultural resources, that every citizen is a shareholder in USSR, Inc., the size of the annual dividend depending on the success of the company and on the decisions of the managers. To all this one might possibly add a certain residual right to privacy which is exercised in such matters as the choice of a mate and, to a limited degree, the choice of an occupation.

All these rights are qualified by the proviso that they must not be abused. Participation in public affairs must not disrupt the regime's determined policies. Personal property must not be used for private gain. More generally, the Soviet code of citizens' rights and duties forbids placing individual rights and interests over public ones (as defined by the Party). In a contest between rights or claims, the individual must voluntarily yield to the public authorities. Freedom must not be taken absolutely; for absolute freedom disrupts the socialist order.[1] Nor can the regime allow freedom to be "abused" by anyone inimical to communist rule. The constitution and the laws do not protect those Soviet citizens opposing the Soviet system.

Behind this is a conception of citizenship very different from that prevailing in some Western countries, especially the United States. Here, the individualistic ethos prevails, according to which citizenship consists in the right to exercise personal choice and pursue individual interests by participating (or even by not participating) in public political life. Citizenship means contesting with fellow-citizens for advantages. It means being alert, watchful, and critical in guarding one's personal interest, and with deliberation placing the weight of one's vote and influence into the scale of politics. Of course, it also means obeying the law, paying taxes, serving in the armed forces when drafted, and risking one's life against foreign enemies. But these obligations are so basic an attribute of citizenship everywhere that they do not give citizenship in the United States a markedly different character. What does determine its nature in the United States is the emphasis on individual rights and the pursuit of individual interests. In the liberal conception, individual citizens' rights are rights *against* the government, even

[1] ". . . socialist democracy differs essentially from the unlimited, uncontrolled 'freedom' of which anarchists love to chatter. Such 'freedom,' incidentally, exists only in their heated imagination, but not in society. As for socialist democracy, it is not directionless democracy, but *directed democracy*, i.e., democracy directed by the party and the state to further the development of socialism and the building of communism. This is stated by the Communists straightforwardly and openly." *Fundamentals of Marxism–Leninism*, p. 599.

though, perhaps paradoxically, the political system is designed to guarantee them.

Citizenship in the USSR reverses the emphasis. Although certain rights remain with the individual—residually, as it were—the stress is on duty toward the government and toward the community of fellow-citizens, most important among them the duty to do socially useful work, i.e., a job designated as useful. The assertion of individual rights and interests or of the individual personality is regarded as corrosive and destructive by those who have absorbed the ethos of Soviet socialism. Those rights that have been granted are secured, not by struggling against the system, but by relying on it and collaborating with it. "The most substantial guarantee of these fundamental rights of the Soviet citizens is the Soviet regime itself. . . ."[2] A life devoted to the pursuit of personally defined goals —be this a career, money, status, power, eternal salvation, sexual satisfaction, or what not—such a life must appear profoundly immoral to the well-socialized member of the Soviet system. If the word "socialism" means anything to them, it means the rejection of the individualistic philosophy.

To be sure, many Soviet citizens obviously have not quite accepted this idea for themselves and continue to manifest individualistic strivings. Also, the system rewards the individual for his performance, as we have seen, and thus stimulates his collaborative effort by the promise of individual advantage. Moreover, on a higher level of abstraction, it is possible to reconcile the collectivist emphasis on duty, on obligation, on work for the common good, with an individualistic self-interest: the well-socialized Soviet citizen may tell himself that work for the community ultimately means working for himself and his children—hence, that cooperation coincides with individualism, as obedience does with freedom. This collectivist ethos sounds far more convincing to the average Soviet citizen than to the average American. To the outsider it may seem as if every Soviet citizen is a civil servant, an employee

[2] A. Denisov and M. Kirichenko, *Soviet State Law,* p. 321. I have translated *sovetskaia vlast* as "Soviet regime."

of the state, a person in bondage to the community; but many such a servant may feel that at the same time he is also an integral part of the collective employer and sovereign, and is beneficiary of the joint labors.

PARTICIPATION

Citizenship in the USSR, ideally, means active participation in public affairs. In the eyes of the Party leaders, the ideal Soviet citizen, indeed, is loyal and obedient. But he is not a silent automaton who lets the authorities do everything with utter passivity. Instead, the ideal citizen is the *activist* who participates as much as possible. From all the preceding chapters it must be clear that the scope of this activism is carefully circumscribed. The activist is expected to participate in executing or fulfilling the commands of the hierarchy, although in doing this he is to show imagination and initiative. His contributions are to be positive and constructive. He should develop leadership qualities, but use them for the purpose of guiding, leading, inspiring his fellow citizens to follow the commands of the authorities. "What is required from the builders of communism, and still more from members of communist society, is not mere compliance with established regulations, but initiative, creative activity and the ability not only to work intelligently at one's place of work, but also to take part in deciding matters of state and public affairs."[3] Obviously, the ideal society as imagined by the Soviet ruling elite is a bureaucratic system which combines the hierarchic command principle of *edinonachalie* with maximal involvement of all citizens in the administration of enterprises and organizations, a bureaucracy in which the lower ranks carry out the commands of the hierarchs cheerfully and expeditiously because they themselves have "participated" in formulating them.[4] At the risk of plagiarizing that Madison Avenue genius who coined the term "people's capitalism" we might give the name "people's

[3] *Fundamentals of Marxism–Leninism,* pp. 684–685.
[4] This ideal is stated clearly in the decree of the November 1962 Plenum of the Party's Central Committee. *Spravochnik Partiinogo Rabotnika,* Issue 4 (1962), p. 195.

382   CONTROL OVER BEHAVIOR OF CITIZENS

bureaucratism" to the ideal discussed at such length in current Soviet publications.[5]

For any citizen who wishes to participate in this people's bureaucracy, whether his motives be idealistic or careerist, the Soviet system offers a host of organizations and activities. In his place of work, the citizen can take part in one of the many committees formed by his union.[6] In his community, he can help organize or run parent-teacher associations (called Councils for Assistance to School and Family), neighborhood courts, or perhaps an occasional *ad hoc* committee for some badly needed improvement. Civic duties which demand activists include elections, rallies, and drives, court assessor service, and work with local and provincial Soviet standing committees. From civil defense and civilian military training to adult education or organized entertainment, there is a broad range of activities demanding the participation of citizen activists.[7] The many different organizations within which the rank and file of the citizenry can participate in this fashion are called "public organizations" or "mass organizations" in the Soviet Union. The Party has been inclined to lay greater and greater stress on the importance of such organizations; its spokesmen assert that more and more governmental functions will be transferred to such agencies as Soviet society moves closer to the communist ideal of the state's withering-away. Whether or not we concede that increased participation in mass organizations conforms to our notion of democracy, we must be aware of the growing importance of these institutions for the Soviet political system.

To this, one might perhaps add one other kind of participation, namely, public opinion. True, the Soviet political system permits no free formation and exchange of opinion on public affairs. Opinion leadership, like leadership in all other matters, is claimed by the Communist Party as its exclusive right, as is the monopoly right

[5] See the chapter on "The Role of Public Organizations" in *Fundamentals of Marxism–Leninism,* pp. 528–529.

[6] See pp. 433 ff.

[7] In addition one could list town or neighborhood committees for the maintenance of housing facilities, production conferences, and *kolkhoz* brigade councils.

over all communications. But the Party has nonetheless shown some interest in the moods of the citizenry. Through the police and, more recently, through polling devices, the Party has sought to gauge these moods.[8] Having one's opinion surveyed might be regarded as some indirect and passive form of participation. But it would be important only if the polling methods were sufficiently refined and if the leaders allowed the results to influence their policy-making. Of this there is no evidence. The regime may be interested in receiving feedback on its activists and communications from the population. But it is not in the habit of *consulting* the people. Indeed, there are workshop conferences with foremen and workers; *kolkhoz* meetings, perhaps, with genuine discussion; selection processes in which the Party does eliminate obviously unpopular candidates. In short, the Soviet system involves some consultation with the citizens on a level commensurate with their limited work (or life) experiences, although even this apparently is done rarely and reluctantly. On national issues, however, public opinion is consulted rarely, and then only in ceremonious or perfunctory fashion. The law concerning abortion, in 1936, was submitted to the public for discussion and was then passed, despite evidence of overwhelming popular opposition. Similar public discussions of the 1936 Constitution yielded minor amendments. On such things as foreign policy, missile programs, or the seven-year-plan, there can be little genuine consultation.

From all this it is clear that the citizens' participation in public life is not supposed to be, and cannot be, free participation. Because it is possible only within the framework of approved associations, groups, and institutions, it is in fact carefully controlled. No association in which activist citizens are expected to participate can legally be formed without clearance from or planning by the Soviet authority having jurisdiction over the sphere of life with which

---

[8] One of the most interesting of these experiments so far has been an open questionnaire about the attitudes of Soviet youth administered by the youth newspaper, *Komsomolskaia Pravda,* in January 1961. More recently, there has been extensive polling of industrial workers to investigate job dissatisfaction. See Jay B. Sorenson, "Problems and Prospects," in *Problems of Communism,* XIII, 1 (January–February, 1964), 28–29.

the association plans to deal. No meeting can legally be held without approval of the authorities. In the final analysis, all organizations are creations of the Party. All of them function in prescribed fashion, according to prescribed or patterned plans of organization and by-laws.[9] All organizations function as transmission belts for the Party because their core is always the Party's primary organization or caucus, which often makes decisions before they are submitted to general discussion. Hence if there is discussion, debate, or other grass-roots participation, it is rarely more than a prelude to the adoption of policies formulated by the leadership.

Citizens' participation in public affairs therefore does not serve to provide free reign for individual or group interests. Instead, it is designed to mobilize the citizens, that is, to enlist their services for purposes and interests defined by the Party.[10] It is to utilize individual creativity and leadership for this goal; it wishes to tap resources hidden among the population for the Party. Moreover, it serves the purpose of elite recruitment; through participation in committees and associations, suitable activists are discovered who might rise to positions of higher authority. For all participants, whether or not they are made of leadership material, participation serves a socializing function: it introduces them to the political system, its values, priorities, forms of organization, and pattern of operations. In addition, the many opportunities for participation which we have discussed undoubtedly provide satisfaction for various personality types which must abound in Soviet society as they do in ours— joiners, operators, careerists, as well as service-minded idealists— and does so in a fashion which furthers the goals of the Party. Finally, it may be of value also as a safety valve through which popular discontent may vent itself without harm to the political system.

[9] For a Soviet discussion of the structure and functions of mass organizations, see B. M. Lazarev and A. I. Luk'ianov, *Sovetskoe gosudarstvo i obshchestvennye organizatsii* (Moscow, 1960).

[10] For an excellent discussion of mass organizations as mobilizing agents, see Hartmut Zimmermann, "Der FDGB als Massenorganisation," in Peter Christian Ludz, *Studien und Materialien zur Soziologie der DDR* (Köln: Westdeutscher Verlag, 1964), pp. 115–144.

SAFETY VALVES

How valuable mass participation is to the regime can be seen in an examination of the institution of *samokritika* (self-criticism). This word connotes public criticism, by individuals, of their own conduct or performance, and also public criticism of an organization by its own members or leadership cadres. *Samokritika,* in other words, includes criticism from below of the activities and failures of some collective body within Soviet society.[11] Self-criticism is usually voiced, in a somewhat formal or ritualized manner, in pre-arranged public meetings. Such meetings represent, perhaps, an effort on the part of the leadership to include mass participation in decision-making, or to give the appearance of such mass participation. In a *samokritika* session, management itself is facing its subordinates, and it does so without the usual managerial prerogatives. All sorts of complaints and grievances may be aired and must be answered, as the British government must answer questions in the Parliament.

Although discussions in such meetings may be rather free, there usually is planning even behind the seeming spontaneity of such criticism from below; truly spontaneous self-criticism would doubtless be considered too dangerous by the Party. Instead, *samokritika* doubtless is an effective method of using discontent among the citizens for the purpose of putting lower and middle-range officials under pressure and keeping them in line—even to terrorize them, if that expression is not too strong. *Samokritika* sessions therefore are also safety valves because they allow popular discontent to discharge itself in controlled fashion, so that it does not hit those higher up and does not challenge the political system itself.

There are several other safety valves at the disposal of the regime, i.e., channels through which citizens can voice complaints and give vent to negative feelings without endangering the regime. A person who is very upset about injustices done to him or failings of

[11] It also includes a form of official humor which in the USSR is called satire. This takes the form of cartoons, anecdotes, or jokes designed to lampoon or ridicule persons or institutions that do not live up to the expectations of the regime.

administrators has a number of agencies to which he can turn with a letter of complaint—his soviet deputy, his Party secretary, his trade union, his public prosecutor, his newspaper.[12] In short, the individual citizen has numerous formal and informal channels providing access to, or communication with, authoritative decision-makers in the Party or the government. The agency set up to receive the complaints coming through various formal and informal channels is the recently created Committee of Party and State Control and its field organizations.[13] All evidence suggests that complaints are treated with some respect and followed up by investigation and, at times, remedial action.[14] At the same time, one must assume that undoubtedly the inspecting authorities acquire a sense for telling which complaints come from the pens of cranks and which deserve attention. Moreover, this form of complaining itself is risky for the individual. It may get him in trouble with the administrator or the agency he is criticizing; indeed, it may get him in trouble with the regime as a whole because it may make the authorities believe that he is disloyal or a grumbler and trouble-maker. The use of out-of-channels communications for the purpose of voicing grievances is therefore a safety valve that dissatisfied citizens will probably use only when all the more formal methods have failed. These channels do exist, and they are used; perhaps that is all that should be said.

[12] The press, especially the local and regional press, plays very much the role of the muckraker and often appears to take the initiative in this or to be prodded by complaints from readers, while in general it undoubtedly responds to the cues of the Party. Whoever gives the cues and provides the prodding, however, the newspaper editor easily finds himself in a cross-fire and must tread warily lest he offend agencies or administrators to which he is vulnerable, and against whom his appeals to the Party, the courts, or other protectors will not avail him. For the complaint of a local newspaper columnist whose muckraking was rewarded by considerable harassment, see the letter to the editors of *Pravda* (November 16, 1960), p. 6.

[13] *Pravda* (January 18, 1963) printed a Party communique on this. The communique stresses the need to have representatives from all the mass organizations participate in the Committee's field organizations and obliges the Committee to render regular accounts to these mass organizations.

[14] Perhaps it would be better to say that complaints of this sort are sometimes treated seriously, but are often neglected. See the Central Committee decree "About Serious Deficiencies in the Review of Letters, Complaints, and Revelations coming from the Toilers," in *Pravda* (August 26, 1958).

Part Five

Government in Action: Economic and Social Problems

Chapter XVII
The Economy and the Plan

In the efforts of the Soviet political system to perpetuate itself, grow in strength, and control the behavior of its citizens, a number of social and economic problems face the regime. We must now pay at least some attention to them.

We shall begin with issues relating to the structure and functioning of the economic system, with considerable misgiving, to be sure, for it is questionable whether a book on the Soviet *political* system ought to deal with economic problems at all. Obviously the goals, structure, and working of the economy cannot be separated from the political order; on the contrary, they are most intimately related to it, as I hope many of the preceding pages have shown. This is true of any society, but especially the USSR, where virtually the entire economy is government-owned and -operated, and where the nature of the entire political system is so clearly a function of the Party's economic goals. Many problems of economic planning and management, in the USSR as anywhere else, are so technical that their discussion must be left to trained economists or engineers; and still, even in some of the most technical matters, politics creeps in by the back door, either in the form of ideological biases and predispositions or in the guise of specifically Soviet forms of bureaucratic organization and social relations. For instance, an ideological preference for giant enterprises has had an appreciable influence on Soviet engineering practices; the bureaucratic chiefs' fear of responsibility has, I believe, helped determine the manner in which Soviet engineers construct many projects; a strong ideological block against the use of interest calculations in investment planning has led to chronic difficulties in weighing the long-range advantages and disadvantages of investment alternatives; the bureaucratic nature of the entire political and economic system has affected planning and management procedures in a host of ways, as we have seen already. The centralized command system doubtless has many advantages and disadvantages; bureaucratic competition and empire-building increase both efficiency and inefficiency, savings as well as waste. The bureaucrats' penchant for secrecy conflicts with the need for adequate statistical information. In myriad ways, the nature of the political order thus affects the country's economy.

Despite our serious misgivings, therefore, this book must include at least a bare sketch of some of the issues of economic planning and management.

THE STRUCTURE AND FUNCTION OF THE ECONOMY

A nation's economy might be regarded primarily as a mechanism for regulating the allocation of resources, with the understanding that resources are not abundant. Precisely how resources are to be allocated and distributed depends, among other things, on the overriding purpose served by the economic system. Such purposes may be any of the following: (1) the maximization of profit for those who own the chief resources; (2) the strengthening of the nation's defenses; (3) rapid economic growth, with priority given to the production of capital goods; (4) balanced economic growth; (5) the satisfaction of consumers' wants. Although the system itself predetermines to a considerable extent which of these purposes it will serve, the structuring of the system, and hence the choice of primary purpose for the entire economy, is in the final analysis a political choice, usually made in the course of the revolution that creates the economic order. The various goals enumerated above (and some important goals that an economy may be pursuing have perhaps been omitted) are not necessarily mutually exclusive. For instance, classical economic theory claims that free enterprise promotes at least two of the above goals (maximization of profit and consumer satisfaction), and also a third, namely, balanced economic growth. Since free enterprise has never existed anywhere in its pure model form, this claim may be considered by some to be somewhat academic.

In the Soviet Union, most of the economy is publicly owned and operated;[1] furthermore, the regime has for some decades been committed very firmly to the principle of public ownership and management, which it calls "socialism." The preservation of this socialism and its extension or intensification into something called "communism" is, therefore, one of the goals of the Soviet system. Below this we might list several other aims pursued by the regime, in the order of their importance: (1) rapid economic growth, (2) defense, and (3) consumer satisfaction. Some Western observers would doubtless change the order of these goals by placing defense considerations ahead of economic growth. Others might argue that both defense and economic growth are more important to the leaders of the Communist Party than the preservation of socialism. Furthermore, subsidiary goals of the economy, such as the demands made by science, foreign economic relations, modernization, the need for reserves and stockpiles, must be weighed against the overriding goals and against each other. The Soviet economy is thus strained by pluralistic claims on all available resources, by conflicting major objectives and conflicting high priorities. Precisely how the regime finds formulas for balancing out these conflicts must remain hypothetical so long as we cannot look more closely into the workings of the political system and the minds of its leaders.

The complex goals of the Soviet economic system could perhaps be restated as follows: The task of the leadership in organizing and managing the economy is to devise routines of planning and to manipulate bureaucratic incentives so as to promote economic growth which is both very rapid and has a necessary minimum of balance, at the same time satisfying various special sectors not

---

[1] The major exception is farming, where a nominally cooperative form of enterprise prevails, with remnants of private enterprise mixed in. Cooperatives also exist in various crafts, and private enterprise of a semilegal character is practiced in certain professions, such as medicine.

directly related to economic growth, such as defense, science, consumption, overhead, and a multitude of other services. In order to achieve these goals, the economic system must be designed in such fashion that it enlists maximum individual effort from all citizens and at the same time promotes teamwork between all persons and agencies involved in it. It must do all this in an environment of chronic scarcity, hence of frantic urgency, which has had the effect of putting the Soviet economy into a state of permanent emergency similar to a wartime economy, as Alec Nove, among others, has pointed out.[2] In turn, this climate of emergency has led the Soviet leadership to neglect other purposes it might have pursued, and which might seem very important to Western economists. One other way in which this might be expressed would be to say that the Party must forever seek to impose political decisions (concerning economic priorities) over economic laws or societal pressures which keep asserting themselves. We have here another instance of that struggle between the decision-making hierarchy and the professional specialists which takes so many forms in all bureaucratic structures.

In the management of the economy, this struggle between political and economic principles expresses itself also in a chronic disparity between the planners' objectives and actual results, or in a strong tendency toward such a disparity.[3] Again, this is nothing else than the usual pattern in bureaucratic command structures: the hierarchs seek to impose tasks on their subordinate organizations. The subordinates, competing with each other, are interested primarily in out-performing all other individuals and agencies within the same system. The hierarchs, in their turn, must structure the system so as to be able to assess and compare performances. This is done through a complicated system of success indicators, such as quantity of output, quality of output, labor productivity, profit, and others. But any measurable definition of performance standards is an oversimplification of the actual objectives the hierarchs pursue,

[2] See Alec Nove, *The Soviet Economy* (New York: Praeger, 1961), p. 22.
[3] For a discussion of that problem, see David Granick, "An Organizational Model of Soviet Industrial Planning," *Journal of Political Economy* (April 1959), pp. 109–130.

as was noted already in Part Three of this book. In turn, a skillful subordinate who knows precisely how successful performance will be measured is likely to manipulate the system so as to maximize his success indicators. The incentive system every bureaucracy must develop, as we saw, skews the results sought by the topmost authorities.[4] A more specific discussion of how this problem applies to the Soviet economy must be left to the professional economists. Here we shall only cast a brief glance at the basic structure of the economy and some aspects of its operation.

Within the nationalized sector, the most enduring institution has been the enterprise, or firm. This need not astonish anyone; after all, modern technology must play a significant part in determining the organizational framework within which production can be accomplished. Given a similar technology, a sardine cannery, a tractor factory, or a steel mill in any one social system will look very much like those in other social systems.

And yet, the similarities are rather striking. The enterprise in the USSR resembles the Western corporation in more than technology, equipment, and work processes. It is established very much

[4] Despite the multiplicity of success indicators, Soviet managers as well as their superiors have shown a tendency to concentrate on mere quantity of output. But even here there are various measuring sticks, each with its skewing effect. Let us take the easy example of a shoe factory. If output is measured by price, the manager will concentrate his firm's efforts on the most expensive items, on luxury footwear. If it is measured by weight, he will use the heaviest materials and will make the heaviest, largest, clumsiest commodities, such as boots. If it is measured by the number of items produced, he will make the cheapest and the smallest kinds, such as inexpensive children's shoes. Attempts to curb such irrationalities by defining success criteria in more complicated terms threaten to jeopardize the bureaucrats' control over the individual enterprise. Nevertheless, concern over the poor quality and inadequate assortment of the output in many areas has caused the planners to be increasingly concerned with quality and balance.

For bitter complaints about the great amount of defective merchandise produced, see Khrushchev's speech of April 24, 1963 (*Izvestiia* [April 26, 1963], and a follow-up editorial in *Pravda* [June 26, 1963]). For measures to improve the quality and balance of output, see Max Frankel's article in *The New York Times* (December 18, 1959), and Harry Schwartz's remarks, *The New York Times* (December 19, 1959). An excellent general discussion of success indicators and the problems they create is Alec Nove, "The Problem of Success Indicators in Soviet Industry," *Economica*, N. S., XXV, 97 (February, 1958), 1–13.

like a business firm, as a juridical person, with its own assets in the form of building, equipment, stores, credit, and cash. As a juridical person, it regulates its relations with other firms through contracts. It is litigable; and, as we have seen, a special judiciary branch exists (Gosarbitrazh) for settling disputes between enterprises according to Soviet business law. Furthermore, the Soviet enterprise operates on the basis of cost accounting (*khozrashchet*), according to which it is expected to minimize its cost and maximize its profits.

Nonetheless, despite its juridical autonomy, the Soviet firm is an administrative agency of the central government. The structure of the production organization existing between the Council of Ministers and the individual enterprises at the grass roots has always been complicated, with divisions of functions that were not very clear to the outside observer. Moreover, this in-between machinery has been comparatively unstable, something that can also be said about planning procedures. These have amounted to an ever-shifting method of trial and error, so flexible that many Soviet planners have worried about it.[5] The Khrushchevian reforms since 1957, abolishing most production ministries and setting up regional Economic Councils (Sovnarkhozy), as well as the more recent trends toward renewed centralization in planning—all these experiments with the organization of economic management are but episodes in a chronic search for the most satisfactory organization of planning and management.[6]

Despite this relative instability, certain fundamental principles remained operative. Notwithstanding the legal autonomy of the enterprise, and despite the centrifugal empire-building trends in various superordinate agencies, functional as well as territorial, the entire nationalized economy has always been a command structure receiving its assignments from the All-Union Council of Ministers. Its one principal task has always been to fulfill or surpass the production plans handed down by the central government and broken down

---

[5] For a discussion, see Herbert S. Levine, "Recent Developments in Soviet Planning," in Joint Economic Committee, U. S. Congress, *Dimensions of Soviet Economic Power* (Washington: Government Printing Office, 1962), p. 174.

[6] See pp. 256–263.

into more specific assignments by the numerous subordinate agencies.

Yet even this characterization of the economic structure is an oversimplification. Planning in the USSR is more than mere commands issued at regular intervals by the central government. It is a continuous activity involving all levels of the economic administration, from the All-Union Council of Ministers down to every individual enterprise, farm, and workshop. It requires not only the issuing and enforcement of orders, but also the upward flow of information, advice, and articulation of interest. The planning process must start with the collection of information about capacity from every single branch and enterprise of the economy. Such information is provided by statistical data concerning available machinery, materials, unfinished goods, and personnel, including their past performance records. Since these data must in the final analysis come from the enterprises at the grass roots, and since the managers of these enterprises have a strong interest in concealing their real capacity as much as possible (so as not to be burdened with excessively difficult tasks), this information will always have a certain degree of unreliability, and its collection involves the central administration, or its agents, in an ambiguous bargaining relationship with its subordinates. The central planners and their subordinates have undoubtedly developed a degree of sophistication in discounting pessimistic estimates reaching them from below; or perhaps they simply counter the habit of underestimating capacity with the habit of assigning seemingly impossible production quotas, thus correcting one irrational practice by another. The prevalence of such rule-of-thumb practices in economic decision-making is made more plausible by the incredible volume of economic data with which the planners are continually inundated; it is so large that it seems to be a serious threat to the over-all functioning of the planning mechanism. One reason for this overwhelming volume of information is the typically bureaucratic urge of Soviet planners and top managers to maintain control over the economy by keeping themselves informed and by prescribing every move the subordinates are to make. Ideally, in the Soviet economy, nothing is to be done without plan, and no transaction is to remain unrecorded. This means that every time the smallest item goes from one hand to another, there must be orders, permits, receipts, and reports. To be sure, the same proliferation of paperwork, involving orders, invoices, receipts, shipping tickets, and the like, accompanies the transfer of materials in Western economies. Western economies, however, seem convinced that the glut of paperwork is much more serious in the USSR, because there many more central controlling agencies wish to be informed.

On the basis of information on capacity, the central authorities must weigh alternative uses to which this production potential might be put, and, on the basis of a hierarchy of priorities, determine the "bill of goods" the entire economy is to produce in the coming planning period. The establishment of priorities and the determination of the desired bill of goods should be aided, ideally, by exceedingly complex economic calculations based on a thorough knowledge of how the entire economy functions. Western economists seem to assume that because of its over-centralization and the resultant information glut, and also because of certain ideological blinders, the Soviet economy is innately incapable of making such calculations. Whether or not this is correct (and it might be correct, if only for the duration of a transitional period during which the planned economy establishes itself), one might argue that in any case the establishment of investment priorities is, in the final analysis, a political decision. Hence, even though the economic information and advice must come from statistical and planning experts, it is the Communist Party, or its Central Committee and Presidium, which defines the goals for any long planning period by publishing target figures or planned increases. Thus the Twenty-second Congress of the Party articulated production goals for the next two decades in the new Party Program. More specific target figures are given by the seven-year plans and the subsidiary plans covering shorter periods. It then remains for the government administration to work out the complexities of fulfilling these production quotas.[7]

Complexities inevitably arise, because the output of any one

[7] Soviet terminology distinguishes between long-range, or *perspective,* plans giving broad, general directions, and *current* plans spelling out the concrete objectives derived therefrom.

commodity demands an input of various other commodities (machinery, materials, labor). Hence any output plan commits various sectors of the economy and must therefore foresee and plan the multiple relationships between these many different sectors. The production plan for any one sector, or for any one of its subunits, must thus be supplemented by a host of other plans specifying such things as capital investment, use of materials, use of labor, use of money and credit, expected profits, expected rise in the productivity of labor, and others. The sum total of directives handed down to any enterprise, therefore, will also include a set of planned contracts with suppliers, customers, construction agencies, and other firms.

This is the environment within which production goes on. To it we must add the ubiquitous features of complex organization: multiple overlapping inspection and controls; seemingly endless reports and other paperwork, and a tempo of work which the skillful manager must seek to prevent from lapsing into either of two extremes—dead routine or the frantic state of emergency trying to meet threatening deadlines. Rewards for what is regarded as outstanding performance are high. Managers, like virtually everyone else, are on something akin to a piece-rate wage, because the Soviet system pays substantial cash bonuses to those individuals, firms, or production chiefs who overfulfill their assigned quotas. These material rewards are supplemented by important psychological rewards; and the general recognition which accompanies them leads to higher, more responsible, and more rewarding assignment. More specifically, successful economic managers are the most likely candidates for rise in the Party leadership. Meanwhile, the sanctions for failure remain rather severe.

RECENT DEVELOPMENTS IN ECONOMIC PLANNING

In this, the economy resembles the entire administrative apparatus of the USSR. It does so also in the informal devices of concealment, bargaining, bartering, hoarding, mutual protection associations, and the like, which we discussed in Part Three. In assessing the efficiency of the Soviet economy, the outside observer has the choice of concentrating on the inefficiences of this process, the duplication and waste, the shortages, bottlenecks, and failures to meet objectives; or he may wish to point out that the most basic requirements of the regime have been met by this system, and that on the whole the Soviet economy has made spectacular achievements. Conversely, even Soviet spokesmen no longer hesitate to point out that the successful crash program of industrialization has led to serious imbalances in the economic structure, both within the economy as a whole (where overdevelopment in some sectors is matched by underdevelopment in others now considered vital) and also within each enterprise (where, typically, some of the most modern techniques are used side by side with medieval methods of production).[8] To be sure, party ideologists have bragged for many years that socialism is superior to capitalism because it achieves proportionality by rational planning (whereas capitalism achieves it by a blind process of trial and error and at great cost); but even they have now admitted that this is easier to say than to realize and that, in fact, even for socialist planners the difficulties in promoting balanced growth are tremendous, and that the whole idea, in fact, may be unrealistic. The reason for this is that even in socialist society ". . . there are no eternal proportions. There can never be any permanently fixed proportions between the branches of the national economy. Stability in this sphere would not be a sign of health but an alarm signal, for it would mean that the volume of social production remains constant, that production is moving within the same circle and is not expanding at all."[9] In short, Soviet planners have begun to see a fundamental logical flaw in the very idea of balanced economic growth, and rightly so, for it may be as meaningless, unattainable, and deadly as the "perfect bureaucracy" which reduces all life to regularized procedures. Perfectly balanced growth, indeed, requires the total bureaucratization of the economy; and that, we have asserted, is itself a pipe dream.

[8] See Khrushchev's speech of April 24, 1963, reported in *Izvestiia* (April 26, 1963). See also Allan Ballard, "Sovkhoz Kuban," *Survey*, 48 (July, 1963), 71, for a telling example.

[9] *Fundamentals of Marxism–Leninism,* p. 573.

In focusing on the problem of balanced growth, Soviet economic planners have implicitly challenged the overbureaucratization of the economy. They have expressed criticism of the perpetual air of emergency that pervades the command economy and have shown their increasing readiness to re-think Stalinist dogmas and Marxist assumptions.

Stalin's economy had been completely centralized in its planning and preoccupied with production of priority items. Once the planners had the necessary capacity information (however crude their estimate may have been), they established production priorities and, in thoroughly bureaucratic fashion, set targets. From the point of view of Western economists, such behavior flies in the face of economic rationality. But in claiming that socialist planning could replace the "law of values" Soviet ideology brushed aside the warnings of "mere" economists. In the planners' eyes, the victory of rational planning over life implied the supremacy of politics over economic laws. In the light of the most urgent needs of Soviet economic growth, they may have been right. A crash program of industrialization, the demand for rapid growth in the production of capital goods, are probably hindered rather than helped by paying attention to the laws of the market. Moreover, the political commitments of the Soviet regime made it imperative to eliminate all forms of private property, even at the expense of economic irrationality. But the advantages were matched by the ills of bureaucratic hypertrophy: over-centralization, especially in the allocation of materials; cumbersome, overlapping jurisdictions amounting to a messy administrative tangle; and, more generally, the self-defeating attempt to prearrange the functioning of a machinery so complex that it did not lend itself to bureaucratic control.[10] This, in summary, might be an economist's explanation and criticism of

[10] "The one-year plan is a work of several dozen volumes with thousands of pages and hundreds of thousands of figures. The nomenclature of centrally allocated commodities in 1960 contained 13,105 items. . . . In 1962, 18,000 specified commodities were being allocated centrally. . . ." A. Birman, "Sto millionov gaek," *Ekonomicheskaia gazeta*, 13 (1963). See also N. Fedorenko, "Khimicheskaia industriia i ekonomika," *Kommunist*, 4 (1963).

Soviet planning methods.[11] We have talked about them in the past tense because they have all the marks of Stalinist thinking. But in the main Soviet planning still proceeds in this fashion; and Soviet planners and economists are increasingly frank in expressing their worries about the fundamental irrationality of decision-making in the USSR. More and more they focus their attention on the communications problems that inevitably arise in over-centralized bureaucratic structures. The centralization of planning implies the need to control the flow of all commodities, down to the last nut and bolt; for without such careful accounting, how can rationality prevail? But the resultant volume of information and the glut of paperwork have for a long time been entirely unmanageable. As a consequence, major decisions, including those concerning output targets and the allocation of resources, are made on the basis of hunch rather than adequate information. Other consequences are over-control and evasion; lack of coordination and resultant gluts and scarcities, which snowball into chain reactions of bottlenecks; waste of motion and waste of resources.[12]

One way out of the difficulty is to decentralize. The central planners would continue to coordinate the economy, but they would refrain from fixing production targets and from allocating all resources. Production managers would be on their own. Guided in their over-all operation by a national plan, they would be guided in day-to-day operations by some sort of market structure—hence by what Western economists would call economic rationality.

Proposals to this effect have been made more and more insistently by Soviet economists. It may be that the increasing demand for skilled manpower has impressed on Soviet planners the fact that they can no longer operate as flexibly and with as much sovereign authority as in the past. Even more, the crude old planning methods

---

[11] See Alec Nove, "The Politics of Economic Rationality—Observations on the Soviet Economy," *Social Research* (Summer 1958), pp. 127–144; also Herbert S. Levine, "Recent Developments in Soviet Planning," Joint Economic Committee, U. S. Congress, *Dimensions of Soviet Economic Power* (Washington: Government Printing Office), p. 183.

[12] For a discussion of these difficulties, and Soviet sources, see Leon Smolinski, "What Next in Soviet Planning?," *Foreign Affairs* (July 1964), pp. 602–613.

became obsolete as a result of the increasing difficulty of weighing the ever-growing number of economic priorities against each other. Now that the industrial base has been laid, the regime faces a great number of pressing commitments—consumer goods, agriculture, science, defense, new industries, foreign aid, urban renewal and housing, to name the most outstanding—which strain the resources of the economy. To cope with this strain by introducing a rational price system and other market features into economic planning and management has been the effort of several leading economists in the USSR in the last few years. On September 9 and 21, 1962, *Pravda* printed proposals by two professors, which were then discussed at the plenary meeting of the Central Committee in November. In effect, these proposals asked for the introduction of limited freedom for individual enterprises. An incentive system based on profits should guide their operations. Central planning of such things as wages, the use of labor, production cost, and the productivity of labor should be discontinued, and so should the system of bureaucratic material allocation. Enterprises should be free to develop their own way of fulfilling production goals and in dealing with other enterprises.[13]

Within the last two years, the Soviet economy has put some of these proposals to practical test by releasing certain enterprises from the established planning procedures and placing them within a market situation in which production is determined by the demands of the consumers rather than by bureaucratic fiat. The experiment started with two ready-to-wear clothing plants, one in Moscow, the other in Gorki, in the spring of 1964. After a thorough stock-taking

[13] For this continuous search for the most satisfactory organization of a system combining central planning with economic rationality under the form of some sort of market economy, see the article by Alec Nove cited in footnote 11, p. 400; also Alec Nove, "Revamping the Economy," *Problems of Communism*, XII, 1 (date); and Gregory Grossman, "The Soviet Economy," *Problems of Communism*, XII, 2.

For the Soviet economists' contributions to this debate, see the articles by Zverev, Kazitskii, Kapustin, Al'ter, Plotnikov, and Kapitonov in *Voprosy Ekonomiki*, 1 (1962); by Bor and Liberman in *Ekonomicheskaia Gazeta*, 46 (1962); by Nemchinov in *Vosprosy Ekonomiki*, 11 (1962); by Vaag and Zakharov in *Vosprosy Ekonomiki*, 4 (1962); by Batyrev in *Vosprosy Ekonomiki*, 5 (1962); by Gamovskii in *Kommunist*, 18 (1962); and by Malyshev in *Pravda* (February 7, 1963).

at a meeting of the Sovnarkhoz of the USSR in October of the same year, Pravda on January 12, 1965, announced that this system of production would be extended to the vast majority of all Soviet clothing and footwear enterprises, and that the same manner of operation would also be tried by textile mills, tanneries, and other suppliers. Altogether, one quarter of the enterprises constituting the light industry sector of the Soviet economy will operate semi-independently, in a market economy, by the second half of 1965. As outlined in the relevant Soviet discussions, the autonomy granted to individual enterprises in this new manner of operation goes considerably beyond the proposals made in 1962 by Professor Liberman. Nor is this likely to be the entire story. A similar transformation of management patterns seems to be in the offing for the Soviet food industry; and a *Pravda* editorial of November 13, 1964 even suggested that the same market principles ought to be allowed to determine production in heavy industry.[14]

In various ways, the structure of the Soviet economy thus seems to be moving in the direction of decentralization in management. At least, this is a clearly discernible tendency. A contrary trend is not at all incompatible with it: even if individual enterprises and entire industries are given more freedom, and this freedom is cemented by a price system based on the market rather than on bureaucratic price-setting, the basic decisions will still be made at the center. A development which will make centralization possible without once again inviting chaos is the increasing use of the electronic computer. Soviet planners and economists have become keenly interested in the possibilities opened up by the use of computers and in the development of cybernetic models of management. A newly established Institute of Management and Resource Allocation (Nauchnoissledovatel'nyi institut organizatsii upravleniia i normativov) established by the Council for the National Economy (Sovnarkhoz) of the USSR appears to pay considerable attention to such problems, to judge from the articles in its journal, *Organizatsiia Upravleniia i Normativy*. No wonder, for the use of com-

---

[14] See also Kosygin's report to the Supreme Soviet of December 9, 1964 (*Pravda* [December 10, 1964]).

puters makes it possible to bring order into the fantastic glut of information that used to paralyze the planners. Already a Soviet computing center is said to have worked out a three-year production plan for the entire country in a calculation involving 360 million electronic operations, according to a report by Theodore Shabad in the *New York Times* of April 13, 1963. In addition to working out the input-output relations between various sectors of the economy, the report went on, computers are also used for investment planning, including determination of the most effective geographic location of new plants.

The relationship between decentralization and consumer sovereignty, on the one hand, and centralization through computers, on the other, remains to be studied. One might argue that the Soviet economy at this moment is at a crossroads, where it might turn either in the direction of further decentralization or renewed centralization. Yet one might also see the two trends as complementary and mutually reinforcing methods of rationalization, in which the use of computers will make it possible to concentrate highly intricate planning operations for the entire national economy precisely because farther below a more rational system of management prevails. Thus, by extending limited freedom of enterprise to its units in the field, the central government may be able to gain more complete mastery over the entire economy.

Chapter XVIII
Agriculture

"Always the same old story. It really was a vicious circle! In order to produce a decent return for a day's labour people would have to work—what other source of funds did the farm have? But in order to make people work there had to be a decent return for the day's labour.

"Where was the way out?

"In the district committee they said: you're a bad manager. Your agitational-education work is weak. But how were you to 'agitate' today's collective farmer? No amount of propaganda reached him unless there was money in it. You argued it out with him: did we buy two tractors? We did. Do we need money for lorries? We do. What about the new cattle yards? And didn't we bring radio into the village? Wait a bit, and we'll get round one day to the wage packet. But the kolkhoznik can't wait. He doesn't want to wait any longer. That's the trouble."

Fyodor Abramov, ONE DAY IN THE "NEW LIFE"*

Despite some serious structural and operational inefficiencies, the Soviet system has promoted industrial growth so rapidly and successfully that most Western observers credit it with quite spectacular achievement in this respect.[1] In contrast, agriculture is usually considered to be the system's most spectacular failure. Whereas in industry the productivity of labor has grown tremendously, it has remained virtually stagnant in the countryside.[2] Farming methods have not kept pace with the technological revolution which is transforming manufacture and which in the United States has pro-

---

* Fyodor Abramov, *One Day in the "New Life"* (New York: Praeger, 1963), pp. 86–87. Reprinted by permission of the publisher.

[1] In this context, the reader should keep in mind that, after all, inefficiencies and tremendous wastes are built into the Western economy as well.

[2] The Party has at times admitted this. "As a result of the last war and also of mistakes made in the past and failures of leadership, the country's agriculture has found itself in a grave situation. The low level of output of agricultural produce could hold up the development of the Soviet economy and seriously affect the welfare of the nation." Resolution of the

foundly changed large-scale farming. The economic backwardness of Soviet agriculture is complemented by political backwardness, from the regime's point of view: the peasantry still has not allowed itself to be transformed into that new socialist man the Party has wished to create. In fact, the Party's failure to win over the peasantry is usually considered to be the most important example of the limits of totalitarian or authoritarian government. Among the reasons for this failure are some naturally given conditions of soils and climates, and also some hard economic decisions the regime has had to make in planning investments. Throughout the industrialization period of the Soviet regime, investment has been concentrated on heavy industry, agriculture being most clearly regarded as the stepchild of planning for economic growth.[3] All this is of no more than incidental interest in a book on the *political* system of the USSR. Instead, our attention must be directed to the human relations of agricultural management, that is, to the Party's policies toward the peasantry as a class.

THE REGIME'S ATTITUDE TOWARD THE PEASANT

The aims underlying these policies have been complex and, to some extent, mutually contradictory. For one thing, the Party was for a long time unable to make up its mind about its broad political attitude toward the peasantry. It was torn between the desire to mend political fences by gaining the peasants' confidence and allegiance and the desire to neutralize or totally destroy their political influence. The former attitude was dictated by political necessity, the

---

Twenty-second Congress of the CPSU, October 31, 1961, in *Spravochnik Partiinogo Rabotnika,* Issue 4 (1963), p. 16. See also the appeal to the nation made by the March 1962 Plenum: "The party openly tells the people: the rates of growth in agriculture . . . do not correspond to the rising needs of the population." *Ibid.,* p. 179.

[3] "While the development of machine construction in our country is on a high level, the production facilities for putting out tractors, agricultural equipment, and storage facilities have increased only slowly; new enterprises for this purpose are not being built. In recent years, while demand has risen, the production and procurement to our agriculture of corn and silage harvesting combines, seeders, cultivators, and other machinery has fallen. . . ." Decree of the March 1962 Plenum, *ibid.,* p. 172.

feeling that in an overwhelmingly rural society the Communist Party could not maintain itself in power without making concessions to the peasantry. The latter, more negative, aim might be ascribed to impatience with precisely this need for adjustment, and the fear that coddling the peasants would only make them stronger, hence even more dangerous politically. Deeply felt hostility against the peasantry as a political force, moreover, is a part of the Marxist intellectual tradition that has been extremely strong and persistent. When communist programs demand the elimination of the difference between the city and the country, we must interpret this statement to mean that the country must give way to the city, and that the peasant as a distinct social class must disappear. Precisely what he should become has also been controversial in the Communist Party. Those who have advocated a policy of adjustment to the peasants' aspirations and interests seem to envision his gradual transformation into an independent farmer, at least for a certain period. Those who wished to urbanize agriculture would like to see him turn into something resembling a worker.

This is not a clash of merely political attitudes, but a broad cultural problem. At stake is the very existence of the peasant way of life, despised and held suspect by the Communist Party. The cultural revolution that Lenin demanded in 1922 aims to eradicate this traditional culture pattern, and the conflicts in the Party are little else than disputes over the speed and the methods for this imposed change. Whether the peasant would become an independent farmer or an agricultural proletarian, or, perhaps, if a compromise solution were to be found, the Party wanted to lift him out of the Middle Ages or the timelessness of the peasant life into the modern age—in any case, the Party had to expect resistance.

Apart from the alternative aims of securing the peasants' allegiance, transforming them, or destroying them, the Party has always been compelled to adjust its agricultural policies to its economic needs: perhaps the most immediate aim of the Soviet regime in its relations to the peasantry has always been to secure ample supplies of food and fiber for the growing cities and the armed forces of the country. This ever-growing need for agricultural produce entails several difficult tasks which at times get into each other's way. First, methods have to be found to make the peasants work rather than remain idle. This goal can, of course, be promoted by a great variety of devices, ranging from force to psychological, political, or material rewards. Second, the regime must seek to raise the productivity of agricultural labor, or the per-acre yield, a problem that also has its psychological and political as well as economic and technological sides. Making the peasants work and rendering them more efficient, however, is not enough, as the Communist Party found out in the 1920s. Means must also be found which will enable the regime to procure the agricultural produce, to channel food and fiber away from consumption by the producers and into the mouths or hands of the city population (or, perhaps, into industry or the export market, if this is what the Party decides to do with it). For this purpose, too, there are a number of methods. But, in choosing between them, the regime has had to take into consideration the relatively low state of development of the entire economy and the consequent need to devote all possible resources to investment rather than consumption. To put this more bluntly: the Party has for a long time searched for effective ways of securing a maximum of agricultural produce without paying the peasants more than a bare minimum of reward. In its preoccupation with this problem, the task of raising agricultural productivity has tended to be neglected; in fact, the policy of the Soviet regime toward the peasants has been a long series of uneasy compromises satisfying neither the peasantry nor the Party leadership.

We can trace this condition back to the revolutionary year 1917, when the Bolsheviks, seeking to cash in on the boundless radicalism of the peasantry, came out in support of anarchic policies and processes of land redistribution of which in their hearts, as Marxists, they disapproved. As a result, agricultural Russia was transformed into a society of independent small producers, differentiated by the size of their holdings and other property. During the civil war, when in the cities and in the Red Army food was desperately short, the regime extracted agricultural produce from this new peasantry by unleashing bitter class warfare in the village, setting the poor against the well-to-do, and by applying force in seizing all available food stuffs. These measures were as desperate as the need that had evoked them, and, by alienating the peasantry from the regime, they created more problems than they solved. The coercive requisitioning of grain was therefore abandoned as soon as the wartime emergency was over. In 1921 the Soviet regime made an abrupt turn-about when Lenin introduced the NEP in an attempt to give the peasantry material incentives for the production and marketing of food. A period ensued during which the regime sought to promote the revival of agriculture by catering to the peasants' interest in free enterprise and a free market, even while it tried to prevent the formation of a prosperous upper stratum of *kulaks*. Meanwhile, through education, indoctrination, and political manipulation, the peasantry was to be raised to a higher level of political and economic sophistication. Withal, the NEP was a period of all-pervasive compromise and hesitancy—an interregnum during which the Party lacked a clear sense of direction. This feeling of being politically at sea was increased by the fact that the compromises contained in the NEP did not, in the long run, yield the expected beneficial results. The NEP was designed to raise agricultural production and promote general economic growth. However, because of serious imbalances in the economic system, the regime saw itself unable to match the rise in agricultural production with a corresponding increase in available industrial goods. Hence it could not give the peasant a fair return for his produce; consequently, the procurement of food for the cities was threatened once again. The specter of starvation once more raised its head. In the eyes of many Party leaders, free enterprise in farming, and the very existence of a strong peasantry, more than ever appeared as a threat to the existence of the communist regime. Although contemporary Soviet spokesmen claim that the major reason for doing away with private enterprise in agriculture was its technological backwardness, its inability to make use of modern equipment, hence its inefficiency as compared to large-scale farming, they do admit that the coexistence of private enterprise in one sector of the economy with socialist management in another was untenable in the long run.[4]

Once the Communist Party had decided to begin its program for industrialization, Stalin and his lieutenants apparently deemed this threat intolerable. The first five-year plan for industrial development was therefore accompanied by a drastic, revolutionary, and bloody restructuring of agriculture and the peasantry. Gradually at first, but soon with an irresistible sweep, using promises, persuasion, then threat, and finally deadly violence, the Communist Party and the Soviet government virtually wiped out private enterprise in agriculture, deprived the peasants of most of their property in land, implements, and farm animals, and made them pool these resources in producers' cooperatives of a decidedly collectivist type. Called collective farms (*kolkhozy;* singular, *kolkhoz*), these cooperatives are still the dominant form of organization in the countryside.

THE INSTITUTION OF THE *Kolkhoz*

For these *kolkhozy,* the Soviet peasantry, and indeed the entire nation, paid a very high price in human lives, happiness, and material welfare. The ruthlessness with which Stalin exacted this price betokens his impatience with the previous agricultural order. If thirty years after the end of collectivization the *kolkhoz* is still the prevailing form of rural enterprise, it must have proven itself sufficiently useful in solving the regime's most pressing problems. At the same time, the persistent technological backwardness of collective farm methods, the recurrent evidence of the peasant's dissatisfaction with his status, and the repeated efforts of the Party to reform the system—all these phenomena demonstrate that the advantages of the *kolkhoz* system are limited and that they are

[4] P. I. Nikitin, *Osnovy politicheskoi ekonomii,* 2d ed. (Moscow, 1962), pp. 212–213. Western economists have concentrated more on the economic difficulties of the regime—the vanishing agricultural surpluses, the unfavorable price structure which led to increasing consumption on the part of the peasantry, the crying need for exportable surpluses, and the need for mobilizing additional agricultural labor for work in the cities. See Maurice Dobb, *Soviet Economic Development Since 1917* (New York: International Publishers, 1947); Alexander Erlich, *The Soviet Industrialization Debate* (Cambridge: Harvard University Press, 1960); Lazar Volin, *A Survey of Soviet Russian Agriculture* (Washington, D.C.: USDA, 1951).

attained at the expense of other interests vital to the Party.

A collective farm ostensibly is a cooperative enterprise having at its disposal the various means of production that the family units constituting its membership have surrendered to it. Title to the land ultimately remains with the public authorities, but, according to *Kolkhoz* law, the government grants usufruct of the land to the collective farm "in perpetuity." Buildings, implements, supplies, and farm animals are the property of the *kolkhoz*. The individual family, meanwhile, retains ownership of its modest dwelling, a garden plot of varying size (normally around a half-acre), hand implements, limited numbers of fowl and other small animals, and even a family cow. Short of selling or leasing these residues of private property, the individual family is entitled to work on this garden plot and care for its own animals at its own discretion and to dispose over the resulting produce freely. Most of the meat, milk, eggs, fruit, and vegetables yielded by this free enterprise find their way to the so-called *kolkhoz* market in the nearest town, where the urban dwellers can purchase them from the farmer at prices determined solely by the law of supply and demand. Here the farmer may also offer for sale the fish he may have caught or the mushrooms and wild berries he may have gathered on his own time.

Apart from this residual free enterprise, the *kolkhoz* is a collectivist enterprise which uses its land through the application of organization and teamwork.[5] Management of the farm is in the hands of a *kolkhoz* director ostensibly elected by, and responsible to, the assembly of *kolkhoz* members, but in fact appointed by higher authorities and responsible to a bewildering array of governmental and Party agencies which directly interfere with his planning, management, and operations. Within the farm, the director can work with the entire *kolkhoz* assembly, but ordinarily he relies on his cadre of administrative aides, farming specialists, and team bosses ("brigadiers").

---

[5] The *artel* form of cooperative organization which, after some experimentation, became standard for collective farms, means that resources (land and equipment) were pooled, labor was rendered collectively in work gangs or teams, but remuneration went to each individual and was not equalized.

Farm operations have to conform to the national production plans, in general, and agricultural priorities, in particular. Central bureaucratic agencies therefore determine what should be grown and often also prescribe methods or even the timing of specific farm operations. A host of governmental and party organizations with grossly overlapping jurisdictions and authorities supervise, guide, and control the collective farms in their attempts to fulfill their assigned production plans. In the past, these have included agencies directly responsible to federal or republican ministries, *obispolkom* agricultural inspectorates, *raion* authorities of both government and Party, as well as still lower organizations, such as Party primary organizations. This agricultural bureaucracy has been cumbersome and inefficient and has been subject to a number of very thorough reforms within the last ten years.[6]

To all those involved in this machinery, from the individual farmer, through the *kolkhoz* chairman, up to the chief government executives and Party secretaries in provinces and republics, production figures covering farm operations are an important indicator of success. But an even more important figure for all of them is that which describes the agricultural produce that has actually been acquired by government procurement agencies; and, similarly, the obligation of the individual *kolkhoz* to deliver to the government in fact appears more important than that to produce. Each farm is obliged to sell to the government (at prices fixed artificially low) a quota of its produce which the government assesses on the basis of the acreage the farm has under cultivation. The precise method of assessment of this compulsory procurement quota has been subject to change, depending on the needs of the government and its disposition to exert pressure on the peasantry. Once these compulsory deliveries have been made, the *kolkhoz* has still other obligations. It must set aside certain fixed quantities of its produce for seed and feed, as well as for planned reserves. It may have tax obligations that might be satisfied by additional deliveries. Once all these obligations have been met, the *kolkhoz* can, again within limits, dispose freely of its surpluses. The entire system, instituted in the early 1930s, was designed to stimulate

[6] See Part Three, Chapter II and *passim*.

production by giving the collective farms an incentive to increase their surpluses. These surpluses over compulsory deliveries, taxes, and the like, can be distributed to the *kolkhoz* membership in kind, or they can be transformed into cash by being sold to the government at higher prices than those paid for quota deliveries. The specific rights of disposition over these surpluses have also been subject to change. Of course, even after all obligations to the government have been met, the *kolkhoz* chairman will have to reserve a certain portion of his disposable surpluses for such purposes as construction, repair, purchases of equipment, cultural or educational endeavors, and administrative overhead. Only then can he begin to think about paying off the collective farm membership.

In short—and this is the overriding principle of the entire system —the need to deliver assessed quotas and provide for other planned needs of the economy is higher than the need to take care of the collective farm's own requirements. Delivery quotas, especially, are sacrosanct. They must be met even if meeting them seems an impossibility because of crop failure. Hence it is possible that a *kolkhoz* may have to purchase, at high prices, grain or cotton or potatoes so that it may be able to sell them, as part of its delivery quota, to the government at a far lower price. Inefficiency or natural disaster, therefore, are not likely to cause disastrous drops in deliveries, but will lead only to empty stomachs among the *kolkhoz* peasants. The collective farmers carry all the risks and burdens of their profession, while a regular flow of food and fiber continues to go into the cities.

It is indeed the individual members of the farm who carry this risk, because their remuneration for services rendered to the *kolkhoz* can only come out of the farm's disposable surpluses. If these are absent, the farmers receive no pay, because theirs is the last of all the claims on return for the work that has been done on the farm. Hence the garden plot may be a life-saving source of subsistence staples or cash. When surpluses are there to be distributed, the individual *kolkhoz* member receives pay for the precise amount of work-time he has contributed to the collective effort. Each individual is given credit for the number of "work days" or "labor days" he has rendered to the farm. A labor day, however, is not necessarily one full day's actual work. Instead, various jobs that need to be done are measured differentially, according to the skill or training they require; twelve hours' work of operating complicated farm machinery, let us say, may be counted as several labor days, whereas the same number of hours spent in herding goats or even such arduous but simple a task as harvesting potatoes may be counted as no more than a fraction of a labor day. At the end of the year, when the *kolkhoz* distributes its surpluses either in kind or in cash (or both), it does so in strict accordance with the number of labor days with which each individual member has been credited.[7] The collective farm system, like the Soviet economy in general, thus operates with a sharply graded system of wage differentials, the purpose of which, of course, is to stimulate production, encourage the development of skills, and punish slackers. Like all other devices at the disposal of the Soviet administration, this system of rewards can be and has been changed from time to time in response to the peasants' behavior. The government also has experimented with various ways of organizing collective-farm work gangs. For instance, in what may have been an attempt to appeal to the peasants' individualism, the government in the years after World War II sought to break up the impersonal brigades into much smaller teams. But these experiments were halted rather abruptly in 1950. Many observers believe that the brigade system does run counter to individualistic strivings among the peasants, while at the same time the sharply graded wage differences offend their egalitarian or collectivist sense of justice. Occasionally, the Soviet press has reported cases in which collective farm managers have violated the rewards system

[7] Karl Marx described the labor day as a ruthless method of feudal exploitation: ". . . every Wallachian peasant owes to the so-called landlord . . . 14 [labor] days in the year. With deep insight into political economy, however, the working day is not taken in its ordinary sense, but as the working day necessary to the production of an average daily product; and that average daily product is determined in so crafty a way that no Cyclops would be done with it in 24 hours. In dry words, the Réglement itself declares with true Russian irony that by 12 working days one must understand the product of the manual labour of 36 days, by 1 day of field labour 3 days, and by 1 day of wood carrying in like manner three times as much." Karl Marx, Capital, Vol. I (Chicago: Charles H. Kerr, 1906), pp. 262–263.

and distributed their surpluses in much more egalitarian fashion.

Until a few years ago, the institution of the Machine-Tractor Station (MTS) played a crucial role in this system of riskless exploitation. If the labor day seems to have been borrowed from feudal practices as described by Marx, then the MTS looks like a direct application of the Marxist principle that ownership of the essential means of production gives the owner power to exploit and dominate the actual producers. The MTS was a motor and equipment pool operating in a rural district and directly responsible to a central ministry. It owned tractors and implements, as well as repair shops to provide for their upkeep, and each MTS would service a number of *kolkhozy* by placing this equipment—essential for large-scale farming—at their disposal. Merely by maintaining control over the deployment of this machinery, the MTS could keep all the collective farms in its district in a state of dependence. Because of this unequal relationship, it could, in addition, serve a number of other important functions.[8]

Foremost, the MTS until its abolition served as the collecting agency for all compulsory deliveries of *kolkhoz* produce. If, in carrying out this task, the MTS acted as the representative of the central agricultural planning organizations, it did so also by interfering directly in the management of *kolkhoz* operations, as well as by providing agricultural extension services through its staff of agronomists and farm experts of various kinds. The MTS thus functioned as the most important bureaucratic link between the government and the collective farms. The activities of this link organization, however, were not only economic, but also political. Given the chronic weakness of the Communist Party in the *kolkhozy*, the MTS, with its Party primary organization, was the focus of Party activity at the grass-roots level in rural areas, engaging in that great variety of activities constituting the sum total of Party work. More generally, therefore, the Machine-Tractor Station was an outpost of the city in the countryside, of the machine age in a backward rural society, a missionary post of urban communism

---

[8] ". . . at a certain stage of development, it was the MTS which in a certain measure functioned as the organizer of kolkhoz production." From the Decree of the March 1962 Plenum of the Party Central Committee, in *Spravochnik Partiinogo Rabotnika*, Issue 4 (1963), p. 175.

among the dark people of the pagus or the heath. As such an outpost, the MTS sought to convert the peasantry by promoting the cultural revolution in the village, introducing the peasants to machine shops, accounting, bureaucracy, and Party lore. By serving as a training ground for upward-mobile members of the rural youth, finally, it provided one of the most convenient channels for draining the more enterprising young villagers away from the overpopulated countryside and into the city working class.

The MTS has been abolished, but the main features of the *kolkhoz* system has been retained. The arrangement carries some obvious advantages for the Soviet economy. Primarily, it has assured the government of a steady supply of farm staples as food for city dwellers, raw material for industry, and, in good harvest years, marketable surpluses for export, while those who can afford it may relieve the scantiness and monotony of their diet by more expensive (and time-consuming) purchases on the *kolkhoz* market. The system compels the peasants to work both on the collectively owned land and also on their private plots, while managing to keep their rewards down to the lowest possible level. In making this relationship possible, the collective farm system was an essential precondition to the program of rapid industrialization.

The disadvantages of the system have always been obvious to those who devised and perpetuated it. Chief among them is the low productivity of *kolkhoz* work. It would be a mistake to explain this disappointing yield of Soviet collective farming exclusively by reference to its organization and management. On the contrary, one major cause for the backwardness of Soviet farming has been the regime's deliberate neglect of this sector of the economy in favor of industry. Agriculture decidedly has been the stepchild of Soviet investment policies. More generally, rural society has been the stepchild with regard to all other outlays expended by the Soviet state. With regard to housing, schooling, medical facilities, transportation, and public services of many other kinds, quantity and quality rapidly decrease as one goes from urban centers to the Soviet countryside; even the Party now concedes this. Says the official ideological text: ". . . for a long time after the victory of socialism the cultural level of the peasantry still lags behind that of the working class and the rural mode of life is inferior to the urban,"[9] although it then points out that this situation is being remedied. It is, of course, a fact that rural life is poorer in most or all industrial societies; but the contrast in living standards is much sharper in the USSR than in Western Europe or North America. The differences are not only material, but psychological and even legal. The prestige and status of the rural dweller in the Soviet Union is low; in many regards he is subject to a different system of laws and regulations—a clear echo from the feudal past. More than in the West, therefore, the rural dweller must feel himself to be a member of an underprivileged class. This feeling is intense among ambitious or enterprising Soviet citizens as well as among the rural youth. Soviet writers themselves have pointed out that anyone who is bright, capable, and ambitious leaves the collective farm for industrial employment.[10] Especially since the last war, there has been a steady drain, particularly of young men, from the country. Combined with the serious manpower losses of World War II, which eliminated millions of young males, this migration from the countryside has led to a predominance of women and old people among *kolkhoz* farmers in many areas. Among the educated, assignment to rural posts is regarded as virtually a form of punishment. Many Party and government officials, including teachers, physicians, and other professionals, seek to avoid or evade such posts. This general tendency results in a chronic shortage of skilled and capable personnel in many areas of rural administration.

All these factors go far to explain the low productivity of Soviet collectivized agriculture. So long as these conditions prevail, i.e., so long as agriculture is the stepchild of Soviet investment priorities because trips to the moon are more important than tractors and chemical fertilizer, the *kolkhoz* system will fail to provide effective incentives for hard and good work. The typical *kolkhoz* member has an insufficient stake in working hard or in working at all for the

[9] *Fundamentals of Marxism–Leninism*, p. 591.

[10] See V. Zasukhin, "Pod goriachuiu ruku," *Komsomolskaia Pravda* (August 15, 1963). Also Fedor Abramov, *One Day in the "New Life"* (New York: Praeger, 1964).

collective effort, since the return for himself is so uncertain. In the words of the party ideologists, "An excessive increase in the rate of accumulation . . . may weaken the material incentive of those engaged in production and ultimately affect the rate of growth of labor productivity."[11] Nor does the regime appear to have succeeded in complementing the insufficient material incentives with a collectivist ethos or a moral feeling of obligation toward the *kolkhoz*. Collective-farm members therefore have tried to shirk their legal obligation of putting in a predetermined minimum of work days. The quality of the work they do often is poor. Their real effort goes into the care of privately owned animals, the cultivation of the family garden plot, and the marketing of the resulting produce. Recent Soviet statistics reveal that this private sector of agriculture still produces a surprisingly high proportion of the meat, milk, eggs, and vegetables consumed by city dwellers. Furthermore, recurrent complaints and countermeasures attest to widespread attempts on the part of *kolkhoz* members to enrich themselves at the expense of the collective, by pilfering, private use of *kolkhoz* land or equipment, and similar abuses. An especially threatening erosion of collective farm discipline, followed by a sharp crackdown, took place during World War II.

To these economic and organizational causes of inefficiency one might add the complexities of the bureaucracy responsible for planning, coordinating, and supervising agriculture, the jurisdictional squabbles, the possibility and widespread use of evasion devices, and the sad fact that nature or local conditions often frustrate plans and schedules which may look eminently sensible to some chair-borne manager in a central office. To all this we must add the resistance which the older generation of peasants especially has shown to the political and cultural penetration of the countryside by the communist regime. Altogether this amounts to an impressive catalog of difficulties.[12]

[11] *Fundamentals of Marxism–Leninism,* p. 571.
[12] For summaries of these complaints, by a short-story author, by an economist, and by Khrushchev, see Leonid Ivanov, "V rodnykh mestakh," *Novyi Mir,* No. 3 (1963); M. Lemeshev, "Voprosy uskorennogo razvitiia sel'skogo khoziaistva," *Voprosy Ekonomiki,* No. 6 (1962); and Khrushchev's speech of March 12, 1963, in *Pravda* (March 14, 1963).

ATTEMPTS AT AGRICULTURAL REFORM

Hence it is not astonishing to see that the zeal for experiments in reform, so lively in the USSR since Stalin's death, has been particularly active in agriculture. Actually, the *kolkhoz* structure even during Stalin's life was subject to frequent experimentation. Toward the end of his life, Stalin himself indicated that the collective farm was only a temporary form of organization, which in the future communist society would have to yield to more collectivist structures. He seems to have believed, however, that a considerable span of years would have to pass before the *kolkhoz* had outlived its usefulness. Not so some of his advisors. In the course of a campaign to merge existing *kolkhozy* into fewer and larger farms, which was launched in the spring of 1950 and proceeded for an entire year, N. S. Khrushchev proposed a more ambitious reorganization of farming. He suggested that collective farmers be resettled from their present villages into larger agricultural towns, so that collective farm management and operations might be more centralized. Presumably, urban services to the population might be improved through the establishment of such "agro-towns" (Russian, *agrogorod*). At the same time, the private garden plots would be relocated around the towns and reduced in size. Undoubtedly, such a relocation of personnel and land would have strengthened the hand of farm management in imposing *kolkhoz* discipline on the peasants. Perhaps this is a typical Soviet example of trying to solve a problem bureaucratically (i.e., through reorganization), which in the final analysis is economic.

The *agrogorod* scheme aborted. Since then, however, the regime has succeeded in greatly reducing the number of collective farms through a prolonged merger movement. In successive steps, the number of collective farms has been reduced from around 254,000 in 1949, to about 80,000 in 1956, to somewhat over 41,000 in 1961.[13] This urge to consolidate undoubtedly is more than an ex-

[13] According to Khrushchev, the merger movement culminated in 1960 and got out of hand, leading to the creation of giant collective farms which turned out to be unmanageable. Speech of March 12, 1963, in *Pravda* (March 14, 1963).

pression of spleen, which some Western scholars have called
"gigantomania."[14] Obviously, it promotes centralization of management, as well as the urbanization of farm life in general. It thus
speeds the cultural revolution and at the same time permits deeper
penetration of the Party into the countryside. Party organization
among the peasantry, as we saw earlier, has always been weak; only
a minority of the more than 250,000 *kolkhozy* existing in 1949
had their own primary organization. With the successive mergers,
this picture changed. Party members who had been scattered too
thinly over many collective farms now were thrown together
in far fewer enterprises, and of the 40,000-odd *kolkhozy* existing
today only a small minority is without its primary organization.
This increase in grass-roots strength made possible (and, in turn,
was greatly aided by) an even more revolutionary step taken by
the regime in 1958. This was the abolition of Machine-Tractor
Stations. Although Stalin had warned, not long before his death,
that the MTS was a vitally necessary tool of the regime for controlling and transforming the peasantry, the Khrushchev government surprised its own citizens (as well as the Western world)
by doing away with this seemingly essential institution and allowing
the *kolkhozy* to purchase the equipment, for cash or on credit.
Apparently, the collective farms had become so large that sharing
tractors and implements with other *kolkhozy* led to excessive friction and inefficiency. With greater size came larger and more
specialized staffs, as well as Party primary organizations right in
the farm. The various functions carried out by the MTS could
therefore be taken over by the several collective farms. The success
of the merger movement permitted a modicum of decentralization.[15]

The picture, however, is far from simple. The abolition of the
MTS was only one dramatic step in a series of reforms and reorganizations that has been going on for more than ten years and

[14] This is the assumption, made by Marxists almost *a priori,* that the
efficiency of any economic enterprise inevitably increases with its size.
[15] For Western comments, see Roy D. Laird, "The Demise of the Machine
Tractor Station," *American Slavic and East European Review* (December,
1958), 418–425; also Laird, Sharp, and Sturtevant, *The Rise and Fall of
the MTS as an Instrument of Soviet Rule* (Lawrence, Kansas: University of
Kansas Governmental Research Center, 1960).

has brought with it rather sweeping changes in the exceedingly complicated structure of planning, managing, and controlling organizations, most of them somehow related to the decentralization and "recentralization" reforms in other sectors of the economy. What has emerged is far from clear to the outside observer, because obvious overlaps of authority and jurisdiction between various levels of government and between government and Party offices continue to exist, the most recent key organization being a Territorial Production Administration which, in agriculture, seems to correspond, vaguely enough, to the regional councils of the national economy (*Sovnarkhozy*). If there is one outstanding aim in these organizational reshufflings, it might be an increased emphasis on raising the productivity of agricultural labor.

Various other recent measures and trends apparently pursue the same aim. They include vigorous and manifold attempts to improve farm methods, partly on the basis of Western experiences and practices, as well as repeated starts in the direction of increasing capital investments in farming or in industries serving the farmer, such as the production of chemical fertilizers. Efforts have also been made to eliminate the greatest injustices or hardships to individual *kolkhoz* members. Thus collective farm chairmen have began to substitute cash payments for payments in kind, to make regular advances of such payments to their members, and even to guarantee the individual a certain minimum wage. In short, the regime has begun to give the *kolkhoz* peasant a modicum of material security, although still with a great degree of hesitation and with obvious fear of giving in to the peasants too much.

Two other major developments deserve mention to round out the picture of recent farm policies. One is Khrushchev's drive to put to the plough vast areas of virgin lands in the area of Northern Kazakhstan and Southwestern Siberia. The other, somehow related to the former, is the rapid growth in the number of state farms (sovkhozy). State farms are agricultural enterprises owned directly by the government and operated in a manner similar to that of industrial plants. In fact, cereal-producing *sovkhozy* have sometimes been called "grain factories." Salaried farm hands (statistically counted as workers, rather than peasants) perform the labor in the fields and stables. They are employees rather than cooperative partners, and they do not own private garden plots. Their full labor time belongs to their employer. In its entire structure and operation, the *sovkhoz* corresponds to the Soviet pattern of industrial management, whereas the *kolkhoz* is a compromise that peasant stubbornness and recalcitrance have forced on the regime. The Party leadership is therefore likely to regard the *sovkhozy* as the more desirable organization, perhaps as the organization of the future—a pattern for agricultural management which corresponds to a greater intensity of agricultural investment and to a more advanced state of urbanization and technical education. Opening up millions of acres of hitherto untilled land gave the USSR an opportunity to increase the number of such enterprises significantly. Moreover, some *kolkhozy* appear to have been reorganized into *sovkhozy* in the course of recent mergers and other reorganizations; and, in general, one might assert that other recent reforms in *kolkhoz* management go in the direction of assimilating the collective farm to the state farm.[16] The experiments with a guaranteed wage for kolkhoz farmers is one of such measures. Perhaps we are at present witnessing the beginnings of a long-range effort to extend such a change to a majority of collective farms (most likely the more efficient and prosperous ones). Perhaps, indeed, Soviet agriculture is now entering a period during which it can seriously contemplate the elimination of the *kolkhoz* altogether. Its replacement by, or transformation into, state farms would undoubtedly lead the Soviet leadership to claim that the peasant class has been assimilated into the working class and that, therefore, Marx's demand for an elimination of the differences between city and country has been fulfilled.

To be sure, the short-lived administrative reforms of November 1962 divided Party and government into two separate branches—one for industry, another for agriculture.[17] This might be interpreted

[16] The Twenty-second Party Congress, in October 1961, passed the following resolution: "The Congress approves the course in the direction of further strengthening and growing similarity between the nationalized (*obshchenarodnoi*) and collective-cooperative forms of socialist property." *Spravochnik Partiinogo Rabotnika,* Issue 4 (1963), p. 19.

[17] The decree creating the new territorial production administrations for agriculture is printed in *Spravochnik Partiinogo Rabotnika,* pp. 321–331.

as an admission that the differences between city and country still were considered very real. At the same time, however, it could be regarded as the first serious step in the assimilation of the country to the city, because it was an ambitious attempt to extend to agriculture bureaucratic management principles tried out in industry. At the March 1962 Plenum of the Party Central Committee, Khrushchev attempted to explain the poor productivity of Soviet agriculture by asserting that agriculture, in the past, had been marked by a curious mixture of autonomy and control, a pattern in which risk-taking and investment policies were left to the *kolkhoz,* while bureaucrats at various levels were exercising political and social control. "On the one hand, we meddle directly and immediately with many aspects of cooperative life. But when it comes to the organization of production, on the other hand, i.e., to the decisive factor in the life of the *kolkhoz,* we preach the principle of non-interference in cooperative affairs."[18] The remedy he proposed was to forget about the myth of noninterference altogether, to form administrative organizations for planning and supervising and managing agricultural farm production—in short, to rationalize farming by imposing agronomic expertise and sound business management on the production units. This, however, is nothing else than the elimination of the differences between *kolkhoz* and *sovkhoz* and, in the long run, between the country and the city.

For the time being, the contrast between the city and country remains great. While the Soviet economy continues to develop, agriculture has remained its sick sector. The year 1963, with a poor performance in regard to virtually all major crops, turned out to be disastrous. Instead of exporting cereals, as usual, the Soviet government had to purchase large quantities of grain abroad. Dramatic setbacks of this kind may easily be repeated. One can therefore expect the Soviet regime to continue its efforts to find more satisfactory methods of organization and management in agriculture.

[18] *Pravda* (March 6, 1962).

Chapter XIX
Labor

"A minor but vocal opinion in corporate circles goes beyond reluctant acceptance. Where unions are no longer battling for survival, where a kind of modus vivendi *has been established with management, their positive use as agencies of communication and as agencies of industrial government may be recognized. I have heard some industrial executives—not many, but some—say, 'I don't know how we did without them.' The union, enforcing standards of conduct by the pressure of peers rather than the imposed discipline of superiors, concerned with working out satisfactory rules rather than defeating the enemy, may become a more intimate part of corporate government than the stockholders became or could have."*
Wilbert E. Moore, THE CONDUCT OF THE CORPORATION

"The trade unions, which Lenin called a school of administration and economic management, a school of communism, acquire particular importance. The trade unions have to raise the communist consciousness of the masses, organize emulation for communist labor, and help the working people in learning to manage the state and social affairs. They must encourage the activity of factory and office workers in the efforts for technical progress, for higher labor productivity, for the fulfillment and over-fulfillment of plans and assignments. The trade unions have big tasks in regard to protecting the interests and rights of the working people, raising their skill and improving working and living conditions."
FUNDAMENTALS OF MARXISM–LENINISM

The preceding discussion of the agricultural problems facing the Soviet regime may have demonstrated, among other things, the possibility of approaching any question from various directions. For the Party leadership, agriculture poses problems that are economic, organizational, and cultural. Investment policies, administrative structuring, personnel recruitment and training, as well as fundamental attitudes toward the peasantry as a class must enter into the discussions. Nor can these different sides of the problem be separated from each other. On the contrary, any policy that deals with any partial aspect of Soviet agriculture will inevitably make its impact on the entire range of related matters. Still, for a book concentrating on the political sociology of the USSR, the organization of farming and the treatment of the rural population as a class are the most interesting problems.

A discussion of the peasantry and its relation to the Soviet system, however, must then be complemented by a discussion of how other classes or groups of the population have fared under the communist regime. We shall, therefore, deal (however briefly) with several additional groups: labor, the national minorities, and the professional intelligentsia.

THE STATUS OF WORKERS
IN THE EARLY YEARS OF THE REGIME

Collective farms, though ostensibly independent cooperatives, are yet linked with the administration of the Soviet political system through a multitude of ties and controls. Similarly, urban workers are organized in unions which are, in form, independent public associations, although actually their policies, organization, and personnel are controlled by the Communist Party; in fact, as administrators of the social security system and in several of their other functions, labor unions are direct agents of the government.

Whether or not labor unions should have a function in a proletarian state, and what this function might be, became controversial questions in the Party soon after it came to power. Workers' spokesmen of a strongly syndicalist orientation argued that the revolution had been a workers' revolution, that its aim had been to give political and economic sovereignty to the proletariat, and that in the organization of the newly created proletarian state unions should be given a prominent place. If the Communist Party and the soviets were to be organs of political self-government for the working class, then the labor unions ought to be organs of proletarian democratic government in the economy: unions should take over the industrial establishment from the former capitalist owners, and unions should manage these plants and factories for the working class.

Against these spokesmen for trade union sovereignty, or "workers' control," as it was called, stood a number of communist leaders who argued that a socialist state had no place whatsoever for trade unions. Unions, they maintained, were fighting organizations created by the working class for the purpose of resisting capitalist exploitation. Such exploitation had now been eliminated because the victory of the proletariat had led to the nationalization of industry. Hence unions had altogether lost their *raison d'être* and should be dissolved. Or, if they were to be continued, they, too, might be nationalized and turn into something akin to a national communist labor army. The ensuing controversy, which raged at the time of the civil war, was resolved by a compromise in which the Party conceded limited functions to the unions in the socialist state, even though they were denied the right to operate the industrial establishment. Perhaps the chief reason for maintaining a system of trade unions was Lenin's desire to keep alive mass organizations which could serve as convenient transmission belts between the Party and the workers.

In order to understand the bitterness of the controversy at that time, one has to be aware of a strong ambivalence in the relation between the Russian workers and the Bolshevik party, even before the revolution. Although urban labor unions in Russia tended to be affiliated with the Marxist movement, an unquestioning identification of the unions with Marxist political aims and strategies could not, for many reasons, be taken for granted. Moreover, the Marxist movement was divided; and many unions that did follow Marxist leadership or guidance were under Menshevik, rather than Bolshevik, control. The Bolsheviks, in turn, nursed strong doubts about the value of labor unions, even though they sought vigorously to utilize and dominate them. These doubts expressed the Bolsheviks' overriding interest in the political struggle, which made them distrust the labor unions' preoccupation with the fight for economic and social gains. Union leaders and Bolsheviks, in short, had a tendency to regard each other as seducers of the working man, as people trying to lead the workers in false directions. Though this is a grossly oversimplified summary of a complicated story, it may suffice as background for a relationship between labor and the communist regime that has had its share of tension and trouble.

During the civil war the working class, supposedly the victor in the recent revolution, diminished in numbers. The misery of half-starving cities, the call of the Red Army, and the harsh labor discipline imposed by the Bolsheviks cut into the ranks of the urban working class—this, even though the workers were exalted ideologically. Hailed as the new ruling class, they were given political as well as economic privileges—higher rations, a direct voice in the soviets, educational and other opportunities for rapid rise in status and power. From the resultant mixture of genuine revolutionary enthusiasm and bitter disappointment about actual conditions of life, it would be exceedingly hazardous to generalize about the feelings of the workers during these years.

The NEP brought a reaffirmation of economic rights for the unions, together with a continuation of political and cultural privileges for the working class in general. In the management of industrial establishments, union leaders participated on an equal footing with representatives of the Party and the government. Thus, in industry the unions had gained for themselves something akin to the right of codetermination. Labor was recognized as a legitimate interest group within a political and economic order which in so many ways sought to effect compromises and a stable balance of forces. Still, for the workers, the NEP was not nearly so much the "golden age" it retrospectively appears to have been for the peasantry and for some elements of the intelligentsia. Industrial production was lagging. The procurement of agricultural produce for the cities ran into difficulties. The burden of these and other difficulties often fell with disproportionate heaviness on the shoulders of the workers, because at several junctures the Party did not feel it could afford to let them be borne by the peasantry. The whole industrialization program had as one of its aims to remedy precisely these ills. Certainly, according to the pronouncements of the leadership, the rapid growth of industry was to ensure the political and economic ascendancy of the workers over the peasants.

The immediate effect of the five-year plans, however, was to worsen the conditions of labor, for several reasons. Among them was the Party's determination to spend every ounce of available resources for capital outlays rather than consumption or distribution. In addition, the revolutionary transformation of agriculture led to temporary difficulties in providing food; indeed, the rather sudden abolition of private trade may, for some time, have led to serious malfunctions in the distribution of consumer goods. Large numbers of surplus agricultural population were forcibly transplanted from the country to the city, with little regard for their welfare. In general, the growth of cities in numbers of inhabitants was so hasty that the improvement of living conditions and the provision of services essential for such large aggregates of people did not keep pace with this influx. In imposing such conditions on the working class, the Communist Party appealed to their communist convictions, their spirit of cooperation, self-abnegation, and sacrifice, and to the hopes for the eventual material rewards the entire society would soon reap as the fruit of these labors. Attempts to stimulate individual enterprise, energy, and ingenuity were made by singling out as heroes of the industrialization effort those individual workers who by their record achievements had earned the title "shock workers" (*udarniki*). Such appeals to the communistic spirit were soon reinforced by efforts to arouse individual and group self-interest in higher material rewards. The Soviet regime abandoned its egalitarian rhetoric and restructured the system of workers' wages so as to reward outstanding performance very highly and to punish slackers. Since this wage policy went hand in hand with a successful effort to raise the standard production norm determining each worker's pay, Soviet industrial enterprises turned into institutions remarkably similar to what Western trade unionists would have called sweat shops; every individual production worker now was paid by piece-rate wages. The system developed in the 1930s and still prevalent today customarily provides for a basic salary which is paid for individual output conforming to a general production norm for the particular job performed. Substantial increments are paid for output exceeding the norm, whereas wage deductions or other penalties may threaten those whose work does not come up to the production standards.

This wage policy was reinforced, during the 1930s and later, by laws providing sanctions against absenteeism, lateness, unauthorized job mobility, and other breaches of labor discipline. The precise provisions of these laws and enforcement devices has varied greatly, and so has the severity of their application, pressure and relaxation varying according to the needs of the regime. The first five-year plan, World War II, and the early years of postwar reconstruction were the most desperate periods of the Soviet economy, and therefore the times of the strictest labor discipline. One of the most effective devices to ensure labor discipline has been the labor book, introduced in 1940. This is something akin to a military service record which belongs to the individual worker but is retained by the employer. It provides a convenient summary of his past assignments and performance. Moreover, since the worker cannot be hired without having it in his possession, the employer retaining it can prevent his workers' moving to a different job. Such stringent measures, however, were used mainly in the 1940s. During those years of perpetual crisis and acute labor shortage, the society which called itself a workers' and peasants' republic resembled much more a giant workhouse in which the proletariat toiled under conditions of coercion, competition, and squalor that recalled descriptions of working-class life during the early decades of nineteenth-century capitalism. Since then the situation has improved steadily. The real wages of the workers have risen. Their work load has tended to diminish; the official work week has been shortened from 45 to 41 hours and is to be further cut to 36 hours, according to official announcements; and there is to be an upper limit to the hours of overtime workers will be permitted to put in. In many other ways, the regime during the last ten years or so has striven to relax the harsh labor discipline previously enforced and to replace "administrative" methods (i.e., coercion) with positive incentives.[1] Recurrent complaints in Soviet publications and meetings indicate that the transition is not being made altogether smoothly.[2]

THE ROLE OF THE TRADE UNION

In the execution of the regime's labor policy, the unions play an important part. These are industrial unions federated in the All-Union Central Council of Trade Unions (VTsSPS). Between this central organization and the locals there is a sizable bureaucracy of councils, committees, and other supervisory organizations, set up for the purpose of regulating the activities of the unions within their jurisdiction. Higher organizations within this trade union bureaucracy have the right to review the activities of subordinate organizations, to demand reports, to exhort and cajole. The Central Council may issue decrees (*postanovleniia*) regulating the activities of all unions. Superordinate organizations also control union personnel. Nonetheless, this entire bureaucracy gives the outsider a certain impression of powerlessness, of impotence. The decrees of the Central Council do not seem to have the full force of law, even though, in the final analysis, they are backed by the authority of the Communist Party. The intermediate union bureaucracy seems somehow to be hanging in mid-air between the top command of the party and the rank-and-file membership of the union locals. Union officials have complained that the coordinating committees and councils are out of touch with the locals, do not check on their work, give them no assistance, do not inform them of their rights and powers, and do not allow them any initiative. They pre-

[1] For a compilation of recent documents that are pertinent, see "Principal Current Soviet Labor Legislation," Bureau of Labor Statistics Report No. 210, U. S. Department of Labor (January 1962); also N. Aleksandrov, ed., *Trudovoe pravo v svete reshenii XXI. s"ezda KPSS* (Moscow, 1960); and Jerzy G. Gliksman, "Recent Trends in Soviet Labor Policy," *Monthly Labor Review* (July 1956).

[2] Such complaints are made in *Trud,* (November 25, 1961), p. 2, and in a statement issued by the All-Union Central Council of Trade Unions, in October 1962, *Spravochnik Partiinogo Rabotnika,* Issue 4, pp. 631–632.

sent an image of union bureaucrats working in a void, ignorant of the real problems of the industrial locals and accomplishing nothing.[3]

Virtually the entire population of wage earners belongs to the appropriate union, including farm workers employed in state farms (*sovkhozy*), who are considered members of the working class rather than the peasantry. This almost total membership seems to be due to habit rather than compulsion. Everyone apparently takes for granted that upon entering employment he becomes a union member, just as anyone changing his place of residence registers with the nearest police precinct as a matter of course.[4] Since employees not belonging to their appropriate union miss out on certain social security payments and perhaps other fringe benefits, there is a certain incentive to join.

The role of the trade unions in the relationship between the workers and the society fits in with the general pattern governing the structure and functions of so-called mass organizations in the USSR. As we have seen before, such organizations are used as transmission belts conveying the aims, spirit, policies, and guidelines of the Party to the rank-and-file members of society, at the same time channeling the latters' special interests and aspirations up to the leadership. Mass organizations, in short, provide communication between the elite and the citizenry—in this case, the workers. Nominally autonomous and democratic, their leadership cadres are elected by the members with the help of the Party's *nomenklatura* system, and the union's work is kept within the confines of Party policy by the Party caucus within the organization. High union officials have usually been picked from among members of the professional Party *aktiv*. V. V. Kuznetsov, for instance, who served as Chairman of the VTsSPS between 1944 and 1953, was a Party leader with broad experience, especially as a steel industry executive. Despite these customary devices of Party control, auton-

[3] See the complaints made at the Plenary Meetings of the VTsSPS in November 1961 and December 1962, in *Spravochnik Partiinogo Rabotnika*, Issue 4, pp. 579 and 636.

[4] There is a difference: failure to register changes in domicile is against the law. Failure to join the union is not.

omy and democracy do govern union life within narrow limits. At least at the lowest level of union organization, in factories, shops, offices, and other places of employment, the membership has the opportunity to speak up, to participate in committee work, and to help select the lower officeholders or, at least, to eliminate the least desirable names from slates of candidates prepared higher up.

In their role as transmission belts, the unions perform Agitprop functions of a general nature. More specifically, they operate to enforce labor discipline and help organize socialist competition. In other words, the unions seek to mobilize the workers for more intensive and sustained work. This is the unions' part of their bargain with management, which leads them to collaborate with management in measures of prevention, education, rehabilitation, sanctions, and rewards. It involves, among other things, the organization and supervision of disciplinary tribunals, such as the Comrades' Courts and grievance committees staffed by representatives of the unions and management; it also involves organized efforts to stimulate the workers' interest in the success of the enterprise, encouragement of suggestions and innovations and of participation in so-called production meetings, and even of criticism in cases of managerial inefficiency or waste. Because of this, the unions serve, among other things, as a controlling agency over management, though probably a rather weak one. Since 1958, the unions have experimented widely with attempts to promote workers' self-discipline through loyalty to small collectives. Throughout the country, Communist Work Teams (*Brigady kommunisticheskogo truda*) have been organized or may have organized themselves. They consist of qualified workers, who (it is hoped) are attuned to each other or will become close-knit teams, competing joyfully against other such collectives.[5] Finally, the unions help to organize and maintain cultural, recreational, and recuperative facilities for their members, including sanatoria, rest homes, resort facilities, club houses, and dance halls.

At the same time, they represent the workers and are thus trans-

[5] In 1961, a high-ranking trade union official claimed that one third of the country's labor force belonged to this "movement for communist labor." See *Trud* (October 22, 1961), p. 2.

mission belts in reverse, though their freedom in this regard is more limited than that of their Western counterparts: the main weapon of labor unions, the right to strike, is denied them.[6] Still, the VTsSPS participates, in an advisory capacity, in the setting of wage rates, production norms, safety standards, and other conditions of work, matters for which the State Committee on Labor and Wages has final responsibility. Union locals, in their turn, actually bargain with management over the precise manner of fulfillment of these employment standards, and in some matters they have formal rights of participation or even veto; for instance, in cases where management wishes to dismiss a worker or employee, the union local must be consulted. At the same time, national standards strictly limit the range within which bargaining remains meaningful; hence, the union's chief function must be in pressing management to conform to such national or industry-wide standards. In line with this, the local ("factory-shop committee") may also bargain or press for such fringe benefits as housing, medical services, vacations, canteens, nurseries, or recreational facilities for its members. Recurrent complaints in Soviet publications indicate that the locals often do not exert this pressure very resolutely.[7] What limits the range of bargaining demands and the force of bargaining pressure, of course, is not only the industry-wide agreement reached by higher headquarters, but also the clear knowledge of all those involved in the bargaining process of the Party's wants and priorities. No responsible union official will make demands he knows the Party will regard as excessive (just as in the West, the prevailing climate of opinion provides broad limits to the demands that unions and management can effectively make); and complaints by high Soviet union officials that their lower organizations do not do their job of protecting the worker is either pious chatter or may be a hint that

[6] Wildcat strikes occur occasionally. Strictly illegal, any such spontaneous strike is a symptom of truly desperate workers' grievances. For examples, see Albert Boiter, "When the Kettle Boils Over . . ." Problems of Communism, XIII, 1, 33–43.

[7] See, for instance, the decree of the Eighth Plenum of the VTsSPS of November 24, 1961, in Spravochnik Partiinogo Rabotnika, Issue 4, p. 574; and the complaints of V. V. Grishin, Chairman of the VTsSPS, printed in Pravda (June 20, 1963).

the Party does indeed want the unions to press harder for benefits.

Like their Western counterparts, furthermore, the Soviet trade unions represent their members in the case of grievances against management. Grievance procedures are handled informally by conferences between representatives of management and the union —perhaps the complaining employee's foreman and shop steward. If no satisfactory settlement is made, a labor disputes committee composed equally of management and union officials may hear the case in a more formal setting. If after that an appeal is made to the regular courts, the union may provide its member with legal counsel.

Finally, the unions serve an important function in administering the social security system, with its accident insurance, pension plans, vacation arrangements, and the like.

All the unions' various activities at the grass-roots level are carried out through committees established within each enterprise. A typical union local thus might have special committees dealing with wages, housing, grievances, social security, recreation, and innovations or suggestions. Since the workers have a good deal of opportunity to participate in union work through such committees, the unions, like all Soviet mass organizations, also fulfill the important functions of political socialization and elite recruitment. Through such participation, the worker is socialized to the processes of Soviet administration; and by organizing this kind of participation, the leadership is able to discover activists with various kinds of talent who can then be recruited for more responsible work. In turn, the opportunity to participate in public life which this system offers to any worker must be a source of considerable satisfaction for great numbers of workers and give them a personal interest in "their own" enterprise.

Factory work, asserts Harvey Swados, is degrading. It kills all dreams of ever leading a decent, worthwhile life; and it becomes ever more degrading the more middle-class values and white-collar sophistication permeate the society.[8] I am sure this statement is as

[8] Harvey Swados, "The Myth of the Happy Worker," *The Nation*, CLXXXV, 4 (1957).

true for the USSR as it is for the United States. If we accept it as a fact, then two major problems follow for the managers of the enterprises or of the society as a whole. They must recruit people into the industrial working class; and they must maintain discipline as well as morale among those who work in the production line, at the same time raising the productivity of labor, i.e., increasing output. Our society solves the first problem by placing those who fail in academic work into manual labor. Soviet society does this too. But it also recruits for industrial work those young men and women from rural areas who show skills and aptitudes above the rural average. Thus recruitment for industrial work may constitute downward or upward mobility. As for the problem of productivity, the Soviet regime faces the same dilemma it is now confronting in so many other areas: In the past, it has relied almost exclusively on tough measures—terror, criminal law, the threat of starvation, social ostracism, forced indoctrination—for instilling discipline, raising output, and if not creating, then at least simulating, high morale. Although many interests within the Soviet system argue in favor of continued reliance on tough methods, considerable pressure now exists from many quarters, and for many reasons, to use concessions instead. In labor policy as in many other fields, the conflict between the hard and the soft managers will remain the overriding political issue for a long time to come.

Chapter XX
National and Religious Minorities[*]

NATIONALITY POLICY

The multinational composition of Soviet society has always presented problems to the Soviet political system. When the Party
came to power in 1917, it had a conflicting set of objectives regarding the national minorities. On the one hand, the Bolsheviks had
sought to gain followers among Russia's subject nationalities by
resolutely defending (though not advocating) the break-up of the
tsarist empire: the rather Wilsonian slogan of "national self-determination" (which in fact was coined before Wilson's fourteen
points and may indeed have inspired them) therefore was part of
the Bolshevik platform. On the other hand, this liberal aim was
qualified by very strong reservations. The communist leaders wished
to keep the former Russian Empire together as much as possible;
and, far from favoring decentralization, federalism, or any sort of
national autonomy, even if only in the cultural realm, they believed
in strict centralization, presumably based on the international solidarity of all workers and toilers. To complicate matters, the Party
harbored many members and leaders who sharply disagreed with
Lenin's liberal slogans or his centralist predilections, or both.[1]

[*] This chapter has been rearranged and expanded from my lecture,
"The Problem of National Minorities in the USSR," in William J. Bossen-
brook, ed., *Mid-Twentieth Century Nationalism* (Detroit: Wayne State
University Press, 1965). Reprinted by permission of the publisher. Copyright © 1965 by Wayne State University Press.

[1] The resolution of these conflicts was made more difficult because of
considerable ambiguities in the views of Marx and Engels concerning nationalism and national minorities. See Solomon F. Bloom, *The World of
Nations* (New York: Columbia University Press, 1941), which deals with
these views exhaustively.

In practice, circumstances, including the dictates of geography and the fortunes of war, forced compromises on the Soviet regime. As a result of the revolution and civil war, Poland, Finland, and the Baltic provinces made themselves independent. Georgia, Armenia, and, to some extent, the Muslim principalities of Central Asia, enjoyed brief periods of autonomy or independence but were reconquered and incorporated in the Soviet state in the early years after the revolution.[2] Some twenty years later a similar fate befell the Baltic provinces and portions of Poland and Rumania. The resulting political structure was given the shape of a federal union, as we have seen.

One other major element of the compromise effected after the Empire had been regathered was the promotion of cultural autonomy in minority areas—precisely the policy which, before the revolution, the Bolsheviks had repudiated. This consisted in the vigorous encouragement of the various minorities to use their languages and to cultivate their national heritage in art, literature, history, folklore, and customs. The communist regime adopted and pursued this policy of cultural decentralization in a period when its dictatorship was comparatively lax, and when in addressing social problems it experimented with a variety of solutions that might be labeled avantgardist, progressive, or libertarian. However, once the government embarked on its ambitious crash program of industrialization, avantgardist experiments and easygoing relationships became dysfunctional, and cultural autonomy henceforth was severely curbed. Although never clearly repudiated, it was reinterpreted so as to suppress any views or practices likely to jeopardize administrative centralization and the pursuit of over-all national objectives. The entire nation's culture was now to be "socialist in content, and national in form," to use the regime's own phrase.

Behind this phrase, we may detect a number of subsidiary views and objectives. The central goal that overrides all others is that of industrialization and urbanization. It implies the intention to coordinate all the nation's activities by central plans for the purpose

[2] See Richard Pipes, *The Formation of the Soviet Union* (Cambridge: Harvard University Press, 1954), for a full account of this process of regathering the scattered parts of the Russian Empire.

of bringing the machine age, the city, and the urban way of life to all corners of the country. Of necessity, this implies a profound hostility to all aspects of national culture that do not fit in with the regime's conception of modern life, of industrialism and of socialism.[3] Perhaps we can add to this some reference to the galloping bureaucratization of life in the Soviet Union and the rise to power and authority of people with a bureaucratic frame of mind— organization men and authoritarian personalities who tend to be suspicious of all heterogeneity and are unable or unwilling to cope with it, except by annihilating or suppressing all those people who do not fit their own stereotype of normal citizens. Such an un-focused intolerance is different from popular prejudice against specific nationalities, such as certain widely held antagonism against Jews, Armenians, and Gypsies. Western scholars have often felt that, on many an occasion, the Soviet regime has manifested some readiness to cater even to such latent feelings of discrimination, or to give in to them in structuring educational opportunities and career lines. Yet the average Soviet citizen does not seem to have strongly developed racial prejudices; and the Great Russians do not generally show strong feelings of national superiority over other Soviet citizens. Under Stalin, they were proclaimed to be the country's leading nationality; and in Chapter One we ventured to say that in Soviet society the Great Russian was in a fashion the equivalent of our White Protestant Anglo-Saxon—more equal than others in a society of equals, or slightly favored in any competition with otherwise similarly endowed citizens. This is no more than an impression, and it would be difficult to document.

To the extent that national consciousness presents a threat to the political integrity of the Soviet state, the Party seeks, naturally, to curb or neutralize it. At the same time, there have been occasions when the regime seems to have promoted nationalism so as to set various minorities off against each other in the manner of the slogan, *divide et impera*. For instance, in Central Asia, a relatively homoge-

---

[3] Thus a decree of the Presidium of the Supreme Soviet, dated May 24, 1955, obliges Procurators to ensure the full and uniform application of all laws regardless of local cultural differences and influences. National culture must not interfere with Soviet law.

neous native population was divided into several nationalities, each
with its own Union Republic and language, with the obvious aim of
weakening pan-Turanian tendencies prevalent in this region. Moreover, the promotion of national consciousness and separateness has
at times given the Kremlin minor advantages in its dealings with
other nations of the world. Still, by and large, Hugh Seton-Watson
seems correct when he says that the Soviet regime's long-range
aim is a "war of extermination against the principle of nationality."[4]
The Communist Party wishes to weld Soviet society into a more
homogeneous whole and seeks to make its country into a thoroughly
effective melting pot of nationalities. The Party platform adopted
in 1961 makes this fairly clear:

> Attaching decisive importance to the development of the social-
> ist content of the cultures of the peoples of the USSR, the Party
> will promote their further mutual enrichment and rapprochment,
> the consolidation of their international basis, and thereby the
> formation of the future single world-wide culture of communist
> society. While supporting the progressive traditions of each
> people, and making them the property of all Soviet people, the
> Party will in all ways further new revolutionary traditions of the
> builders of communism common to all nations.[5]

Again, this urge for social homogeneity can be understood most
easily as part of the country's industrialization drive. The central
planning this drive necessitates calls for the curbing of regional
autonomy. The tasks of administering a large and complex industrial society require that all citizens understand each other; hence
to homogenize the country means to russify it, at least to a degree.[6]
Most of all, industrialization requires a population which is attuned
in its very habits and outlook to the way of life of the machine age.
It therefore demands the neutralization of preindustrial patterns

[4] Hugh Seton-Watson, "Soviet National Policy," *Russian Review*, XV, 1
(January, 1956), 3–13.

[5] From the Program of the CPSU, part II, chapter IV.

[6] In the first decade or two of the regime many communists apparently
assumed that the language of the future communist world would be a new
international tongue such as Esperanto. Today they take it for granted that
Russian will be this *lingua franca*. See p. 443.

of living; and these are intimately related to national peculiarities and traditions. Seen in this fashion, the cultural revolution demanded in 1922 has an antinational bias.

RELIGIOUS POLICY

This is particularly evident when we realize that religion is part and parcel of virtually every national culture. Hence hostility against one implies hostility to the other. To promote national culture while combatting religion means to promote national culture very selectively and with considerable ambivalence.

The antireligious tendency of the Soviet regime is explained in part by the heritage of Marxist philosophy and its dogmatic atheism. Among the Russian communists, this was reinforced by the fact that, historically, religious institutions were associated with political reaction and counterrevolution. The churches were part of the old order which was to be swept away. The attempts of the regime in the 1920s to destroy religious organizations by jailing the clergy, closing down houses of worship, confiscating church funds and treasures, and persecuting believers, were based on this deeply ingrained antagonism to all organized religion.[7] More recent attempts to destroy or harass the churches were undoubtedly reinforced by the realization that religious practices interfere with the industrialization effort and with the Soviet way of life in general. For one thing, religious practices interfere with daily work. Religious holidays constitute a disruption of the citizens' duties. Fasting weakens their efficiency. Regular prayers mean time out from work. Many religious practices of Christians, Buddhists, Muslims, Jews, and others, may be contrary to the commands of modern medical knowledge and hygiene. Religious food taboos and other dietary practices interfere with the regime's food distribution system; any special consideration given to religious believers thus threatens the ef-

[7] "Freedom of conscience was established in the Soviet state immediately after the October Revolution. The Soviet regime, however, had to wage a resolute struggle against those religious organizations and groups among the clergy which resisted the gains of the October Revolution." A. Denisov and M. Kirichenko, *Soviet State Law* (Moscow, 1960).

ficiency of the political and economic bureaucracy. Furthermore, the efforts of churches and religions to shape the entire personality of their believers squarely clash with the claim the Communist Party makes on all the citizens, with its effort to shape the new Soviet man. Religious law may come into conflict with Soviet law, and must therefore be outlawed. Religious education is opposed to Soviet education. Religious organizations dealing with any problem of secular life compete with bureaucratic agencies and mass organizations of Soviet society. And what has been said about religious laws, traditions, and organizations applies more generally to national traditions and to the entire national way of life, religious or secular.

Once all this has been made clear, one must be aware that three decades or more of struggling against religions has not eliminated religious practices among the various national minorities any more than among the Great Russian majority. Broad strata among Soviet Russia's Muslims, Buddhists, and other non-Russian faiths seem to carry on at least part of their traditional rituals, adapting their practices to the prevailing pattern of Soviet life and to the degree of grudging tolerance shown by the Communist Party. This is true also of at least part of the population in the Russian and Ukrainian areas, where Russian Orthodox Christianity is the prevalent faith. Partly because the militant atheism promoted in earlier decades did not have enough success, and partly because the church turned out to be a useful ally in the war effort, the regime in 1943 found a modus vivendi with organized religions. The arrangement made at that time placed their organizations and personnel under Party supervision and control; it permitted them to carry out religious services and other religious activities so long as they had a purely sacramental character, enabled them to train priests and issue publications for the faithful, at the same time preventing them from extending their work into areas such as education, social work, charity, or even social life. The churches, in short, are tolerated so long as they keep within the narrow limits that have been set for their activities. To be sure, the tolerance is grudging. Concessions which the regime has made to the churches can be taken back, and since

1943 the actual treatment of organized religion has varied.[8] Meanwhile, the Communist Party has never ceased subjecting all religious beliefs to the most scathing criticism and preaching atheism as the only scientific creed.

NATIONAL DIFFERENCES VS. RUSSIFICATION

In the broader area of national culture and national customs, the practical solution betrays a rather more generous or, at least, less suspicious attitude. Those habits which are utterly out of tune with the Soviet way of life have tended to disappear. Those that can be tolerated or adapted have tended to maintain themselves and be cultivated, many nationalities apparently clinging fervently to those of their own behavior traits which they are allowed to keep. This is true of national costumes as well as living habits. It applies to the careful cultivation of national or folk traditions in art, music, literature, and history. All these elements of national culture are promoted to the extent that they do not conflict with the Soviet way of life. This means, among other things, the elimination of the religious element from art and the careful falsification of history, or, as the Communist Party platform of 1961 puts it, opposition to any "idealization of the past and the veiling of social contradictions in the history of the peoples."

How significant a concession to national culture this is remains controversial. On the one hand, the imposition of standardized Soviet patterns of life has meant the destruction of national cultures as they previously existed. Settling nomads in collective farms, converting Gypsies into factory workers, eliminating private trade in Armenia and Southern Central Asia so thoroughly changes the way of life of the people affected that their very identity and survival are threatened. If, nonetheless, the external trappings of their old national culture are preserved and cultivated, they will have

---

[8] Treatment varies not only from one period to another, but also from one religious denomination to another. Although the major faiths are tolerated, various religious sects not conforming to these faiths are outlawed, and their practitioners are persecuted. The Soviet government thus finds itself in the curious position of being the protector of religious orthodoxies.

become stage props in the manner in which hillbilly music and cowboy craftsmanship in our culture have become stage props. We view them during leisure hours for our amusement, and perhaps for the purpose of nostalgically transporting ourselves into a pre-industrial setting. This would imply that members of the national minorities ought to be regarded as Soviet citizens in national garb, just as some people would define the people of contemporary Japan as kimono-clad Westerners. In some cases, the Party's handling of national and religious customs is similar to what the Christian church did with pagan ones: it absorbs them.[9]

On the other hand, there are indications that national differences persist and are deepening, so that the minorities in various areas are in fact remaining distinct nations with no more than a superficial Soviet varnish. Again, some observers would similarly say about contemporary Japan that it has remained a distinct national culture with but a thin coating of Western living patterns. The conflict between these two views is not merely a dry academic exercise. It expresses a difficult problem of great interest to contemporary social science, namely, the question of how much weight to assign to the persistence of different cultural traditions against the homogenizing influence of modern industrialism.

One long-range development in the Soviet Union, to which we have alluded already, seems likely to undermine the persistence of national culture patterns. This is the trend toward russification. It takes several forms in the USSR. One of these might be called "colonization"; by this term I mean the movement of Russians or, more generally, Slavs and other non-natives, into areas predominantly inhabited by some minority. This process has proceeded so rapidly in some parts of the country that in some Union Republics the native population is today outnumbered by Russians. This appears to be the case in Kazakhstan and the Kirghiz Republic, as well as in the Western portions of the Ukrainian and Bielorussian

[9] Thus the Christmas tree is transformed into a New Year's tree; certain traditional lenten dishes become seasonal special foods retailed by governmental stores; the marriage ceremony, complete with rings, becomes secularized. For these and other examples, see Klaus Mehnert, *Der Sowjetmensch* (Stuttgart: Deutsche Verlagsanstalt, 1958), p. 247.

republics. Another aspect of russification is the widespread use of the Russian language and its imposition as the second language all school children are expected to learn. To be sure, primary schools and many higher educational institutions conduct their classes in the language of the dominant minority; and the native tongue may be used in all official business within each Union Republic. Nor has there been a general decline in the use of the native languages in the last three or four decades.[10] Nonetheless, a person unfamiliar with Russian will be handicapped because many schools, public institutions, and places of work have mixed clienteles; and in such cases Russian necessarily becomes the *lingua franca*.[11] Its exclusive use in such agencies as the armed forces promotes this development further. In many subtle ways, through new vocabulary and the use of the Cyrillic alphabet, even the minority languages themselves are in a slow process of russification.

One might argue further that the weight of the Russian Communist Party and the Russian republic within the entire political system are so overwhelming, and that this system is so tightly centralized, that in effect the national minorities are politically subordinate to the Russians. More specifically, Russian supremacy even in minority areas is secured by the policy of assigning Russians (or at least non-natives) to some of the most important positions of authority in the several Union Republics. The fact that the First Secretary of republican and provincial Party organization in Central Asia usually is a native, whereas the Second Secretary is a Russian, Ukrainian, or Georgian, seems a sure indication that the

[10] Richard Pipes, "The Forces of Nationalism," *Problems of Communism*, XIII, 1 (January–February, 1964), 1–6.

[11] "In the Soviet Union all peoples, great and small, are guaranteed free development of their language and national culture. No restrictions are imposed, there is no compulsion to use any particular language. Every citizen is free to speak any language and to teach it to his children. If the Russian language is widespread it is not because it has any privileged position, but owing to the needs of life itself. Many millions of people learn Russian because they regard it as a means of acquainting every nation and nationality with the cultural achievements of the Russian people and all the other peoples of the USSR, and with world culture." *Fundamentals of Marxism–Leninism*, p. 677. See also I. P. Zamerian, "Razvitie natsional'nykh otnoshenii v period razvernutogo stroitel'stva kommunizma," *Voprosy Filosofii*, No. 7 (1959).

First Secretaryship in these areas is a ceremonial office, and that decisive control resides with the Second Secretary.[12]

The summary of methods by which russification or at least control is achieved remains incomplete unless we call attention to the regime's readiness to use force in imposing its will on the national minorities. We have already mentioned the violent methods used in trying to destroy organized religion. Of course, the same methods were applied against the Russians themselves; but, perhaps, their impact on the national minorities may have been more traumatic. Similarly, the years 1936–1938 were a period in which an entire generation of civic leaders was decimated in the Great Purge. Here, too, the police terror seems to have made a cleaner sweep of the national elites than it did of the Russian. The Great Purge appears to have been far more savage in Central Asia and the Ukraine than in other areas of the USSR. In later years, too, selected nationalities were subjected to sweeping punitive or preventive police methods which at times differed little from actual genocide. Entire nationalities suspected of widespread disloyalty to the Soviet regime were wiped out during and after World War II; and mass deportations to labor camps or remote regions decimated the ranks of the people in areas added to the Soviet Union in the 1940s.[13]

Instead of speaking about the resultant tendencies as russification, one might use the image of the melting pot familiar to Americans. All the policies enumerated above seem to weaken the cohesion and strength of the national minorities, if only because the Soviet system dilutes the purity of minority populations. The homogenizing process is speeded up by the sheer physical scrambling of the nationalities. Not only do Russians colonize the minority areas; the minorities, in turn, are on the move. Their educated members are mobile because the Party or the government may assign them to posts all over the USSR. Common work and common schooling integrate people from all nationalities. So does military service; and so, finally, do the forced-labor camps or

[12] For a thorough discussion of Russian domination of the Party and government bureaucracy in Central Asia, see Michael Rywkin, *Russia in Central Asia* (New York: Collier-Macmillan, 1963), pp. 118–152.

[13] Most of these liquidated nationalities were reinstated in early 1957.

other punitive measures throwing together people from different areas of the USSR.[14]

Against the many factors contributing to the Soviet melting pot, there are, however, some countervailing tendencies. One of these is the remarkable tenacity with which some of the minority peoples cling to cultural patterns not in conflict with the Soviet way of life. We have already mentioned this strength of national culture. While it may be a clinging to externals, it is matched by the pronounced clannishness many minorities exhibit. Social contacts between natives and non-natives are infrequent in many minority areas. A cultural gap is maintained by both. Intermarriage in some of these areas is the exception. In Central Asia, for instance, intermarriage between Muslims and Christians makes the young couple outcasts in both parent communities.[15]

Turning to the educated elites among the minorities, we confront a highly complex attitude. To some extent, they are likely to be uprooted and alienated from their own societies, without necessarily being integrated into Russian culture. Instead, we can expect them to be thoroughly acculturated to both twentieth-century civilization and to over-all Soviet behavior patterns. Many of them will be torn between the desire to assimilate and their loyalty to their own native culture. Pipes, in the article just referred to, sees them as mediators between the minorities and the regime—a thankless and difficult role. Conversations with educated Soviet citizens from Central Asia and the Baltic republics seem to give glimpses into a very ambivalent attitude, in which genuine gratitude to the Soviet regime (for its educational opportunities and career possibilities)

[14] "Closer intercourse between the nationalities in the Soviet Union was assisted in no small measure by the realization of such gigantic national-economic projects as the development of the virgin lands, the construction of large hydropower stations in thinly populated places, etc. By bringing together tens and hundreds of thousands of people of different nationalities, uniting them in joint labor, the construction projects of communism at the same time influence national relations in the country, accelerating the overcoming of survivals of national narrow-mindedness among people and promoting the most rapid development of common features of their spiritual make-up." *Fundamentals of Marxism–Leninism*, p. 676.

[15] See Richard Pipes, "Muslims in Central Asia: Trends and Prospects," in *Middle East Journal*, IX, 2 (Spring, 1955), 147–162, 295–308.

is mixed with bitter resentment of purges and deportations that wiped out entire generations of friends and relatives. Both these feelings are tied together by a fierce pride in the cultural progress made by their own nationality.

That cultural gaps between the various nationalities persist has by now been acknowledged by the leadership of the Communist Party, and that they will be difficult to eradicate is conceded as well. The Party platform of 1961 declares, "The obliteration of national distinctions, and especially of language distinctions, is a considerably longer process than the obliteration of class distinctions." Similarly, the principal ideological textbook in several places admits that it will take unflagging attention and hard work to do away with problems arising out of national differences.[16]

What, then, is the total effect of Soviet nationality policies? Obviously, it too is ambiguous. Melting-pot trends in the direction of the development of a new Soviet nationality are matched by the intensification of national consciousness—if not among all the country's nationalities, then certainly among some of them. The differentiation and centrifugal tendencies resulting from this growth of national consciousness are sufficiently strong that in recent years even some high-ranking Party leaders have wondered aloud whether nations will disappear even under full-fledged communism.[17]

Soviet nationality policy has at times been compared with colonialism because the regime's relation to its minorities has involved conquest, domination, and exploitation; and still today there is a strong residue of mutual antagonism and suspicion between natives and settlers, between Russians and non-Russians. Yet, there is no legal discrimination against minorities. Moreover, it cannot be asserted that domination and exploitation are prac-

[16] *Fundamentals of Marxism–Leninism,* pp. 606 and 678. See also I. P. Zamerian, "Razvitie natsional'nykh otnoshenii v period razvernutogo stroitel'stva kommunizma," *Voprosy Filosofii,* No. 7 (1959), who concedes the legitimacy of asking whether there is a nationalities problem in the USSR, and then goes on to say that, strictly speaking, there is no such problem, but in practice there is the persistent problem of strengthening the brotherly bonds between the various Soviet nations.

[17] See Aleksandr Yurchenko, "The New Party Program and the Nationality Question," *Studies on the Soviet Union,* New Series, II, 2 (1962), 17 ff.

ticed for the purpose of perpetuating such unequal relationships. On the contrary, the whole effort of the Party is to cement all Soviet nationalities into one common culture. Soviet rule seeks to bring its minority subjects (and the Russian peasants as well) into the twentieth century. It wishes to act as an agent of Western civilization. In the short run, this may continue to promote the development of national consciousness and thus further strain the fabric of Soviet society. If in the long run a new Soviet nationality emerges, the Soviet variant of colonialism may well be of a self-liquidating kind.

Chapter XXI
The Intelligentsia

Chapter II of this book, in its attempt to survey the group structure of Soviet society and to indicate special interests impinging on the political system, presented the educated elite as a group having especially contradictory and ambivalent attitudes toward the regime of the Communist Party. It should not astonish anyone that the interests of the Party and the treatment it has afforded the Soviet intellectuals reflect and reciprocate this troubled relationship. In discussing this relationship one must begin with the trite observation that the services and advice of highly trained specialists in a great variety of fields are absolute necessities for a modern industrial society. The Soviet government simply could not function without armies of scientists, engineers, and doctors, together with specialists in the management of organizations, social life, culture, education, entertainment—judges, historians, artists, journalists, and many others. Barrington Moore some years ago wrote that the Communist Party has never been able quite to make up its mind whether to coddle the intellectuals or to shoot them. From what we observed earlier about the origins and interests of the professional intelligentsia, this ambivalence of the Party is easily understood. In some branches of professional or intellectual endeavor, the family ties of the Soviet intelligentsia with the pre-revolutionary elite are still surprisingly strong. More important, intellectual training and professional expertise engender attitudes and dispositions that disturb bureaucratic hierarchs and political operators. Professional expertise requires autonomy of thought and judgment of anyone who is to perform adequately. In fact, professional training in many fields includes training for intellectual independence. For truly creative work in certain areas even this is not enough. Intellectual autonomy in this case is only the first step toward that iconoclasm and mythoclasm, that suspicion of authorities and traditions, which leads to discovery, innovation, and creativeness—at least according to notions about creativeness and intellectual progress current in the Western world. It may very well be that these notions are themselves provincial and time-bound. Perhaps they are generalizations based on excessively narrow experience or on commonly accepted myths. Even if this possibility be granted, it would still be true to assert that such notions concerning the creative function of intellectual autonomy and, if you please, deviancy, are widespread among professional intellectuals, including those of the USSR. They are part of contemporary intellectual tradition in a number of important fields of science and art.[1] This in itself deserves to be reiterated: that the various professional fields possess conventions and traditions of their own which apply to training, knowledge, practice, and vocabulary. They make all the members of certain professions into closely knit communities or subcultures, having structures and hierarchies that may conflict with those of the political or administrative community. The members of these professional communities are often devoted, at times narrowly and single-mindedly—not to say (in the original Greek meaning of the word) idiotically—to special professional goals which are insufficiently attuned to the needs of the entire society as expressed by representatives or administrators of the public. As every professional who has clashed with an administrator or money-controller knows, expertise often defines its own

[1] For instance, Russian science by tsarist times had developed a strong tradition of free enterprise within the bureaucratic state. To be sure, the ideology and political needs or anxieties of the state did set certain limits to free scientific inquiry. Hence, pure science flourished, whereas applied fields and such subversive areas as economics ran into difficulties. Nor were scientists permitted to draw atheistic conclusions from their research; or, more generally, they were discouraged, to say the least, from being philosophers. Despite these handicaps, Russian science attained highest achievements in a variety of fields, from mathematics, physics, and chemistry to soil science, aerodynamics, and rocketry; and in some fields this high tradition was continued throughout the Soviet period.

goals and norms of behavior, which may conflict with those of the public authorities. The conflict of goals confronting the Soviet physician (discussed in a previous chapter) is only one of countless possible examples.

Conflicts of this kind are not explained by peculiarities of the Soviet political structure, by its "totalitarian" nature, as the phrase usually goes. On the contrary, they occur in all modern societies, where the complexity of the division of labor and the expertise required for manifold tasks demands the collaboration of a great variety of people with different training, skills, and outlook. But they take different form in the USSR because that society is distinct from many other industrial societies in its political structure. In it the struggle for power has, for the time being, been decided. The Communist Party has placed itself in charge. It claims the exclusive right to define goals and work out policies; it alone is entitled to express the interests of the public. It must therefore oppose any professional claims that come into conflict with its own sovereignty and to reject them as inadmissible or incorrect. This means that the Party will seek to impose political and intellectual conformity to many views and attitudes on all professional experts. It will be tempted to consider goals, standards, and the very solidarity of various professions as dangerous and antisocial. Nor will it hesitate to interfere in and decide controversies among experts which the latter may consider to be matters quite internal to their profession. The Party is not willing to concede to any group of experts that its professional problems could ever be purely internal matters. In the eyes of the sovereign, all problems are the concern of the entire public. Again, this situation is similar to that in Western societies, where professional opinions and public policy are inextricably enmeshed. But in the looser and more heterogeneous political structures of the West, power is scattered rather than concentrated; hence the autonomy of any one interest group is very much greater and the outcome of group conflict is less easily predicted.

The treatment the Soviet regime has given its intelligentsia in the nearly fifty years of its existence has thus been determined by these considerations: The Communist Party has been aware of the need for trained experts in many professions. It has distrusted them. It has often regarded them as disruptive, antisocial, or hostile; and it has sought by various measures to bring their activities and thoughts under Party control, to subject them to guidelines the Party considered binding for the entire society.

THE INTELLIGENTSIA AFTER THE REVOLUTION

During the civil war, members of the intelligentsia shared the fate of the former ruling classes: the regime treated them as pariahs who did not deserve to survive and were scarcely tolerated. And yet, the regime did need many of them and sought their services—engineers, economists, and managers for industry, teachers for the schools, painters, sculptors, actors, and poets to practice their arts in the service of the revolution, professional officers to help create and lead the proletarian army. These and other members of the prerevolutionary intelligentsia in Soviet services were called bourgeois specialists (*spetsy*). The government rewarded them for their work with ration cards, quarters, and other material preconditions for survival. But many communists distrusted, hated, and harassed them. Hiring them or relying on them got high-ranking communist leaders in trouble with proletarian purists in the Party. The very practice of hiring *spetsy,* in short, was controversial and had to be defended by leaders from Lenin on down. The status of the bourgeois specialists thus was precarious. It remained so during the interregnum of the 1920s, even though in these years the Soviet regime tolerated the old intelligentsia much more readily than during the civil war. The Party's demands now became somewhat more modest: so long as any group declared itself loyal to the October Revolution and willing to collaborate with the existing regime, it could expect to be tolerated and even supported with public means. In many fields, especially in the arts and sciences, therefore, the prerevolutionary intelligentsia during the 1920s was able to pursue its various activities relatively free of either material worry (outside of the generally low standard of living plaguing the entire society) or political supervision. The intellectual community was divided within itself through some of those controversies in which scientists, artists, and other men of the spirit or of learning customarily engage. Hence its organization, too, was heterogeneous or pluralistic—all with the proviso that outright opponents of the communist order did not enjoy these liberties; and the vigilance of the Party and the OGPU kept even the relative freedom of the intelligentsia within well discernible limits.

The period of the first and second five-year plans ended this era of relatively peaceful coexistence. From the very beginning of the industrialization campaign, bourgeois specialists were singled out as unreliable collaborators in the attempt to drive on toward communism. Show trials and other Agitprop devices sought to unmask them as reactionaries who would restore capitalism and were sabotaging the industrialization effort. In a grand sweep, the Soviet economy and administration rid itself of many members of the old intelligentsia still serving them. Meanwhile, in the fields of science and the arts, the Party for the first time decisively interfered in professional disputes, lending its support to the radical spokesmen of a "proletarian" culture, who wished to place all intellectual and artistic pursuits exclusively at the service of the industrialization effort. For the first time, artistic and scientific controversies were settled by decisions of the Communist Party's Central Committee. Here, too, the victory of the radical Marxists led to a change in the composition of the Soviet intelligentsia, because it swept away large numbers of people from the prerevolutionary educated elite who heretofore had maintained themselves in academic chairs, editorial offices, studios, theaters, and similar places. But the triumph of the radicals was short-lived. The cultural counterrevolution of the mid-1930s eliminated these same radicals more thoroughly than they had removed the residues of the old intelligentsia. In fact, they were forced to yield their places among the practitioners of science, art, and entertainment to some of the people they themselves had denounced and cast out because of their bourgeois origins. Thus, after the hectic experiments with radical Marxist orthodoxies, the old intelligentsia made something of a comeback not only in the cultural pursuits, but also in various technical professions. Bourgeois *spetsy* ousted in the late 1920s or early 1930s were reinstated. They made this cautious comeback at a time when an even more violent storm shook Soviet society and particularly affected the various Soviet elites: the cultural counterrevolution coincided —and not by coincidence—with the Great Purge. And this purge had a decided effect on the relationship between the regime and the intelligentsia.

RECENT TREATMENT OF THE INTELLIGENTSIA

Any of the intelligentsia members who between 1935 and 1940 returned to public service or entered it for the first time, did not receive even the shadow of professional autonomy they or their colleagues had enjoyed a decade before. Instead, they came back cowed and tamed, fully aware of their thoroughly precarious position and of the claims the Party now made on all professions. What did the Party now claim? It demanded the recognition that professional views and values must always be subordinate to the views, values, and interests of the general public (as expressed by the Communist Party)—that political considerations outweigh all expert opinion or knowledge. From making this demand the Party since the mid-1930s has never desisted. This has therefore been the ground rule concerning the relationship between the intelligentsia and the Soviet political system.

We shall now turn our attention to the devices by which the system secures and perpetuates this service relationship of the intelligentsia. Perhaps the most obvious remark to be made here is that all professional work in the USSR depends on government support. Personnel, funds, equipment, jobs, and work assignments all come from the public authorities, Party or government. They are the sole employer of all professional personnel, the exclusive supporter of arts and science. It goes without saying that this monopolistic position as sole employer and supporter gives the regime wide control over all professional activities.[2]

[2] Soviet ideologists do not tire of lamenting the sorry plight of the creative intellectual under capitalism who is robbed of his independence by subtle

ECONOMIC AND SOCIAL PROBLEMS

In addition, the regime has sought very strenuously to educate
and re-educate the intelligentsia for their servant role. In all fields
of endeavor, the Party impresses on all professional personnel that
their thoughts and activities, their theories and applications, are
meaningful and valuable contributions only if they are imbued
with party spirit (*partiinost*), socialist convictions (*ideinost*), civic-
mindedness (*grazhdanstvennost*), and other attitudes of loyalty and
devotion. Similarly, the Party seeks to convince the intelligentsia
that the professional autonomy it grants them, which expresses
itself in the numerous professional associations, guilds, unions,
and the like, must not be misinterpreted as a license to deviate from
accepted Soviet policies, differ with the Party, or develop narrow
professional group interests. On the whole, the Party seems to
have been eminently successful in this educational effort. Although
there may be some angry young men who reject the system, deny
the Party the right to inject its interests into intellectual pursuits,
or proclaim the intellectual's right to turn his back on the public
interest (whoever may define it), the current ferment within the
Soviet intelligentsia is not a revolt against the Party's command
that the educated must work in the service of the public. On the
contrary, a sensitivity to some "social command" was very much
alive already in the prerevolutionary intelligentsia, and this has
survived (perhaps with some changes in emphasis) and grown in
strength in the present intelligentsia. The Soviet professional person
thus tends to be a good organization man. Only the methods of
public control, the delineation of competencies in this relationship
between political authorities and professional staff personnel, have
today become controversial.

The educational efforts to coordinate the intelligentsia's work
with the aims of the Party is strongly supported by the material
and psychological rewards the educated receive, which tie them to
the regime. As we have observed earlier, a higher education carries
with it great prestige, much responsibility, and appreciable ad-

but effective means, including job control and indoctrination. See *Fundamentals of Marxism–Leninism*, pp. 22 and 288–289. For the much more
direct subjection of the Soviet intelligentsia to political control, these ideologists find only words of praise.

vantages with regard to the opulence of life. In this fashion, the regime makes loyal service attractive to the intelligentsia. At the same time, legal and extralegal sanctions aplenty are at the regime's disposal for use against any recalcitrant or rebellious members of the educated elite.

Finally, the professional men, like all other members of Soviet society, are held in line by a variety of organizational controls. First, every field of endeavor has its own professional association or union. Membership in such associations is essential, as a rule, for anyone who wishes to practice his profession. A writer not belonging to the writers' union cannot get his books published; a physician not belonging to the medical association is not likely to be hired; and so forth for most higher professional activities. Hence these professional associations can function as disciplinary organizations (just as a medical association or a bar association in the West has disciplinary powers over its members), and, more generally, as transmission belts for the Party's interests. Needless to say, their higher cadres are subject to the *nomenklatura* system; and those who are at the very top of their professions, organizationally, are not necessarily its outstanding practitioners. Instead, like their colleagues in the West, they are much more likely to be its outstanding political operators, with due regard for great differences in the process of selection. To this we have to add one other method of organizational control. The various higher professions, we must realize, do not in the USSR work independently, except in rare cases. Engineers or physicians cannot open their own consultant firms. Lawyers cannot simply hang out their shingle and then drum up a clientele. Like a great many of their Western colleagues, the Soviet intelligentsia work for some large organization in which they themselves occupy something like a staff position. Teachers in schools and universities are subordinate to directors and deans. Doctors work in clinics and hospitals; engineers, in many kinds of enterprises and agencies; judges, in courts; artists, on commissions or even according to a production plan; and so forth. In almost all of these cases, the professional occupies a subordinate position in an administrative or bureaucratic structure which may often be under the command of a professional administrator, a generalist assigned to his post by the Party. Even if this administrative chief comes from the ranks of the profession to which his subordinates belong (e.g., a physician who has become director of a hospital), we know from our own experience that the professional who turns administrator tends to lose touch with his profession and to become an outsider; and those who make the appointments to administrative line positions tend to choose the "operators" or "politicians," i.e., those who have already shown that they aspire to careers as bureaucratic hierarchs rather than practitioners of their professional skill. In his place of work, therefore, the man of higher education finds confirmation of his role as servant and, hence, firm limits to his professional autonomy.

Even though most Western observers would probably agree with this summary of the place of the intelligentsia in the Soviet political system, it is becoming more and more fashionable among Western social scientists specializing in Soviet studies to see the intelligentsia or various groups within it as political forces which claim and assume greater and greater autonomy within the Soviet system. The intelligentsia or various parts of it, such as the scientists, the military, industrial managers, students, artists and writers, more and more appear in the discussions of Western scholars as interest groups with a certain amount of power—how much power is the subject of considerable controversy or guesswork. Those stressing the totalitarian nature of the communist dictatorship are likely to discount the influence of professional or any other special groups; those who stress the similarities between highly industrialized societies regardless of ideology or formal constitution will look for evidence of a well-developed system of interest-group politics. The attempt made in this book to forego both models in favor of a comparison with large bureaucratic structures is, perhaps, the alternative which subsumes insights offered by both those theories without succumbing to the exaggerations of either.

We do have much evidence that many professions possess a certain independence or autonomy of judgment, that there are points of view which distinguish specific groups of professional experts

from the political elite in the Soviet Union. The evidence is provided by the countless controversies that have been going on,
especially since Stalin's death, in virtually all fields of inquiry and
professional activity, whether military strategy, architectural style
and city planning, economic management and economic analysis,
education and the treatment of the young, problems of law and law
enforcement, journalism, farm organization, foreign policy, and a
host of other fields. In all these areas, professional experts, within
the last ten years or so, seem to have *taken the initiative* in urging
rethinking of old dogmas and reform of established practices, often
with the hidden implication that they, the experts, are the ones who
should solve problems falling within the realm of their expertise.
This hundred-pronged attack on the universal competence of the
professional decision-makers in the Communist Party is one of
the basic features of the so-called revisionist rebellion that broke
into the open after Stalin's death. The Party has opposed this
revisionism and won victories over it; yet, from the viewpoint of
the old orthodoxies of past decades, its fight against revisionism
looks like a continual defensive battle, a steady retreat before an
enemy with plenty of strong reserves. In almost every field of
thought and activity the professional experts have won partial
victories over the dogmatists, and the Party line has softened.

Despite the ubiquitousness of such retreats, they are no more
than circumstantial evidence. To answer the question about the
actual relationship of the intelligentsia to the top decision-making
machinery we simply have not got enough information. We cannot
know precisely how much, how often, and under what circumstances the men of the Party Presidium, the Secretariat, or the
Central Committee consult experts in various fields. We do not
know the channels through which such consultation takes place,
the directness of access professionals have to the top politicians, or
precisely what kind of experts do, and do not, have access. We
have insufficient knowledge of any tests of strength that might have
taken place or of the forms which such tests might have assumed.
We take it for granted that in any real test of strength the Party
will inevitably win. This would mean, to give a concrete example,

that the military, in the USSR, are weaker than the peasantry. For the peasants have been effective in their resistance against the *kolkhoz* as it was originally conceived. The present-day collective farm and many farm policies represent a compromise. Has the Soviet regime, within the last thirty years, ever been forced to make compromises in the face of a recalcitrant military establishment? Would such a necessity arise in a real conflict of interests (for instance, if the political leadership decided that complete disarmament was a desirable goal for the immediate future)? Or could the Party leadership abolish this military establishment and "convert" its personnel to peaceful use?[3] Could the Party leadership (or would it dare) reimpose on writers and artists the canons of socialist realism in their most rigid stalinist form? Or, to go to a different field: what precisely is the process of give-and-take (if there is one) that determines budgets for scientific enquiry, especially for so-called basic research, which means research not promising immediately useful results? These questions cannot be answered, partly because the decision-making and the conflicts of interest go on behind closed doors, but also because they assume that simple, generalizing answers can be given to describe a relationship which must have become extremely complicated and fluid.[4]

Perhaps we can say no more than that the Communist Party and the Soviet intelligentsia need each other and are dependent on each other, even while their respective outlooks and goals may not always coincide. Their relationship is therefore ambiguous, tense, and changeable. There have been times when individuals in one of these groups thought they could dispense with the other. Conversely, the clash of goals is not always manifest; the Party has absorbed the leading cadres of the intelligentsia, while the latter,

[3] Just a few years ago, the regime drastically reduced the size of its military forces and, in the course of this, dismissed thousands of career officers, redeploying them in other occupations. What difficulties stood in the way of this rather bold step, and what political repercussions it may have had, remains a subject for speculation.

[4] For an interesting discussion of the pressures on Soviet scientific institutions to work on applied problems and coordinate research with economic growth, see Nicholas DeWitt, "Soviet Science: The Industrial Debate," *Bulletin of the Atomic Scientist*, XVI, 6 (June 1960).

on the whole, is loyal to the regime and accepts it as legitimate. The typical Soviet engineer, judge, journalist, agronomist, teacher, etc., is probably as conformist as his Western colleague.

This applies even more to certain specialties of tremendous importance for a political regime, hence subject to the most cautious personnel recruitment practices. The police and the military come to mind as the most outstanding examples of such highly sensitive specialties; the foreign service is another. One can be sure that into these areas the regime will not admit any but the most trusted and loyal citizens. These services are so very sensitive politically because their highest officials have tremendous amounts of power. In the foreign service, this may be no more than the power of betrayal. In the armed forces, power lies in the equipment over which they dispose, whereas the power of the police lies in the secret information they possess about every member of the society. Both the armed forces and the police are particularly essential and particularly dangerous to every political order. Since in the case of the armed forces this special relationship was made even more complicated by initial ideological problems, perhaps a few words should be said about the place of the military in the Soviet political system.

THE ROLE OF THE MILITARY

Because it was born in revolution and civil war (complicated by foreign intervention), the Soviet state from its very beginning faced the need to defend itself militarily. Together with this undeniable need, however, came a dispute within the Party leadership over the methods and organization of this defense, because a number of leading Bolsheviks argued that every class has its own way of waging warfare, and that therefore methods of combat and the organization of military command practiced by armies heretofore should be abandoned in favor of a new, revolutionary, proletarian art of war. In the course of the civil war, this controversy was decided in favor of conventional strategy, tactics, and organization. Consequently, the Soviet state at once required large numbers of trained military commanders, experts in warfare, and these could come only from among men who had served as commissioned or noncommissioned officers in the tsarist forces. This is in fact the group from which the Red Army recruited a large proportion of its commanders. Tsarist officers were placed in charge of Red Army units and remained in prominent, and at times highest, places for more than two decades. Thus a problem confronted the Soviet regime more starkly than most other political systems (even though all systems do face it): how to protect itself against its own troops or its own generals. As in the case of all other professions, a system's protective devices against its professional elites must not be so stringent that they paralyze those elites in their actions and therefore deprive the system of their services. The military commander whom the regime does not trust must be prevented from using his weapons and troops against the regime, but must remain free to train and use them effectively against external or internal enemies.

In the first years of Soviet rule, the regime took a number of measures to achieve this end. Most important among them was a dual command system, according to which all military units had two commanders—a military specialist (commander) and a political head (commissar)—who had joint responsibility for their unit and its operations. No order was valid that was not signed by both. Where differences in background, education, political views, military experience, and other matters were as great as they were between military specialists and Bolshevik commissars, this system was likely to operate only with a great deal of friction. But this was a price the regime had to pay for its safety against its own armed forces. As an emissary of the Party, the commissar had direct access to Communist Party authorities and could play them against military headquarters, in case of conflict with his co-commander. The Party caucus or cell within any unit, meanwhile, acted as an additional check on the commander. This Party cell, of course, was the principal channel of communication between the commissar and the troops. He could thus rely on support from below as well as above. The revolutionary traditions of the Red Army further weakened the professional officer's position. It injected into the armed forces strongly negative attitudes against military discipline, rank-consciousness, and the previously prevalent caste spirit. Soldiers as well as commanders were told that the officer was a servant rather than a figure of authority; attempts were made to do away with officers' privileges and distinctions outside of duty hours—all this in order to weaken the commander's status as an authoritarian figure. Needless to say, the regime supplemented these devices by the customary police supervision, by political education, by psychological rewards for the faithful or successful, and by the effort to train new military cadres from among the working class, who might soon make it unnecessary to hire specialists trained by the tsarist army.

Like so many other things in the USSR, some of these policies were reversed in the 1930s. Abandoning its egalitarian rhetoric, the regime reintroduced ranks and rank-consciousness, sharp discipline for subordinates, conspicuous privileges for commanders, traditional military spirit and old military traditions. The institution of the commissar was subjected to much experimentation. Commissars were abolished, reinstituted, and abolished again. The Great Purge thinned their ranks and those of the military specialists alike. What emerged from the experiments was the institution of the *zampolit*.[5]

The *zampolit* is the unit's deputy commander with special authority in political affairs. Unlike the old commissar, he is usually a career officer with professional military training. But in addition to this the Party has also trained him for his political role. The *zampolit* thus plays two roles and is directly responsible to two bureaucratic agencies. As deputy commander, he belongs to the staff of his superior officer and is subject to his authority just like any other subordinate. His duties to his commander are strictly military; and the fortunes of battle may compel him to function very intensively as a professional military man. Even in his capacity of political affairs officer, he is responsible to his commander. His duties in this regard are to maintain the unit in a high state of

[5] An institution analogous to the *zampolit* existed within the forces of the regular police (*militsiia*), until this political control organ was abolished in June 1956. For the pertinent decree, see *Spravochnik Partiinogo Rabotnika*, Issue 1 (1957), pp. 408–409.

morale. To this end, he is obliged to give political instruction to the personnel of his unit, either personally or (in a larger unit) through his subordinate information and education staff. He is supposed to observe the unit's state of morale, report on it regularly and frequently, and seek to improve it, not only by political instruction, but also by maintaining recreational facilities and perhaps even by acting as an informal channel for complaints and grievances. Yet, the *zampolit* is also the Party's direct representative within the unit. With respect to political matters, he reports directly to the next higher *zampolit* and his political staff, in a chain of command that ends in the Military Department (Main Political Administration) of the Party's Central Committee (and even here the relationship between military and political matters remains ambiguous, because this particular segment of the Party apparatus is simultaneously a division within the USSR Ministry of Defense).[6]

Whereas the Great Purge and the ensuing pattern of government under Stalin asserted the sovereignty of the political over the military leadership, the changes in the treatment of the officer corps signify a changed relationship between the regime and the armed forces. In the first fifteen years of Soviet rule, the gulf between the Party and the army was deep and wide; mutual suspicions were strong, and the commissar system symbolized this gulf. Today the regime and the armed forces have approached and probably accepted each other. The higher officer is very likely to be a Party member. In turn, the Party acknowledges military commanders as leading citizens; and during wars or military emergencies, Party

[6] Below the Central Committee's Main Political Administration, and above the hierarchy of line unit *zampolits*, army groups, military district commands, air defense commands, and fleets had Political Administrations, the chiefs of which were *ex officio* members of the commander's war council, just as the *zampolit* is *ex officio* an assistant commander. These political chiefs, as well as the *zampolits* subordinate to them, were formerly appointed by the Main Political Administration. In 1960, however, the Political Administrations were transformed into Party committees run by bureaus whose personnel was, at least formally, elected by the members. It is not clear whether this formal rearrangement has any substantive importance.

For a Soviet discussion of these institutions, see B. Korshunov, "Politicheskie organy, partiinye i komsomol'skie organizatsii Sovetskoi Armii i Voenno-morskogo Flota," *Kommunist Vooruzhennykh Sil*, No. 5 (1960).

leaders have assumed or been given high military rank. In order to make clear the resulting relationship between the regime and its military specialists, it might be useful to compare the USSR with other political systems. Obviously, the Soviet armed forces are not a ruling military establishment (as is that of the South Korean Republic or some recent revolutionary regimes in the Near East). Nor are the armed forces the domestic mainstay and police force of the communist regime, in contrast to most Central American and some African governments. There is no evidence, either, that the military are hostile to the regime, as, for instance, the Reichswehr was in the 1920s. Perhaps the closest equivalent to the Soviet pattern exists in the United States. Here, until World War II, the armed forces were virtually out of public political life; their officer corps were underpaid and had a comparatively low social status, even though they felt themselves to be an elite and a caste— entirely a world apart. Today, public respect for the military has risen. Higher pay, complicated weapons systems, and improvements in the military educational institutions have made it necessary and possible for the armed services to be more demanding in recruiting their officers. The military commander is generally accepted as a civic leader, and he takes a far more active part in public life— local government, service organizations, social affairs. Upon retirement he has plenty of opportunity to move into some leading position in industry, politics, or education. Despite major differences between the two political systems, this, roughly, is the position of the professional military man in the USSR. He, too, is a member of a self-conscious caste wherein recruitment and promotion depend on ability, performance, and a special bearing. Although there is a natural division of labor between civilian politicians or administrators and military commanders, the senior officers, as members of the professional elite, as leading citizens, and as symbols of government authority, are prominent in national, regional, and local government, if only as coordinators of recruitment, reserve, and civil defense matters and as authorities over paramilitary citizens' organizations. Thus they are integrated in public affairs in a variety of tasks. Their uniforms, their training, the caste spirit fostered among them—all these do keep them apart from the civilian authorities. Yet it is unlikely that Soviet generals and admirals have less disagreements and conflicts of interests than their Western colleagues. In such conflicts, the Council of Ministers and higher Party authorities must function as courts of last resort, as arbiters and makers of final decisions. Hence a single unified "military lobby" is no more likely to exist in the Soviet political system than in the United States. The supremacy of the civilian authorities over the military, of the politicians over the specialists in warfare, seems as firm in their government as it is in ours.

Part Six

A Review and Evaluation

Chapter XXII
Bureaucratic Government
and "Totalitarianism"

The ideological mark of The Fourth Epoch—that which sets it off from The Modern Age—is that the ideas of freedom and of reason have become moot; that increased rationality may not be assumed to make for increased freedom.

C. Wright Mills

The difference between capitalism and socialism is this: Capitalism entails the exploitation of man by man. Under socialism the relationship is reversed.

Soviet joke

In the preceding pages we have attempted to survey the Soviet political system, its origins, its component parts and structure, and its manner of operating and functioning. Occasionally, we have even ventured timid guesses about trends of development or possible modes of change. Perhaps we should now try to ask these questions once again in a much more general way, to summarize the whole book by making a final broad statement about the nature of the Soviet political system.

The main theme of the preceding chapters has been that the USSR is best understood as a large, complex bureaucracy comparable in its structure and functioning to giant corporations, armies, government agencies, and similar institutions—some people might wish to add various churches[1]—in the West. It shares with such bureaucracies many principles of organization and patterns of management. It is similar to them also in its typical successes

[1] Others might refer to Western wartime economies, either to compare the USSR to the United States-at-war, or to compare the problems of Soviet managers to those of American plant managers in wartime. See Lynn Turgeon, *The Contrasting Economies* (Boston: Allyn & Bacon, 1963), p. 213.

and inefficiencies, in the gratifications and frustrations it offers its constituents, in its socialization and recruitment policies, communications problems, and many other features. The Soviet Union shares with giant organizations everywhere the urge to organize all human activities rationally, from professional life to consumption patterns and leisure activities. It has in common with them a thoroughly authoritarian political structure, in which the elite is independent of control by the lower-ranking members of the organization, even though all or most giant bureaucracies in the modern world insist that their rank-and-file constituents participate in the organization's public life. Both in the USSR and in large organizations elsewhere, the individual finds himself thrown into a situation in which unseen and uncontrollable authorities ceaselessly impose social change unwanted by the constituents. All human beings must live in a world they themselves did not make; but in modern bureaucracies, they live in worlds someone is constantly seeking to remake.[2]

In thus describing the USSR as a modern bureaucracy writ large, we are rejecting two other interpretations with a certain amount of currency today: that which assumes the Soviet Union is on its way to becoming a so-called "open society," and that which refers to it as a "totalitarian" government.

The term "open society" is used loosely today, with ill-defined or imprecise meaning. But we may nonetheless be able to select a few basic features that everyone who uses the term attributes to it. Among these are heterogeneity and conflict: whoever speaks of the open society appears to assume that it is pluralistic in structure, that conflicting interests can be attributed to the individuals and groups composing it, and that therefore there is in fact a continual clash of interests, even though a well-functioning open society will have available methods to alleviate conflicts, to find compromises and preserve the community. But, since heterogeneity and conflict can doubtless be found in all societies, those who speak of "open

[2] For a more elaborate discussion of the similarities, see Alfred G. Meyer, "USSR, Incorporated," *Slavic Review* (October 1961); and Alfred G. Meyer, "A Political Scientist Views the USSR," *Graduate Comment*, VI, 3 (April, 1963), 4–9.

societies" would have to add that this pluralism has to be free and spontaneous, that the ability to fight for individual or group interests must not be limited, and that there must be no arbitrary authority which can decide conflicts by imposing a decision on the contesting groups. Instead, ultimate authority for all decisions affecting the community lies in the community itself—which means in the contesting groups. Although people using the term would undoubtedly admit that the power of different groups decides the outcome of conflicts of interests (and power may be a function of the group's wealth, size, prestige, access to policy-makers, economic role within the community, or other factors), the notion of the "open society" seems to assume that normally the various interests within the community will tend to balance each other, that the open society therefore maintains itself in a continually changing equilibrium. Hence conflicts within the community will normally be resolved by compromise. Intimately related to this postulate of dynamic equilibrium, finally, is the concept of freedom as an essential condition of the open society. Examined closely, freedom in this context seems to mean nothing else than the absence of a universally binding scheme of values (except, perhaps, a commonly held resolve to preserve this very condition). The "open society" implies a refusal to acknowledge moral absolutes. It is relativistic, individualistic, and perhaps in a certain sense amoral. Again, this moral relativism can be described in positive terms as a commitment to freedom, individualism, or antiauthoritarianism—hence as the expression of a strong humanistic ethic, which the citizens remember well because they appeal to its lofty ideas whenever they assert their freedom and defend it against encroaching authoritarian demands.

It would be going too far here to investigate whether this image of the open society corresponds to any existing political system past or present. But it seems perfectly justified to assert that centralized control, homogenized patterns of organization, and a universally binding set of values and priorities still prevail in the USSR and distinguish it from industrial societies of the West. To be sure, in this book we have repeatedly noted trends toward the formation of groups and special interests. We have referred to a clash of outlooks and values between various segments of the population. We have noted that the elite itself has become aware of the disadvantages of terror, thought control, and overcentralization. There is looseness, elasticity, and heterogeneity in the vast structure of the Soviet political system, as in any giant bureaucracy elsewhere. But the system remains unified under one command, coordinated by one universally binding set of goals, guided and controlled by one central hierarchy. The bureaucratic ethos is incomparably stronger than the libertarian.

Again, we have noted the intelligentsia's yearning for professional autonomy, the increasing dependence of the Party on technical experts whose work they cannot really understand, and the leaders' reluctance to resort to Stalinist methods of terror. We can expect the Soviet system to go on decentralizing its administration, to place more and more technical details in the hands of lower organizations, including citizens' groups at the grass roots. But we should not expect the Party to yield its sovereign command position without a serious struggle, in which it would have at its disposal many effective devices. And even if the Party were replaced, it would take more than a mere change of power elites to give the USSR that pluralistic structure of groups, interests, and ideas we see (or at least think we see) in some Western societies. Organization seems still to be far stronger than pluralism; command and duty, superior to interests and rights. Despite the ever more frequent and open disputes among the various elites, the Soviet system will doubtless be able to present itself as a unified bureaucratic command structure to the outside world as well as to its own citizenry.

Because of this, many Western scholars have called the USSR a "totalitarian" government—a term this book has avoided or used only with the utmost reluctance. The word "totalitarianism" has been in use among Western social scientists since World War II. It represents the effort to define features characterizing the rule of both Stalin and Hitler and perhaps some of their allies and satellites. This effort is related to the abrupt change in foreign policy when the Western allies, after just defeating the Axis powers, found themselves engaged in a fierce cold war against their former ally. It was not an altogether successful undertaking, because in its attempt to find common denominators it tended to neglect essential differences in origin, structure, aims, and functioning of the two regimes. Moreover, it may have been unnecessary to use the word. New terms must be introduced into the discourse of social science when new phenomena appear which old terms do not adequately denote. The use of a new word clearly implied that Hitler's Third Reich and Stalin's USSR, together with some similar systems, were something unique and totally new—a claim which appears highly dubious.

Precisely what was new in these political systems remained controversial. The few important attempts to define totalitarianism do so in divergent fashion. But a term which upon closer examination turns out to have varied meanings should be rejected. To be sure, all those who use it might agree on a very broad and vague definition; but terms that are too vague become useless. Attempts to give the word more specific meaning have caused difficulties. In efforts to list the specific features which the Third Reich and the USSR had in common, the fact that both systems underwent changes was perplexing. Is a single party with a monopoly of power an essential feature of totalitarianism? In the Third Reich, the party played a more negligible role. Is police terror a necessary ingredient of it? In the USSR the importance of terror has declined, as have, perhaps, the intensity of indoctrination, the mania for centralization, and other features thought by some to be essential elements of Soviet totalitarianism. Western scholars still using the term therefore have begun to talk about a mellowed totalitarianism, enlightened totalitarianism, or totalitarianism with a new look, thus indicating that the term in itself is not quite satisfactory.

A definition on which all who write about totalitarianism might, perhaps, agree would be as follows: those political systems are totalitarian which seek to politicize all human endeavor, to organize and plan all human relationships. In such systems, the outside observer detects something like creeping coercion, a silent transformation or perversion of all beliefs, values, attitudes, and patterns of human life according to a preconceived design. In effect, this amounts to the extension of bureaucratic principles of organization, decision-making, and control over all aspects of human existence. This presupposes, of course, the presence of a sovereign elite or hierarchy powerful enough to effect such a restructuring of the entire society.

If totalitarianism be thus defined, we obtain once again the impression that the USSR can best be understood as modern bureaucracy writ large. To be sure, one might argue that in the process of being writ large, bureaucracy as we know it in Western societies undergoes a very significant change: it becomes virtually all-powerful. In the West, bureaucracies customarily exist within larger societies, which limit their effectiveness. In the USSR, bureaucracy has taken over the society and thus is subject to no checks. No Western bureaucracy can wield the kind of terror practiced by German or Soviet police organizations. No Western corporation, agency, army, or other bureaucracy has as much power as the Soviet regime over virtually all areas of life. If anyone feels the urge to dramatize this difference between bureaucracy-simple and bureaucracy-writ-large by labeling the latter totalitarian, so be it; still, the word has been used with so many divergent meanings that it may, on balance, confuse more than it enlightens.

One might perhaps argue that such a definition of the Soviet system as total bureaucratization fails to incorporate one principle of operation that pervades all its parts. That is the frantic pace of action which the regime wishes to impart to all citizens and all organizations. Soviet government is very intense government. It seems to find itself in a never-ending state of emergency. Several factors impart this impression. One is the fluidity of Soviet institutions, the Party's readiness to change or abolish them, the rapid turnover of cadre personnel, the elite's ability to make sudden changes in policies or views without much psychological preparation. Another is the weight of the demands the regime makes on the citizens. The outsider gets the impression that the Soviet system pegs individual and group achievement norms too high, that it demands more of its citizens in performance than they can deliver, and that it expects them to adjust and change their personalities, their thoughts, their way of life, more quickly and thoroughly than is humanly possible.

Now even this phenomenon is familiar to students of modern large-scale organization and bureaucracy and has been the subject of considerable comment. Hence the fact that Soviet citizens are harassed, that the regime claims their total personalities and seeks even to change their very nature, is not sufficiently new or different to warrant the use of a new word.

Again, many Western social scientists might define totalitarianism as the end of politics. Whether or not this is acceptable depends on the definition of politics. Soviet writers would probably be inclined to identify the political with conscious and long-range planning, with rational decision-making based on a "scientific" study of historical trends and the interests of mankind. In line with this, they would have to claim that their system represents the triumph of politics over economics and all other human activities, the primacy of conscious planning over spontaneous life. Western scholars, in contrast, would tend to define politics as the struggle of interests in the process of making decisions binding for the entire system. Now in the USSR this kind of struggle has not been eliminated, but goes on just as it does in every complex bureaucratic system. To be sure, it is not pursued quite in the open, and only a small minority of citizens participate in it with any effect—but the same can be said of many Western bureaucracies, public as well as private. We can therefore say that bureaucratization dampens or mitigates the political process and removes it both from public view and from the hands of the "common man," but does not eliminate it altogether.

Finally, politics can be defined as the struggle over fundamental principles of human relations, as a continual collective attempt to organize society, to define the aims of government and the public interest, in the broadest sense. This kind of conflict rages in some Western political systems, but far less openly and freely than apologists for constitutional democracy at times seem to think; this kind of political struggle can best be observed at present not in the governments and societies of Western Europe or North America, but rather in the so-called emergent nations now engaged in the revolutionary effort to constitute themselves as political systems. As for the Soviet Union, it is done with this kind of discussion as much as any other bureaucratic organization. In all bureaucratic systems, the basic aims are given. They have been defined by those who make all the final decisions. To be sure, they might be redefined; and on occasions the leadership, prompted by sharp crisis or by rapid changes in society, will have to debate this problem. Still, in the main, bureaucracies of all types operate under the assumption that fundamental, searching discussion of goals and interests is superfluous and disruptive; and in this sense bureaucracies spell the withering away of politics.[3] They cannot, however, succeed in eliminating it forever, because human beings, individually and in groups, are too autonomous, the goals of the hierarchs themselves are too contradictory, and the perfectly functioning bureaucracy is a pipe dream. Hence the chronic strain between formal and informal organizations, regulations and execution, paper plans and reality. The complexities of human affairs frustrate and limit all forms of bureaucratic rule. Students of "totalitarianism" are therefore obliged to point out that totalitarianism never exists in its pure form, but must always remain an aim or a tendency.

What I have been trying to tell the reader is that the Soviet political system, in its structure and functioning, in the character

[3] This is not the same as the withering away of the state; in fact, it is the exact opposite. The withering away of the state symbolizes the democratic ideal of Rousseau and his followers, who believed that the state must merge into society, that politics must turn societal, and government must respond perfectly to the people's "will" and interests. The bureaucratic model of government also foresees a merger of state and society. But, instead of government turning societal, society is to turn political. Planning is to govern over spontaneous life. All human activities are to respond to the bureaucratic direction of a ruling hierarchy.

One reservation must be made in passing: Contrasting planning with "life" is misleading. What appears to the bureaucrat as spontaneous and natural often is no more than an ancient artificial pattern, originally imposed, possibly by "totalitarian" methods, which in time has become habit and second nature. Thus bureaucratization is not really the imposition of an artificial life pattern over a natural one, but of a new over an old artificiality.

of the people active in it and even in its basic goals, is quite similar to some social organizations with which we in the United States are very familiar; and that the Soviet way of life therefore is similar in many essentials to the American way of life.

This is, of course, a one-sided presentation. First of all, I have deliberately neglected the striking differences between the Soviet and American political cultures and over-all political frameworks. Surely, a bureaucracy which encompasses all human endeavors must be different from one that functions within a markedly pluralistic constitutional system. Even the traditional American company town or military post, to which I have compared the USSR, must feel, somehow, the impact of the democratic-libertarian political culture within which it exists as a seemingly autonomous autocratic enclave. But then, it may also be that echoes of this same political culture, which after all has become world-wide, reach the Soviet Union and have an impact on its system of government.

Second, I have deliberately neglected (though not forgotten) dissimilarities based on determining factors unique to the Soviet Union. Many of these determining factors have been discussed in Part One—traditional Russian culture in the broadest sense; the Leninist revolutionary heritage, its goals, prejudices, insights, thought patterns, the very language of politics and its impact on the actions of leaders and citizens; the country's economic and cultural backwardness; problems of foreign relations; the Stalinist heritage; and others. In relegating these specifically Russian or Soviet factors to the background of the political system, I have proceeded on the assumption that industrial society, or the industrial way of life, has a structuring effect on political and social life which, in the long run, is bound to be stronger than political culture, history, and ideology. Differences will undoubtedly remain, but they may be characterized as differences in style. A book concentrating on these differences would have to make an attempt to define or describe national styles in political and human relations. But the methodological difficulties standing in the way of such a comparison are formidable.

One other reason that prompted me to classify the Soviet system as I have was my endeavor to preserve a somewhat balanced judgment despite my biases, to counter the self-righteous implication that the Soviet and American political systems find themselves at opposite ends of a classificatory continuum which coincides with a scheme of moral evaluation. Despite my deep appreciation of the many blessings of Western constitutionalism, I shun complacency because too many serious ills beset us. In stressing the similarities between the Soviet and American ways of life, I want to alert the reader to an awareness of some of these ills, not by "rehabilitating" the Soviet system, but by drawing attention to the beam in our own eyes. It might even be useful to realize that scholars in other parts of the world might conceivably construct different continua of classification and evaluation, schemes in which the USSR and the U.S. might find themselves grouped together at one end, with other political systems at the opposite.

Chapter XXIII
Standards of Evaluation

No one who has read this book can conclude that its author is an apologist for the Soviet way of life. On the contrary, one might say that I have written it in a spirit of criticism, if not ill will, which my hostility toward analogous authoritarian systems in the Western world does not necessarily mitigate. In the Introduction, I hinted at the quixotic or romantic attitudes lying behind this hostility to the admittedly useful and beneficial mechanization of life processes and relationships. My bias was based on some image of human relationships free of coercion, domination, and deception; a collectivist society of autonomous individuals in which human relations could be direct and spontaneous; a life in which rationality and the free reign of natural drives need not persistently come into conflict. Admittedly, this is a romantic utopia. Yet political systems can be evaluated against the standard even of utopias, if we realize that some come closer than others to the fulfillment of such dreams, or that various political systems depart from them in quite different fashion. All evaluation, after all, is a comparison between an ideal model and things as they exist in real life.

I cannot assume that my readers share the bias that has affected my own method of analysis and interpretation. Some readers, indeed, may claim to have no bias whatsoever, except for the honest wish to investigate and understand the Soviet political system scientifically, without any ideological ballast of preconceptions and value judgments. But I have never seen any research in the social sciences which was not influenced by the scholar's passions and preconceptions; and I do not think I ever will. Still, even if we could imagine a social science free of hidden value judgments and yet yielding significant results, I should argue that no description of a political system, however "scientific," is quite complete without a discussion of the manner in which it might be evaluated.

Since this entire book is written under the spell of those biases which I have tried to state, I wish to close by offering or suggesting a few alternatives to my views, different attitudes with which one could approach the Soviet system. In each case, an ideal, a model society, is assumed with which the actual Soviet Union is to be compared.

Let us begin with the official Soviet view, because, on first sight, it seems to be an evaluation of a different kind, one implying no comparison of reality with an ideal model. Instead, Soviet ideology fully approves of the system; hence if there is an ideal model, it happens to coincide with reality. At most, some shortcomings are acknowledged, and a higher stage of development is envisioned. But this higher stage has been redefined so that it looks surprisingly like present-day Soviet society, minus some of these residual shortcomings. We can say then that, instead of comparing its system critically to an imaginary ideal system, Soviet ideology seeks to *idealize* the existing order. It elevates prevailing relationships to the status of moral norms. All apologetic ideologies do this.

As for the pathological features of Soviet government, on which I have dwelled, Soviet spokesmen would not deny them; they could not do so because they themselves discuss them all the time. But they would dismiss them as mere deviations from the norm, as aberrations from the general workings of the system, not negligible perhaps (because they do provide unwelcome disturbances), but incidental to it. At the same time they would call attention to the many serious inequities of political and social relations in the West. Yet, in order to emphasize the contrast between the evils of capitalism and the blessings of the Soviet way of life, they usually posit the malfunctioning and the injustices of the Western world against the potential or promised benefits of socialism. Such procedure is of questionable legitimacy. Far be it from me to devalue the goals of socialism; I subscribe to many of them, despite nagging

reservations. Nor would I deny that some specific practical consequences of the Soviet way of life are ethically superior to analogous consequences of free enterprise, oligopoly, and interest-group
democracy. These would include the welfare state features of the
Soviet system, the relative openness of the ranks of the elites to
people coming from the bottom of the social order, and the sense
of ownership, of a real stake in the system, which many citizens
apparently have developed. But at the same time, I claim the
right to point out that actual political systems rarely become anything but caricatures of the utopias in the name of which they have
been created, and that the actuality of Soviet socialism discredits
the socialist idea no less than the actualities of the West discredit
the ideas of free enterprise and constitutional democracy.

The critical views of many Western writers on the subject represent a direct reversal of official Soviet views. In much of Western
literature, Soviet government is unfavorably compared with something called democracy, the open society, or the free world, which
purports to be a description of Western political systems, but is
in fact a naive and unquestioning idealization of them. Those who
depict the USSR as an absolutely inhuman form of government
often are blind to the inhumanities of their own political order, just
as the Soviet public relations experts will acknowledge no moral
blemish for their own regime. Both views refuse to acknowledge
that their own social systems may violate important ethical norms.
Both are pharisaic in their explicit or implicit claims to have attained something close to perfection.

A less self-righteous method of comparison would be to construct
a system of values and then examine how close different political
systems, including the USSR, come toward fulfilling them. Such a
framework of standards would have to incorporate a possibly large
number of norms relating to freedom, equality, and respect for
human dignity. Every person would have to arrange these norms
into a system of scales—his personal utopia, as it were—with
which to measure different political orders. The likelihood is that
no such order would measure up as superior to others in every
one of these criteria. One could think of many ways in which, to

any one reader, the USSR appears preferable to tsarist Russia, contemporary China, France, South Africa, Sweden, Paraguay, or the United States, not to mention societies of the past—England in 1830, France under Louis XV, Prussia under Frederick William I, Caesar's Rome, the Athens of Pericles, or the Egypt of the Pharaohs. I submit that a value perspective for judging any political system is gained only by keeping at least the possibility of such comparisons in mind. There is no need to exhaust all the possibilities; but neither should we limit our imagination too much.

One other standard by which one can measure and evaluate an existing political system is the interests or goals of its own members. In doing this, it is necessary to be aware of the fact that goals may change and that different groups within a society are likely to have conflicting interests and views. Accordingly, it would be misleading to ask how the Soviet system compares to the wishes of the Soviet population, because it would probably be impossible to attribute one universal political philosophy to all Soviet citizens. Instead, one would have to ask how beneficial or hateful it appears when measured against the hopes and aspirations, the needs and fears of workers, peasants, and a host of other groups, including the leaders of the Communist Party and other elite groups, as they have been summarized in Part One of this book. Similarly, the Soviet regime would also have to be evaluated by comparing it with the goals and aspirations of 1917, in other words, with the ethos of the revolution.

Any attempt to provide an evaluation of the Soviet system which does justice to only a few of these different points of view would be formidable, if possible at all. This book therefore closes with unanswered questions; and it does so deliberately, so as to suggest to everyone dealing with the subject—students and teachers, readers and writers—that their work, however careful, must remain fragmentary, inadequate, partial. Humility, self-criticism, and doubt are among the most essential equipment of all who wish to study the Soviet political system.

BIBLIOGRAPHICAL NOTE

An adequate bibliography for the Soviet political system would fill many hundreds of pages. Since such bibliographies exist, I feel no need to duplicate the efforts of their authors. Even to list only those books and articles pertinent to this study which I have managed to read within the last fifteen years or so would be a formidable task; and since it may reflect the caprices of the author or the accident of a book's availability or non-availability, I doubt whether it would sufficiently benefit the reader.

But such considerations should not deter even those whose interest is, comparatively speaking, casual from seeking further information, if this book has aroused either their interest or antagonism. I have been tempted to provide such readers with a relatively small guide to pertinent literature, but desist because the task is not solvable within the confines of this book. A meaningful guide ought to be annotated; but an annotated selection of readings would be much too selective. A mere listing, without comment, of a larger selection, however, would combine the disadvantages of all courses open to me.

More competent advice can be obtained by consulting up-to-date bibliographies:

The American Bibliography of Russian and East European Studies (Bloomington: Indiana University Press, 1957 annually to the present).

Fisher, Harold H., ed., *American Research on Russia* (Bloomington: Indiana University Press, 1959).

Horecky, Paul L., ed., *Russia and the Soviet Union* (Chicago: University of Chicago Press, 1965).

—— *Basic Russian Publications* (Chicago: University of Chicago Press, 1962).

Kolarz, Walter, *Books on Communism* (London: Ampersand, 1963).

Maichel, Karol, *Guide to Russian Reference Books* (Stanford, Calif.: Hoover Institution Bibliographical Series, 1962).

Miller, Wright W., *USSR* (Cambridge: Cambridge University Press, 1961).

These bibliographies, some of which list additional bibliographies, are fully satisfactory guides to literature about the Soviet political system in English and other Western languages, as well as Russian, even though they too must be selective and do not include every reference some other scholar might have thought important.

Less thorough, but nonetheless extensive, bibliographies can be found appended to a number of books dealing with the USSR and related topics, for instance:

Clarkson, Jesse D., *A History of Russia* (New York: Random House, 1961).

Fainsod, Merle, *How Russia Is Ruled* (Cambridge: Harvard University Press, 1963 Revised Edition).

Kulski, W. W., *The Soviet Regime* (Syracuse: Syracuse University Press, 1956).

Meyer, Alfred G., *Communism* (New York: Random House, 1962 Revised Edition).

One important kind of printed source material for the study of Soviet society likely to be neglected by many students is the fiction and even poetry produced in the USSR, much of which has been translated into Western languages. Horecky's *Russia and the Soviet Union,* listed above, provides an extensive listing not only of this kind of literature, but also of Western works dealing with its history and significance.

The literature dealing with modern bureaucracy is extensive and cannot be listed here in adequate measure. Any college textbook on public administration or problems of management is likely to give at least introductory guidance to the major works on this subject. In contrast, the much-abused concept of totalitarianism has not yet even been defined satisfactorily, and literature about it remains rather scanty. The most interesting attempts to define the concepts are found in:

Arendt, Hannah, *The Origins of Totalitarianism* (New York: Meridian Books, 1960).

Daniels, Robert V., *The Nature of Communism* (New York: Vintage, 1962).

Friedrich, Carl J., ed., *Totalitarianism* (Cambridge: Harvard University Press, 1954).

Friedrich, Carl J., and Zbigniew K. Brzezinski, *Totalitarian Dictatorship and Autocracy* (Cambridge: Harvard University Press, 1956).

Kornhauser, William, *The Politics of Mass Society* (Glencoe, Ill.: Free Press, 1959).

Neumann, Sigmund, *Permanent Revolution* (New York: Harper, 1942).

Talmon, Jacob L., *The Rise of Totalitarian Democracy* (Boston: Beacon Press, 1952).

For critical discussions of these and other works, see Peter Christian Ludz, "Offene Fragen in der Totalitarismus—Forschung," in *Politische Vierteljahresschrift*, 1961, II, 4, and the same author's "Entwurf Einer soziologischen Theorie Totalitär Verfasster Gesellschaft," in P. C. Ludz, ed., *Soziologie der DDR*, Köln–Opladen, 1964, Westdeutscher Verlag, pp. 11–58.

On this subject, too, an extensive reading of fiction will doubtless stimulate our imagination and deepen our understanding of the phenomena which have impelled us to add the word totalitarianism to our vocabulary. Among the great wealth of pertinent works, I mention just one that has made a lasting impact on me and is unduly neglected in this country: Constantin Virgil Gheorghiu's *The Twenty-Fifth Hour* (New York: Knopf, 1950).

In recent years, it has become fashionable to make comparisons between the Soviet Union and the Western world. Much in the present book conforms to this fashion, though perhaps in a somewhat non-conformist manner. Other interesting attempts at comparison have recently been made, for instance:

Brzezinski, Zbigniew K., and Samuel Huntington, *Political Power: USA/USSR* (New York: Viking, 1963).

Turgeon, Lynn, *The Contrasting Economies* (Boston: Allyn & Bacon, 1963).

INDEX

A NOTE ON THE TYPE

The text of this book was set on the Linotype in a face called TIMES ROMAN, *designed by Stanley Morison for The Times (London), and first introduced by that newspaper in 1932.*

Among typographers and designers of the twentieth century, Stanley Morison has been a strong forming influence, as typographical advisor to the English Monotype Corporation, as a director of two distinguished English publishing houses, and as a writer of sensibility, erudition, and keen practical sense.

This book may be kept

FO'